# *Just Conflict*

# Just Conflict:
## *Transformation through Resolution*

Rev. Dr. Mark Lee Robinson

Maps for Harnessing the Transformative Power of
Conflict to Create Mutually Accountable Relationships

Epigraph Books
Rhinebeck, New York

**Just Conflict: Transformation through Resolution**
© 2009 by Rev. Dr. Mark Lee Robinson

Printed in the United States of America

Book and cover design: Rob Fieldhouse & Lee Robinson, Playground Creative

Library of Congress Control Number: 2009939030

ISBN: 978-0-9825255-7-9

Epigraph Books
An Alternative Publishing Imprint of
Monkfish Book Publishing Company
27 Lamoree Road
Rhinebeck, New York 12572
www.epigraphPS.com
USA 845-876-4861

*To Joan*

# Acknowledgments

It is quite literally impossible for me to name everyone who has contributed to this project.

My thanks to my many clients who gave me their trust and taught me how to support them, when I could, such that they might discover how to construct their own healing. They more than anyone else are responsible for the wisdom in this book.

My thanks to those who helped in the production of this book. To my many readers who gave me such excellent feedback about the earlier drafts and helped me to clarify the message and translate from the class I have taught for many years into this book. I especially want to name my colleagues and friends, Mary DuParri and Carol Klooster, whose painstaking reading and editing have tightened the prose in a manner which I hope will be invisible to others but which I see clearly.

My thanks to Greg Kiger who has been my student and friend and my biggest cheerleader for writing this book and has also supplied the picture of me for the cover.

My thanks to my daughter, Lee Robinson, and her partner, Rob Fieldhouse, for their work on cover design and interior layout. And my thanks to my whole family for their support but especially to my wife, Joan, who is also one of the readers and editors and cheerleaders but is most of all my partner.

MLR
St. Louis
October 2009

# Contents

# Introduction

All conflict can be resolved.

This is not to say that all conflict *will* be resolved. New conflicts arise moment to moment. But it is possible to resolve every conflict. This may be something you can accept in theory but in practice find hard to accept. We have all encountered conflicts we couldn't resolve, indeed which we concluded were beyond resolution. We can give up on a conflict anytime we want. We may decide resolving the conflict is more effort than it is worth. Nevertheless, all conflict can be resolved.

When we resolve conflict we engage in an act of creation which transforms the world.

While the scale of the transformation we cause when we resolve a conflict depends upon the nature and complexity of the conflict itself, we are in small and grand ways ending turmoil, constructing justice, discovering power, and bringing ourselves into harmony with the will of the divine order. As hard as it may be to resolve conflict, it is worth the effort.

Everyone is able to resolve conflict.

You resolve conflict all the time. Life presents us each with an endless series of conflicts and we have been learning from infancy how to name, address, and resolve those conflicts. We are gaining greater and greater mastery at conflict resolution everyday. We may not recognize all of the conflicts arising for us. We may not even name them conflicts until they appear to be something we don't yet know how to resolve. But we all resolve conflict all the time.

Nevertheless, there are times when a conflict arises for us which we don't know we can resolve and we flinch. We back away, not because we don't care enough to address the conflict, but because we don't have the confidence that this time, with this conflict, we will be able to construct a resolution. It is the goal of this book to bolster your confidence about your competence to resolve conflict.

## Conflict resolution is a learned skill.

As with any skill, we get better with practice. The more we practice with conscious attention, the better we will get at conflict resolution. As with anything we learn, we move through stages in our growth toward competency. Just as our math teacher gave us problems for homework which were a bit harder than we could easily solve, so does life give us problems we cannot yet easily solve. That is how we grow.

This book will help you learn to resolve the conflicts you do not yet know how to solve. It is a set of tools you can apply to any conflict that arises for you so that you can gain greater and greater mastery. While conflict resolution can be very complicated and difficult, there are a series of simple steps which anyone can do which will increase your ability to resolve all of your conflicts.

## We can help others resolve their own conflicts.

We cannot resolve a problem which is not our own. We cannot resolve others' conflicts for them. But we can create a context in our relationships with others which supports their growing ability to resolve their own conflicts. In this book we will look at what we can and cannot do to support the transformation of others.

# What We All Already Know About Conflicts in Our Relationships

We all have many relationships and we all long to have them be safer and more satisfying. We may think others have an easier time with their relationships; they somehow do it better or it comes more easily for them. This is not true.

Some people insist that they have no conflicts. It seems to me those who say they have no conflicts fall into one of two groups. The first group is those people who are so skilled at conflict resolution and so attentive to their circumstances that they immediately know as conflicts arise and address and resolve them with such grace and ease that they don't even show up as conflicts.

The second group is those of us who minimize conflict in our lives by

- only being around people who share our perspective on most things,
- not caring too deeply about anything which might be a source of controversy, and
- being able to deny our feelings when we get agitated.

If I minimize my contact with people who are different from me, have different views, come from a different culture, and have different life experiences; then I will be less likely to discover conflicts. This is increasingly difficult to do in some respects as the globe shrinks and we can easily learn about people whose circumstances are very different from our own. But in other ways it is becoming easier to isolate as we can only relate to our "friends" on our social networking site about fashion and popular culture. We don't have to be aware of the diversity which surrounds us.

If I can keep my attention on things that don't matter, I can prevent myself from caring about anything controversial thereby avoiding conflict.[1]   I can remain detached. Then I can remain calm and unruffled as everyone around me freaks about climate change and hunger and globalization and a bunch of other things I don't understand but am pretty sure I can't do anything about.

If, when I do become so aware of a conflict that it begins to disturb me, I

---

1    I have always been a bit dismayed by the prevalence of physical violence between sports fans who follow rival franchises. Here are people who care very deeply about something which has no lasting significance and are willing to brutalize the very others they are most like. I have to wonder what they are really so angry about.

can just push it out of my awareness, than I might deny that I was bothered in the first place. If my denial mechanism is well developed and I can implement it at the slightest twinge I can sustain the notion that I have no conflicts to address.

But few of us are so isolated, apathetic, and insensitive that we are unaware of any conflicts in our lives.

There is another thing about conflicts in relationships which we already know but mostly ignore or deny: conflict resolution builds relationship. It creates intimacy.

Join me for a moment in a simple little thought problem.

> *Think of a time in a significant relationship when a conflict arose and each of you were able to clearly name what the conflict was, hear the other's perspective and concerns, and were able to come to an agreement about what you would each do. Just take a moment before reading on to get the memory of such an event firmly in mind.*

Not everyone can find such a memory. But among those who do (and even many who cannot) nearly everyone has the same response to this next question.

> *Consider the relationship in which the conflict arose, and think about how close and durable and satisfying the relationship felt at each of three points in the resolution process: 1) before you discovered the conflict, 2) as you addressed the conflict, or 3) after you had resolved it. At what point did the relationship feel the strongest?*

In asking hundreds of people to participate in this exercise, almost without exception, everyone agreed that the relationship feels strongest after the conflict is resolved. Certainly it doesn't feel all that safe or secure as we are in the midst of addressing it; but the work of naming, addressing and resolving the conflict actually results in a more durable relationship than we started with.

I say nearly everyone because in some circumstances what the process of addressing the conflict reveals to us is that the conflict stems from the fact that we do not share with the other party an agreement about what we want the relationship to be like. We discover that we have very different expectations and, when neither of us is willing to abandon what we are looking for in the relationship, we decide to move apart. While this does not result in a closer relationship, it does create a healthier and more satisfying one.

Since we know that resolving conflicts builds healthy relationships, it makes sense that whenever a conflict arises in a significant relationship we think to ourselves, "Oh goody, what a wonderful opportunity to strengthen our relationship."

No, of course, this isn't what we think. We don't think this, not because we haven't witnessed that resolving conflicts builds healthy relationships, but because we don't trust that *this* time, in *this* relationship, with *these* issues, we are going to be able to move to resolution.

Thus the central issue in the task of building healthy relationships is learning to have more confidence in our competence in conflict resolution. What we will do together in this book is discover the skills to address any conflict that arises in any relationship and to move it towards resolution.

## The Promises of Becoming a Conflict Resolution Master

Conflict resolution is hard work. There are specific and valuable benefits we will acquire from the effort. Here are my promises to you regarding what will come to you as you become more and more masterful.

- You will have fewer and less intense conflicts in your personal life, and you will be less upset when conflicts arise.
- You will greatly enhance the quality of your relationships and you will get much greater satisfaction from them.
- You will come to know yourself better and will have greater integrity in all of your actions.
- You will know your true place in the created order and will experience greater and greater harmony with the energy and the intelligence of the Creator.

Each of these sets of promises arises in a different dimension of our lives. To keep them differentiated we will refer to them as the personal, the interpersonal, the intrapersonal, and the transpersonal realms.

## Personal

The personal realm is that area of our lives which is most focused on our physical experience of being. It is the realm of our physical bodies and the sensations and desires which arise from having our consciousness centered in the material world. In order to resolve conflicts in the personal realm we must know what is happening to us and know how to act to create safety and satisfaction. When we are able to resolve conflict we feel as though the conflict has gone away.

## Interpersonal

The interpersonal realm is that area of our lives which is focused on our relationships with others. It is the realm of our roles with others and the rights and responsibilities which accrue to us and are demanded of us by the relationships we create and have forced upon us. In order to resolve conflicts in the interpersonal realm we must know what others' expectations are of us and respond to those expectations in a manner which is consistent with our own integrity and ability. When we resolve conflict we feel the relationship grow clearer and stronger.

## Intrapersonal

The intrapersonal realm is that area of our lives which is focused on our relationship to ourselves and our interior awareness. It is the domain of our feelings and fantasies, our intuition and imagination. In order to resolve conflicts in the intrapersonal realm we must know the many aspects of ourselves, particularly those which appear to be in conflict with each other, and clarify who we might be and how we might act such that all aspects of who we are find expression and satisfaction. When we resolve conflict we find we are more centered and whole and powerful and safe.

## Transpersonal

The transpersonal realm is that area of our lives which is focused on our place in creation and our relationship to the whole created order and the source of that creation. It is the domain of our apprehension of the divine and our knowledge of the purpose we each have in the larger scope of the cosmos. In order to resolve conflicts in the transpersonal realm we must know the suffering of the world and respond with compassion and care. We must see the divine longing for justice as our own longing and know how we are in harmony and unity with the energy and intelligence which creates the world.

These levels or realms[2] are all present for us all the time whether we focus on them or not. What we mean by conflict and what we might experience as resolution will be different depending on which domain we are attending to at the moment.

In the personal realm conflict appears as our experience not being what we want and resolution is the assurance that we can construct what we need. But in the interpersonal realm conflict is whenever others are not as we would have them be or we are not as they want us to be. Resolution is not about getting them to do what we want or doing what they want us to do, resolution is becoming able to see how the other is viewing what is going on and see the other's perspective as valid for them. Similarly we want to know that they see our perspective as one which is valid for us.

## Seeing from Multiple Perspectives

Albert Einstein famously stated, "No problem can be solved from the same level of consciousness that created it.[3]" When we look at any circumstance or event, we do so from a particular perspective. This is one of the great discoveries of post-modern philosophy. Einstein is pointing out that there are many levels of consciousness, perspectives, points of view, or paradigms through which we can observe whatever is happening in our experience. The way we think about whatever is arising shapes how we deal with the event. Some of these ways of seeing actually create problems for us because they don't take into account all of the relevant variables. We end up doing things which create the opposite of what we need. What we most need is not a better strategy, but a better way of seeing. The reason we have not been able to resolve the conflict is that we have

---

2    In some places I will refer to these as "tiers" as they do tend to have a sequence to them and build upon each other.

3    Sometimes this is quoted as "level of understanding," and sometimes as just "consciousness." I have not been able to find the original source of this quote.

not yet found the perspective through which resolution can be seen.

There are a theoretically infinite number of points of view. When what we are doing is not getting us what we need, we have good evidence that the way we are looking at things isn't from the best possible perspective.

Whenever an event arises in our perception we make meaning of it. This is what humans do. We are meaning makers.

We make meaning by consulting the cognitive maps we have constructed out of our past experience. If the map I am using is not one which accurately describes the current terrain of my life, I am likely to make poor choices. If, for example, I grew up with a dad who was bitingly critical of me when he was angry, I might well conclude that when someone is critical of the choices I have made, this means they are angry. However, suppose my new boss is trying to help me understand my job better and is giving me some feedback about how I am doing. He is being critical. And suppose I conclude that he is angry with me and I become afraid of his anger. If I then quit the job, my map isn't helping me understand and navigate this territory.

All of our maps are partial and incomplete. Reality is far more complex than our ability to map it. From time to time we find one map which fits together with another map and we get a fuller vision of reality. We have an "ah hah" moment. This requires that we acknowledge the validity of both maps.

There is an ancient tale which has variations in many cultures about a group of blind men who become curious about the creature called an elephant. They decide to go and "see" it for themselves. Each lays hold of a different part of the elephant and assumes each has a full sense of what an elephant is. Each has a part of the truth. None has the whole truth. This is the nature of truth. We cannot ever grasp the whole of it. All cognitive maps are partial.

## Conflict and Resolution

What appears to us as a conflict, and what occurs to us as a resolution of the conflict, will be different depending on our perspective. When a six year old boy watching TV is told by his father to get to bed, the boy's perspective is that the conflict is caused by Dad telling him to get to bed and the resolution would be for Dad to let him watch TV. From Dad's point of view, the conflict is that the kid is still up and the resolution is for him to get to bed.

However, suppose the boy has night terrors and doesn't really care about TV but is afraid of sleep. Suppose the boy's mom has been expressing displeasure that Dad hasn't been looking out for the boy's welfare. These are complicating factors. Conflict can be very complicated. For that reason we are going to need some fairly robust maps to help us understand and address the complexity.

Simply put, *conflict* is when we don't like what is arising in our experience. We are not experiencing what we want or expect or believe we have a right to experience. *Resolution* is when we have what we want restored or created for us. We are now getting what we like, expect, or deserve.

However, one person's resolution can easily be another's conflict. The purpose of this book is to tease apart the multiple perspectives and make clear the complexity so that we can address our conflicts in a durable and satisfying manner.

> There is a retreat center near my home where I have spent many a weekend doing deep emotional work with colleagues. As one of the people responsible for gathering provisions for the weekend, I have purchased many boxes of tissues. We assume that deep emotional work will include the expression of tears and the presence of the boxes is an invitation to do the work; to express the feelings.
>
> One weekend I was in the same space but with a different organization. Members of this group were operating with different cognitive maps. During a moment of emotional sharing, a woman seated near me began to tear up. I looked for the tissues, and, seeing none, reached into my pack for a small packet I carry with me. I set the packet close to her.
>
> She quickly moved through the emotional moment and then, not addressing me directly, expressed her anger that people would try to shut down her expressiveness. She took my offer of tissues to mean, "Mop it up, lady. We don't want to hear it."

What my gesture of making the tissues available meant to me was, "Your feelings are valid and we are completely open to hearing them fully." What my gesture of making the tissues available meant to her was, "Your feelings are unwelcome and intrusive and we would rather not hear them." Obviously these are very different ways of making meaning of the same event. The question is, which one of us is right?

Of course, we both are right. We each looked at my gesture completely differently and came up with very different meanings, both of which are valid and true. Mine came from the map of my experience and hers came from the map of her experience. I have no doubt that she has been rejected during prior attempts at open expression of her feelings. She imposed that meaning on my gesture.

While there was a part of me that became angry and ashamed that I had my intentions so badly misunderstood, it was also helpful for me to discover my incorrect assumption that she would make the meaning I intended. It is entirely possible more people would have taken it the way she experienced it than the way I intended it.

Whenever we get into a conflict with someone, we each are looking at the same event and making it mean something different. Many times we are curious about the difference and use the difference to enhance and enlarge our perspective on the event. We gain depth. However, when we have very strong emotions about the event, we may become acutely anxious and we may be unable to see or acknowledge the perspective of the other. We may invalidate the other's point of view. When we do this we hamper our own ability to see with depth the events that are arising in our common life.

Much of this book is dedicated to learning how to gather as many perspectives as we can so that we can see with as much depth as possible. We want to have the greatest diversity of perspectives.

This is not to say that all perspectives are equal. Maps are tools and some tools are better for some tasks than for others. When we find a conflict which appears to be irresolvable, all this means is that it can't be resolved from the level of consciousness from which we are currently looking at it. We have to find a better map, that is, one that helps us navigate this territory in a manner that moves us toward what we need.

## Conflicts in Organizations

For the most part this book considers conflicts between two people. It is easier to see and describe the dynamics in a simple system. But all of the principles are equally applicable to the more complex systems of families, faith communities, associations, corporations, and nations.

In my early training in conflict resolution I was taught that conflicts in dyads were different from conflicts in groups. I have not found this to be the case. The difference between conflicts in simple systems and more complex ones is that it is easier to see the complexity in the ones we have labeled "complex." Even what appear to be "simple" systems are far more complex than they first appear.

Organizations are just as timid about addressing conflict as are individuals. Churches fear admitting their experience of conflict will make them appear unfaithful. Corporations fear acknowledging conflicts within the corporate structure will scare investors and customers so tend to adopt a stance of rigid denial.

I was active for many years in a federally funded project to address and resolve the conflicts between the family courts, child protective services, and the domestic violence intervention community in the ways those three systems deal with families with children when there is adult intimate partner violence. The reason for the project was the awareness that conflicts between the perspectives and strategies of the three "partners" resulted in harm to battered women and children.

Despite the clear mandate for the project and the premises on which it was built, and, despite a clear recommendation from one of the consultants to the project, the project never developed, much less implemented, any guidelines for how we would address the conflicts between the parties. We were so afraid of the conflict getting out of hand if we named it that we danced around it for years.

All of our relationships experience conflict. Our biggest conflicts arise in the relationships we have that matter the most to us. Whether at home or at work or in our faith communities or at the gym, conflicts arise. Naming, addressing, and resolving them results in personal, relational, social, and spiritual transformation.

## Sources for This Curriculum

I have been teaching most of this material for nearly thirty years. Beginning in the early 80's I provided individual and group therapy with men who battered their female partners and men who sexually abused their own children. There are several important things this experience taught me, but the central one has to do with attitudes about how conflict resolution shapes relationship.

We tend to assume that men who are abusive in the context of intimate relationships are not only comfortable with conflict, but that they seek it out. This is decidedly not true. These men all found conflict to be scary and they assumed that any attempts to address the conflicts would result in them losing. As a consequence, the only strategies they could rely on were various ways of making the other lose. Manipulating, bullying, dominating, discounting are all ways of disempowering the other. They are not ways of getting what we need.

And so I set out to figure out ways of teaching these guys new tools for addressing and resolving the conflicts that arise in their relationships. What I learned was that there are ways to act which genuinely do resolve conflicts and that it is possible to break the process down into small enough steps that anyone with sufficient motivation can learn them. This caveat about "sufficient motivation" is an important one. This is very difficult material which requires a perspective very different from what one hears "on the street." This is genuinely hard to master.

I also learned that the tools I was trying to teach these men are ones that very few of us have or know how to use. It has been a continual source of dismay for me that many of my colleagues in the field commonly display the same cognitive distortions as the men we are trying to help. These men are the visible tip of the iceberg, but they are not qualitatively different from the rest of us.

About fifteen years ago I began to pull this material into a set curriculum which I have been teaching as a twelve week class. It has gone through a couple of major revisions, and hardly a week goes by when I don't adjust something about sequence or content.

Where I know the sources for an idea in this curriculum I credit it, but I confess to not being a very good scholar and so don't always know my sources. In many cases I have found others saying the same things I have been saying but we didn't know about each other. I believe this is because we have each found a helpful perspective independently. I have included a bibliography of the books and articles which I find to best support or inform the argument of the book.

# Some Notes to the Reader

As you have already seen, I will sometimes shift the font and the margins for a portion of the text. This is a way of indicating that I am speaking from a different "voice." If you find this distracting, please just disregard it. It is intended to help, not to confuse.

Many of these shifts in font come as we get to know the Johnson's—Jane and Joe and their two sons, Jack and Jesse. These are fictional characters meant to illustrate some of the concepts in the book. You will also meet some other characters who, while patterned after real people, are disguised to protect their privacy.

This material was initially developed in the context of a class with not more than a dozen students. As such it is intended to be experiential in nature. To aid you in experiencing the material viscerally, not just cognitively, I have included some of the class assignments for you to try on your own. I strongly urge you to explore the material in this way. But this is not primarily a workbook. I will write a companion book to be a more hands on self-help sort of text. This book is the theory which supports the practice.

At the end of each chapter you will find a summary which is designed to briefly recount the essential flow of the argument. If, as you read the summary, you find a portion which doesn't make sense to you, I suggest you go back to the section it seeks to describe and review it. This is a way for you to be sure you are getting the essential points in each chapter.

You may find it difficult to use the material in this book. We are so powerfully constructed by the culture which surrounds us that making the shifts in perspective which Creative Conflict Resolution invites in us are very hard to sustain. We tend to be who those around us expect us to be even when being that way isn't working for us.

For that reason I strongly encourage you to talk about this book with others. Start a discussion group or just find one other person with whom to dialogue. If you can't find anyone close to you to engage with around this material, join an online discussion. Options are available through the web site at www.CreativeConflictResolution.org.

# Part One:
# Motivation for Transformation

All conflict can be resolved. We cannot resolve conflict without transforming ourselves. We cannot change others but we can allow the conflict to change us. Creativity is a process of conflict resolution.

# 1

# Becoming a Conflict Resolution Master

H ere is some good news and some bad news.

> *The good news is that all conflicts can be resolved. The bad news is you will have to change yourself to resolve your conflicts.*

There are things you can do—indeed, you are already doing—which lead to the resolution of the conflicts that arise in your life. This book will set forth a series of simple steps which will lead you to become a conflict resolution master. You may decide that some conflicts are so massive that you are not yet ready to address them. You may decide that some conflicts are so small they are not worth your time. But, if you decide it is impossible to resolve a given conflict, you are mistaken. For it to become possible, however, you will have to be dedicated to your own transformation.

> *The good news is that it is possible to transform yourself such that any given conflict will be resolved for you. The bad news is that, while simple, the steps are not easy. Indeed this could be the hardest work you will ever do.*

Becoming masterful at resolving conflicts is the product of the diligent application of a set of disciplines which will transform the way you see yourself, others, and your relationships with them. It is not unlike training in a martial art where you practice over and over a set of moves until they become second nature to you. As you master these tools and become able to see from the perspective of Creative Conflict Resolution you will find that, as new conflicts arise, you will greet them with curiosity and enthusiasm to see what new lessons they will offer you. Everywhere you go you will find new opportunities for conflict resolution.

Becoming masterful at resolving the conflicts which arise in our awareness allows us to transform ourselves and our lives and, in the process, transform the world in which we live.

> *The good news is that when we act to transform ourselves we create what we need and in the process create what everyone around us needs. And to this, there is no bad news.*

## Paths to Becoming; Adopting Constructive Practices or Disciplines

At its most basic level, Creative Conflict Resolution is a set of techniques for naming, addressing and resolving the conflicts that emerge in our day to day contact with others. It is designed to be as simple and straightforward as such a difficult and complicated process can be. It is an effort to break down into specific and discrete steps a process anyone can use to address and resolve any conflict in any relationship.

In practice it is much more. If you decide you want to learn to use the tools of Creative Conflict Resolution, you will discover it is a process for transformation which will result in you becoming more truly your Self in all of the dimensions of your being but most especially in who you are emotionally, relationally, and spiritually.

If you are someone who has practiced hatha yoga and are coming to Creative Conflict Resolution from that perspective, then you are already familiar with how stretching yourself, maintaining balance, and holding your concentration can improve your physical wellbeing while at the same time improving your total spiritual health. The disciplines of Creative Conflict Resolution are much like asanas for your relationships with others as well as for yourself. This discipline is a form of karma yoga. You will gain concentration. You will feel stretched. You will find balance.

If you are someone who is trained in one of the martial arts then you are already familiar with the importance of certain skills: finding your center and remaining in it, anticipating how others approach you and practicing how you will respond, and at all times carrying yourself in a manner that will protect you without harming others. Creative Conflict Resolution is just such a system for disciplined self-care but in the emotional realm rather than the physical. You will become more centered and you will gain a capacity to respond easily and immediately to others in ways that not only get you what you need but support others in getting what they need as well.

If you are someone who has experienced psychotherapy as a tool for guiding you through difficult times in your life and helping you to heal from the effects of trauma, then you are familiar with how going into your own deepest thoughts and feelings can give you insights about why you make the choices that you make and, thus, help to free you to make better choices in the future. Creative Conflict Resolution can be seen as a form of psychotherapy in that it helps to identify patterns of conflict in significant relationships and then uses them as a way into our interior experience of meaning-making. It is a means of self-discovery of the ways our past experiences shape our current relationships. Through the tools of Creative Conflict Resolution you will become able to make choices that are both freeing and healing.

If you are someone who has used a twelve-step or another spiritually-based program for addressing problems with addiction, then you are familiar with how a comprehensive set of tools which are applied in the context of a supportive community can totally transform your life. Creative Conflict Resolution is also a technology for transformation but it starts where recovery leaves off. Indeed, while Creative Conflict Resolution can help those who are battling addiction to discover why they are having trouble with recovery, people who are active in their addiction will not be able to master Creative Conflict Resolution.

Students of Creative Conflict Resolution come to the practice for many different reasons. You are invited to join them.

## Maturity and Mastery

If we are to become better at creating resolution for the conflicts which arise we will have to make more mature choices at the very time we are feeling the greatest stress. We will have to learn not to act impulsively, but to construct carefully the circumstances by which we nurture what we need. It is very hard to get ourselves to do this if we believe we are already grown. We must come to understand that the reason to grow is not because we are bad the way we are, but that more is available to us if we continue to mature.

Becoming able to see how such conflicts can be resolved and to then become someone who can actually embody these strategies is the goal of mastering conflict resolution. Becoming a CR Master is a bit like studying for a black belt in a martial art. There is a certain amount of understanding that one must develop, but mostly it is a matter of practicing over and over the moves, parries, throws, stances and holds that make up the content of the art.

As a martial art is a physical discipline that also requires emotional and spiritual discipline, so Creative Conflict Resolution is an emotional discipline that also requires physical and spiritual discipline. There are ten specific disciplines or practices which you will learn to use to build your skills as a CR Master. The more you practice these disciplines, the greater your ability will be to address creatively whatever conflicts arise in your experience.

This is a process that requires both focus and surrender. You must pay keen attention and let go all at the same time. Just as Luke Skywalker practiced long and hard with a light saber under the tutelage of Yoda, so will you have to keep your Bothers Me Log every day and do your Anger Workout. But for all of his practice and his reliance on the technology available to him, when it came to his one shot at the Death Star with a photon torpedo, Luke flipped up the targeting scope and trusted the Force. At some point we must all let go of the outcome and simply trust the process. We focus…and we surrender.

It is this surrender which allows us to discover the spiritual nature of this discipline, for it is the design of the creation we all inhabit that we can all have what we need. As the bumper sticker says, "there is enough for everyone's need, just not enough for everyone's greed." When we make the choices which move us toward what we need and when we do so in a manner that is not at anyone else's expense, we actually create the qualities which allow for everyone to have what they need. This is not a zero sum game. When we play to win, everyone wins.

# Identifying my "Self"

The first thing you learn in a martial art is not a throw or a hold, but a stance. The first thing you must master is the ability to find and hold your center. If you are off balance it will be easy for your attacker to knock you over. When you stand with your knees slightly bent and feel the inertia of your solar plexus as the seat of your power you become so rooted that you cannot be moved.

Just as we find safety and power in knowing our physical center, we also discover security in knowing where we come from emotionally and mentally. We become adept at conflict resolution largely by nurturing a keen awareness of who we are.

There are many aspects of ourselves we will get to know as we nurture our self awareness, and we will explore many of them, but for the moment we want to notice how we locate who we are.

> *Remember for a moment your second grade classroom. Bring it as clearly to mind as you can. Try to visualize yourself at the doorway, or in the room, or peering in the window. Look around the room and notice whatever you can remember. What events happened in this room? What impact did they have on you? Give yourself a few moments to explore this and see just how much you can recall.*

Now, consider a few questions about what you have just observed:

- How long has it been since you thought about your second grade classroom? What impact do you suppose the length of time has had on how easily you brought it to mind?
- When you were looking around the room trying to recall what it looked like, were you looking from the perspective of who you are now, or from the point of view of who you were as a second grader?
- What impact do you suppose your life experiences since second grade have had on what you were able to observe about the classroom or your experience in it?

It is unlikely that you have been thinking a lot about your second grade classroom recently. Nevertheless, if you are like most people you probably found something that you could remember about the room and the events that happened in it. That is, you could focus your attention on an event which was not at the forefront of your awareness. You could find it when you went looking for it. We all have the ability to *focus our attention* on whatever we decide to focus on. This is a choice we all have the capacity to make, though it is easier for some of us than others to hold our attention on any given thing.

As you brought your attention to bear on these memories, you looked at them from the perspective of who you were then, or who you are now, or perhaps a combination of both. When I ask a group to do this exercise I usually get about half seeing from the perspective of who they are now and half from who they were then. There is no right way. But what we see is different depending on the place from where we look. This is the *locus of our identity*.

You may also have noticed that you have a different perspective now than you had at the time. You may be an educator and noticed something about the way the teacher taught. You may be an architect and noticed something about the layout of the room. You may be a child psychologist or a sociologist and the perspective that you bring to your observations today may inform what you know about what happened to you then. These are all lenses or perspectives we can choose to look through now which inform what we are able to see. We get to choose the *perspective* through which we look at whatever arises in our experience.

As we construct our current awareness we decide where we will look from, what we will look at, and what we will look through. As we change our choices and look from a different place, or move our attention to a different focus, or see through a different perspective, who we understand our *self* to be will change. The "I" that we are at any given moment will change.

It becomes very important to recognize that we can do this because we tend to assume we can't change who we are. Certainly there are some things about me which I cannot change. But my age and blood type are not generally the sources of the conflict I experience. We have a tremendous power to shape who we are even moment to moment by the choices we make. Knowing and using this power is fundamental to becoming a CR Master.

# Strategies, Events, and Qualities

We think conflicts cannot be resolved because of what we understand the nature of conflict to be and how we conceive of the process of resolution. As we develop a fuller understanding of the nature of conflict, possibilities for resolution open up to us.

We may say to ourselves about a troubling situation, "I won't say anything. I don't want to start a conflict." By *conflict* in this context we mean, "I don't want to start a fight." "What I have to say about what is bothering me will hurt her feelings and then she will respond in kind and then we will be caught up in trying to make each other lose and I don't want to go there, so I just won't say anything."

In another sense, however, the conflict exists whether I say anything about it or not. The other is doing something which bothers me. There is a quality to our relationship I don't like and it is not serving my needs. The other has made or is making choices which create events which create a quality in our relationship which is not good for me or for our relationship.

While I may think of the conflict as *the fight we might get into if I say anything*, we may also think of the conflict as *the condition that exists already as I contemplate what, if anything, I will do to respond.* For our purposes in learning to more fully resolve conflict, it is necessary to separate out

- the condition or event that triggered my awareness of the problem, and
- the response that I consider making to the problem.

So we will talk about *conflicts* and *strategies for addressing conflicts* as different things.

My awareness of the problem may have been triggered by any one of a number of co-occurring circumstances. The other may have made a choice I didn't like. An event may have occurred which was not what I expected or what I believe serves my needs. The qualities in our relationship may have shifted such that it is no longer safe or satisfying. Thus I may see a conflict as a *choice* or *strategy*, an *occurrence* or *event*, or as a *quality* or *condition of the relationship* itself. Let's look at a simple example of this.

*Suppose you are driving on a crowded Interstate highway on your way home after work. You get over into the right hand lane to join the queue for your exit. As you are slowing, cars continue past you on your left and one of them suddenly cuts in front of you.*

*You notice feelings of anger arise in you as you hit the brakes to avoid the other car. You notice thoughts about the other driver as one who is selfish and entitled and dangerous. You entertain thoughts of flashing your lights or your horn or riding the car's bumper to express your feelings.*

At one level the conflict may be seen as the result of the choice of the other driver to cut in front of you. This driver has a *strategy* of pulling past other drivers in the queue to save a few seconds on his or her way home.

At another level the conflict may be seen as the *event* the choice created. The abrupt appearance of a car pulling into your lane caused you to have to brake, to have concerns about your safety, and to worry that the car behind you may not have seen you brake and could slam into you.

And at the third level, the event created tension, alarm, fear, anger and the awareness that others on the highway are not as concerned about the common welfare as you would like. Others are not looking out for your best interests. These are not the *qualities* that best serve you or those around you.

We may then think of the conflict as

- the *strategy* that the other used,
- the *event* or *interaction* that the strategy created, or
- the *quality* or *need* that results from the event.

All three of these are perfectly valid perspectives. But we want to focus especially on the *qualities we need*. This is the perspective which will most help us know how to act in ways that get us what we need, which will serve to resolve the conflict.

When a conflict arises in our awareness, we experience it as a problem to be solved so we try to figure out what to do. We go looking for a *strategy*. Whatever strategy we settle upon will create an *event*. Something will happen. As that event unfolds it will create *qualities* in our relationships with others. But if we pick a strategy before we know what qualities we are trying to create, we are likely to do something that will get us the opposite of what we need.

Flashing your lights or horn or riding the other car's bumper or flipping off the driver are all things that many of us do and most of us at least fantasize doing. But let's look at what those choices create. They raise your heart rate and your blood pressure, they distract you from other things that are going on, and they put your car in dangerous proximity to a car whose driver we already know shows poor judgment.

If, on the other hand, we start from the point of view of the qualities we are trying to create we can see that what we are looking for is a calm and safe ride home. We want to be on a highway where people are attentive to others and considerate of their needs. The strategy of flashing lights and horn does nothing to create these qualities and, in fact, creates the opposite.

Ultimately we will have to settle on a strategy for responding to the conflicts which arise for us. Even deciding to slow down and take a deep breath and give thanks for good reflexes is a strategy. But whatever strategy we choose will create a new event. And whatever new event arises will generate new qualities. It is the qualities we are after.

When we know which qualities are missing in the circumstances we call conflicts, then we can choose strategies that will create what we need, that will create those qualities. This resolves the conflict. Very simple. And actually very hard to do.

## Complexity of Conflict

Perhaps in the circumstance of someone cutting us off in traffic the resolution is simple. But getting cut off in traffic is an event which arises often and does so in a relationship of low significance. This driver is a stranger, so we don't have an investment in repairing the relationship or trying to get him or her to change. Getting cut off is something that happens over and over, so we have lots of opportunities to practice how we will deal with it.

Consider instead the situation of a man who is known to have an "anger problem" who discovers that the shared printer in his home has a jam and he cleans it out. The paper that is stuck turns out to be the second page of the letter that his wife has written to her "friend," a guy who plays in a local band whom she often goes to see "because she likes the music." When the text on the crumpled paper describes her attraction to and wish to be with the musician, what does the man do? What strategies will create what he needs in this situation?

- At one level the conflict the man has is with the paper and the printer. They are in a problematic relationship and when he has cleared the jam, the conflict goes away.
- At another level he has a window into his relationship with his wife and he learns that his understanding of their relationship is not the same as hers. He suspects that she is not entirely honest with him.
- At still another level there is a part of him who is desperate to preserve the relationship and so argues that he should just ignore this information, but another part of him feels as though he is becoming a cuckold and wants to protect his integrity by addressing this issue with his wife. He is thus in conflict with himself.
- At still another level he wonders about his place in the relationship and with his children and in the world and he wonders if this is his punishment for times when he has been dismissive toward his wife. He fears the marriage may end but he has made a vow before God to stay with her "'til death do us part."

Each of these aspects of the conflict will have to be fully addressed and resolved if he is to feel fully satisfied with the outcome.

You will recall the promises that I made in the Introduction.

- You will have fewer and less intense conflicts in your personal life.
- You will greatly enhance the quality of your relationships and you will get much greater satisfaction from them.
- You will come to know yourself better and will have greater integrity in all of your actions.
- You will know your true place in the created order and will experience greater and greater harmony with the energy and the intelligence of the Creator.

And you will recall that each of these sets of promises arises in a different dimension of our lives—the personal, the interpersonal, the intrapersonal, and the transpersonal realms—and conflict and its resolution appear differently in each of them.

| Realm | Conflict | Resolution |
|---|---|---|
| Personal: physical-material | Conditions in my experience are not what I consider to be optimal for me | The situation is corrected and the conflict is gone |
| Interpersonal: relational | Others are not doing what they "should" or they are not approving of me | Our expectations are clarified and met. The relationship is solid and satisfying |
| Intrapersonal: internal | I'm not happy with myself. I'm of two minds. I am anxious and uncertain. | I can see and appreciate my own complexity and accept myself without denying aspects of who I am. |
| Transpersonal: metaphysical-spiritual | I don't know my place in the world. I feel abandoned by God. The suffering we experience has no meaning. | I can act confidently in harmony with my place in the grand scheme of Creation. |

## Disciplines or Practices

Whenever one takes on as a goal the development of a new capacity or ability, one takes with it the awareness that this mastery will require practice. We will have to practice if we are going to become masters at conflict resolution.

This book is primarily about the mechanics of conflict resolution. It is not a workbook. But for you to understand the mechanics you will have to have a feel for how they might be applied. As I stated in the Introduction, I will be offering a companion to this book in which I will focus on the practical application with references to the mechanics. In this book we are looking at the mechanics with references to the practices which support them.

So that you may get a feel for what is possible for you, I will introduce to you ten disciplines which I have found to be very helpful in mastering the skills of Creative Conflict Resolution. You will find in hard to make sense of what I am saying if you do not have a personal experience of what I am talking about. For this reason it is essential that you at least try each of these disciplines. Indeed it is only with persistent effort that you will find the benefits that they promise.

In the book, *Living Deeply*[4], the authors share their discovery that all personal growth disciplines have what they call the "four essential elements of transformative practice." Let's look at these four elements in the discipline of learning to hit a baseball with a bat.

*Intention:* All practices or disciplines have a quality of intentionality. We enter into them with an intention to have some quality of our lives be different. If we do not actively will that change, we won't change.

It is my intention to meet the incoming baseball with the broadest part of the bat just a few inches from the end of the bat. I want to propel the ball over the head of the pitcher and between the second baseman and the shortstop so that it falls shy of the center fielder and I can get on base.

*Attention:* We will have to pay attention…close attention…attending to things we haven't noticed before. We will not create transformation in our lives without focusing.

I have to remember to see the ball all the way to the bat and not begin to look at where I want it to go or at the pitcher. It is just me and the ball. But I also want to note that it may not come in as a strike so I don't want to commit to hit it unless it is in or close to the strike zone.

*Repetition:* Getting it right once is not going to be the end of it. We will have to do it over and over and over. We will have continue to do it until it becomes second nature…to where it becomes not just something we are doing but an aspect of who we are.

I will not hit the ball the first time I swing at it. I will have to practice my swing and practice watching the ball and attempt to hit it several thousand times before I really come to competence. Hitting the ball is ultimately an act of luck,

---

4    By Schlitz, Vieten, and Amorok. See the bibliography for the full reference.

but one's luck improves the more one practices.

*Guidance:* We will not know best how to do this all on our own. We have to be able to ask for help and then accept the guidance we are offered. Others have gone before and learned some things which will make this more easily available to us if we simply open ourselves to their guidance. But there is another source of guidance which comes from within. We have an inner knowing which can also guide us.

The coach told me to choke up a bit and remember to keep my weight on my back foot and swing level. The coach knows how to hit a ball and if I listen to him I will do better. But I also need to listen to myself. I can't think through whether this is a strike, I have to simply know. I don't have time to think about it but must cultivate an inner knowing which will guide me.

So batting a baseball is a discipline and it is a collection of disciplines. I have simplified the process here for the sake of the example, but a professional ball player can tell you that you can't hit a left handed pitcher the way you hit a right handed one. We can break this larger practice into sub-practices, all of which we must master if we wish to gain competence at batting a baseball.

In just this manner mastering Creative Conflict Resolution is a discipline and it is a set of sub-disciplines. The ten which I will discuss in this book range from very simple to quite complex. They are all aimed at helping you become a CR master. In the largest sense then Creative Conflict Resolution is a discipline which has these four elements.

**Intention:** It is our intention to respond to the circumstances of our lives in a manner which creates what we need (as opposed to what we want) and to trust that when we do so, with no expectation that others will change, we will not only create what we need but also create the circumstances in which others will get what they need.

**Attention:** We will note whatever it is that bothers us, as it is those irritations which alert us to the fact that we are not getting what we need. We will pay attention to how our behavior affects others so we can be certain that we are creating the outcomes we desire. And we will pay attention to how others' behavior affects us so that we can fully appreciate how we are constructed by our relationship to the world around us.

**Repetition:** Recognizing that the world continually arises for us in ways we don't like, and noticing that there are patterns of conflict which arise for us, we will select those patterns which bother us the most or which appear most frequently to practice on such that we can know clearly what it is that happens, how we are affected, what we need, and what we can do to construct what we need. We will welcome each opportunity to refine our skills at Creative Conflict Resolution.

**Guidance:** This book is intended to provide the external guidance—a map for the territory of the conflicts we all encounter. But there is an internal guide we will learn to listen to. It is the core of our being, our true Self, which ultimately can confirm whether what we are doing will construct what we and all of creation need.

❧

There are many personal growth disciplines which will help you improve the quality of your life. The ten presented here are certainly not the full list of disciplines you will want to have in your own life. We are not, for example, going to talk about the discipline of being clear about your diet. What we eat is crucial to our wellbeing. I hope you are paying attention to the things that make you sick and not eating them. You should likewise be getting regular exercise composed of both weight training and aerobic exercise in alternating periods within the week. You should be engaged in a meditation practice. I recommend you be part of a faith community or some community that has clear shared values and is acting on behalf of the larger community.

There are many things you can do to improve your wellbeing. All require a regular practice of specific activities. What we are focused on here are some practices which will greatly improve your ability to name, address, and resolve the conflicts which arise in your life.

# The Mindfulness Disciplines

The first five disciplines or practices are essentially tools for paying attention. They are designed to enhance our capacity to pay attention to some crucial aspects of our experience

**#1 – The Bothers Me Log** is a practice for tracking whatever bothers us. We can do a much better job of attending to what is bothering us if we know what it is.

**#2 – The Anger Workout** recognizes that very few of us have a healthy relationship with our anger and that anger often interferes with our ability to respond well to conflict. No matter how clear we are about how we would like to address conflicts, if we are being controlled by our anger we are likely to make a mess of things.

**#3 – Cultivating Critical Feedback** recognizes that we cannot see ourselves without a mirror and we can harvest some very good information from the perspectives of those around us if we can learn to listen to them.

**#4 – Suspending Self-soothing** acknowledges that we have to settle ourselves down when we are anxious but sometimes we are so good at calming ourselves that the issues which are stirring us up never get addressed. When we can suspend the soothing until we know the source of the anxiety then we can address the cause of the problem, not just the symptom.

**#5 – Self Care Routine** notes that we are always caring for ourselves to some degree but we are also denying ourselves things we need. This practice helps bring to the surface our internal conflicts about what we genuinely need.

# The Practical Disciplines

The second five disciplines are guidelines for what to do when a conflict arises. They are focused on the choices we have available to us.

**#6 – ACE: Anticipate, Create, Evaluate:** Most of the conflicts we deal with in our day to day lives are the same thing over and over again. Since it has happened before and is going to happen again, we can observe what we know about the issue to help us prepare for next time.

**#7 – Statement of Accountability:** Accountability is an essential quality of healthy relationships. When we make choices which harm others we have violated the other and damaged the relationship. Even if the relationship is destroyed there is much we will want to learn about the choices we made and how we can transform ourselves so as to reduce as much as possible the likelihood that we will make such choices in the future.

**#8 – Apology and Forgiveness:** When we make choices which harm others, or when they make choices which harm us, we experience the relationship as having been damaged. If we are going to have healthy relationships we are going to have to be able to repair the damage in such a way that we can become more confident that we will not harm or be harmed in the future.

**#9 – Framework for Creative Conflict Resolution:** Acknowledging that we cannot change others and that conflicts arise over and over in even our most intimate relationships, this framework clarifies what we can do to transform ourselves so that we are constructing what we need without expecting or depending on the other to change.

**#10 – Conflict Resolution Meeting:** When we do have a relationship in which the other is also committed to addressing and resolving the conflict, what do we each need to be able to do to clarify the relationship, acknowledge the issues, hear each others' perspective as valid and construct agreements which will move us toward what we all need?

As you can see, the Disciplines are numbered in order of complexity. They are also developmental in so far as your ability to do the later disciplines will depend to a fairly large degree on your ability to do the earlier ones.

There are copies of the handout sheets for these disciplines in the Appendix and there is much more available about them online at http://JustConflict.com. We will look at the Practical Disciplines in some depth in Chapter Eleven and will introduce the Mindfulness Disciplines as we go along. Here I will to introduce the first two.

# Discipline #1: The Bothers Me Log

If we are to be aware, we will have to become aware of the things that we are trying not to be aware of. Mostly, we don't want to be aware of the things that are bothering us. We don't want to be bothered. But we don't know what is bothering us until we notice there is something bothering us. So the first discipline is to notice, everyday, whatever is bothering us. Set aside time everyday to allow your attention to rest on whatever you notice is bothering you. Then, just write a brief note to remind yourself of what it is that is bothersome. This is not a journal, just a list.

From time to time people tell me that nothing bothers them. "What about the way people drive," I ask. "Oh that," they say, "I just don't let that bother me."

If you don't let things bother you, simply make a list of those things you don't let bother you. That is your Bothers Me Log.

The purpose of the Bothers Me Log is to raise our awareness of what is bothering us. We always have things bothering us. We fear that if we focus all of our attention on what is bothering us we might be overwhelmed. We are challenged to be fully aware and to be able to filter out things that aren't important enough to deal with so we can bring enough attention to bear on our problems such that we can solve them. The problem is that there arise many things which bother us which we don't solve because we don't sufficiently notice they are bothering us.

A colleague of mine who took the Building Healthy Relationships class as a form of professional development was brave enough to take on the discipline of doing the Bothers Me Log. One day as she was sitting in her office making brief notes about what she was aware was bothering her, she noticed that for the third day in a row she had been bothered by the crooked picture in the halfway to her office. She set down her pen and went out into the hallway and straightened the picture.

When she reported this event in the class the following week she was a bit sheepish, as though it seemed petty to allow something like a tilted picture to bother her, or that this exercise should be reserved for bigger things. In fact, she was doing it just right.

Fully half the things which are bothering most of us are just such little things as the crooked picture. These are things we already know how to deal with. We don't fix them because we are not sufficiently aware that they are bothering us. Once we notice that we are bothered, we address them, resolve them, and the bother goes away. But we don't straighten the picture until we notice it is crooked. We don't take off our shoe before we know there is a rock in it.

Even when we know there are things that are bothering us, and even when we experience those as things we can change when we bring our attention to them, and even when we can resolve them and get a sense of mastery, even then, we often don't want to notice what is bothering us. We don't want to be bothered. We don't want to expend the effort paying attention takes. We all want to protect ourselves from the threat of emotional overwhelm that can come when we get too bothered.

We have seen what it can be like when we get really angry and we don't like what we are capable of doing. We know what other people can be like when they are very angry and we don't want to be like them. And we know how others have often treated us when we were very angry and we don't want to leave ourselves open to that. So we protect ourselves by not letting ourselves get bothered.

> *Someone does something that bothers me, but, rather than letting myself get all worked up about it, I just stuff it. And then someone else does something and I stuff it. And then a driver on my way home cuts me off and I stuff it. And the kid left his tricycle in the driveway, again... and I stuff it. And then I am relaxing watching the news when my wife walks in and changes the channel and I no longer stuff it. All of the stuff I have stuffed comes billowing up and we fight and I spend the night on the couch. I should a' stuffed it.*

When our anger management tactic is keeping it all in the stuff sack, what do we do when the sack is full and we decide to express our anger? We have no where to go. If our only option is to stuff it or to blow up, then we have no appropriate or helpful or healthy option.

## Discipline #2: The Anger Workout

The Anger Workout is designed to change the relationship we have with our anger, not so that we will not be angry, but so that we will become able to express ourselves in a manner that moves us toward what we need when we are angry. Let's tease that apart a bit.

Anger is a natural, normal, and necessary emotion. It is what arises whenever we experience others as making choices which are harmful to us. If someone does something which hurts me, I am going to feel angry. But no matter what I feel, I am still free to choose what I will do. Just because I am angry doesn't mean I have to cuss or slam doors or put my fist through a wall.

A part of what is confusing for us about anger is that we use the word *anger* to refer to both the emotion and the behavior. When someone tells us not to be angry, they mostly mean that they don't want us to act towards them in the manner they are used to people having with them when they are angry. But the emotion is not something we can control. When people talk about getting in control of their feelings they either mean being able to act appropriately no matter what emotions arise (which we can learn to do), or they mean learning to stuff their feelings (which only works in the short run).

So, anger is both an emotion and a behavior. We get to choose our behavior but we don't get to choose our emotions. When it comes to emotion our only choice is whether we will feel it or not. We get to be aware or numb. If we choose awareness we are going to become more aware of all of our feelings, and that includes anger. The reason we tune our feelings out is not because we experience too much joy or satisfaction, but because we want to avoid fear, hurt, sadness, anger and guilt. We don't want to feel anger because we don't want to act the way people act when they are angry.

Now, let's do another thought problem.

> *Go inside your own awareness right now and see if you are angry. Just feel into your feelings and see if it is true that you are angry.*

> *Okay now, if you are not angry, just check and see if there is anything you have anger about or anything towards which you might hold some feelings of anger. Just see if you have any anger.*

This is a distinction that the guys in the Abuse Prevention Class taught me about their anger. There is a difference between the *anger we are* and the *anger we have*. Or another way to put this might be that there is a distinction between the *anger that we have* and the *anger that has us*.

When I *am* angry, it is at a time when all of the other emotions fall back and the one that dominates my awareness is anger. Anger comes up and grabs me by the throat and tells me how to act.

When I *have* anger, it is at any time I am aware of circumstances which hurt me or those I care about and when I see those circumstances as a consequence of a choice. I have anger all the time and it arises from time to time in my awareness in all of my relationships, including my relationship to me.

The goal of the Anger Workout is to help us be so aware of the anger we carry all of the time that we don't let anger sneak up on us and grab us by the throat and take control of our behavior. When you do the Anger Workout consistently you will begin to notice some changes in how you act when you get angry and how you relate to your anger from day to day.

To do the Anger Workout, find something to do everyday, perhaps something you already do, at which time you can become very aware of your anger as a sensation. This can be while you exercise or while you walk from where you park your car to where you work. Continue to bring your awareness back to your anger for at least five minutes but not more than twenty minutes at a time. Following this attention to your anger you may find it helpful to focus on your gratitude or some other more comforting emotion before you enter into contact with others.[5]

The first thing you will likely notice is that you are less reactive when people make you angry. You will have a greater sense of control over how you behave when people "push your buttons." You won't have such a tendency to overreact.

The second thing you will notice is that you have anger all the time. You will begin to feel the anger in even the small things. This doesn't mean you will be more angry, only that you will be more aware of the anger that arises for you all the time. You will not have such a need to stuff those feelings.

But the third thing—and this is really big—is that when you are angry about something and you decide to address it with someone—the very someone who is acting in ways that hurt you—you will be more and more able to do so in a manner which doesn't come across to them as you being angry. You will

---

5    For more information about this and the other disciplines you may consult the Appendix in this book or go to JustConflict.com and click on the Disciplines tab.

become more able to be calm and direct and effective in addressing the issue that is bothering you.

The ways anger impacts our capacity to build healthy relationships are so important that we will return to anger and all of the passions in Chapter Eight. But I want to introduce the ideas here because it is important to get to know our own anger early on so that we can actually apply the concepts of the later chapters. It takes a while to train our anger dog well enough that he doesn't always bark and scare people away.

## Qualities of Shalom and Esuba

In the broadest sense, there are two competing qualities which arise from time to time in all of our relationships. When the transactions we have with those around us are ones which meet our needs such that we feel safe and satisfied, we experience *Shalom*. When those transactions are ones which fail to provide for us and others such that we feel hurt, we experience *Esuba*. When we address the Esuba and resolve the circumstances which cause the harm, Shalom is naturally restored.

> When I was in my twenties, my dog, Henry, and I, with four of our friends, "did" Hunter Island in Quetico Provincial Park in Ontario just north of Ely, Minnesota. In the maze of glacier dug lakes that is the park, there are two points on Lake Sagonagons that drain to the west. These two rivers come back together many miles away in Lac La Croix. The area in between is Hunter Island."Doing Hunter Island" is a matter of circumnavigating the area between those rivers and lakes.
>
> We completed a two week trip carrying all of our food and gear. It took the first couple of days to get the loads balanced between the two canoes, but by day four as we headed up Kawnipi we were into a rhythm. When we got out into the open water, the wind came up confronting us head on.
>
> When canoeing, especially with a heavily loaded canoe on a lake, wind is a curse. You have to keep the canoe straight into the wind. If you get only a few degrees off, the wind will catch the canoe and spin it broadside and then try to turn

*you over. There was no place to rest. Stopping would only push us back and possibly swamp us. We paddled on for hours.*

*It was probably about 7:00 P.M. when we got to the island that was our destination. We unloaded the canoes, gathered firewood and started a fire for dinner, set up the canoes as a camp table, set up the tents, and while the water was coming to a boil for dinner I pulled out my personal pack, pulled off my soggy boots, and put on dry socks.*

*Ah, dry socks. What a glorious feeling.*

There is a word for that feeling…for that quality in our lives.

I have a coffee cup in my consulting room that has *shalom* emblazoned on it in both English and Hebrew. Beneath the word is a quote from Isaiah about turning swords into plowshares. We tend to think of the word as a synonym for peace but it is actually much more than the absence of war or conflict. *Shalom* is about there being enough, distributed to everyone. It is about a sense of well-being and confidence about the future. It is about wholeness and fulfillment.

*As I pulled on my dry socks I felt a deep sense of shalom.*

We tend to think of objects as having qualities—they can be blue, or heavy, or old—but we less frequently notice that relationships between objects also have qualities. The quality of shalom that arose for me as I pulled on the dry socks was not so much about the socks or even about my cold and wrinkled feet as about the relationship between the socks and my feet.

Bring to mind a time when you had an experience of shalom. Allow yourself a few moments to bring to mind a time in your life when you felt deeply safe and satisfied and that all was right with the world. If you have been able to bring such a time to mind, you are also probably aware that such experiences can be fleeting.

*After dinner when we had finished washing the dishes and had laid them out on the rocks to dry, the wind shifted and we retreated into the tent. That cold north wind was mean.*

Just as we experience shalom, there is also a kind of anti-shalom that arises as a quality of our relationships. I have searched for a good word to capture this but all of our words for such unpleasantness come with a moralistic tone I want to avoid. So for the purposes of this conversation, I will call the quality in a relationship where there isn't enough or where we don't feel safe *esuba*.

You have probably been with a group of friends having a great time and then something happened which brought everybody down. Perhaps someone joined you who was an esuba generator. We all know people who just give off esuba anywhere they go. It rolls off them like a fog. Like the cloud of dust around Pigpen[6], these people have tension follow them around.

Perhaps you are aware that, from time to time, you yourself become an esuba generator. You may just be having a bad day, but those around you can't escape the fact that you are bringing them down; you are bringing the quality of esuba into the relationship.

Even when we have the best of intentions we can unwittingly become an esuba generator. When I handed the packet of tissues to the woman at the retreat[7], I was consciously working to create shalom. I wanted her to feel safe and accepted. But, instead, what I did caused her to feel rejected. My action created esuba in my relationship with her and her response spread it around the room. We want to create more and more experiences of shalom and yet all of our relationships experience esuba.

One other thing to note: I put on dry socks almost every morning. But the feeling of shalom that arises for me is not like what it was that evening many years ago on an island at the north end of Lake Kawnipi. The *shalom* which is greatest is created out of the deepest *esuba*.

We tend not to want to notice when esuba is arising in our relationships with others. We make up all kinds of excuses for not paying attention. Mostly we don't think there is anything that we can do about it so we try "not to let it bother us."

If I am walking down the street and kick up a rock and it gets into my shoe, the rock will irritate my foot. I can say to myself, "There is no rock in my shoe." I can say, "It isn't a very big rock." I can say, "I don't have very far to go." But none of these things will alter in the tiniest bit the effect which the rock is having on my foot.

---

6    A character from the comic strip "Peanuts" who was always dirty and surrounded by a cloud of dust

7    A reference to a story in the Introduction

When I acknowledge there is a rock in my shoe and it is harming me I already have the technology for solving the problem. I sit down on the curb, take off my shoe, and let the rock out. But I don't take my shoe off unless and until I acknowledge the rock.

I notice the rock because of the esuba it is generating in my experience. If we want shalom, we have to notice the esuba and address it. When we have addressed the esuba, shalom arises.

## Summary

All conflict can be resolved but to do so we have to transform ourselves. This transformation is possible through a consistent application of some specific practices or disciplines. These disciplines help us to develop the ability both to focus clearly on our perceptions and choices and to surrender fully to the outcome.

The central feature of each of these practices is that they move us ever closer to the core of who we are. They connect us more and more to our essential Self. As we come to know ourselves we discover a set of choices we each make which constructs who we are . These choices are the focus of our attention, the locus of our identity, and the lens or perspective through which we observe our experience.

Conflicts can easily be overwhelming because they can be quite complex. One aspect of this complexity is that what we experience as a conflict is both the condition which arises for us and the response we hope to create. This response is to invoke a *strategy* which will create an *event* which will establish certain *qualities* we are missing. When we settle on a strategy before we are clear about the desired qualities we are likely to select a strategy which will get us the opposite of what we need.

Further, these desired qualities appear in different domains or realms of our experience.

In the Personal Realm the focus of our attention is in the physical experience of having enough time, or food, or shelter to meet our needs. When the need is met, the conflict goes away.

In the Interpersonal Realm the focus of our attention is on the qualities of our relationships. When the need is met, our relationships are restored and strengthened.

In the Intrapersonal Realm the focus of our attention is on our internal experience of our feelings, hopes, dreams, fears, and so on. When the need is met, we are clear about who we are and what we are doing.

And in the Transpersonal Realm the focus of our attention is on our place in the grand scheme of creation and our awareness of the suffering of others. When the need is met, we see our role in perspective and we appreciate the essential harmony of the universe.

There is great personal, relational, and social benefit to becoming skilled at identifying or naming the issues which arise for us in each of these realms, addressing the problems we find there, and making the changes required to construct what we need. These skills are worth cultivating. Doing this requires discipline. We must have a clear intention about what we are trying to create, pay keen attention to whatever arises, engage the disciplines over and over, and do so within the framework of the guidance we get from learned others and from our own interior wisdom.

The ten disciplines we will learn allow us to become more mindful and skilled at addressing specific common circumstances. The first two disciplines have to do with noticing what is bothering us as a way to attend to what we need, and noticing how we relate to our strong feelings like anger as a way to be fully aware of our emotions without letting the emotions make our choices for us.

When we and those around us have what we need we experience a sense of peace and wholeness we call shalom. When we or those around us are not getting what we need we have a troubled feeling we will call esuba. If we ignore esuba it will not go away but it will grow and become more troublesome. When we attend to the source of esuba and create what we need, esuba dissolves and shalom is restored.

# 2

# Mapping Our Reality

Very early in life we become able to recognize the face of our mother. We see many faces, but we know which one belongs to Mom. We have in our awareness a sort of map of the colors and shapes that make up the face of Mom and we identify it and respond differently to it than to any other faces we see.

Each day we build upon our internal representations of the world around us so we can make new distinctions and anticipate more events. We hear footsteps outside our room and we know that one of our parents is there. We see the color of the puree in the food bowl and we know that we are getting strained peas for dinner. We learn the streets from home to school so we can walk to and from by ourselves. We learn the rules for chess and become able to play. We learn to solve differential equations.

At every moment we observe the world around us and anticipate what is likely to happen. When we are right, our cognitive map is confirmed. When we are wrong, we adjust the map so that it more accurately predicts what will arise in the real world.

This is the essence of the scientific method. We are curious about what is happening in the world around us. We create a hypothesis, a sort of tentative map, and then venture out into the world to see if the hypothesis holds. If it does, we hold onto that map and use it to build other maps. If it doesn't, we put it aside, perhaps making a note to ourselves to be wary of that kind of map in the future.

Remember what Albert Einstein said; "a problem cannot be solved with the level of consciousness which creates the problem." What he is pointing out to us is that the way we look at a problem constitutes a level of thinking, a perspective, which is necessarily an imperfect map of the territory. The errors in the map create problems which the map can't solve. We need to find better, more comprehensive, and often more complex maps to solve the problems which seem irresolvable.

My youngest son had to struggle to learn to read. One day we spent several hours on some basic words which he was finally able to get. He was able to see the letters *s, t, o,* and *p* and to know that when they were in that order, they meant *stop*. He knew the spoken word *stop*, but this day he became able to look at the printed letters and know they represented the word. The pieces of his cognitive map fit together.

The next day we had some errands to run and as we drove through the neighborhood he pointed and shouted, "Look, there's one! Stop!" And then as we approached the next corner he again shouted with glee, "There is another one." For him, the stop signs had not existed before that day. Once he had the cognitive map for making meaning of the sequence of those letters, there were suddenly signs on every corner.

Our verbal language is a lower order map. By "lower order" I don't mean less important, but rather more basic. It is by our language that we form the building blocks of more complex maps. Language itself doesn't fully solve our problems, but without language we don't have the basic tools with which to even name the problem, much less to solve it.

The way we talk shapes the way we think. The way we think shapes the way we act. The way we act builds our relationship with those around us. If we are to repair our relationships with others, we have to change the way we act. To change the way we act, we have to change the way we think and talk. We have to change the words we use and the maps which form our understanding of the world.

These conceptual maps we use are ones we have carefully crafted out of our life experience. They are the best maps we can find to help us navigate the waters of our daily circumstances. They help us find our way around. They help us know how to tie our shoes, whether to raise our hand, and how to hit the pitch. They are an internal representation or symbol of the external reality and we use that representation to know what to do.

We form a map when we discover something we believe to be true which we want to apply to a future circumstance. Since I will need to tie my shoes again I will remember to "put the right end under the left, pull them tight, make a loop on the right, make a loop on the left, wrap the left loop around the right loop and pull them tight." Since I will be called on if I never raise my hand, I will be sure to raise my hand whenever I know the answer but not when I don't. If I want to get on base I have to follow the pitch with my eyes and not look at where I want the hit to go. We have thousands and thousands of maps in our glove box.

## Perspectives and Conflict

So what does all this have to do with conflict resolution? What do cognitive maps have to do with settling disputes and creating justice in the world?

In the personal realm conflict is about things not being as we want and resolution is getting what we want. But in the interpersonal or relational realm conflict is about confusion in our understandings with others and resolution is the restoration or the healing of the relationship. Perspectives have everything to do with healing relationships.

There is an old and great fable about a group of blind men going to "see" an elephant. This fable exists in many cultures but the most famous version is the poem by John Godfrey Saxe.[8] In the unlikely event that you are not familiar with the premise, the story is about a group of blind men who have heard of this creature called an elephant and so resolve to check it out for themselves.

Upon arriving at the elephant, they each lay hold of a different part of it and conclude that the whole elephant is just more of the part they "see." Thus each one thinks it is like a big snake (the trunk), or a tree trunk (a leg), or a rope (the tail). Convinced at the accuracy of their own perception, they then proceed to argue with one another about the nature of an elephant. Each is certain that he is right and the others are fools.

It is significant that this fable is so present in every culture and so well known to this day. It speaks to a very common and destructive proclivity we seem to have when it comes to our own perspectives. When we decide that our own is correct, we then assume that all others are wrong. We believe that there is only one valid perspective and it is the one we hold.

---

8    This is easily found on the Internet. There is a fine overview of the story at Wikipedia.

Resolving conflict in the Interpersonal realm depends upon our ability not only to see our own perspective and to assess accurately its validity, but also to be able to see the other's perspective and, at the very least, to know that it may also be valid. If we can, we do well to see how the other has come to hold to the validity of the other's perspective, and if we want to do really well, we might even take some aspects of the other's perspective and incorporate it into our own.

In the Interpersonal or relational realm, conflict resolution depends upon the capacity to see the validity of the other's perspective for the other. For this reason it is vital that we become clear about our own perspectives and be able to accurately assess the validity of these perspectives. We can then apply that same skill to the perspectives of others.

## Types of Cognitive Maps

There are many kinds of cognitive maps. There are some we want to pay particular attention to as we work at becoming masterful in our ability to resolve conflicts. Some maps help us know *where we are*. Some are better for helping us figure out *where we want to go*. And others are best at helping us know *how to get there*.

A literal printed paper map which shows a geographic area may work well for all three purposes. We pull out the map to figure out where we are. Then we see if we can find where we want to go on the map and then we use the relative positions of those two points to decide in which direction to go.

But suppose I am trying to figure out if my teenage daughter is lying to me. What map do I use to decide what is going on when she tells me she is going to spend the night with her girlfriend but I can't get the girlfriend's mom on the phone to confirm the plans?

Or suppose I know that she is invited to spend the night with her friend and the friend's mom confirms the invitation and that they will be supervised, but I am afraid she is spending too much attention on her social life and not enough on her studies. How do I know how much is enough or too much?

Or suppose I am clear that she is not doing well enough in her studies and I am not willing for her to stay with the friend when I know they won't get any sleep and she should stay home and work on the big project due Monday. How do I tell her that in a way that won't result in all of her energy going into hating me instead of doing the work?

Each of these tasks requires a different cognitive map. There are many maps of many types and we have a lot at stake in the task of finding and using the best ones.

## Words

As we have already noted, a word is a kind of basic map. We have created language –a shared meaning for a set of symbols and sounds and by those symbols we communicate with each other and with ourselves. Our words form the symbols on the pages of our maps.

There are many words which we will use in a very specific way in this book. We have already introduced the words *shalom* and *esuba*, and pointed out that there are many meanings for the word *conflict*. We have clarified that, for the purposes of our conversation here, *conflict* refers to the conditions in the relationship, not the strategies for addressing those conditions.

## Disciplines

We have also begun to introduce the idea of self transformation through the use of disciplines or practices. A discipline is a map in much the way that a recipe is a map. If I want to make cornbread, I have a favorite recipe in a particular cookbook and I check it to make sure I am using the right proportions and not leaving out the baking powder.

The Disciplines of Creative Conflict Resolution are a set of actions we can take to create a specific circumstance. They form a map for our behavior to help us get to a particular outcome.

## Distinctions

A distinction is a kind of map which helps us distinguish this from that. When I go to weed the zinnia bed I have in mind an image of a zinnia seedling. I hold in my mind a visual map of what zinnia seedlings look like. Anything which isn't a zinnia has to go.

A screwdriver is different from a bottle opener. I have used a screwdriver to open bottles and a bottle opener to turn a screw, but they each work best for the tasks for which they were designed. A distinction doesn't say that one thing is better than another...just different in a way that matters for the task before us.

We will return to the matter of distinctions later in this chapter.

## Other Maps

We have then three major categories of maps for negotiating the territory of our internal awareness and our relationships with others, words, disciplines, and distinctions; but these do not exhaust the kinds of maps we will be introducing and using. There are many other maps. For example, we have already introduced and will return to again and again the map of how to resolve a conflict. While there is a lot of detail in the map we have not explored yet, the broad outlines are that we name, address, and the resolve the conflict. Those three steps have to be done in that order. We will sometimes dismiss a conflict as irresolvable when we haven't fully named it yet. We have to name it in order to address it. We have to address it in order to resolve it. [You may want to explore the index for a list of some of the other maps or go to the web site for the book at www.JustConflict.com.]

## Believing and Believing In

One of my favorite stories is about the Baptist preacher who was asked by one of the members of his church if he believed in infant baptism. "Believe it," he replied horrified, "I've seen it!"

I admit that many of those I tell this to greet the story with puzzled silence. While some may not be aware that a central feature of the Baptist tradition is that the sacrament of baptism is only administered to those who have attained the age of reason and thus reject the baptism of infants, I think mostly the silence comes from the expectation that there is more to the story.

The story, to my ear, is the distinction between what we *believe* and what we *believe in*.

We *believe* what we find to be a true fact. We *believe* in what we find to be a true perspective or frame of reference. In either case we are referring to what we experience as an accurate representation of reality. But the *belief* has to do with an item of that reality and the *belief in* has to do with a much more complex map. When we believe in something we are looking out at the world from within the frame of the belief system.

When people say they "believe in Jesus" they are not saying simply that they believe that there was an actual historic person named Jesus; they are saying that they hold to a complex set of beliefs about him, about the nature of God, about the purpose of life, and so on.

When people say that they don't believe in divorce, they are not saying they don't believe people get divorced, they are saying they will not choose divorce for themselves and they may even be implying a critical judgment of those who do so choose.

## Getting it

When there is a complex way of looking at the world which is shared by a group of people—that is, when there is something in which they all believe—others may or may not see or become able to see from that complex perspective. When those who share the perspective encounter those who do not they may say about those who do not that they just "don't get it."

In some cases we may find ourselves listening to someone tell a story or joke and at some point others begin to laugh and we can't figure out what is funny. We "don't get it."

When my son became able to read the word *stop* and thus it suddenly appeared on nearly every corner he became someone who "got it."

But sometimes the crowd holds a perspective which we used to hold as well and which we have since abandoned as a faulty map. In this case they see us as not getting it when we see them as not getting it. We follow different maps.

## **Choosing the Best Map**

With all of these maps in the glove box of our awareness it is important that we grab the best one. As we have already noted, there are essentially three things we look to create with the cognitive maps we hold. We want to be able to find out where we are, where we are going, and how we might get there.

Sometimes a single map will help with all three tasks but sometimes we will need different maps.

Where am I? What is my current situation? What is actually happening? What is reality? We are not going to be able to do anything without a clear picture of the present circumstances. This is why the Freedom of Information Act is so important to so many causes. It allows people a greater access to matters which affect them. One of the ways we can keep others from self-determination is to hide information from them. We will return to the issue of secrecy in addressing conflict when we explore the notion of oppression.

Where do I want to go? There are several maps we will introduce to help with this task. One is the distinction between what we want and what we need. We will explore a series of maps for helping us identify what we need in Chapter Ten. We will find that the chances of getting what we need are greatly enhanced by knowing what we need.

What can I do to get there? Ultimately we will have to change our behavior. We will have to do something different from what we are already doing. This requires that we have a strategy. The third part of this book is about strategies. Strategies create events which create the conditions which allow certain qualities to arise. It is important to remember that getting what we need requires certain qualities be present in our relationships. Don't pick a strategy until you are clear what the qualities are you are trying to create.

## How Do We Use These Maps to Help Us Make Choices?

Whenever an event arises it affects us. We notice the circumstance or the issue and we try to make meaning out of it. We are meaning makers and we do this by finding a map which is a way of thinking which explains the phenomenon we are observing. We all struggle to make meaning but we don't all use the same maps. As we will see, we don't even each use the same maps consistently. Based on the meaning we have made, we come to an interpretation of an event and then choose a behavior as a response to the interpretation.

There are a series of steps we go through over and over again as we move through our lives attending to the experiences which arise for us.

- What is going on? What do my senses tell me about the current reality? What will I pay attention to and ignore? There is a real experience happening that I am not in control of and I want to respond appropriately.
- What does it mean that this is happening? Which map I am going to use to make sense of this territory?
- How will I apply the map to the perception such that I come to an interpretation?
- Then finally, what am I going to do in response to my interpretation? How will I act to get what I need?

So we have a conceptual map here in four steps which leads from the event to our response to the event.

1. We have the *perception* of what is happening.

2. We retrieve the *core belief* or *cognitive map* which we think best gives meaning to the perception.

3. We use the map to create the *interpretation* of the event.

4. We make the *choice to act* in a particular way in response to the event.

This process happens over and over from moment to moment in our daily existence but it becomes most crucial when applied to the conflicts which arise repeatedly in our most significant relationships.

## How Do Maps Get Broken?

All maps worked to some degree when we first created them or we would not have chosen them. But just because a map had some utility in the past doesn't mean it is a good map now, and it certainly may not be the best map available now.

Some maps that used to be great are just out of date. My old city map doesn't have some newer roads on it. The map I used to figure out how to please Mrs. McKinley, my first grade teacher, didn't work at all with Mr. Wolfe, my ninth grade teacher.

Some maps are great for some problems but don't work at all for others. My Kansas City map doesn't help with St. Louis. My map for how to be successful as a psychotherapist doesn't help me much in dealing with my family. They just tell me to quit acting like a therapist. My map for teaching my dog to fetch isn't going to work with my cat.

Some maps are either too simple or too complex for the task at hand. With a web-based mapping program we can scroll in or scroll out to get the level of detail we are looking for. I don't need the names of the side streets when I am trying to get to Chicago. But once I get to Chicago, I need more detail to know where I am going. Newtonian physics works great for simple tasks of calculating the properties of objects in motion when they are my size, but it doesn't work for sub-atomic properties or the motion of planets.

So we find that we have maps which don't work as tools for solving the problem at hand. They may have worked before, or they may work in a different context, but for this problem they don't bring clarity. So we set them aside. Except that sometimes we don't. Sometimes we cling to an old familiar map even though it isn't working for us. When we do this, the map becomes what we call a *cognitive distortion*.

## Cognitive Distortions

All maps are simplifications of reality which help us know what is going on, what we want to have happen, or what we must do to create the outcome we desire. No perspective is perfect. We are seeking perspectives which balance ease of use with accuracy. The more accurate the point of view, the harder it is to see from it. The easier the paradigm, the less complexity it has and thus the likelihood it is to be accurate. Again, as Einstein pointed out, we want to find a way of looking at things which is as simple as possible, and no simpler.

Thus, every perspective is also inaccurate. It has flaws or limitations. It may be said that all cognition is to some degree distorted. But we are going to limit our use of the term *cognitive distortion* to a narrower meaning, one that takes into account not only the flaws of the map, but the flaws in the process by which we choose a particular map.

I may well choose a perspective or paradigm only to discover that it doesn't help me solve the problem I am trying to address. When it doesn't fit, it is best for me to put it down and find a better map. But, from time to time, we find that a point of view doesn't explain the reality we are viewing and yet we cling to the point of view and insist that the experience we are having must be wrong. We choose the map over the experience we are trying to explain. These are cognitive distortions.

We all harbor cognitive distortions. We all view the world in which we live in ways that don't match the reality we are experiencing and, yet, we cling to the perspective and insist it must be right. We all do this. And we don't know when we are doing it. We are all blind to our own cognitive distortions.

The most pernicious cognitive distortions come from a willfulness not to see. We may have reason to know that something is affecting us and our circumstances and yet we choose not to look at it. The man who flies into a rage at his wife may then apologize and tell himself that it is over and assumes that things are fine between them. The company pays someone to haul off the toxic byproducts of its manufacturing and gives no thought to where the toxins will end up or who they will poison. The civilization sates its thirst for energy by mining carbon from the ground and discharging it into the atmosphere and then only looks at the "progress" this theft creates.

If we don't come to recognize our cognitive distortions we will continue to do the same things over and over and expect a different result. My grandpa, a wood pattern maker, used to tell of the carpenter who said, "I've cut that board three times and it still isn't long enough." If cutting a board is something one does to make it the right length, then cutting it should work.

The global economic meltdown in 2008 happened, in part, because the experts in understanding the market in mortgage derivatives were people who stood to gain financially from the accuracy of the forecasting models they were using and promoting. They had reason to favor the cognitive maps they were using and didn't have an incentive to discover the shortcomings in those maps. They were blinded by the chance to make money and, thus, didn't see their own cognitive distortions.

Since becoming able to see our own cognitive distortions is essential to our own safety and satisfaction it is important that we explore some ways we can make our own distortions more visible to us. We can sometimes spot our cognitive distortions by listening to the ways we talk about things. If we notice the words *should*, *ought* and *supposed* to we can sometimes catch ourselves in our own cognitive distortions. If we say that something *should* be a particular way, we can then try the same sentence without the *should*. If we know the resulting sentence is false, then we know it is a cognitive distortion.

For example, try the statement, "Children should do what their parents tell them to do." Most of us would agree with that statement. But what if we take the *should* out. "Children do what their parents tell them to do." No they don't. Not always. In some families it is not even usually. Children do what they want to do, just like the rest of us. Children do what we tell them to do when they want to please us and when they know how to do what we want. And when they don't want to or don't know how to, they don't.

Let's look at a somewhat more complex example of a cognitive distortion in Joe and Jane's relationship.

> As Joe and Jane are getting dressed for work on a Wednesday morning, Joe notices how beautiful Jane is. He feels his desire for her and he wishes they could take the day off and be together. He tries to give her some affection and she pushes him away saying, "I'm late!"

> Joe has an early day so he picks up the boys from day care and is home by 4:30. Jane gets off at 5:00 and is usually home by 5:15. When she isn't home by 5:20, Joe starts to worry. At 5:25 he starts to pace and by 5:30 he calls her mobile phone and doesn't get an answer. He can't figure out what is going on.

Joe has a choice of maps he can use to interpret the meaning of these events. He can use the one he got from his dad when his dad was upset with his mom for hanging out at the local bar. That one is a lot like the one he built for himself when in high school he dated the captain of the cheerleading squad who dumped him at Homecoming to be with the star quarterback. By this map he can see how much he is at risk of losing Jane to some other guy and how careful he must be to let her know he is watching her.

Or he can use the cognitive map he built for himself the year he worked on the other side of town past the highway construction that caused huge traffic jams every evening. It took hours to get home. By this map he can see how stressed she must be and how much she is at risk driving in this traffic and how scared he should be for her safety.

In either case he will be using his perspective on what is happening to help him decide what is going on, what he wants things to be like, and what he will do to create what he wants. His behavior will be a product of how he interprets his perceptions.

The perception Joe has that Jane is late is a product of his expectations. But he doesn't see this as his choice. He sees that she *is* late. It is true that she isn't home and she does get off work at 5:00 and she works 15 minutes from home and she left home looking really good this morning. Those are all simply observations of fact. Joe gets to decide whether he will pay attention. And he gets to decide to what he will pay attention. But he doesn't get to decide what is actually happening. We all have the opportunity to choose whether we pay attention and to what. But we are simply noticing what has already happened.

We do, however, get to decide what the event means. We filter our perceptions through our core beliefs in order to construct an interpretation of what these events mean. We get to select a map by which we will determine the meaning of the events we observe. Then based on the interpretation we have come to as to the meaning of this event, we will choose our behavior.

Thus, Joe may be all up in Jane's face when she gets home wondering who she has been with and why she isn't answering her phone. Or he may be concerned and attentive and urge her to sit down and put her feet up while he fixes her a cup of tea and tells her how glad he is that she made it home safely. Each is a potential action he may take. And there are infinite other options of how he can interpret the data and choose to respond.

## Discipline #3: Inviting Critical Feedback

We are now ready to introduce the third of the ten disciplines. Remember these are simple ways we can increase our mindfulness and our skill at conflict resolution.

We all harbor cognitive distortions. We all have a way of looking at what is arising for us and interpreting what it means in ways that don't actually fit what is going on. These bad maps lead us to poor choices...to choices which don't actually construct what we need. Still, we cling to these bad maps because they once worked, we get comfort in the familiar, and they are the best we have.

*Mapping Our Reality*

One very common map is the one called, "But I didn't do anything wrong!" This is one we use to protect our sense of our own goodness and rightness, and to shield us from blame. We may have looked at the way we intended to show up and can see that we are being very close to who we intend to be and, thus, conclude that what we did was not a mistake. "This really is who I intend to be and I am a good person so what's the problem?"

The problem is that what I am doing is not getting me what I need. The problem is that what I am doing is harming another or my relationship to another. And the problem is that I can't see it. I am only seeing from my own point of view. The only way I am going to "get it" is by seeing from another's perspective.

The good news is that we are always getting feedback from others about how they see the events in our relationship and how they see us. The bad news is that we are not always open to the feedback and sometimes the feedback itself is a product of the other's cognitive distortions. So then what do we need to do to be open to the feedback and how can we tell if it is any good?

First we must be clear that we will benefit from getting the feedback. We must be clear that this is data which will help us see from a more accurate perspective and thus be able to make better choices.

Second we must know that just because others see things differently doesn't necessarily mean that we are seeing things wrong. There are lots of perspectives which may all be accurate but partial. Remember the blind men and the elephant.

Third we have to be able to sort through the data we get by our openness to other's points of view to find the ones which are really good for us. There are a couple of things which help here. One is to notice that when lots of points of view agree they are all pointing to the same reality. The more we keep getting the same feedback from different sources, the more accurate the feedback is likely to be.

If I go into the fun house at the carnival there is a room with lots of twisted mirrors. Some make me look fat...some make me look skinny. But if they all show me wearing a red shirt, I probably have a red shirt on.

When radio telescopes gather data from distant stars they get a reading from a whole array of antennas. Then the data from each antenna or dish is fed into a computer and the signals are compared to each other. The signals that all of the antennas share are considered the real signal and all the rest is noise.

When we get the same feedback from many different sources it is probably good feedback. That doesn't mean that if we only get it from one source it is bogus. Maybe the feedback is about something only some people can see. Or maybe the feedback is from a really good source.

Some sources are from the perspective of people who seem to be making really good choices in their own lives. When the source is someone who is doing well at constructing their own needs, chances are he or she is someone who sees clearly. If the source is someone whose own life is a mess, chances are the feedback is less helpful.

Still, remember that all sources can be golden and all can be fool's gold. It takes practice to discern the difference. But we have to be paying attention and open to the feedback. When, from time to time, you make choices with which the other doesn't agree, would you like to;

- know what it is you have done the other finds troubling,
- know what it is about the choice which is troubling to the other, and
- know what the other sees as more helpful in those circumstances?

If you don't want that, then you won't be able to harvest this good information.

For Joe to be able to get the best outcome, there are some distinctions he will need to be able to make between the various maps that are available to him as he tries to make meaning of Jane's late arrival home. To start with, let's be clear about what distinctions are.

## Making Distinctions

Our ability to distinguish *this* from *that* is one measure of intelligence. Standardized IQ tests measure one's ability to know how one thing is different from another and even how the difference between A and B may be like or unlike the difference between C and D. Scoring well on such tests may not be a good indicator of one's ability to get on in life, but being able to distinguish between things is a necessary skill if one is weeding a garden or preparing a meal; that is, can I tell the difference between and weed and a radish, or between salt and sugar.

Distinctions are not between *what is good* and *what is bad* or between *what is right* and *what is wrong*. It is not that one is better than the other. They are only different in ways that may not be easily apparent. So why make the distinction? Because while they are not right and wrong, there are ways in which one may be more effective at creating a satisfying outcome than the other in a particular context.

For example, we have noted that it is important to make a distinction between a *conflict* and a *fight*. This is hard because we sometimes use those words as synonyms, as when we talk about an international conflict when what we are referring to is a war. Certainly a war is a kind of fight. For our purposes, though, we want to be able to notice that there is a condition in a relationship that we call a *conflict* even before we begin to do something about it. A *fight* is one of the strategies that people use to address conflicts, but the conflict exists before the fight starts and we can choose not to fight even if there is a conflict. A *conflict* is a condition in a relationship in which one or both parties don't like the way the other is being. A *fight* is a way of addressing a conflict in which the goal is to try to make the other lose.

So while we sometimes use the word *conflict* to mean *fight* there is a useful distinction we can make between them. Most people, once the distinction has been made for them, are able to reliably continue to see and make the distinction. But there are some distinctions that are much harder to make consistently. One example is voiced by the Serenity Prayer with which many are familiar. There are variations, but the one I am familiar with is:

> *God grant me the serenity to accept the things I cannot change,*
> *The courage to change the things I can, and*
> *The wisdom to know the difference.*

Personally, I think it should be referred to as the Wisdom Prayer as the crucial capacity is the ability to distinguish *what I can do* from *what I cannot do*. This is a distinction which is very hard to make. It seems simple, but it certainly isn't easy. And, as the popularity of the prayer can attest, it is very important to know the difference.

## Perceptions and Choices

At one level we can make a clear and simple distinction between those things which are within our control and those which are not. I can notice that it is sunny or rainy today but my choices are not going to change the weather. I can decide what I will wear based on the weather, and I will be more comfortable in my rain jacket if it is raining. My choices construct my experience. But if the weather changes, so will my jacket.

We are, thus, going to talk about two aspects of our experience: our perceptions and our choices. Further, we are going to note that the more we give attention to our perceptions, the more we will construct awareness. The more we give attention to our choices, the more we will construct mastery. That seems simple enough.

But the attention we give to our perceptions which results in awareness is a product of our choices. And the more we practice attending to our perceptions the more mastery we develop in the art of constructing awareness.

Similarly, since we have far more experience than we can fully attend to at any time, the choice to attend to something creates our perception. You didn't perceive your second grade classroom until you accepted my invitation to focus your attention there. Then you were able to bring to mind the memory of the room and to apply to it the tools of perception you have developed since the last time you were there. The choice created the perception.

So our experience of our perceptions which we cannot change (only notice or not notice) and our choices which we can change (though not as easily as we might like) are closely related to each other. They can at times appear as different sides of the same coin.

As with any distinction, heads are not better than tails (unless I have already called one or the other). But as I hold the coin in front of me one side is toward me and the other is away from me. My observation that it is rainy was accurate and my choice to wear my rain jacket was a good choice when I made it. Now that the sun has come out the jacket is too warm. My perception has changed so I will make a new choice. I will take off my jacket. There is a chain of perceptions leading to choices which lead to perceptions.

There are a couple of medical terms which I hope will help to clarify the mix of perceptions and choices. These are the terms *distal* and *proximal*. They have to do with the relative positions of two parts of the same thing, the two sides of the same coin. One is closer (proximal) and the other is farther away (distal). When I smile, the part of my tooth you see is the distal side, the side my tongue rests on is the proximal side. A shoulder is proximal to the elbow, but the elbow is proximal to the wrist.

This distinction between what is closer and what is farther away will help us appreciate some aspects of five distinctions that are important to master if we are going to become skillful at resolving conflict.

## Five Crucial Distinctions

1. *Event* from *Meaning*: What happened is different from the story that I tell about what happened. How I make meaning about the events in my life is very important. But the meaning I make and the story I tell about the event (proximal) are not the same as the event itself (distal). Indeed, others who experienced the same event may find it to mean something very different from what it means to me.

2. *Feelings* from *behavior*: Just because I may be experiencing a particular feeling or set of feelings doesn't mean I will behave in any given way. Feelings (proximal) are not the same as behavior (distal).

3. *Effect* from *Cause*: What effect the event had on me is different from what I think caused the effect. Can I be aware of what is going on within me (proximal) as different from what I believe is going on around me (distal)?

4. *What I want* from *what I need*: I want others to be the way I want them to be (distal). What I need is to have certain qualities in my relationships with others (proximal).

5. *What I can do* from *what I cannot do*: When I focus on what I cannot do anything about (distal), I feel powerless and hopeless. When I focus on what I can do (proximal), I discover how immensely powerful I really am.

Let's see what happens as we apply these distinctions to the choices Joe makes as he decides how to respond to Jane arriving home later than he expects her to.

- **Event from Meaning:** Joe knows what happened. But if he thinks what happened is what he makes it mean, then he is reacting to his meaning, not to the events. For example, he may think Jane dressed to impress some other guy. He knows that she left home looking good, but he doesn't know whether she was making a special effort today or why. He may think that Jane decided not to pick up when he called her. He knows that he called and that she didn't answer, but he doesn't know if she was in a dead zone, had her ringer off, or was talking to someone else and decided not to click over.
- **Feeling from Behavior:** Joe is feeling scared. He may not know this. He may think he is angry (and, of course, he is feeling that too, but the core of his concern is his fear of losing his beloved) and he may well think that he must let his anger out by yelling, accusing, slamming things around. If he doesn't know that he is free to decide what he wants to do no matter what he is feeling, he may not slow down enough to make conscious choices about his behavior.
- **Effect from Cause:** Joe knows he is deeply affected by the events that are happening (or not happening) but the focus of his attention is not on his own interior awareness, but on what he sees happening around him and the meaning he makes of it. If he was able to notice his fear, he might then be able to wonder what he is afraid of and to assess what he can do to protect himself and those he cares about. But as long as his focus is on the cause of his distress he will not notice just how it is affecting him.
- **Wants from Needs:** Joe *wants* Jane to be home. He *wants* to have the reassurance that she is okay and that she remains committed to him and to their marriage and family. Each of these depends on her being different in ways Joe can't determine. He *wants* her home because he enjoys her company and *needs* the intimacy they create with each other. He *wants* her reassurance because he *needs* a relationship with her which is characterized by trust and mutual support. But if he cannot see these distinctions between what he *wants* and what he *needs*, then all he knows is that he wants her to avoid conversations with male colleagues at work. Thus he will likely try to get her to behave differently in ways that will have the opposite effect. He will become shrill and demanding and she will withdraw.

*Mapping Our Reality*

- **Can Do from Cannot Do:** Joe cannot make Jane answer her phone. He cannot make her drive safely or arrive home when he expects her. As long as the focus of his attention is on Jane making these changes, he will be disappointed. When we try to change the things we cannot change, the natural consequence is that we feel helpless and hopeless. When, however, Joe decides that what he needs is a caring and attentive and intimate relationship with Jane, he can create that by listening to what happened with her today and see what she says kept her later than Joe expected. When we focus on what we can do to create what we need, we discover just how immensely powerful we really are.

There is one other broader distinction that will help Joe as he discovers how he can respond to Jane's arrival home later than he wanted.

## Expectations and Standards

We often use the terms *expectation* and *standard* interchangeably. Indeed they can be synonymous, but I want to suggest a way of making a very helpful distinction which can support our ability to select the best possible map for a given situation. To that end I suggest we use the terms in the following manner.

*Expectation* refers to the map we use to anticipate what is most likely to actually happen (perception).

*Standard* refers to the map we use to guide how we actually want our own behavior to be (choice).

Please notice that neither of these maps refers to *how I want the other to behave*, only to *what I actually have reason to expect the other will do*.

We want our expectations to be as close as possible to exactly what is actually going to happen. We, of course, can't always know what is going to happen, so we are sometimes surprised or disappointed. The closer our expectations are to reality, the more we can accurately anticipate what our experience will be. We want our expectations to be spot on. If things don't go the way we expect, we want to alter our expectations.

Standards on the other hand are the way we hope we will be able to behave and, thus, are just a bit better than what we have actually been able to do. Standards are the adjustable supports that hold the bar in the high jump. They can be set at different heights depending upon the ability of the high jumper. The height is set just slightly higher than the last jump the athlete was able to make. Ideally, we want to have our standards be just a bit beyond what we are usually able to do. If they are too low, we sell ourselves short. If they are too high, we set ourselves up for continual failure.

Joe was expecting that Jane would be home by 5:15. He was expecting that when he gave her some affection that morning it would be returned. He was expecting that when he called her she would answer. None of these expectations were met.

Joe could see this as evidence he is not making accurate maps. As he builds his expectations he is failing to take into account that Jane may be distracted by concerns about work and thus rushed in the morning when he wants to play with her. He is not adequately taking into account the demands which may keep her late at work, or may slow her progress home, or may have sent her into a store to get something for dinner while leaving her phone in the car.

Joe may forget that he cannot appropriately set standards for Jane and may try to tell her when she should be home, how she should dress, and with whom she should and should not talk. Or he may remember that standards are about his own behavior and focus on how he wants to act when he is disappointed and afraid.

Still, he is feeling upset. He is afraid and angry. These feelings seem to him to be coming from Jane and her choices. Indeed, it was her choices which created the events which evoked these feelings in Joe and allowed these qualities to arise for him in his relationship with her. But the feelings are actually coming from the tension within Joe which he is projecting onto Jane. This strategy of projection is one we all use to protect ourselves from unwanted feelings. The problem with this strategy is that it disowns the feelings and thus inhibits us from addressing them at the source. We will return to this problem in Chapter Five.

## Summary

We are meaning makers. We make sense of the world by giving meaning to events and circumstances. This meaning is a form of conceptual map. We don't all have the same map for understanding the world in which we live. When we are operating off of a different map than those around us, we find ourselves in conflict with them.

Repairing our relationships requires that we use the best possible maps. There are many maps we will introduce in this book. They all have to do with developing a perspective or a lens with which to see and to make sense of what is arising for us so that we can make the best possible choice so as to create what we need.

But there are no perfect maps. All maps are by their very nature a rough approximation of reality. Thus we must be careful to understand the limitations of our maps. Sometimes we become so attached to a familiar map that we insist that it is more real than the experience it is supposed to explain. When we cling to the map rather than the reality we are creating a cognitive distortion. We all do this from time to time and we can't see our own distortions. We have to be able to get external feedback to be able to see what we are doing.

To be able to attract that external view we can use the third discipline to cultivate critical feedback. This requires that we be able to acknowledge that others may have a different perspective than our own and that there may be value to us to know how their perspective is valid for them. We will have to develop the skill of knowing and trusting our own perspectives well enough that we can set them aside and genuinely hear the perspectives of the other with openness and appreciation. This skill is essential for resolving conflicts in the Interpersonal Realm.

One particular type of map we make great use of is the ability to make a distinction between two similar things. There are five distinctions which are crucial to our ability to address relational conflicts. There is another distinction, that between expectations and standards, which helps us to see that the conflicts we may think we have with others are actually conflicts we are having with ourselves which we are projecting onto others.

# 3

# What Makes it so Hard to Change?

Many of the things which bother us are the choices others make. What they choose to do really matters to us. We can act as though we are not bothered, but we really are. Their choices have a genuinely negative impact on us and we wish they would change.

Still, we have tried many strategies and none of them seem to work to get others to be different. We don't seem to be able to make others change.

Some people actually do believe they can make others change because they relate to them in a way that shifts their behavior. When this works, it works because the other actually wants to be pleasing or finds the new way of being more satisfying in its own right. When we are simply creating compliance—bullying—the change doesn't last and the troubling behaviors will return.

We assume, therefore, there is nothing we can do. "The others are causing the problem. I can't change the others. I am helpless." This is a way of looking at the problem which makes the problem impossible to solve.

We each have a part of us who is willing to do whatever it takes to improve our lives. We have another part that is keen to preserve our self-esteem. If we start trying to change, the self-esteem part reasons, "it is like saying there is something wrong with me the way I am. I try hard; I am a 'good person.' I shouldn't have to do anything differently."

No, I don't have to do anything differently. I can continue to be just as I currently am. But if there is any part of my life in which I am not fully safe and satisfied, then there are things I can do differently that will help me get what I need.

# Changing Myself and Not the Other

The simplest thing about the perspective of Creative Conflict Resolution is also the hardest for most folks to fully take in.

*In order to get what I need I have to change what I do.*

What makes this so hard to fully comprehend is that we think we already know it. Indeed we do. But that doesn't stop us from trying to change others. It is fine to want them to be different. It may well be in their best interest that they make different choices too. But the degree to which my goal is to get others to change, or even the degree to which I gauge the effectiveness of my own changes on how it makes others be different, is the degree to which I am sabotaging my own ability to create what I need.

We will say much more about that last point as we move along. Let's, for the moment, look at some of the common ways we resist changing ourselves.

- **I can't change. This is just the way I am.** There is, of course, some truth to this. There are some things about who I am and how I am which I simply will not be able to change. And some of these things have a huge impact on the kinds and qualities of relationship I am able to build with others. I can't change the timbre of my voice. I can't change how tall I am or the color of my skin. I can't change my sexual orientation. There are even some aspects of how the culture in which I grew up powerfully dictates how I will experience the events in my life. But I can become more aware of my feelings. I can notice how I am of two minds about some of the events and choices that appear to me. I can learn to express my anger in ways that feel safe to others.

- **Why should I have to change when I didn't do anything wrong?** We have all had people tell us we should be different because they see us as bad or wrong the way we are. If we were to change it would be like admitting they were right. We all have a part of us which is proud of who we are and what we have been able to do. "Sure, I haven't always been perfect. But I know, at heart, I am a good person. If I change, isn't that like saying the way I am is bad?" No, the reason to change is not because I am bad or wrong the way I am, but because I am not as satisfied with my life as I would like to be.

- **I can change all I want but if my partner doesn't change, what good will it do?** Our reasoning is that, if the relationship is created by the choices we are both making, then the only way to change the relationship is for both of us to change. There is a kind of logic to this. Embedded in this is the notion that, if I am the one to change, then isn't it like an admission that I am the one who is making the problems? No, actually, that isn't true. If I am the one to change then that is a declaration that I am the one who most wants things to be different. Certainly, if both parties are in agreement that there are ways they want the relationship to be different and they are willing to work together to create those changes, then they can expect it will be an easier and quicker transformation. We would prefer it to be that way. But what if the other is not as motivated to have things be different as I am? While I cannot change the other, I can change the relationship. All I have to do to change the relationship is to be different in the relationship. The trick is to figure out how to be different in a way that will move me toward what I need without expecting or depending upon the other changing.

The prospect of fully resolving our conflicts makes a promise so compelling that we have to wonder why anyone wouldn't want to make these changes. And yet, as we try to apply these principles, we find they are devilishly difficult to maintain. We keep slipping back into old habits.

There are some powerful reasons this change is so hard to sustain. Not only are we stubborn and defensive, but we also live in a culture that tells us who we are to be and how we are to act. Much of what makes it so hard to change is that to do so we have to go against the culture.

## Cultural Barriers to Change

Culture is the collection of expectations and agreements which shape who we are to be in any given context. Whenever we start a new job, we check to see what other people are wearing. Do we really have to be here on time? What happens if we call in sick? Do people expect everyone to go out to eat at lunch, or is there a lunch room, or do people eat at their desks?  These are all perceptions which arise in the Interpersonal or relational realm.

We are all members of many different cultures.  There is the family we grew up in, the religious institution where we worshipped, the schools we attended, the kids we hung out with, the pacts we made with our friends, the festivals our community celebrated.  Every relationship defines a culture.  Often we will only use the term culture to mean ethnicity or country of origin, and certainly those cultures are very powerful at shaping our identity and our behavior, but a culture is the container of expectations we create as we construct relationships.

There is another meaning for the term *culture* we often hear.  Any longstanding community has forms of artistic expression which help to communicate the expectations and values which form the culture.  Thus the cuisines, the graphic art, the music, the literature, the dress, the dialect are all expressions of the culture (art) of a given culture (community).

This communication of values and practices is even present in the micro-culture of a couple in a marriage.  I can remember as a child noticing that my dad never left for work in the morning without kissing my mom goodbye.  They kissed with a pattern of three kisses.  It was always the same.  These days, when my wife leaves the house for work, I make it a point to kiss her goodbye.  I don't feel right when I am busy with something and she gets away without getting a kiss.  I also need to give her a kiss before we go to sleep at night.  It is a ritual, a pattern of three little kisses.

ॐ

I remember the first time I went to Church Camp.  I had been to Scout Camp before, but Church Camp was different for a lot of reasons I couldn't figure out as a kid.  It wasn't just that it was a different place with different people.  It wasn't just that we were in cabins instead of tents.  It was that at Scout Camp I was around people I had known well for a long time.  At Scout Camp I was with the boys in my patrol and my troop.  These were guys I met with every week.  At Church Camp I was with a couple of kids I sort of knew from my own home church, but mostly these were people whom I didn't know and who didn't know me.

At Scout Camp, my big brother was the Patrol Leader and my dad was one of the adult leaders. Everyone knew I was Bob's son and Bruce's little brother. At Church Camp, I was just one of the kids from Prairie Village, whatever that might mean. Church Camp was my first experience of people relating to me solely on the basis of how I appeared to them in the moment, not their beliefs about who the Robinsons are.

Of course, as a kid, I didn't understand what it was that was different. But I did have a growing sense all week that I was coming to see myself differently as I came to understand how others saw me. They listened to me. They were curious about me. They saw me as a leader. As the second son, I hadn't been a leader before; I had only been a little brother. So I tried on being a leader. I kind of liked it.

I remember the opposite experience in my first semester of college. I was just far enough away from home that I couldn't easily return every weekend, so the first time back was over Thanksgiving Break. I had been at college. I was a college man now. I was an adult. I ran my own life, kept my own hours. And then I went home. And when I walked into my mother's kitchen, I was suddenly eight years old… or maybe ten. That confident college man was gone.

It is hard to overestimate the power of culture. The culture of that church camp brought out a part of me I had not known. The culture of my mother's kitchen dropped ten years off my maturity. The culture of a mob can get otherwise gentle and reasonable people to act horrendously. The culture of a sanctuary can slow our breath and calm our anxiety.

## The Three A's: Awareness, Acting in our own Behalf, and Accountability

The culture around us has an immense power to shape our expectations of ourselves, of others, and of the appropriate nature of relationships. Though the power of culture is largely positive, when cultural values promote behavior that is contrary to our own best interest, it can be extremely difficult to surmount.

While there may be many ways that our culture tells us how to be which aren't really in our best interest, there are three particularly problematic lessons we all get every day.

- Don't let it bother you.
- Don't be so selfish.
- Don't admit it when you mess up.

Each of these common messages contains a kernel of wisdom. Getting worked up about everything that happens is tiring and tiresome. Only being concerned for your personal interests denies your connection to others. Taking on responsibility for everything that happens is unrealistic and harmful to one's own self-esteem. But when we only see from this perspective, we end up sabotaging our relationships and ourselves.

## Awareness

We begin with the question of whether we pay attention and, if so, to what. We are told to pay attention at least as much as we are told not to let it bother us. We should "pay attention to what we are doing" if, by so doing, we are less likely to bother someone else. But if someone else does something that bothers us, we should "not let it bother us."

The position of Creative Conflict Resolution is simple… notice everything. Notice what pleases you, notice what bothers you, and notice what you do that pleases or bothers someone else. This is all important data. Don't let it slip away unnoticed.

The power of our culture to induce us not to pay attention is so incredibly great, especially when the short term benefits of not knowing are so high, that if we are to genuinely make changes which will improve the quality of our relationships, we are going to have to be very intentional. Just as we have to get into training if we are going to meet athletic goals, so will we have to engage in a conscious discipline if we are going to meet relationship goals.

## Acting in our own behalf

We are told not to be selfish. Some of us are labeled as part of the "Me" generation that is all about itself and that is a bad and self-centered thing. We should put others first. We especially hear this from the others who want us to put them first. We are told by people close to us who are not getting the attention they want, "This isn't all about you!" By implication, it is all about them.

The position of Creative Conflict Resolution is that we have an equal responsibility for the welfare of all, but we don't have an equal ability to act on behalf of all. The bulk of our effort should go where we can do the greatest good. The person whose needs I can best understand and am in the best position to address positively is myself. I will not be much good to others if I am not getting what I need. So we must act in our own behalf without it being at the expense of others.

Thus, our first responsibility is to take care of ourselves. This comes across to many as profoundly self centered, so I want to offer a distinction between *being self-centered* and *being centered in your self.*

Let's try another thought problem:

> *Think back into your past relationships and see if you can remember a time when someone accused you of being self-centered. Most of us have had this happen to us at one time or another.*
>
> *Now, consider how it felt to you to hear this accusation. You most probably didn't like it, but did it seem just, did it fit for you, or was it wholly untrue and wrong?*

Most people respond to this thought problem with a mix of observations. There are ways in which the accusation fit—I do sometimes think of myself without considering others—and ways in which it does not fit—I am very considerate of others.

We all have times of being so consumed with our own interests that we cannot make room in our awareness for the needs of others. Hopefully these times are rare, but they are most likely to arise when we are under the greatest stress. When we are well satisfied in ourselves, we have the emotional space to open up to consider others. For us to care for others, we must have our own wellbeing sufficiently addressed that we have room in our awareness for the needs of others.

On the other hand, sometimes we do such a poor job caring for ourselves, we become so out of touch with our own wellbeing, that we don't know what we need. We might insist we have no needs, but the truth is only that we don't know what they are.

It may be that our needs are not being met at all and, therefore, we are so stressed and disoriented that we aren't of any use to anyone, including ourselves. Or it may be that we are getting our needs met because others are taking care of us. If we are getting our needs met at the expense of others then we are needy and others may see us as self-centered precisely because we are not adequately caring for ourselves.

If we are genuinely committed to our own welfare, pay keen attention to what we need, and act immediately to generate what we need without trying to get it from others—then we are not needy, are centered in ourselves, and are able to act on behalf of others.

The antidote for being self-centered is to be centered in your self.

Whenever we fly on a commercial airline, while the plane is taxiing out, the flight attendant recites a statement about safety concerns that are mandated by the FAA. "Here are the wing exits, this is how the seat belt works, you can use your seat cushion for flotation." Then, near the end of the speech the flight attendant will say something like, "In the unlikely event of a sudden drop in cabin pressure, a mask will fall in front of you. Extend it to its full length, place it over your nose and mouth and breathe normally. If you are traveling with small children..." What do they say? Do they say a) make sure to get the mask on the child first, or b) put your own mask on first?

Time's up. The answer is b) put your own mask on first. And why would that be? Because if you are responsible for the child and you don't have sufficient oxygen, you won't be making clear and calm decisions. If you are struggling with a terrified child to get the mask on the child then neither of you is going to get what you need. But the FAA knows that most people will try to care for the children first, so they go to the trouble to remind us every time we fly; take care of ourselves first.

Anyone who has ever taken any sort of martial arts or self defense class knows that the first lesson is not a move but a stance. The first thing we learn is how to be centered; how to find our *tan dien*. When you are centered no one can throw you. When you are off center, you can easily be toppled.

Creative Conflict Resolution is a martial art for relationships. We don't know what sort of challenges the relationship will throw at us, but we want to respond from a place that is strong and centered and from which we can take care of ourselves without harming others.

## Accountability

One of the characters who appears from time to time in the comic The Family Circle is *Not Me*. In the comic *Not Me* looks a bit like a ghost but is the spirit which appears whenever the children are asked by a parent who it was that did a particular deed like breaking a lamp or scribbling on the wall. "Not me," they say together. We know at an early age to try to minimize our responsibility by making excuses for ourselves or to somehow shift it off onto someone else.

The position of Creative Conflict Resolution is that the best way to build healthy relationships is by claiming a stance of full accountability. We must notice how we affect others and how others affect us.

One can hardly open the newspaper without reading another story about how some corporation or politician has denied responsibility for something. It seems that the nature of public life is, for many, about shifting the blame. Ford blames Firestone; Enron blames Arthur Anderson; George W. Bush can't find anyone who leaked the news about Valerie Plame; Bill Clinton wonders what the meaning of the word "is" is.

Still there are dramatic examples of public accountability.

- Someone dies from tainted Tylenol and Johnson and Johnson not only pulls the entire product line off the market, it invents tamper-proof packaging thus changing the industry.
- A submarine surfaces off the coast of Hawaii and scuttles a Japanese fishing boat with a crew of trainees. At the court of inquiry the captain of the submarine, Commander James Waddle, faces the families of those who were lost and declares that, even though his decisions were not the only ones which constructed the disaster, as the captain, he is accountable.
- A boy in the custody of the Department of Social Services of the Commonwealth of Massachusetts is killed as a result of the apparent negligence of his foster parent. The Director of the Department goes to the funeral for the boy and affirms responsibility for the death and commits to a full inquiry.

These are not the ways we normally do things, but this is what we do when we are committed to building healthy relationships. The notion of what we might mean by accountability and what it might take to create it are topics we will return to once we have a few more concepts in place. For the moment, though, I will assert that our culture supports efforts to limit liability not simply to keep others from harm, but to avoid getting into trouble when harm finds them. Everyone in the corporate hierarchy knows that C.Y.A. stands for "cover your ass."

From the perspective of Creative Conflict Resolution, accountability is a prerequisite for creating the durable agreements that construct healthy relationships. We have to take into account not only how our choices affect others but also how others' choices affect us.

## Relational Barriers to Change

All of the cultural barriers to change we have just named also exist in the micro-culture of a given relationship between two people. Just to reiterate, these include:

- We have been taught how things are supposed to be:
    - *Who I am:* my characteristics, what I am expected to do and not do (my roles and responsibilities.)
    - *Who others are:* the characteristics of the other and what I can expect the other to do or not do.
    - *What relationships are like:* the qualities or characteristics that are attached to various kinds of relationships and how rights and responsibilities are distributed in those kinds of relationships.

- We are told daily what we are supposed to do:
    - *Don't become Aware:* don't let things bother you and don't pay attention to the things which irritate you.
    - *Don't Act in your own behalf:* don't be selfish and don't make it all about you.
    - *Don't be Accountable:* don't admit when you screw up; the important thing is your image and that you mean well.

As the level of intimacy in the relationship grows, the power of the expectations of the other grows with it. We most want to please the people we are closest to, and we are the most displeased when those closest to us aren't the way we want them to be.

In any relationship we are confronted with choices about whether we will act to preserve or improve the relationship, or whether we will act in our own interest separate from the relationship. We ask ourselves, "Will I be who the other wants me to be, or will I be who I choose to be." While we typically experience this choice as one between what the other wants and what we want (occurring in the Interpersonal realm), it is really more a choice between what a part of me wants and what another part of me wants (occuring in the Intrapersonal realm). A part of me wants to please the other, and another part of me wants what I want. Our most special relationships are different from ordinary ones. We are can be so urgent to create and sustain them that we are more than usually willing to abandon our own interests.

One of the things we will explore more fully in later chapters is the awareness that our conflicts with others, especially with others we are close to, are always conflicts we are having with ourselves which we experience as something out there in the relationship. This is not to say that we are making it all up. People really do things we don't like. But our capacity to change such that we can resolve the conflict depends upon our awareness of our inner conflicts and our willingness to name, address, and resolve them. We cannot fully address the interpersonal aspects of our conflicts, especially with those we are very close to, without first addressing the intrapersonal aspects of those conflicts.

The distinction between what is going on around us and what is going on within us can sometimes get very muddy and can result in some potentially destructive behavior when confronted with conflicts. Sometimes a relationship is so important to us, the other is so important to us, the success and stability of the connection to the other is so vital to us, that we lose a sense that we are separate from the relationship. We come to believe in some sense that "without this relationship I am nothing."

This is what happens to us when we become obsessed by a relationship. In some respects such an obsession feels wonderful. It is an intense feeling of connectedness to another. There is something that feels deeply spiritual about

*What Makes it so Hard to Change?*

this loss of self boundaries as we become "blended" with another.

But it is also something which causes us to do crazy things. This is what happens with people who become stalkers. They imagine they are so connected to the object of their attraction that they deserve to be with them and that the other really wants to be with them. This is what happens with men who kill the families they are afraid of losing and then kill themselves. They say to themselves, "If I can't be family with them, then I am nothing. But they are me so they are nothing. So I will annihilate us all."

Fortunately very few of us become so gripped with obsessive love that it leads us to murder, but many of us do things which look crazy to others. Others can't figure out why we are still married to that person, or dating that person. We may even decide that we are going to change how we are in the relationship and then find we can't because, if we do, we may lose the relationship and, consequently, some essential aspect of who we are.

This energy of attraction we find in our most significant relationships can be a force-field which keeps us stuck in ways of being which are not in our own best interest or even in the best interests of the other. It is possible that we can use the energy to actually promote our own transformation but that will require deeper awareness of the conflicts within.

## Personal barriers to change

While there are cultural and relational barriers to change, ultimately the only person stopping us is ourself. There are lots of things that bother us which we are simply not going to do anything about. Whatever we can think of to do may require more effort than we believe the problem deserves. Getting ourselves to move from noticing that we are bothered to actually doing something about it is a huge hurdle. Let's look at all the steps that it takes to get us to act.

1. **There is a problem.** I notice there is something wrong. Even as I try to "not let things bother me," the bother arises in my awareness. Lots of things may be wrong, but they don't appear as problems to us until they are big enough that we notice them. What we notice may be a circumstance with another or sensations arising within us.

2. **It is my problem.** Even if I recognize the existence of a problem, I am not moved to do anything about it until I own the problem. The only problems I can solve are my own. Until and unless I take it on as a problem of *mine*, I am not going to act. If it is a big enough problem for me that I want to do something about it, but I am denying that it is *my* problem, then I create a situation in which I hobble my own ability to address the problem. If this is a problem for me, what part of it is my problem? My part is the only part I can solve.

3. **It is a big enough problem that I want to address it.** If I am sufficiently aware of my own circumstances I will notice many things that bother me. If I have insight into my own internal ecology I will know what it is about this circumstance that I find bothersome. But it will have to rise to a level of importance above a certain threshold before I am willing to act. This point depends on many factors in my life but, in general, the more frantic my life, the higher the threshold. If I am experiencing a lot of chaos around me I will only address the really big things. When things calm down, some of the stuff that I have been ignoring will rise to the surface.

4. **I have an idea of what I can do to address it.** Having decided that this is something that will hold my attention and shape my behavior, I will now need a plan of action. I will have to at least have a plan that I have some reason to believe will be successful. If I find myself saying to myself that I have already done everything, then I will talk myself out of acting.

5. **I am willing to change myself in order to address it.** No matter what the plan is, it will require me to act differently than I have been acting. There are some strong reasons why we stop ourselves from any choices that focus on changing ourselves. One of the largest is our assertion that the only reason anyone should have to change is if they are bad or wrong the way they are. If I am not at fault, then this is not my responsibility. In fact, the reason for me to change is not because I am bad or wrong the way I am, but because the way I am is not getting me what I need.

*What Makes it so Hard to Change?*

6. **I have confidence in my ability to address it.** Even if I have a plan, and even if I am willing to change myself in order to implement it, if I don't trust that I can actually do what I intend, then I will stop myself in order to avoid failure. It is only when I am reasonably confident in my own ability that I will act. But if, as I envision myself enacting my own plan I think, "I am going to blow it," then I am going to spare myself the embarrassment and do nothing instead.

7. **I am worth the effort it will take to address it.** Still, this may take a lot of effort. And if it is really all about getting me what I need, and if I am not all that important, then, why bother? Those of us who were raised in families where we were precious and protected, know that we are valuable and don't have any trouble acting in our own behalf. But those of us who were neglected or abused as children don't have that same sense of our own worth and thus find it very hard to care for ourselves.

It is only when we have all seven steps in place that we will actually do something. If any one of these is missing, we don't act. These seven steps will come up again and again throughout this book. We can have all of the insight in the world, but until we actually change our behavior, nothing changes.

> I am walking down the street and I notice a sensation along the instep of my left foot. I think this is caused by a rock in my shoe. I don't know how the rock got there, but I am quite sure it won't go away without intervention. It is my foot which will be harmed if I don't do something. I only have a couple more blocks to walk to meet a friend; I could deal with it then. But here is a bench I can sit on to take off my shoe. It will mean stopping for a moment to deal with it and I don't want to be late, but I also don't want a blister. I'll stop here.

The simple act of stopping to let the rock out of my shoe is predicated on my having noticed that there is a problem, owning it as my problem, deciding it is big enough that I want to deal with it, having a plan, deciding that I can change my current way of being to address it, and knowing that I am both competent and worth the effort. So I do it.

Let's take another example, this time in the lives of the Johnsons.

*Joe is sitting watching the news when he hears his wife, Jane, engaging their son, Jack, over his failure to take out the trash. Joe notices that the sound is distracting him from the news but he also knows that this dispute could escalate into an issue that will spoil the whole evening. He could close the door so he doesn't hear it, but he will still know it is going on, and he will still be afraid of the longer term consequences. Closing the door will meet his immediate needs, but he has a larger problem.*

*If he skips the part of the process where he figures out what his problem is he can easily trip himself up by trying to get them to change. He might go join forces with his wife to get their son to take out the trash, or he might stick up for Jack by getting Jane to "give him some slack", but in either case this only shuts things up for now—and sets up a bigger blowup in the future.*

*If Joe can figure out that his problem is that his family is not as he would have it be—that what he needs is a family in which they all work happily together to meet their common needs—then he may decide on a plan that helps both his wife and his son figure out what isn't working for them in this circumstance. He may decide to approach the situation with curiosity and to wonder what it was about his mother's request that Jack wasn't able or willing to comply with. He may wonder what it means to Jane when their son hasn't done what she asked him and to see if there might be another way of understanding that moves him to a calmer and more productive outcome.*

*Yes, but he just wants to hear the news. Why should he have to disrupt his life just because they can't work it out?*

*He has to disrupt what he wants to do because what is going on within his household is far more important than whatever is on the news.*

*But if he walks in there he is going to get drawn in and if he doesn't jump to his wife's side then she will be angry and then they will have a horrible evening. Sure, he wants to be the peacemaker; but he is so angry, he thinks to himself, "I'll probably just make things worse."*

*What Makes it so Hard to Change?*

*No, he can take some deep breaths and monitor his own feelings and stay
focused on what he needs and be fully present to both of them. They are his
family and nothing is more important to him.*

❧

So Joe works through the seven steps and decides to act to address his problem
that his family is not as he wants it to be by creating the qualities he needs in his
relationships with his wife and son. Very simple, and very hard to actually do.
More typically we do what we always do and get what we have always gotten.
Or we decide that there is nothing we can do and become frozen. Neither
choice gets us what we need. How can we find our way from where we are to
where we want to be? We need some better maps to guide us.

## Changing Ourselves by Changing Our Maps

If we are going to change ourselves in ways that create more and more of
what we need, we have to change what we do. What we do is a product
of our interpretation of what is happening to us in the world at the moment.
If what we are doing is not creating what we need, then we want to shift what
we are doing in the direction of creating more of what we need and that shift
happens most effectively by finding a more helpful map. We change what we
do by changing how we see the world around and within us.

None of our maps is perfect. The best map is a simplification of reality
which helps us focus on the relevant items which support our ability to know
where we are, where we want to go, and how we can get there. When we have
struggled to construct a complete map we may begin to think it is *the right
map*. I may feel like I really understand my 12 year old so when his teacher
describes him in ways which aren't familiar to me, I may decide she doesn't
actually know my son. Instead, if I want to expand the library of maps I have
to help me know my son, I can try to learn the map his teacher is using to see if
it has value for me.

When we are experiencing conflict with others we are reading from different
maps. We are observing the same event and making different meaning of it.
Resolving the conflict depends upon our ability to validate each others' maps.

We don't have to take them on as our own, though we may, but we at least must see how the map is valid for the other.

Some maps may be too complex for us. They are at a level of development beyond what we are currently able to make sense of. Those maps are not yet helpful to us. Other maps are too simple. They used to be helpful but now they are just simplistic.

We need to keep changing our maps so we always use the ones which are most appropriate to our current circumstances. Remember, maps are tools. Use them, don't worship them. If they aren't getting you what you need, trade them in for better ones.

## Summary

As we work to break down the complicated business of resolving conflicts into a set of simple steps it is easy to get fooled into thinking this process is easy. Simple is not the same as easy. This is very hard to do and is hard for some very good reasons. If we forget those reasons we can easily get discouraged when we discover this is harder than we thought.

Even though we know we can't change others, we don't stop trying. We don't see what we are doing as an attempt to make them change. We assume this is the only thing we can do. It is not. There are many things we can do but the effective ones all have to do with changing ourselves. Nevertheless, we don't have faith in our own ability to change. We don't think we can, we don't see why we should, and we don't see that it will help.

Additionally, we live in a culture which has already told us how we are to act and it will be very hard for us to challenge those cultural expectations. We already know that we shouldn't let things bother us, shouldn't be selfish, and shouldn't admit if we screw up. But what actually helps is to notice whatever is bothering us, act on our own behalf, and become accountable for the consequences of our choices.

In the micro-culture of our most intimate relationships these forces are amplified by an intense wish to make the relationship work at the expense of our own integrity and authenticity. We choose for the relationship and abandon ourselves, thus sabotaging the relationship.

Even as it comes to the relationships we construct with ourselves, we find it very hard to act in ways that create what we need. As it turns out, there are a series of seven things we need to have in place for ourselves before we are willing and able to change how we have been acting.

It is very hard to change what we are in the habit of doing. But it is possible. It becomes more possible the more we make the interior changes of adjusting the focus of our attention, the locus of our identity, and the perspective through which we are looking. These perspectives are maps for making meaning and we want to have the best possible maps.

# Part Two:
# Maps for the Journey

To find our way to resolution we have to use the best maps and these are often not the maps we have been using. Here are some perspectives which are quite different from the traditional wisdom we have been taught about addressing and resolving conflict.

# 4

# Transformation and the Orders of Self

Our maps will change as we change and as the world around us changes. This is a book of maps. For most who read it, these maps will be new and perhaps challenging. Some may be ones which are immediately useful and some may take work to become accustomed to. Hopefully, they will someday be ones you have outgrown.

## The Proximal Self

The more we move our awareness toward our own center, the more power we have to create a positive effect on ourselves and others. We will see many examples of this as we move forward but I hope this is a premise that is simple to understand. When we are off balance, we fall over.

It is essential then that we find our center and we come from a place of being centered. Our life circumstances can easily knock us off balance so we need to be good at restoring our center. We have to have mastered certain centering skills.

This is clearly true for us physically as material beings with bodies, but it is also true for us in our non-material aspects. We have an emotional center, a relational center, and even a spiritual center. Each of these different centers is available to us and we do well to seek them in the four realms we have already described:

- my physical center and the place of my body (the personal or material),

- my place in my family, community and culture and my sense of belonging in my primary relationships (the interpersonal or relational),
- my awareness of my own sensations, emotions, thoughts, wishes, intuition, and imagination (the intrapersonal or internal), and
- my awareness of my place in the grand scheme of creation, awareness that I am an insignificant nothing and the most precious and powerful being in the universe (the transpersonal or spiritual).

Our capacity to be conflict resolution masters depends completely on our ability to find and hold each of these centers. Indeed, we are at our best when all of these centers are in alignment.

In each of these realms there are two things we need to do to restore our center. We have to know what is happening—where we are and where the center is—and we have to have a choice we can make which will move us toward the center. Thus, we must have accurate perceptions not contaminated by cognitive distortions and we must have skills we can call upon to construct the qualities we need so that we can restore our ability to be centered. We have *perceptions* and *choices* by which, as we give attention to them with proper intention, we build *awareness* and *mastery*.

I am trying to make this as simple as possible but this really is a very complicated reality. We will need a somewhat detailed map if we are going to find our way. This map will be a framework which helps us know where we are, where we are going, and give some guidance about how we might get there.

Where we are going is toward a greater mastery in the face of the inevitable conflicts which arise for us. To create that mastery we must be centered in our selves. This is the self which is closest to my center, that is, the proximal self. So this is a map for finding the proximal self and restoring our ability to be centered there.

This self is not the distal self which we show to others or which we hope others will see. This is not about how we hope to be seen; this is about who we know ourselves to be. This core Self we will distinguish by capitalizing the spelling when we speak of it.

This Self arises in our physical being, our relationships, our feelings, and in the awareness we have of the ultimate. So we have one center in each of four realms and we seek to find that center by attention to both our perceptions and

*Transformation and the Orders of Self*

our choices. We thus end up with one map with four parts each divided into two parts, or eight aspects. These eight are each a unique state of mind.

The state of mind I am in when I am trying to figure out what is upsetting my partner (interpersonal – perception) is different from the one I am in when I am practicing my jump shot (personal – mastery). We have a theoretically infinite number of states of mind so we are greatly simplifying things here when we limit them to only eight.

As we look for a way to organize these eight States of Mind, we discover that they are not just random. They are actually a developmental sequence. It is this quality of our map—that it is developmental—that will help us discover how we can act to foster our own transformation and the transformation of our relationships and, indeed, the whole creation of which we are a part.

## Stages of Development

All growth happens through stages of development. There are many lines of development, but there are certain characteristics which all of them have. Stages are sequential, cannot be skipped, and cannot be taken out of order. Each stage transcends but includes all the earlier stages and thus each stage is more complex than the previous ones. Subsequent stages may look like a prior stage until we actually reach that stage.

## Stages of Growth

While some stages of growth can be easily observed, others are invisible.

*The summer between first and second grade I began to feel really urgent about learning to ride a bike. I had the peddling part of it down having attained mastery of the tricycle, but I couldn't seem to get that aspect of bicycle riding we call balance.*

*One afternoon I was up the street at my friend Billy's house. He and I were in the same class and always lined up next to each other when we queued up by alphabet as we shared the same last name. But Billy could ride a bike and I couldn't.*

*That afternoon I was very determined that I was going to learn how to do this thing. I knew if Billy could do it, so could I. But I was also a bit baffled about how people on bicycles didn't fall over. That was what always happened when I tried it. Again and again I walked the bike to the top of the hill in his back yard, climbed on and aimed myself down the hill. Little by little I started to get the hang of it. Billy coached me to steer towards the direction I was falling. This made no sense to me at first but then I began to see what he meant. Each run I was able to stay upright longer and more easily than the last. Then, suddenly, I had it. I felt what it was like to balance on a bicycle. It was more that my body learned it than my head did. It still didn't make sense to me that this was possible, but here I was riding down the grassy hill on Billy Robinson's bike.*

*I rode my own bike home. It was a little awkward because the training wheels kept getting in the way and throwing me off balance. When I got home, no one could see the transformation which had occurred in my life. No one could look at me and know that this was a kid who knew how to ride a bike. But I knew. And I asked my dad to help me take the training wheels off.*

Moving to a new stage in our development—undergoing transformation—can be very hard to see. I use this example of learning to ride a bike because it is unusual in that sense. Yesterday I couldn't ride a bike and today I can. I can see and experience the transformation.

More common is my experience at the beginning of eighth grade as I went to the first session of my class in vocal music. As the teacher was calling the role and she read my name and I responded, "Here," she remarked, "Oh, we have a bass." I thought to myself, "No, I sing alto." Or at least I was singing alto the previous spring. Over the summer my voice had dropped. I had not noticed…but everyone else had.

So, one of the characteristics of transformation to a new stage of development is that it is often invisible to us. It is often only as we step back and view change from a distance that we discover that true transformation has occurred.

Systems Theory makes a distinction between orders of change. If I change the light bulb or if I change my shirt, that is first order change. Things are different but the structure remains the same. Second order change is an actual transformation of the structure. Third order change is a change in the way the structure is created.

*Transformation and the Orders of Self*

If the light bulb burns out and I replace it with one just like it I have changed the light bulb but overall I have simply restored the system to its previous state. This is first order change.

It the light bulb burns out and I decide to use a long-life energy efficient bulb I now have a different way of plugging into the power grid to get light. This is second order change.

But if I decide that I am tired of buying light bulbs when there is a sun which provides plenty of light and I put a hole in the roof and install a solar tube I am now off the grid (at least for this light) and am not buying light bulbs. This provides light but gets it from a different source. This is third order change.

Each of these is a response to a system with a burnt out bulb, and each is a response which creates light in the room, but the kind of change is very different at each order. When things are different within a given order, we call that change. When we move to another order, we call that transformation.

All growth happens through stages. Sometimes the stages are clearly delineated as in the life cycle of an insect. Insects grow from egg to larva to pupa to adult. Butterfly larvae (caterpillars) are so easily differentiated from adults that one must be an expert to know which caterpillars become which butterflies.

Oak trees also grow through stages going from acorn to seedling to sapling to adult. While it is easy to differentiate an acorn from a mature tree, it is a bit harder to say when it transforms from a sapling to an adult tree by becoming sexually mature.

In the case of oak trees, they also undergo changes through the annual cycle of dormancy, new growth, fully leaved seed production, leaf change and return to dormancy. That is, they cycle through winter, spring, summer and fall. But these changes are not transformation except that each year another ring is added to the trunk.

## Sequential, Invariant, and Hierarchical

There are three other characteristics of the kind of change we call transformation[9].

---

9    These are identified by James Fowler who has worked with the transformation which occurs for us as we move through stages of faith.

**Sequential:** The stages of development for any process of growth happen in a prescribed sequence. Typically there are many tiny changes which are nearly imperceptible. We group these changes into a cluster which describe a change and which we label as a stage, but the divisions between stages can be seen as somewhat arbitrary. They are simply a map to help us understand the transformation.

**Invariant:** Each of these stages happen in a set sequence which must be taken in order. One cannot skip a stage. One cannot do them in a different order.

**Hierarchical:** Each stage is more complex than the one before it and pulls together the qualities of the preceding stages. There is a certain level of competence which is necessary at each stage before we are able to move to the next one. If the prior competency is lost, the developmental sequence will collapse. We need the prior stages to support the later ones.

The notion that transformation is hierarchical is very difficult for some people to understand and accept. So let's look at an example of this in the lives of the Johnson's.

> Joe and Jane have two sons, Jack and Jesse. Jack is two years older than Jesse and when he was five he would sometimes use his size and experience to dominate Jesse. This would often arise when there was something to be divided between the boys and Jack would get more than his share.

> To address this Joe and Jane established a rule that whenever there was something to be divided between the boys, one of them would make the division and the other would get first pick for which half he wanted. This meant that each had a motivation to make the split as close to equal as possible.

> Still Jack wanted to get as much for himself as possible. So when the thing to be divided was a cookie, he would let Jesse be the one to break it. Jack knew that cookies almost never break evenly, so he could take the bigger half.

> But when the thing to be divided was the last of the juice, he would be the one

*Transformation and the Orders of Self*

*to make the division. Not only was Jack bigger, and so better with pouring (stronger, better coordination), he was also more developed in terms of spatial understanding.*

*He would take two glasses out of the cupboard—one tall thin one, and one short squat one. He would pour into each glass until they both were at just the same height and then he would put the last little bit of juice into the tall thin one to ensure that Jesse would pick that one.*

Jack is able to think in three dimensions and Jesse is still thinking in two dimensions. Jesse can see that the tall thin glass has the meniscus above the one in the short squat glass and that means to him that it has more. Jack is able to think in terms of volume, not just length, so he knows he is actually getting more juice. Jack is at a stage of cognitive development which is more advanced than Jesse.

This does not mean that Jack is better than Jesse, but it does mean that Jack has a way of thinking—a level of understanding—which is more effective for solving the problem "how do I get more" than is Jesse's way of solving the problem. When it comes to the hierarchy of these stages of development, Jack has a cognitive map which is superior to Jesse's.

At some point within the next couple of years Jesse is going to figure it out and Jack will be left holding the tall thin glass.

## Lines of Development

This example of Jack and Jesse shows that, along a line of development which is the capacity to judge amount, Jack has attained a level of understanding which is superior to Jesse's. This does not mean that Jack is better than Jesse, only that his way of thinking is.

We may also consider how developed Jack appears ethically in relation to his brother if he is always trying to get more for himself at his brother's expense. Then again, he is only five, and we don't expect a high level of ethical development from a five year old. If he were still doing this at 25 we would have reason for concern.

There are many many lines of development. Each of us is developing physically, cognitively, emotionally, ethically, spiritually...and each of these areas have sub-areas and each of these is developing at its own pace. As we go through our lives we grow at different rates in different areas of our lives. We may know people who are very smart but are very unethical. Or people who have very poor physical coordination but are very empathic with others. We do not grow equally in all areas.

I am expecting that most of you who read this have already grown physically to adulthood—that is, you would be considered by most to be a "grown up." But I wonder if you consider yourself to have finished growing? Are you done? Or do you wish to continue your growth and development?

Mastering conflict resolution is about learning how to use the conflicts which arise for us as tools for our own transformation, for our own capacity to move to ever higher stages along the lines of development which are opening for us. For us to do this most effectively and efficiently we need to have a good map. The best map that I have been able to construct is one I call the *Orders of Self*.

## Orders of Self

The crux of learning to resolve all conflicts is that we have to transform our selves in order to do so. So *who we each understand ourselves to be* is crucial to this process. This is complicated by the fact that *who we understand ourselves to be* changes as we grow. Who we knew ourselves to be as children is different from who we know ourselves to be as adults. Not completely different—we have a sense of continuity with who we were then. But I am no longer the kid who learned to ride a bike in Billy's backyard. And yet, I am still the kid who learned what balance is and I can still ride a bike. We are both different and the same.

One of the things which transforms through stages of development is a sense of who we each are. There are stages we all move through as we bring into being our sense of ourselves and having a map of these stages helps us know where we are, where we are going, and how to get there.

## First Order

Our sense of ourselves as separate from the rest of the world is something we begin to develop in infancy. We are born without this separate self sense. We

# Orders of Self

Eight Stages in the Development of the Proximal Self

| orders | attitudes | identity | longing for | currency | tier/domain |
|---|---|---|---|---|---|
| 8° | violet | I am one with all | re-union, harmony | conciousness - pure unbounded awareness | transpersonal/spiritual |
| 7° | turquoise | I am a product of the unique circumstances of my being | meaning and purpose in my life; release of suffering of others | compassion - identification with other beings | transpersonal/spiritual |
| 6° | teal | I am the one who chooses which perspectives and abilities to use | mastery over internal conflicts | integrity - ability to be integrated | intrapersonal/internal |
| 5° | green | I am the multifaceted creation of my many experiences | self-awareness in the midst of contradictory impulses | perspectives - holding diverse points of view | intrapersonal/internal |
| 4° | orange | I am the one choosing my roles and relationships | mastery over my role and security in my relationships | intimacy - having deep connections with others | interpersonal/relational |
| 3° | amber | I am my roles and relationships | acceptance of others and security in my role | esteem - knowing worth in relationship with others | interpersonal/relational |
| 2° | red | I am the one having my experience | mastery over what I am experiencing | possessions - having fine things and using them well | personal/mastery |
| 1° | magenta | I am my experience | connection to the material world | experiences - attending to everything that arises | personal/mastery |
| 0° | beige | | | | personal/mastery |

A color version of this chart is available at http://justconflict.com/OSchart.pdf

*Just Conflict: Transformation Through Resolution*

simply have our immediate experience of experience. In response to this intense stimulation, we fall asleep.

While we don't understand all of what sleep is for, it at least keeps us out of harm's way and allows us to conserve our resources. It also creates the context in which we can dream. We all know that babies sleep a lot but it appears they also dream a lot.

Dreaming is a way we work at making sense of what we experienced while awake. We know that babies have long periods of what is known as REM sleep (for rapid eye movements) and that when adults are in that form of sleep, they are dreaming. And while we don't fully understand what dreams are for, they seem to be a way that the brain is processing the information we have received while we were awake. We gather the perceptions while awake and then try to dream them into a map which allows us to make sense of them.

So babies are working hard at building the cognitive map within which to create an understanding of the world around them. The content of that map is far beyond the scope of this book, but I want to lay out just a piece of what we work out as infants so that we can appreciate the complexity and depth of this work.

As an infant I have a sensory experience and try to make sense of it. At the core of intelligence is the capacity to make distinctions...to notice that this is different from that. Among the first distinctions we each make is between the things we like and the things we don't like. I like it when I get a dry diaper; I don't like it when I get wiped with a cold cloth. I don't like it when I get a bath but I like getting wrapped in a warm towel. I don't like when my teeth are hurting, but I get relief when I bite down on a blanket. I don't like it when I bite my thumb. So we begin to distinguish between the things we like and the things we don't like. We distinguish between good and bad.

This separation of experience into the categories of good and bad—what I like and what I don't like—happens very early, even before we have clearly developed the separate sense of self. So while I know that I don't like it when I bite my thumb and I know that I don't like getting a bath, I don't know yet that one is under my control and the other is not. No matter how much I squirm I don't seem to be able to avoid getting a bath.

As I begin to learn that biting my thumb feels bad but biting the teething ring feels good, I begin to recognize that thumb is me and teething ring is not.

As I discover that squirming in the bath means my head goes under water I begin to see that my head is me but the water is not.

But, as the good/bad split forms before the self/other split, I end up with a fourfold division of experience. There is the *good self* that is satisfied and the *bad self* that is hurt. There is the *good other* which satisfies me and the *bad other* which hurts me. Still, as my capacity to observe grows, I discover that the *bad other* who gives me the bath is the same other who cuddles me in the warm blanket afterwards. The other who wipes me with a cold wash cloth is the same other who feeds me. This same other is one integrated person. And so we begin to integrate what was seen as good and bad into the same person.

This integration of good and bad other serves as the template for our capacity to integrate our sense of ourselves as hurt and satisfied into a single sense of Self. When we have parents or caregivers who are very inconsistent and we cannot come to see them as integrated, it profoundly inhibits our ability to integrate our sense of ourselves. This is a theme we will return to when we consider how we are constructed at the $5°$[10].

The task at $1°$ is to be open to the experience of the material world and to be open to that experience without being overwhelmed by it. People with autism are particularly challenged in this regard. They seem to have such poor neurological filters that any stimulus is overwhelming and they have to isolate much more than most of us in order to tolerate the intensity of experience.

The work of developing a Self at $1°$ is to experience fully the material world and to make sense of it such that it is no longer overwhelming.

## Second Order

Even as I bite down on the teething ring or my thumb, I am beginning to move into a $2°$ sense of my Self. I am not just a passive receptor of sensory experience; I am someone whose choices shape my experience. My choices matter. Given sufficient skill and wisdom, I can create the world in which I move and breathe.

The move from First to Second Order is not a sharp bright line which we

---

10    We will use the ° sign to indicate the Orders of Self, thus $5°$ refers to Fifth Order.

cross like the line between not riding a bike and being able to ride one. It is a transition from being passive to being active. It is the move from *being the experience* to *being the one who has the experience*.

At 1° I am tired and hungry. At 2° I am someone who is currently experiencing hunger and fatigue and, when I have eaten and rested, I will be satisfied and restored.

At 2° life is a set of puzzles to solve, of obstacles to overcome. We begin to experience more and more the joy of mastery which comes from encountering a problem and discovering our own capacity to solve it.

Just as we discovered at 1° that there was good and bad, at 2° we begin to discover right and wrong. There is a right way to do things which results in the outcome we are looking for, and there is a wrong way which doesn't get the desired results. We notice that we are not always able to know whether what we are doing is going to work so we are at risk of being wrong.

The distinction between *doing* wrong and *being* wrong is not yet available to us at 2°. If what I do doesn't work, I *am* wrong. If what you do doesn't work, you *are* wrong.

In order to protect ourselves from the pain of being wrong—or of being seen as being wrong—we tend to limit ourselves to relationships with people like us. This is a way of constructing friendships. If a new kid moves in down the street and I want to play with him and I discover that he plays Pokemon, I will take up Pokemon so we have something in common and thus build a relationship.

People who are very different from us make us uncomfortable at 2°. If they are different and they are not bad then we must be bad. But since we are not bad, they must be. 2° doesn't appreciate diversity.

What 2° does appreciate is competence. If this task is one I can do confidently, then I am succeeding at 2°. We learn to tie our shoes and cross the street safely and drive a car and sequence a gene. Bit by bit we gain competence at more and more things. We construct our experience by the choices we are making.

Even as we build this confidence about our competence we discover that there are areas of our experience where we cannot seem to create the experience we want. This is in our relationships with others.

# Third Order

With the shift to 3° we move from the personal realm to the interpersonal realm. At 3° we attend to the experiences which arise for us in the realm of our relationships with others, especially those to whom we are closest.

To begin to develop at 3° we must first have attained a certain level of competence at 2°.

*Joe has told the three year old Jesse to clean his room. Jesse has gone to his room and moved some stuff around in there and then began to play with his new front-loader that he got for Christmas. He is using it to pick up the Legos which are spread around the floor and dumping them in a box.*

*Joe comes to the door and sees Jesse with the toy truck and yells, "Quit playing around and get this room cleaned up." Jesse begins to cry and Joe is startled and angry.*

Jesse experiences his dad's displeasure with him (1°). He wants the feeling he gets when his dad is pleased with him but he isn't sure what he can do to create it (2°). He knows it has to do with manipulating the toys in his room so he begins to do what he thinks will get his dad's approval even as it is a challenge for him to get the front-loader to pick up the Legos.

But Joe is not pleased. He has in mind what "cleaning your room" looks like and what Jesse is doing looks to him like "playing." He is making a 3° demand on Jesse but Jesse doesn't have the 2° skills with which to comply, much less to fully know what it is his dad wants from him.

Joe may even feel as though Jesse is defying him. He may see it as a willful disregard for Joe's authority. Perhaps this scenario will be played out again when Jesse is 13, at which point Joe might be right. But at this point Jesse doesn't have the 3° capacity to even know what is expected of him, much less be able to do it.

It is during our teenage years most of us are focused on developing at the stage we call 3°. We have gained a level of mastery in most of the tasks of living so we imagine ourselves as a person independent of our family of origin. We have our own social milieu and we would just as soon have our immediate family stay out of it.

*Once Jesse turned 15 he got a work permit to have a job after school at Burger Doodle. This gives him a source of income which he intended to save to buy a car but he is having trouble not spending the money on music and fast food.*

*He is a pretty good athlete and has a spot as a starter on a select soccer team. The coach is intent on the team winning the league and pushes the boys hard. He won't tolerate missing practice. If you don't make it to practice, you don't play in the game.*

*Jesse has discovered that girls can be fascinating. He has recently started getting the attention of Susie Carter, the head of the JV cheerleading squad. He believes that Susie expects her boyfriend to be attentive to her as she broke up with the JV quarterback and Jesse thinks this is because he didn't call her every evening.*

*Jesse has a plan to get into a good college and he knows that means he has to have excellent grades. He is good in math and science but he has an American History class that is making him sweat. He is still working on mastering the 2° skill of writing an essay. He can't seem to figure out what the teacher wants.*

Some aspects of essay writing are 2° skills. How do I select a topic, how do I use spell-check, what are the rules of grammar? But the task of knowing what the teacher is looking for is a 3° capacity. Jesse is working on knowing what it is that others expect of him. He has certain responsibilities in each of these roles into which he is being cast.

His manager at Burger Doodle has a task for Jesse to do. He has to show up on time, be dressed in the uniform, be clean, be courteous to the customers and the fellow employees, and do his job well.

The coach of the soccer team assigns Jesse a position to play and expects him to know where to be on the field and how to follow the play. He has expectations about how Jesse will handle the ball and that he be at all of the practices and be on time to the games with his full uniform.

Susie has an idea of how her boyfriend will act and that includes meeting her before and after school and at lunch and that they will chat in the evening. We don't get to select what others expect of us. We can only know what it is they expect and decide whether we will try to meet their expectations.

Thursday morning in American History Jesse learned that there was a paper due Friday that he had forgotten about. He checked his planner and found that he was scheduled for a shift at Burger Doodle right after school at 3:00 and that there is a soccer practice at 4:30 and Susie is expecting him to meet her after school.

Jesse is discovering that he is not able to meet all of the 3° demands of all of the relationships in his life. He is presented with an opportunity to move to 4°.

## Fourth Order

As 3° is the awareness we have of ourselves which is constructed by the expectations of others, 4° is the awareness we have of ourselves which is constructed by our standards for of ourselves. Jesse has a series of choices he can make at this point.

He can decide that his long term best interests are served by doing well on the paper for American History and that the job at Burger Doodle can be done by someone else and Susie will just have to understand that he has other things going on in his life. He can call the manager at Burger Doodle and let him know that he is not going to make it in and ask if he can find someone else to fill his shift. He can let Susie know that she is welcome to meet him in the library after school but that he has some research he needs to do. He can make it to soccer practice and then go home and pull an all-nighter to get the paper finished.

Or he may decide that he isn't going to do well on the paper anyway so he will ask for an extension, skip soccer practice and spend the evening on the phone with Susie after he gets back from his shift at Burger Doodle.

In general then Jesse can move to a more mature position or he can fall back to a less mature one. He can step up to 4° where he decides that he is going to push himself to be a scholar and be disciplined as an athlete. Or he can fall back to 2° where he is going to enjoy the experience of having some cash in his pocket and have the attention of a pretty girl.

While we can root for Jesse doing the hard work of getting the paper done, we should also acknowledge that this is a stretch for a 15 year old. Indeed, many a 35 year old when faced with demands that seem to be too much will just decide to go have a few beers instead.

Robert Kegan's work on these stages of development[11] has clearly determined that most American adults are firmly able to function at 3° but are struggling to consistently construct themselves at 4°. This makes really good sense when we consider how we have learned who we are to be.

In most parts of the world to this day, and even in the most developed parts of the world a hundred years ago, there was little question about what role one would play in adult life. If you are a girl you will be like your mother. If you are a boy you will be like your father. The demands of culture and class do not allow us to be other than that for which we have been bred.

But in the developed world today we have adopted the practice of asking kids "What do you want to be when you grow up?" We invite our children to imagine what they will make of themselves. This is a 4° task.

It may be hard to appreciate how difficult a task this is. Most of us think we have already decided who we want to be when we grow up. Indeed, most of us think of ourselves as already having grown up.

We may, in fact, have decided that we are not going to grow anymore. But this will not stop our life experience from making demands on us that push us past our current construction of who we understand ourselves to be.

> *Anne and Chuck have been married for nine years but separated for the last two. Their daughters, Christy and Zoe, are 8 and 6. They manage to be good parents together but it has been increasingly clear to both of them that they just don't want the same things in life and are not going to reunite. They know how important it is to the girls that they appear as a family so they have not pressed for divorce.*

> *One evening while Zoe is with her dad, Anne and Christy go grocery shopping. In the store they cross paths with a woman who is obviously pregnant and Anne takes this opportunity to talk to Christy about where babies come from. She talks in general terms about sex and the growth of the fetus and childbirth and makes clear to Christy that because sex can result in pregnancy it should be reserved for a loving and committed relationship.*

---

11   "In Over Our Heads"

*Christy is a smart kid and while she thinks of sex as "yucky" she also knows that adults really like it. She knows that her parents have not shared a bed for a few years now so she asks her mom, "Since you and dad aren't together now, are you having sex with someone else?"*

*The question takes Anne's breath away. In fact she has started seeing someone and they have spent the night together on nights when the girls are with their dad. Anne knows that this information will be upsetting to the girls and has decided to withhold it for now. It is certainly not something she wants to blurt out to her daughter in the grocery store.*

*On the other hand Anne has always prized her commitment to speak the truth to her daughters. She has never knowingly lied to either of them. She doesn't want to start now, especially in the context of a conversation about the sacred nature of relationships.*

*She is momentarily speechless.*

Anne is shaped by two different 3° constraints. One has to do with the values of honesty and truth telling. The other has to do with acting in a manner that is sensitive to the emotional and developmental needs of her daughters. Those demands appear to conflict with each other.

In the moments between Christy's question and Anne's response she looks for a "way of being" in her relationship with her daughter which is sensitive to all of the 3° demands and doesn't just attempt a 2° cop-out by changing the subject. How can she balance truth-telling with sensitivity to her daughter's needs?

*Anne squats down in front of Christy so they are eye to eye. She says to Christy, "I know it is hard for you and Zoe that your dad and I are not together anymore. But I want you to know that we both still love you very much and we aren't going to let anything get in the way of both of us being there for you two. I promise."*

Anne hears Christy's question not as a 3° judgment that she is having sex with someone other than her father, but as a 2° concern that someone is going to get in the way of her need for two parents who love her and will be there for her. She is able to find a "way of being" that is sensitive to what Christy needs and is at the same time consistent with Anne's commitment to telling the truth[12].

## Fifth Order

So Anne finds a way of being which works for her and she is able to act on her plan. This is not always something we can do. It is actually two very difficult things to do.

The first is deciding who and how we want to be. Anne was able to use her 1° ability to *hear* and her 2° skill at *listening* together with her 3° understanding of the demands of *how a mother should be* to construct a 4° way of being which she could then act upon. That is, she first made a plan and she then enacted it.

Oftentimes, however, we determine how we would like to be but then find we cannot show up in our lives consistent with that decision. I may have decided that, in this New Year, I am going to be someone who consistently makes healthy decisions on my own behalf. I am going to go to the gym three times a week and not eat sweets. So what, I wonder, is going on with me that I haven't been to the gym in a week and I have a donut in my mouth?

Deciding what I am going to do is essential to constructing myself at 4°. Who I am going to be is created out of the choices I make for myself—my intentions. But just planning to be a particular way doesn't mean that I am going to be able to follow through. Something may be getting in the way. I seem to be of two minds about this.

Indeed, we are of many minds. As we make the shift from the Interpersonal realm to the Intrapersonal realm we begin to discover that we are not as unitary as we may have imagined. One part of me wants to be fit and trim and another part of me wants a donut.

Becoming aware of these different parts of ourselves requires and ability to "go inside." In our interior awareness we begin to discover that we are very complicated. It is essential that we become able to do this as the source of our most durable conflicts is within us. The conflicts we get into over and over with those with whom we are close are always an expression of the conflicts we are having with ourselves which we project into the relationship with another. We will talk much more about this in a bit. For now, though, let's look at why it is so hard to get an awareness of our own multiplicity.

---

12   This vignette is adapted from one in Kegan's, "In Over Our Heads."

- Appearing well integrated: We don't want to appear wishy washy. "There are folks who just can't seem to make up their minds. They are not decisive. Being rational is the way to be and that means not being emotional. Only really crazy people have multiple personalities." So our distal selves are very invested in appearing to have it all together. Acknowledging our complexity runs counter to that appearance.

- Staying in consensual reality: The way we know that something is "real" is by finding out if someone else had the same experience. "Did you hear that?" we ask when we are not certain if we might be imagining something. If I am having an interior awareness I am afraid that there is nowhere to go for validation. I may assume that no one else has ever had that experience and so cannot confirm the reality for me. As we discover, this isn't true. We all have very similar experiences. But since this level of understanding is beyond where most people typically go, it seems like uncharted territory. We are afraid we might get lost.

- Fearing the discovery of aspects of my Self I have tried to forget: On the other hand, we are afraid of what we might find. There are things that have happened to us that we have worked hard to forget about and if we go exploring our interior we might stumble upon something we have hidden and don't want to unearth.

So there are a number of cultural, relational, and intrapersonal barriers to deeply knowing ourselves. On the other hand, there are great benefits to knowing our interior selves, and there are many tools for discovering ourselves.[13]

We are all of many minds about who we are and how we will respond to our

---

13 These include Psychosynthesis, Transactional Analysis, Depth psychology, Self psychology, the Diamond Approach, Voice Dialogue, and Visioning to name but a few. The methodology that I find most accessible and the map I find most accurate is that provided by Internal Family Systems therapy as promoted by Richard C. Schwartz.

I say "promoted" rather than "created" as Dick will be the first to acknowledge that it was his clients who revealed to him the intricacies of our inner working. Dick has been a particularly keen observer of what his clients have shown him about their own interior complexity. He has pulled those insights together into a simple and coherent framework or map for understanding our own interior selves, that is, who we are at 5°.

I offer here a very brief outline of Internal Family Systems theory so that we can use some of its aspects as tools for our exploration of how we address conflicts. If you are interested in knowing more about IFS I suggest you go to the Web site for the Center for Self Leadership. They have some excellent resources available including publications and training events.

life circumstances. We reveal this complexity when we say things like, "A part of me wants to watch TV but I know I should get to work on a project I have been putting off." We are aware of there being different perspectives, values, attitudes, moods, goals, which different "parts" of us bring to any enterprise.

When we are under very little stress and things are going well for us, we lose sight of our multiplicity. Each part of us connects well with the other parts and we function as a unified whole. We feel as though we "have it together." But when we are feeling anxious, we find that we have more trouble making up our minds and getting them all to work together. One part may dominate another perspective or way of being and we may do things which are not typical for us.

When this happens we may say that one or more parts get pushed to an extreme position. The emotional intensity of the situation highlights the inherent conflict between various parts of us and we feel anxious.

While we are all unique in the manner of our internal systems, there are features which are common to all of us. One of these is that our systems function in certain predictable ways when we are under stress. The parts which are moving to an extreme position tend to either step in and take charge of things, or they back off and hide. Sometimes parts are sent into exile by the rest of our internal system.

The parts we call *exiles* tend to carry very strong feelings and are triggered by highly emotional events in our lives. They may be associated with emotional events in our past which we have not been able to face and work through.

We also have protector parts. They are the ones which take over the reins and make our decisions. They can either be proactive, anticipating what is likely to happen and, thus, get us ready for some circumstance; or they can be reactive, finally stepping in when things appear to be out of control. The proactive protectors we call *managers*. The reactive protectors we call *firefighters*.

We have many more aspects to who we are than just the exiles, managers and firefighters. Usually they all function in harmony. But at times parts are pushed to an extreme position and find themselves in conflict with each other. To illustrate this, let us return to the example in the life of the Johnsons from the end of Chapter Two.

As you may recall, Joe is watching the news on TV when he hears Jane engaging Jack about his failure to take out the trash. Joe has a manager who wants to get up and shut the door so he can't hear them but he also has a manager who wants to go in and fix things. He also has a young part which identifies with Jack and remembers the humiliation of being scolded by a parent. And he has an adult part which identifies with Jane being thwarted in her ability to get their son to do a simple task. He also has a firefighter part which wants to explode on both of them for disrupting his ability to listen to the news when he has been working hard all day.

So we can immediately identify a couple of managers, a couple of exiles and a firefighter all trying to claim attention in Joe's awareness and actions as he moves to address the situation with Jane and Jack. How Joe will act in his relationship with his wife and son depends fully on how Joe addresses each of these parts of himself which are being aroused by what he hears from his loved ones.

Before Joe can responsibly address the conflict Jane and Jack are having, he has to address the conflict he is having with each of them. But before he can address the conflict he is having with them, he will have to address and resolve the conflicts he is having with himself, that is, the conflicts between the various parts.

To do this he will have to acknowledge and appreciate each of these parts which are being triggered and pushed to an extreme position.

- He has to notice the manager which wants to simply close the door on the racket and appreciate that this part is trying to take care of him.
- He has to notice the manager which wants to fix things between his wife and son and appreciate that this part wants harmony and to protect the young part of himself who remembers the shame of being scolded.
- He has to notice the exile who is that child part of him who was scolded and still feels the flush of humiliation.
- And he has to notice that part of him which knows what it is like to fail at controlling a child and which is identifying with Jane at the moment. He has to acknowledge that he feels shame at not being the father he thinks he should be.
- But most especially he has to notice and attend to the part of him which wants to "fix" things by venting all the anger he has stored up from a day or a week of not having things go his way. He has to appreciate that

this firefighter is trying to protect and restore him by allowing this way of letting off the steam, but he also has to be so familiar with this firefighter that it will trust him to find a better way to get those needs met.

As Joe focuses on each of these parts he has to come from a different locus of identity than the parts themselves and do so through a particular lens which allows him to approach them with clarity and compassion. He must come from his Self. The Self is not just another part. It is an aspect of our interior awareness which may be thought of as above the parts looking down on them with concern, or it may be thought of as the ground from which the parts emerge, but it is categorically different from a part.

There is an essential shift in Joe's awareness when he changes from "one who *is* angry at Jane and Jack for disturbing him" to "one who *has* anger about what is happening." Is the anger *who he is* and thus is the subjective experience of being Joe, or is the anger *something Joe has* and thus is something upon which he can reflect and act?

This shift in perspective of taking what was the subject of the action and turning it into an object for our reflection and consideration is at the core of all developmental shifts. Let us look at the shift from 1° to 2°. At 1° I *am* my experience. I am hungry. I am happy. I am tired. At 2° [Personal-material: choice] I am someone who *is having* experience. I am one who is experiencing hunger, happiness or fatigue. Further, I am one who can make choices which will impact my hunger, happiness or fatigue. What was subject at 1° becomes the object of the consideration of 2°.

At 2° I am one who is making choices in my life which are creating outcomes. But as I move to 3° [Interpersonal-relational: experience] I reflect on how those choices impact those around me. I transform from just being one who makes choices to one whose choices arise in the context of a set of cultural expectations. What was the subjective experience of being the one who chooses becomes the object of the attention of who I am at 3°. Are my actions consistent with the social expectations in which I live? Am I someone who has honor?

But as I try to remain honorable, that is, as I try to conform to the dictates of the cultural milieu in which I reside, I find that I cannot consistently do that and still meet the demands of my own personal experience. As we saw with

Anne and her daughter discussing sex, sometimes we have to step back from the immediate rules we have set for ourselves and discover a more inclusive and comprehensive way of being.

It is this action of stepping back and looking at the current circumstances that is the core of what we have to do to effect our own transformation. So as Joe gets up from his chair in front of the TV and walks into the other room where Jane and Jack are engaging each other, he must attend to each of these parts arising in him from the perspective of his Self, not from the perspective of the parts themselves.

## Sixth Order

When Joe shifts from feeling the shame of a parent who can't control a child to the shame of a child who can't please his parent he is shifting between 5° perspectives. This is change.

When he steps back from both of those parts and sees that each, while different, is fully valid, he makes a developmental shift to 6°. This is transformation.

In many respects this shift from 5° to 6° is more significant than any of the prior stage shifts. The prior shifts are all huge, to be sure, but this is a shift which puts all of the prior stages into perspective.

At 6° [Intrapersonal-internal: choice] we can see all of the prior stages as having been necessary precursors to the stages which followed. Those stages below 6° are only able to see their own level as valid.

From a 3° perspective, for example, 1° is seen as dangerous. 3° is the realm of clear rules strictly applied. Asceticism is a value and those 1° experiences are hedonistic. 2° is seen as willful and unruly and 4° is not distinguished from 2°. Anything which is not consistent with the law is illegal when viewed from 3°.

But by the time we ascend to a 6° perspective we become able to see that each level builds on the one before it, and each subsequent level includes but transcends the one prior to it[14].

This 6° perspective is very powerful. We deeply know ourselves and

---

14   This is the very shift in perspective that Spiral Dynamics and the developmental perspective of Ken Wilber describe as a movement to Second Tier and Ashok Gangadean refers to as Double Bracket thinking or Global Mind.

understand the reasons for our actions and to reconcile previously alienated parts of who we are. It even allows us to come to an understanding of how profoundly traumatic events in our own history can actually be sources of great strength.

Resting in 6° can give us a very deep and calm sense of power and invulnerability. It is not that we can't be hurt. It is just that even the hurt has a meaning and a purpose in our lives.

❧

Jesus said about himself that he came, not to erase the law, but to fulfill it. He was aware of the need for 3° law but he was inviting his followers to accept themselves and each other in a way that appreciated diversity. He was inviting a Second Tier or 6° point of view.

When Paul wrote to the Corinthians about dietary laws, he noted that violating the laws would be a scandal to those who were operating from a 3° perspective. He acknowledged that food offered to idols was not really defiled because the idols were not real gods, but he suggested that they refrain from eating the food, not because of the nature of the food, but because of the perspective of those they were trying to influence. We should be careful to not inhibit the transformation of those operating from a less complex perspective.

## Seventh Order

As we rest in this safe and satisfying condition we begin to become aware that few of those around us are able to enjoy this same level of calm and equanimity. More and more we notice the condition of those with whom we share the planet. A 6° perspective allows us to see how it is that those who appeared to be our enemies are actually just fellow sentient beings struggling toward their own awakening. The 6° perspective applied to our place in the cosmos propels us into 7° [Transpersonal-spiritual: perception].

At 7° we come to see our physical manifestation as less and less relevant to who we are. Being a white, first world, educated male is no longer a source of pride (or shame). It is not as though those are things I have created. They are accidents of my being. They are important for they privilege me with certain abilities. But those facts simply give me greater responsibilities to use well the power that these accidents of my being bestow on me.

As we come to know ourselves as simply one of the 10,000 things of the manifest world we also come to identify with all of the other manifestations of the divine which make up the existence we inhabit. The suffering of others takes on a huge importance to us and we find our hearts breaking open in compassion for the agony of the world.

Still, even as we are filled with pain for the suffering of the world, we are aware that this suffering is the context in which healing and wholeness can be created and discovered. We remember that sadness deepens our joy and light doesn't exist without dark. There is no *up* without *down* or *in* with no *out*.

## Eighth Order

I confess that I don't actually have more than a fleeting experience of my Self at 8° [Transpersonal-spiritual: choice]. No one I know well can rest there for long. I am going out on a limb here that is constructed by the words of saints and sages through the ages who have testified without exception that we are not actually separate from God, from Spirit, from the Ground of Being, from the Ultimate. We are all manifestations of the one source of energy and intelligence which is the only thing which ultimately is. It is the I Am that was before Abraham and the Father about which Jesus said, "I and the Father are one." Indeed, at 8° we are not many but One. Who I am is none other than God's true face. And so is everyone else.

## **Some Features of This Map**

This has been a very quick introduction to an eight level map of the development of the proximal Self. Let us step back and notice a couple of features which will help us use it better.

The first is that the odd numbered orders have to do with developing a capacity to *accept* what is (perception) and the even numbered orders have to do with *mastering* skills which are creative (choice).

The second feature is that in the first two levels these tasks of acceptance and mastery arise in the *personal* realm, the second two levels are in the *interpersonal* realm, the next two in the *intrapersonal* realm, and finally at Seventh and Eighth Order in the *transpersonal* realm.

At 1° we are the experience we are having in the moment. "I am hungry, I am happy." We do not have a choice about what our experience will be...only whether we will experience our experience. I may not like the fact that it is raining, but I don't control the rain.

At 2° I have an opportunity to do something about the conditions which arise for me at 1°. If I am chilly, I can decide to turn up the thermostat or put on a sweater or do jumping jacks. I have a choice of strategies which will change my experience.

My choices of how to deal with being cold may be constrained by conditions in the social arena—in my relationships with others (the interpersonal realm, that is, at 3°). I may not have paid the utilities bill so turning up the thermostat will have no effect. I may only have sweaters which are out of fashion. I may feel silly (or fear others will see me as silly) if I do calisthenics.

Or I may decide that I will establish a new fashion by the way I dress and wear this funky old sweater. Deciding how I will be while holding an awareness of what the expectations of others are is a 4° capacity. It is attaining mastery in the interpersonal realm.

Still, while there may be parts of me who think this mode of dress is very stylish and trendsetting and perhaps practical, there may also be parts of me that remember when someone who was wearing a sweater like this one abused me and so association with it brings up feelings of fear and shame. As I go inside to the intrapersonal realm I discover aspects of my experience which are not of my choosing. I didn't create these events or these feelings. I can accept and attend to them or I can deny them or pretend they are not happening, but they are not subject to my control. They simply arise in my 5° awareness.

What I can control or have mastery over is whether and how I attend to these aspects of my interior awareness. As I observe from 6° these apparently conflicted parts of me, and identify what they are trying to do for me, and help them relate more fully and supportively to the other parts, the conflicts resolve and I am at peace and am able to act with integrity and harmony within myself and toward others.

I may even notice that not everyone has a sweater and experience a desire to clothe the naked. Or I may notice an awareness of what may have been going on with that person who abused me in a manner which allows me compassion for the suffering that elicited the abuse in the first place. I may move to a 7° awareness of what is in the transpersonal realm. These are all things over which I have no control but can only come to accept, except that I may move to 8° at which I am the one who is naked and I am the one whose abuse arises out of the brokenness of the world and I am filled with love for all manifestations of my Self.

## Centering

We have earlier addressed the importance of remaining centered if we are to be masterful at resolving conflicts. If we are off center, it is easy for us to be thrown by the events which arise for us. We want to find and hold our center. There are a couple of ways that any developmental sequence presents us with a center.

The simplest way to describe a circle is by defining a point which is the center and a radius which defines the outer limit of the circle. We define membership in a group by defining a center and the limits of inclusion. My immediate family is composed of those people who live in my household. I am the center of my family as is each person the center of his or her family.

In the personal realm, the center of concern is me and my immediate experience. It is ego-centric, that is I-centered. In the interpersonal realm the radius of concern expands to include all of the relationships of which I am aware which make demands on me. This is family centric or may expand to be ethno-centric, but it is limited to those I actually know.

We may think that the intrapersonal realm is even more limited being only about what is interior to me. What we find instead is that it is more broadly inclusive than the interpersonal realm. This is because as we connect with the deepest parts of ourselves we develop a greater and greater capacity for empathy. We identify with others we barely know of, much less know well. At the same time we are able to know our own interior conflicts and see how we project them onto others from time to time. We can see that others do this as well. In this sense we may consider this realm to be extra-personal in the sense that we come to know that much of the conflict we experience is not about us.

By the time we move to the transpersonal realm we have a capacity for deep compassion with all beings. This is a level of awareness which is truly cosmos-centric. So the arena of our concern expands as we move to ever higher levels of awareness. The scope of the focus of our attention grows.

## The Developmental Center of Gravity

There is another center, and that is the center of the development of most of those around us. When that center is at a level above where we are, it pulls us up. But once we have risen to that level, it starts to pull us down if we try to continue on.

When Jesse notices that Jack is gleeful when he chooses the glass of juice which, to his mind, has more, it plants in his awareness that there is a way of looking at the amount of juice that is different from his way of measuring in two dimensions. He is given a hint that there may be another and perhaps better way.

Jesse is surrounded by people who measure amount in volume, that is, in three dimensions, so he has modeled for him all the time that there is a developmentally superior solution to this problem. It is just a matter of time before Jack is left with the tall thin glass.

The developmental center of gravity is above where Jesse is. It will be easy for him to rise to that level as his capacity to think and observe grows. Joe and Jane need only wait and watch—and perhaps secretly cheer when he "gets it."

But when the cultural attitudes which surround us are coming mostly from a particular level of awareness and we are presented with a task which can only be addressed from a higher level, we may have trouble getting permission to move to that more comprehensive and effective level.

*When Jesse was sixteen he decided he knew a lot more about life than his dad, Joe, could ever imagine. Dad was just trying to hold him back when he tried to put limits on how much time Jesse spent with his girlfriend. Sometimes their arguments would get ugly and both of them would say things they only partially meant but which they couldn't stop themselves from saying.*

*Joe worked as a lineman for the electric utility. One of those ugly arguments came up about whether Jesse would be allowed to drive to his girlfriend's house*

*Transformation and the Orders of Self*

*in the middle of an ice storm and Joe put his foot down because he knew first hand how dangerous those storms could be.*

*The argument was interrupted by a call from the utility. Joe had to get to work on some downed lines.*

*With Dad gone, Jesse took it upon himself to go over to his girlfriend's house. He knew Dad would be out all night.*

*Jesse made it home just a few minutes after his curfew. He knew right away something was very wrong from his mom's sobs and he couldn't figure it out because he wasn't that late. It took Jack pulling him aside and speaking privately for him to learn that there had been an accident and that their dad had been badly hurt.*

*Joe made a slow but full recovery from his injuries. He was off work for a couple of months but they had health insurance and worker's compensation payments to see them through. But Jesse started having more and more problems. He broke up with his girlfriend and his grades plummeted. He started sleeping all the time unless he was playing video games.*

*Joe and Jane became more and more worried about him. Jane suggested that they send Jesse to a counselor but Jesse said he didn't want to do that and Joe was not convinced it would help. Counseling just wasn't the sort of thing that men in his family would do.*

Jesse was traumatized by his own selfishness. He didn't listen to his dad and then assumed that the distress his mother was feeling was about him. His self-centeredness shocked him. But he was not consciously aware of what was going on with him. On the surface things were fine. His dad was going to be okay. He didn't even get into trouble for disobeying him. What's the problem?

The problem was internal to Jesse in a way he couldn't get to from a Third or even 4° perspective. It would take the kind of 5° approach that psychotherapy provides for him to even know what the problem is, much less address and resolve it. But 5° is too far above where folks in his family, especially the men, find themselves. It is too far above the center of gravity for his family system.

There is a cultural center of gravity which is the point on the developmental spectrum which is the highest point on the bell curve of distribution of those levels represented by those persons in the community. As one grows in a given line of development one first finds more and more support for a perceptual map as one nears the center of the bell curve. But once one comes to the center, it becomes harder and harder to continue to develop as long as one remains in that community.

This is not just about the Orders of Self. This is true for all developmental sequences. Let's look, for example, at how a community of faith supports the faith development of its members. In religious education the children are taught the stories and the principles of the faith. In worship certain values are espoused, as are ways of speaking and acting. The adherents to the religion find that, as they apply the tenets of their faith in their daily life, the quality of their life improves. They become more and more both adherents and proponents of the religion. They tell others, "This is a good faith map."

But at some point they will come to discover that there are aspects of the faith map which don't adequately anticipate or explain certain experiences in their lives. Remember, all maps are partial. Sooner or later we are going to discover shortcomings in the maps we are using. The question is not whether the map will fail us, but what we do when it does. Do we cling to the map in spite of the fact that it doesn't adequately explain the territory; or do we go in search of a better map?

This is made far more difficult when, in order to find a better map, we have to question the central beliefs of our faith community. Some communities see this questioning as a sign of the vitality of one's faith journey and can affirm doubt. These are communities which have a higher center of gravity and can access the collective equivalent of Fifth and 6°. But some communities are operating at 3° and see any deviation as evidence that one is falling back into 2°. Remember that at the earlier orders, all other orders are wrong and dangerous.

So someone who is in a fundamentalist religious community cannot continue to develop in faith without risking the loss of the support of the community. Which is more important to the adherent: to maintain the support of the community, or to continue the faith journey?

Jesse faces a similar dilemma. He has defied his dad by going to his girlfriend's house in the ice storm. He wants to restore his relationship by being obedient to his dad's wishes. He will honor the 3° expectations of his father. But he also can't understand his own depression and his mother thinks he would find benefit by talking to a therapist. He is curious about his own condition but that would require that he move to a 4° construction of himself in relation to his dad and embark on a 5° process of self discovery.

As there is a center of gravity in the faith community and in the family, there is also a center of gravity within each one of us. Each of our parts is constructed at a level of development. We have 1° parts which make sense of our sensory awareness, 2° parts which tie our shoes and program the VCR (or DVR), 3° parts which get us to work on time and remind us to pay our bills and 4° parts which stand up for us when we are unappreciated and which can love our children even when they don't obey us.

Joe has a 2° part which he developed in his relationship with his own dad which chants the mantra, "You just have to pick yourself up by your own bootstraps." This part keeps Joe going when times are tough. It helps him get through.

Joe also has a 4° part which says that "change is good and being open to new things in one's relationships with others allows for transformation." As Joe observes the quandary he finds himself in with Jesse and Jane over Jesse getting help for his depression he can choose from which part he will come. Will he tell Jesse that he should just make himself do what he doesn't want to do or will he be curious about what is troubling Jesse and encourage Jesse to discover himself?

## Going High and Going Deep

It is my sense that we all have an innate wish to be the best we can be. Most folks, as they become aware of various developmental sequences, want to see themselves at the highest possible stage. This is both natural and healthy.

But there are some healthy cautions in how we think about our own development.

- We are all in some sense at all of the levels all of the time. We all have access to all eight States of Mind. Even if I don't have a 5° [Intrapersonal-internal: perception] awareness of the aspects of my self which are constructing my choices at any given moment, I still have the aspects and they are still shaping my choices. Even if I don't know myself at 7° [Transpersonal-spiritual: perception] to be a unique and precious manifestation of the divine just like everyone else, that doesn't mean I am not. We are all at all of the levels all of the time and may, from time to time, get a glimpse at a higher level than we can routinely construct in our awareness.

- While each successive level is more complex and allows for a fuller appreciation of the territory than a lower order map and can, thus, be said to be better, this does not make the person holding the map better. From a 2° [Personal-material: choice] perspective, people like me are good and others are bad or dangerous. But that is a limitation of the maps of 2°. Just because Jack's map allows him to get more juice than Jesse doesn't mean that Jack is better than Jesse.

- Higher levels are built upon the abilities of the lower orders. They transcend the lower orders but they also include them. You can't think in three dimensions without first thinking in two dimensions. When we move more and more to using 4° maps we don't quit using First, Second, and 3° maps. Further, even as we can move to higher order maps, we don't stop needing good maps at lower orders. We may just want to program a DVR.

So while, in one sense, we may see ourselves as developing up the developmental ladder, we also want to go more deeply into our abilities at each level or stage.

1°  How fully can I be aware of my own immediate experience? Can I take in more and more of what is happening without it becoming overwhelming to me?

2°  Can I make sense of what is happening and apply appropriate meaning? Can I understand what it is that I need and act in ways which meet my needs?

3°  Can I notice how my choices affect others and be sensitive to their expectations of me? Can I respond in ways which meet those demands?

4° When others' expectations are not consistent with my own welfare, can I respond in ways which meet my needs but still preserve the relationship and not harm the other?

5° When my behavior is not consistent with how I want to be in my relationships with others, can I become ever more aware of my various aspects and how they are constructing my behavior?

6° Can I be present to all of these aspects in ways which honor them and what they are trying to do for me and help them do their appointed job better, while finding a way of being which has authenticity and integrity for all the parts?

7° Can I treat myself with humility and honor all others while I act from an awareness of my place in the grand scheme of the cosmos?

8° Can I know that what I experience as my separate self is ultimately as separate from God as a wave is from the ocean?

Each of these stages allow for us to go to great depth as we seek to more fully experience our experience. But at each step we risk being overwhelmed by the intensity of life.

## Differentiation and Integration vs. Dissociation and Fusion

As we step back and observe the aspects of our experience which allow for awareness, we construct ever better maps by a process of saying, "well, *that* is different from *this*, but those two fit together this way." We make distinctions or differentiations, and we discover similarities and integrate parts into a whole. There are healthy ways to do this which move us to a higher level and there are pathological ways to do this which move us to a lower level.

Conflicts arise in our awareness when things are not as we expect them to be. When we can look at what is happening and see the things that fit together and the things that are not the same and sort them out and make sense of them, then we can come to a way of being which is centered and calm and creative. But sometimes we find ourselves being flooded by the sensations, emotions, thoughts and wishes which make up our interior experience.

We will explore this process in some depth later in this book, but for now we want to acknowledge that very same stresses which can invite us into a more comprehensive way of being can also push us to regress to a less effective mode.

If we have sufficient confidence in our competence, we can tolerate the stresses of things not being as we want. We can look more closely at the cause of the distress and notice what is happening and not happening and we can differentiate *this* from *that*. But when we are not confident or have already been thrown by a prior upsetting circumstance, we are more likely to decide that we just don't want to look at either *this* or *that*; that is, we will dissociate or dis-associate ourselves from our experience.

Similarly we can notice the various aspects of our experience and put them together into new and novel ways of seeing, if we can tolerate the anxiety of not seeing things the way we always did before. But if we are stressed, we are more likely to choose the old map or to be who others want us to be. We will choose to fuse with old ways of being.

|  | Moving apart | Putting together |
|---|---|---|
| Pathological ways of being when we are under stress | **Dissociation:** choosing not to look at relevant differences, removing our awareness from sources of stress | **Fusion:** holding together things which don't belong, being who others want us to be and abandon our own integrity |
| Healthy ways of coping with complexity | **Differentiation:** being able to see how things are distinct from each other | **Integration:** discovering novel and creative relationships between objects and perspectives |

For this reason we want to remain calm and centered as conflicts arise for us so that we will use the conflict to propel us to a more complex and effective way of looking at our experience, rather than falling back to less effective ways of being.

# Conflict and Transformation

Any transformative work involves conflict resolution. Indeed, any creative work is a process of resolving conflict. "Here is a problem I cannot yet resolve. What can I do to create what I need?"

At each step along the developmental path, be it using the map of the Orders of Self, or any other developmental map, we find there are challenges which our current way of being doesn't adequately address for us. Whether we are playing peek-a-boo, trying to pick the glass with the most juice, settling a disturbance between spouse and child, or opening our hearts to the suffering of the world, there is a conflict between how things are and how we want them to be; there is a conflict between how we are and how we want ourselves to be. It is the resolution of that conflict which moves us higher and deeper.

## Summary

In order to become more masterful at the skill of resolving conflicts we continue to move toward our own centers in each of the four realms. As we do that we notice that some of what arises in our awareness are simply perceptions of what is, and some are choices we have made or may make. But this distinction is tricky. As I make different choices I may notice different perceptions arising. What is in my control and what is not? As I bring more and more attention to bear on my perceptions and my choices, I notice myself becoming more aware and more masterful.

As there are perceptions and choices in each of the four realms, there are eight distinct States of Mind from which we can approach our experience. Indeed all of these are available to us all the time, but some are easier to come to than others. As we explore these eight loci for our identity we discover that they actually arise in a developmental sequence. We have to have mastered skills at an earlier level to rise to the higher one. Thus, these are not just States of Mind but are a developmental sequence we call the Orders of Self.

This map for our self-awareness has a great many uses which we will return to in the rest of the book but we want to notice a couple of its important aspects. While it appears to be a set of discrete steps, in reality it is more like a series of waves. We are never only at a single stage but always in the midst of a sea of waves, each giving energy and direction to the choices we are making.

As we move our awareness to more and more complex perspectives we find we take into our circle of concern not just those close to us who are like us but increasingly diverse people and ideas. We are centered in this circle of concern and we are in communities which have a set of shared perspectives. These perspectives tend to hold us in their sway and it is hard to rise to a higher level of development than the center of gravity in the groups of which we are a part.

Even as we struggle to move to ever higher and more complex perspectives we must not forget to move deeper and deeper at each of the more fundamental levels. Mastery at the earlier levels is essential to our own wellbeing and to stability at the higher levels.

Transformation to higher and more complex perspectives is something which takes great energy and effort especially as we move above the center of gravity of the communities of which we are a part. This energy for transformation comes from the problems which arise out of the perspectives we are currently using which not only fail to solve the problems we face but in some instances are the cause of the problem. It is our efforts to solve those problems, to resolve those conflicts, which carry us to a higher and more complex perspective. It is through the resolution of conflict that transformation occurs.

# 5

# The Structure of Relationships: Power and Agreements

We don't have a choice about whether we have conflicts, only whether we will name address and resolve those conflicts. When we do the hard work of conflict resolution, we experience transformation. The richest opportunities for conflict resolution come in our most significant relationships with others. It is this arena of our relationships with others that we want to examine next. Can we observe what happens in our relationships in ways which allow us to differentiate and integrate, to transcend and include?

All relationships are not structured the same way. A relationship with a lover is very different from a relationship with a parent or child or boss or buddy. These are different kinds of relationships and the conflicts that arise in each of them tend to be different. It will help us to know how to respond differently in each of these types of relationships to know more about the structural differences between them.

We have expectations about the way things will be including what our relationships with others will be like. These expectations come from our culture, our life experience, and the messages we get from others about how things are supposed to be. We have notions about what our relationship with our boss is like, or our relationship with our children, or our relationship with the pastor of our church, or any other relationship that is like any other relationship we have ever had. We have an idea in mind, a map if you will, of what the terrain of the relationship is.

When the map I am using matches the map the other is using we have a reasonably stable relationship and we have a platform from which to address the conflicts which arise in the relationship. When we are not working off the same map we can both get very lost. If we are to find each other and rebuild the relationship we will have to find a way to get back on the same page, to get back on the same map.

This means we will have to be able to structure the relationship in a way that works for both of us. We will have to construct a set of expectations that distribute the rights and the responsibilities we have as members of the relationship in a way that is clear and stable and that promotes each of our needs in the relationship. We will have to be able to appropriately distribute power between us.

## Balancing Rights and Responsibilities

We construct our relationships by having an understanding with the other. In many circumstances this understanding simply arises without much thought on our part. At other times we will carefully construct agreements. A central aspect of these understandings has to do with the ways we balance rights and responsibilities. This balancing is essential for stable relationships. When relationships are out of balance they feel oppressive.

So that one person does not overpower another, and so that we can be clear about how we will distribute power, we construct agreements about how we will balance rights and responsibilities in our relationships. The term *rights* and the term *responsibilities* are ones that have many and varied meanings, so let's start by clarifying just what we mean by them.

In general, a *right* is something I think I can expect is coming to me. It may be a *human right* that I have (or should have) along with every other human simply because we are human. Or it may be a *civil right* that I have (or should have) because I am a citizen of the community. For our purposes we will be talking about *earned rights*. These are privileges that fall to us because of the efforts we have made to fulfill a responsibility.

We will actually describe four different understandings for the term *responsibility* in the next chapter, but for now we will focus on the 3° [Interpersonal-relational: perception] definition which relates to the responsibilities we construct in forming understandings with others. When I enter into an agreement with the gas company to have them supply my apartment with natural gas, I am responsible for paying the bill and they are responsible for keeping the gas coming and reading the meter accurately. They have a right to get paid and I have a right to use the gas. Our rights and responsibilities balance each other.

If I want the right to drive a car I have to be responsible in many areas. I have to buy a car, maintain the car, insure the car, have a driver's license, and drive safely enough to keep it. It is only when I meet all of these responsibilities that I can trust that I will maintain the right to drive a car.

When we are in relationships in which we have lots of responsibilities and not many rights, we begin to feel oppressed. If I am expected to create certain results in my job but I haven't been given the tools or the time to create those results, I am likely to begin to feel that the job is oppressive to me. If, on the other hand I find that I have many rights and few responsibilities, I am likely to feel privileged. If this continues I may begin to expect this will be my lot and I will feel entitled. But when this happens, I am not covering my share of the responsibilities and someone else is getting oppressed.

Maintaining a balance of rights and responsibilities is essential to constructing and preserving healthy relationships. In some relationships this is a simple matter of knowing the rules. If I want to get gas from the pump to fill my tank, I have to pay for it. But in other relationships the rules seem to always be changing. This is especially true in the relationships we construct with our children.

When our children are young they have few rights and few responsibilities. As they grow older they get more and more of both. In fact, it is our job as parents to support them in growing into adults who are able to be fully responsible for themselves and to be able to fully exercise their rights. As little children they may not have the right to cross the street without holding our hand until they show that they are responsible to look both ways. As grade school kids they may not have the right to go play at a friend's house until they show that they are responsible to call when they get there and to come home in time for dinner.

Throughout their lives they are always pressing for more and more rights and it is our job to be sure that they don't get them without also being more and more responsible. When we allow our children to have the rights without having to show they are responsible, or when they show that they are not responsible and we don't respond by removing the rights, we are spoiling them. They "go bad" when they think they have a right to privileges they have not earned, when they begin to think that they are entitled.

On the other hand, if we expect our children to be responsible but then we don't extend to them the rights they have earned, we are leading them to feel bitter and hopeless and to expect a life without promise for them. We teach them to expect less than the best for themselves. Thus parenting is a balancing act where we are trying to be sure we are treating our children with respect by extending to them the rights they have earned while not allowing them to avoid the responsibilities that fall to them. This balance point is a continually moving target.

## Power

Balancing rights and responsibilities is a matter of the distribution of power. Power is the ability to have an effect. If I make a choice, the choice has an effect. Everyone has power. Not everyone has the same amount of power or power in the same arenas.

Power is morally neutral. It is not better to have power or to not have power. Being powerless is not a good thing. Being powerful is not a good thing. *Good* and *bad* come not from the presence of power but from the use to which the power is put. Fire is power. We can use fire to heat a house or to burn a house down. A hammer has power. We can use a hammer to drive nails or break windows. Fire and hammers are morally neutral. What we choose to do with fire and hammers is not.

Everything has power. The chair I am sitting on has power. It has the power to keep me from sitting on the floor. I have more power than the chair. I can move it around, but it cannot move me around.

Some people believe that infants are powerless...until they live with one. If you have lived with an infant, particularly if you have been the parent of an infant, you know how powerful they can be, especially at two in the morning when they have colic or bronchitis. Everyone and everything has power. Everyone and everything has the ability to have an effect.

Not everyone has the same amount of power. As a white first-world educated man I have far more power than an uneducated third-world woman of color. Not everyone has the same kinds of power. I am tall enough to get things down off the top shelf that my wife can't reach but she has smaller hands so can get things out of the disposer that I can't. We each have different ways of having an effect.

## Three kinds of power

The way that power is distributed, the way we have an effect, is shaped by who is making the choice and by who is being affected. When one person or party makes a choice and it affects someone else, we call that *power over*. When a group of people make a choice that affects them all, we call that *power with*. When a person makes a choice that primarily affects themselves, we call that *empowerment*.

### Power over

Most of what we think of as power is *power over*. Parents have the power to tell their children when curfew will be; bosses tell their employees what the quota will be; police tell drivers when to pull over; judges tell them what the fine will be. Even the power that the chair under me has is power over. It has power over my body to keep it upright and in position to type these words. Everyone and everything has *power over*.

### Power with

There is another form of power which is less common but more powerful than *power over*. It is *power with*. *Power with* is constructed by an agreement in which all parties decide to act in ways that construct the welfare of all. *We* have decided how *we* are going to be with each other in a manner that serves *us*.

We speak the same language. This language may be different in different communities or at different times in the same community, but if we are going to understand each other, we have to be speaking the same language. We have decided that we will be governed by the rule of law, that we will honor each other's rights, and that we will act for the common good. These are all examples of *power with*.

Over many generations we have constructed a fabric of social conventions that serve to support the needs of the whole society. We subordinate our individual wishes to the will of the common good because we know we are ultimately served by doing so. When the understandings which create the social fabric begin to crumble, we get very anxious and it becomes more and more likely that we will not get what we need.

In the classic novel *Lord of the Flies*, a group of well bred, well socialized school boys are marooned on a deserted island without adults to structure their common life. At first they maintain their social arrangements but, little by little, the stability of the life they have known decays and they descend into barbarian behavior. When they are rescued, they immediately and gratefully snap back into the safety of civil society. Through the lens of the Orders of Self we could say that the perspectives of 3° were not solidly formed in the boys and they reverted to 2° until the adults returned to restore it.

The United States has in recent years made some efforts to introduce democracy to nations that have not been through the long and arduous process of developing a shared understanding of the nature and purpose of modern social institutions. These efforts have appeared to be successful initially because of the promise of social stability that came with them. But, over time, the institutions have crumbled because the agreements that must be in place to support them have not been secured.

When we have had personal experiences with constructing relationships through understandings of *power with*, we know how to do it and why to do it. We form alliances and associations easily and quickly. When we haven't had such experiences it may not occur to us that it is an advantage to work with others. Paradoxically *power with* is both more powerful than *power over*, and more fragile.

## Empowerment

Most powerful of all is *empowerment*. I am empowered to the degree to which I can construct what I need all by myself. I don't have to get it from someone else. I don't have to build and repair agreements with others. All I have to do is to create what I need. I can feed and dress myself. I can dial a phone and drive a car and make a date.

No wait, I can't make a date by myself. I have to construct an agreement with someone else. I can't create everything I need all by myself. And this is where empowerment runs aground. To the degree to which I can make the choices that construct what I need without expecting or depending on others to change, that is the degree to which I am empowered. I want to be just as empowered as I can be. But some things I can only get by constructing them in relationships with others. I cannot create intimacy all by myself.

| | Who Chooses | Who is Affected | Advantages | Difficulties |
|---|---|---|---|---|
| **Power Over** | I do/ other does | Other is / I am | Easily obtained | Easily abused |
| **Power With** | We do | We are | More powerful | Requires agreement |
| **Empowerment** | I do | I am | Most powerful | Ineffective on relationships |

While we will be pursuing the goal of empowerment, we will mostly be doing it by focusing on *power with*. We live in a world of *power over* and desire a world of *empowerment* and we get there by traveling through the land of *power with*.

One of the most evident ways that we are empowered is in how we care for ourselves. I can, for example, feed and dress myself. Training in this started at an early age.

> As a child I wanted to run barefoot outside. My dad wanted me to wear shoes when I went outside. He was bigger than me. He had power over me such that, if I wanted to go outside, I had to have shoes on.

> One day as I was playing outside with my shoes on, I discovered that one shoe was loose. I played with it and got it off. I played with the other one and got it off too. Then I took my socks off. Ah…barefoot in the grass. I ran and played and kicked the ball. I kicked the ball across the gravel drive but when I chased it, ouch, that hurts. It didn't feel that way when I had shoes on.

*So I called out, "Daddy, shoes."*

*And he said to me, "Get your shoes and socks and bring them to me and I will put them on." And while I did, I realized that I hadn't had to bring him the shoes and socks before. He had always done that. Our relationship had changed. We had gone from power over to power with. Before he wanted me to have shoes on and I didn't but he was bigger than me so he got his way. Now we both wanted me to have my shoes on so we worked together to create what we both wanted. We both wanted Mark to have his shoes on.*

Over time I learned to find my shoes and socks, and then to put on my socks, and then my shoes (I had to know which one went on which foot), and then to tie them, and then to tie them so they stayed tied. Little by little over time I became empowered to put on my shoes and socks. But I did so by going from *power over* through *power with* to *empowerment*.

There is very little of what we have learned to do on our own behalf that we did not learn in the context of a relationship with someone who wanted us to learn. Even when I bake a cake all by myself using only the recipe in a cookbook, I still have an alliance with the author of the cookbook who wrote it so that I and others could cook on our own.

## Three kinds of relationships based on the balance of rights and responsibilities

One way to balance rights and responsibilities in the relationship is to have everyone have the same ones. We all get the same rights. We all get the same responsibilities. We call this a mutual relationship. Another way to balance rights and responsibilities is to give one party the right to act because it has responsibility for the welfare of the other. We call this a fiduciary relationship. But the most common and durable way to build relationships is to construct an understanding by which we decide which rights are balanced by which responsibilities. We call this a reciprocal relationship.

# Fiduciary Relationships

Fiduciary relationships are ones in which one party has rights over the other or the other's affairs specifically because of responsibilities for the welfare of the other. We often think of fiduciary relationships as being like the one that a trust officer in a bank has toward the person or group who has entrusted their funds to the bank. The term *fiduciary* is most often applied in matters of money, but the concept of a fiduciary is much broader and comes from the recognition that, from time to time, one person may be entrusted with the welfare of another. When this is the case, that person, the fiduciary, has the right to act on the other's behalf.

Not everyone has the right to flag down drivers and force them to pull off the road. Police officers have that right because they have a responsibility to maintain public safety. If someone is driving in violation of the law or in ways that endanger others, we want to have someone who can and will address the risk. For that reason we entrust police officers with special powers, special rights.

Not everyone has a right to teach school. Teachers are trained and certified and evaluated to be sure that they are acting in a manner that promotes education, safety, and social development in the classroom. They have rights with regard to our children because they have responsibilities for our children's welfare.

Judges, pastors, doctors, city council members, custodians, computer network administrators all have special rights that others don't have specifically because they have responsibilities for the common good. Perhaps the largest group of fiduciaries is parents. Parents have the right to make decisions about what their children will or will not do because they have responsibility for the children's welfare. I have the right to tell my child to go to bed because I have responsibility for her wellbeing and I know she needs her sleep.

Whenever a fiduciary uses rights in a manner that is not consistent with the welfare of the ones for whom they are responsible, they are committing an abuse. This question of abuse—how we define it and how we respond to it—is a theme of the next chapter. We just want to note at this point that abuses of fiduciary responsibilities are very common and very harmful to healthy relationships. Some of this abuse arises out of confusion about the rights and responsibilities we give to others on our behalf. We may be expecting others to look out for us when they have no sense that they have a responsibility to do so.

> Jane is waiting at a stop light and there is a long line in front of her and behind her. The light changes and the first person in line turns but the second person just sits there. The driver is fumbling with something in the seat next to him and Jane notices that he is on his cell phone. As horns begin to honk, he looks up and guns it through the intersection just as the light changes. Jane is furious. She believes we have a responsibility to look out for others and to pay attention to how our driving behavior impacts others. She believes that when we are driving, our driving should be our first priority. She thinks this guy should only have a right to drive if he is going to do so responsibly. She feels abused by him.

> Henry gets a job in a small manufacturing plant. All the workers there know the economy is slow and that the plant is having trouble getting orders. They value their jobs and their relationships with others and so they are all committed to making sure the operation is successful. When they get notice the factory is closing in a month and the owners are moving the equipment to a new location in Honduras, they are furious. They thought the management had a responsibility to look out for their jobs.

> Joe knows Jane has been stressed about work lately so he plans a nice dinner for tonight. Joe has it mostly ready by the time Jane is expected home. He waits and waits and finally she calls to say she stopped at the mall on the way home and got distracted. She will be home in fifteen minutes. Joe knows she has a right to spend her time the way she wants, but he thought she would be responsible to tell him if she wasn't coming right home. When she gets home and learns about his preparations she is upset with Joe. Jane thinks if Joe is going to plan something special for the two of them he should inform her about it. They are both clear that the other has rights to do as they have each done, but they assumed a fiduciary relationship in which the other would exercise those rights in a manner that would more fully consider their own needs.

# Reciprocal Relationships

A reciprocal relationship is one in which each party bears a responsibility for the welfare of the other and thus each has certain rights. The stability of the relationship comes from how well balanced are those rights and responsibilities. In some sense this can be seen as a set of fiduciary relationships in which each person has rights because of responsibilities to the other.

> Henry hears that they are hiring over at Universal Widget. He has some experience working in a factory and he needs the money. He talks to Frank, the plant manager about the job and they agree that Henry will start Monday. They have formed an agreement that constructs a reciprocal relationship.
>
> Henry will work eight hours a day with a 15 minute break in the morning and another one in the afternoon. He gets a half hour for lunch, paid sick leave after three months, and vacation after a year. His quota is 100 widgets a day. He is to tell Frank if there is anything wrong with the widget machine and to call if he is going to be late. He will be paid $10 an hour.

Frank has a right to know if the widget machine is acting up. Henry has a responsibility to tell him if there is anything wrong with the widget machine. Frank has the right to know because he has a responsibility to support the welfare of the company which gives Henry his paycheck.

Henry has a right to a paycheck. Frank had a responsibility to pay him. Henry has a right to a paycheck because he is responsible for creating the product that keeps the company financially solvent.

Frank has a right to know how many widgets Henry has made in a given day. Henry has a responsibility to tell him. Frank has a right to know because he is responsible for maintaining sufficient output such that the company can continue to employ Henry.

Their relationship is constructed out of a set of understandings that balance rights and responsibilities. If Henry starts showing up late, Frank is going to feel taken advantage of. Henry is not keeping to the agreement. If Henry starts making more than 100 widgets a day, he is going to start thinking about getting a raise. He is being more responsible so he should get more rights. Their capacity to maintain a healthy relationship will depend on their ability to clarify and adjust the agreement so that they maintain the balance of rights and responsibilities. If they are unable to do so Henry will get fired or he will quit. The relationship will collapse.

There is often a hierarchy in reciprocal relationships. In this case Frank is the boss and Henry the employee. Frank has a kind of authority which comes from his rank as the boss. Henry may have a sense that Frank has all of the power but Frank knows better. He knows that if his workers don't show up he is going to have to answer to the owner. Frank has rights Henry doesn't have, but he also has responsibilities Henry may not even know about.

## Mutual Relationships

As we are all humans we all have human rights and thus we have the same rights. We all have the same rights and responsibilities. But beyond that, we sometimes consciously construct relationships around a set of rules or understandings that spell out the ways that we each have the same rights and responsibilities.

Take the players on a baseball team. All of them have the same rights and responsibilities. Each has a right to a turn at bat. Each has a responsibility to field the ball. They may decide to play different positions with different expectations about what each position's responsibilities are; but the players can switch positions. When in the fifth inning the pitcher's arm begins to fade, he can go to right field and the right fielder can come in to pitch. Each player has fundamentally the same rights and responsibilities.

They may select one member of the team to be the captain. The captain has special rights and responsibilities but they are temporary and limited and if the team doesn't like the way the captain fulfills his role, they can vote him out and select a different captain.

The coach on the other hand is in a reciprocal relationship with the players on the team. The coach doesn't have the right to be on the field when the ball is in play, but does get to decide the batting order. The coach has a mutual relationship with the coach of the opposing team but has a fiduciary relationship with the umpire; that is, the ump creates the game[15].

## Strengths and Weaknesses of Each

While all relationships are in some sense mutual, there are many relationships that wouldn't exist if they were not constructed by the formation of a reciprocal relationship. Frank and Henry might have a mutual relationship as they stand around the coffee pot during the morning break talking about the game last night, but at some point Frank looks at his watch and Henry knows it is time to get back out on the floor. They have a mutual relationship as sports fans but their primary relationship is as boss and worker.

Most work relationships are constructed as reciprocal relationships. Some are partnerships (and thus more mutual), but mostly we construct work relationships as reciprocal relationships because they tend to be stable and efficient. As long as everyone knows what they are to do and is able and willing to do it, the job gets done. As the job changes, the system changes, but the people keep doing what they do. The military is a particularly good example of a structure in which stability and efficiency are created though clear understandings. When a decision is to be made, we know whose job it is to make it; they make it; we live with it, and move on.

---

15 *A cub reporter gets an assignment to cover what turns out to be a really dull baseball game. Desperate he looks around the club house and spots the three umpires standing over against the wall. Hoping for a story he goes up to the first one and asks, "How do you call ball and strikes?"*
*"I call 'em as I see 'em."*
*"Oh," he says and shrugs and goes to the second one and asks, "How do you call balls and strikes?*
*"I call 'em as they are."*
*"Uh huh", he mutters and turns to the third umpire, "And you sir, how do you call balls and strikes?"*
*"Sonny, until I call 'em, they ain't nothing."*

The first umpire is allowing his understanding of the game to be shaped by the rules as he understands them. He looks at the rules and at the play and tries to associate them as he sees them. He knows there may be other interpretations but he is centered in the game. He is functioning at 3°.
The second umpire is not allowing for any other interpretation of reality. What he sees is the only reality there is, or could be. He is more ego-centric than the first ump. He is functioning at 2°.
The third umpire is not only saying that there is no other interpretation, or that there is no other reality, he is saying that reality itself is constructed by his experience. He is something beyond ego-centric. He is purely at 1°.

| Characteristics \ relationship type | Rights and Responsibilities | Decision-making | Advantages-disadvantages |
|---|---|---|---|
| Fiduciary | Relationship is created by an agreement by which a "fiduciary" is given rights and responsibilities for the benefit of a less powerful party. | Fiduciary makes the decisions until the agreement is abrogated | Person or party with less power is given the benefit of the power of the "fiduciary" for the term of the agreement. Consolidation of power allows for abuses. |
| Reciprocal | Relationship is created by an agreement by which rights and responsibilities are divided. One party's rights correspond with the other party's responsibilities | The agreement that establishes the relationship determines who makes which decisions. | Creates stability and efficiency but can be impersonal and more easily allows for abuse |
| Mutual | All parties have the same rights and responsibilities | Requires that all decisions be made by all parties together | Allows for the greatest intimacy but coming to a decision can be cumbersome |

Decision-making in mutual relationships, on the other hand, is much harder. Everyone has to make the decision together. When everyone on the baseball team knows what to do with the ground ball and a man on first and they make the double play it will feel really good. But they will have to have rehearsed that play many times to be sure that everyone knows where to go and where to throw. When something comes up which they have never had to deal with before, it might take quite a while for them to come to a clear course of action. So decision-making in mutual relationships is much more difficult.

Intimacy is much easier and deeper in mutual relationships than in authority ones. We are friends with our peers. When a buddy at work is promoted to foreman, we no longer go out drinking together after work. In reciprocal relationships intimacy is actually damaging to the stability of the operation. While dating may be discouraged among peers in a work environment, dating someone who reports to you can get you a sexual harassment suit and job termination.  In the military it is called "fraternization."  It is harmful to morale and will not be tolerated.

Even if it isn't against the rules, we naturally choose to be closest to those who are our equals.  Being able to be emotionally open depends on a level of trust that is much easier to create and sustain in mutual relationships.

## Structure of marriage

So what about marriage?  Is it a *mutual relationship* or a *reciprocal relationship* or a *fiduciary relationship*?  Recognizing there are mutual aspects of any relationship, the question is, "Is a marriage a relationship in which the man and the woman have different rights and responsibilities?"

Almost without exception when I ask this question in my classes, people respond that it is a mutual relationship.  We choose to be in marriages for the purposes of intimacy.  We see ourselves as equals joining into a shared commitment.

But do we really mean that we have the same rights and responsibilities?  Or are we expecting that the man will be the breadwinner and the woman will stay home and raise the kids?  Is he in charge of the lawn and she in charge of the laundry?

In most parts of the world to this day marriage is clearly a reciprocal relationship between husband and wife created by a fiduciary relationship between parent and child.  Marriages are arranged by the families for the purposes of establishing a stable economic unit.  If the bride and groom are able to come to love each other, so much the better.  But the goal is economic stability, not emotional intimacy.  Families know that the heart can make foolish and impulsive choices; better that the parents should pick out a suitable partner.

Even in the developed world we continue the trappings of a culture in which women are property who are transferred from the ownership of the father to the ownership of the husband.  In most weddings even today, the bride will dress in white, wear a veil, and be escorted down the aisle by her father to be given away to her husband.  When was the last time you saw a groom given away?

Still, what we say we want is intimacy and we describe our primary relationships more and more as mutual ones. We can see that they are more nearly mutual than our parents' relationship is or was and certainly more so than our grandparents'. We are in a time of dramatic transformation of how we understand the nature and purpose of marriage. This transformation even happens within a relationship over time.

A few years ago I had as psychotherapy clients a couple who had separated and were contemplating divorce. There was a high level of conflict in the relationship at the time but it had not always been so. They had once been very much in love and had gotten along very well for many years. They had even worked together in his business.

When they married, one of the images they used in the ceremony was a nautical one. He was the captain of their ship and she was the first mate. Over the years, she had changed her expectations and now was asking to be co-captain. He was genuinely dismayed. Things had worked so well all of these years. Why would she want to change things?

At the time of their marriage, being first mate was a huge promotion for her. She had spent her childhood as cabin boy on her father's ship. The prospect of having the authority and respect of being a first mate was a liberating and affirming change for her. But as she grew into her new role she also grew aware that she was her husband's equal and wanted that status to be reflected in their relationship.

I want to acknowledge here that the problems in this relationship were really two-fold. One was that she was changing the fundamental structure of the relationship. They had agreed to a reciprocal relationship and now she was insisting that it be a mutual relationship. The other problem was that he had taken a relationship of authority and turned it into an authoritarian relationship. They are not the same thing.

It is certainly possible to have reciprocal relationships that are not oppressive. This is a distinction that some critics of the institution of marriage have not noticed. Some couples choose to have a marriage that is clearly a reciprocal relationship and they both feel supported and fulfilled by the relationship. In the most traditional of Mormon marriages the relationship is fiduciary. The husband has rights and responsibilities for the welfare of the whole family, including his wife. They are not equals. This is a perfectly appropriate and stable way to create a relationship as long as all of the parties agree.

We can decide whatever kind of relationships we want to have. If a couple wants to have a mutual relationship; fine. If they want to have a reciprocal relationship; fine. A problem arises however when one person wants a reciprocal relationship and the other wants a mutual relationship. Or, as is more common, they both want it to be a mutual relationship at times and a reciprocal relationship at times. They just may not agree on which times.

## Restoring the Balance: Constructing Durable Agreements

In any relationship it is essential that we have the capacity to come to an agreement. As we will see, this is an essential aspect of what it means to resolve a conflict. So let's look as some aspects of what we might mean when we talk about forming an agreement.

*Jane has seen how angry Joe can get sometimes when Jack is not obeying him so she has spoken to Joe about her concern that they respect and "validate" the feelings their children have. She asked him if he also believes that validating the boys' feelings is important and he shrugged, and said "Sure." "And", she added, "I think we should check in with each other when we are disciplining the boys so we know we are on the same page. Again Joe shrugged, "Of course."*

*Early one evening as Joe was just getting home and Jane was working with Jesse on his homework, Joe finds himself irritated that Jack is playing a video game instead of doing his own homework. When confronted Jack states, "It's done. I did it all at school."*

*Joe goes into the kitchen to hang up his keys and notices that the trash is overflowing. He calls to Jack and tells him to take out the trash now.*

*"As soon as I finish this level," replies Jack.*

*Joe storms into the front room where Jack is playing and demands that he put the game controller down this instant and take out the trash.*

*"Dad, I'm almost to a save place. If I quit now I will have to start this level over,"* pleads Jack.

*Jane appears at the doorway and says, "Joe, honey, can we talk?"*

Jane is both angry and scared about what she sees going on with Joe and Jack. She is afraid of what this may escalate into but she is angry because she feels as though Joe is violating their agreement. When Joe realizes that Jane is angry at him, he becomes angry at her. As far as he is concerned, she is violating their agreement.

Jane thought they had an agreement that they would be sensitive to the feelings of their sons and would let the boys know that what they are each feeling matters. They would not just run roughshod over them insisting on them being who they as parents want the boys to be. Further, she can see that Joe is about to impose consequences on Jack but she knows they haven't spoken about it and Joe hasn't invited Jane into the process.

Joe thought they had an agreement that it was Jack's chore to take out the trash when it was full and that they wanted the boys to learn personal responsibility and to set aside their immediate gratification for the welfare of the household. Further, he thought that he and Jane had an agreement that they wouldn't undermine each other's authority with the boys. Her choice to speak to him in the middle of his intervention with Jack does just that.

The process of constructing *power with* others is essentially a process of coming to an understanding of who we are to each other, what we are trying to accomplish together, and what we are going to do to create what we all need. We create these understandings casually and formally.

*I recently had a stretch of fence in my back yard replaced. In order to get permission to do this I had to apply to the city for a building permit. I filled out a form, took and submitted photographs, and paid a fee. I received a form in return that allowed the work to proceed.*

*When the workmen showed up to do the work it was immediately clear that they knew what they were doing and took pride in their work. While they conversed with each other they did not need to talk about the job. With a glance of the eyes or a nod of the head they spoke to the one at the other end of the board or the one with the nail gun. They understood what they needed to do and they did it. It was poetry in motion.*

Coming to an understanding between two (or more) parties requires certain things of the parties. Each is making *requests* about what they want to have happen and each is making *promises* about what they are willing to do.

*I made a request of the city to get permission to replace the fence and promised to have it built in compliance with the plans I submitted. The city requested detailed plans and a fee and promised to allow the construction if it met the promised design. We formalized our understanding with a permit.*

*I made a request of the builder to get a certain style of fence built and he promised to build it. He made a request of a fee for the work and I promised to pay. We formalized our understanding with a contract.*

*The construction crew made a series of promises and requests to each other as they worked together on the job. Their understanding was created and carried out with no formal structure. It was not just unwritten, but, as nearly as I could tell, it was not even spoken.*

In some circumstances, as we try to construct an understanding (and thus create power with another) we find there are power imbalances. This imbalance disrupts our ability to create and maintain a stable understanding. If one party to the understanding feels less powerful in the relationship this imbalance may hamper the ability of the relationship to sustain *power with* and it will degenerate into *power over*.

If one who is perceived to have more power makes a *request*, it may well show up for the other party as a *demand*. In that case, the response of the lesser party may be more about *compliance* than a *promise*.

We may be unaware that the understanding was hampered by the power inequities until we find that the understanding doesn't hold. We find that our expectations are not being met.

*Jane says to Joe, "I thought we agreed we would validate the boys' feelings."*

*"Validate their feelings? What do feelings have to do with this? Jack has a chore to do and he hasn't done it. I thought we had an agreement that he was to take out the trash?"*

*"Yes, it is his job to take out the trash, but when you come down on him with both feet like that you are treating him like his feelings don't matter. Didn't you agree that we would respect the boys' feelings?"*

*"I remember you telling me that you wanted us to validate their feelings. I understand that is important to you. But I had no idea that meant that I was supposed to let him play his game when he has chores to do."*

*"If you weren't sure about what we had agreed, why didn't you come talk to me? You knew I was in the dining room helping Jesse with his homework. Didn't we agree that we would work together when disciplining the boys?"*

*"What? I need your permission to ask our son to do his chores? If I had come and bothered you about this, you would have been angry with me for interrupting and then you would have taken it over and handled it your way. You never consult with me about how you deal with the boys."*

As Joe and Jane discuss this situation they discover just how far they are from having an agreement. There are multiple layers of misunderstanding. What might it mean to validate the boys' feelings? How do they check things out with each other when they are in the midst of addressing issues with their children? Do they have a genuinely mutual relationship around child-rearing or do they each see Jane as the primary care-giver and thus the one with ultimate authority to decide what they will do?

Building durable agreements is very important for the health of relationships of whatever kind, and it is very hard to do. We will be looking at some specific tools for doing this as we explore more of the Disciplines, but, for now, let's identify some characteristics of a durable agreement.

- It must be created in a context in which both parties are committed to having power with the other. Even in a fiduciary relationship there can be a commitment to *power with* if there is a wish to build durable agreements.

  *Jack has much less power than his parents and they have a fiduciary responsibility to be sure he grows into an adult who can know and meet the expectations of others. Having him do chores in the household is a way for him to learn responsibility. But for Jack's part, does he want to be someone who contributes in a meaningful way to the welfare of the family and the household? If he doesn't, then there is a bigger problem here than taking out the trash.*

  *If Joe and Jane approach Jack by saying that he has to carry his weight and he has to take out the trash or else... he will likely be resentful of their power over him. But if they wonder with him whether he is mature enough to begin to help out in the household and see if he thinks he would be able to take out the trash, he is likely to say, sure, he can handle that. Then the chore is evidence of his maturity, not of his servitude. They are constructing power with instead of power over.*

- It must be created in a context in which both parties are clear about the requests and the promises of the other. In some cases this may be formalized in a written document, but more often it is simply a verbal confirmation.

  *When Jane asked Joe to agree to validate the boys' feelings, he had no idea what she was talking about. He knew that he wants them to know they are important to him, and he wants them to be able to know and express their own feelings. But how this might translate into how he deals with them when they are ducking their responsibilities he hasn't a clue.*

- And, it must be created in a context which appreciates the difficulty of maintaining agreements and knows that they will have to be repaired, perhaps many times. Not only do we not know what the other is requesting or promising, we don't know that we don't know. We assume we are fully clear until our expectations are not met.

*Joe and Jane will have to consider how they want to handle these situations in the future. This is certainly not the last time any of these issues will arise for them. They will have to value the agreement and its capacity to build power with more than their wish to be right, to blame and shame each other, and to fall back into power over.*

While we can construct our relationships any way we choose, there are some structures which build durable and satisfying relationships, and there are some which are fragile and frustrating. However we decide to construct our relationships, they will be highly conflicted if we don't agree on the structure.

Some of the elements in the structure of any relationship include the ways that power is distributed, especially how we share rights and responsibilities, and how we make decisions. When we believe we have an understanding but we find that we are still not acting in keeping with each others' expectations, we may need to do some careful work at creating and repairing durable agreements.

## Summary

Our most fertile ground for transformation is in the conflicts which arise in our most significant relationships. For that reason we are giving special attention to those relationships. Relationships are constructed out of the expectations and agreements we have with others. While many conflicts are about the events that happen in the relationship, some are about the structure of the relationship itself.

For a relationship to be stable it has to be just. Oppressive relationships are inherently unstable. Justice requires that the rights and the responsibilities of the parties are balanced. If one party carries more responsibilities than rights, they are being oppressed. If one party carries more rights than responsibilities they are privileged, may see themselves as entitled, and are oppressing someone.

The understandings which construct our relationships are about the distribution of power. Power is simply the ability to have an effect. We have three kinds of power. *Power over* is something everyone has, is easy to understand and use, and can be used to abuse others. *Power with* requires an agreement with others but is more powerful than *power over*. *Empowerment* is personally very effective but doesn't have much traction in relationship building.

There are different basic forms of relationship. Fiduciary relationships are those in which one person or party has the right to make certain decisions because of a responsibility for the welfare of another. Mutual relationships are those in which each party has the same rights and responsibilities. And reciprocal relationships are those in which power is balanced by a set of agreements in which one party's rights are balanced by the responsibilities of the other.

For most of human history the primary relationship of marriage was either a solely fiduciary relationship in which the wife was the property of the husband or a reciprocal relationship in which wives and husbands had different but carefully prescribed roles and rights. It is only in very recent history that we have tried to have marriages be mutual relationships. This is an experiment. It is not surprising we haven't yet mastered how to do it in a way that is both intimate and stable. Intimacy and stability come from the skill of developing and repairing durable agreements. It is these agreements which form the content of the relationship.

# 6

# Abuse and Systems of Oppression

When power is distributed justly and durable agreements are made and kept or repaired, we then have shalom arise in our relationships. From time to time in nearly every relationship, however, we find that power is not distributed justly. We feel oppressed or we make choices which others find oppressive to them. Esuba arises.

Esuba is *abuse* spelled backwards. Abuse is a quality of a choice which results in harm.

Most of us have no trouble recognizing that we sometimes make choices which are harmful to others. It is not that we are bad people. It is just that we are careless or haven't fully considered all of the implications of a choice we are making. Perhaps we are doing what we thought was the right thing because this is how we were taught. Only later do we discover that we have harmed others.

But we resist calling this abuse. Abuse is what abusers do.

*A few years ago I was asked to speak to a men's Lenten prayer breakfast at a local church. They knew that I was a minister and a pastoral counselor who works with men who batter. So I asked them, "How many of you are abusers?" There was a long pause and then one man sort of half-way raised his hand, sensing a trick. Then I asked, "How many of you are sinners." All of the hands immediately went up. They all, being faithful readers of the Bible, knew that "all sin and fall short of the glory of God." It is socially unacceptable in that context not to affirm ones own nature as a sinner. So then I asked, "What is the difference? What is the difference between an abuser and a sinner?"*

Personally, I don't see much difference between sin and abuse. But in the popular imagination there is a huge difference. Sin is a term that is rarely used outside of a specific religious context and then most often the one who is seen as having been harmed is God by the fact that we didn't obey.

If we are to build healthy relationships we need a map which helps us see when we have made choices which are harmful to others, even in very subtle ways, even when we are acting in ways which are completely within the norms of our culture. We are looking for a map which helps us see these cognitive distortions and know how to address and correct them.

## Abuse as a Quality of a Choice

As someone who has worked in the field of domestic violence intervention for the past 30 years I have had a particularly keen interest in understanding just what *abuse* is. I have found especially when working with offenders that it is essential to be very specific about what we are talking about when we use the term *abuse*. It may surprise you to learn that there is no clear and consistent definition within the field for such central terms as *abuse*, *violence*, and *battering*. I will save my thoughts about why this is so, but I would at least note that one of the reasons that domestic violence intervention is not as effective as we would all like it to be is that we are not all operating from the same map.

To that end I want to suggest a map for understanding abuse which I find to be helpful in knowing what is going on, what we would prefer to have happen, and how we might begin to get there. In the process I will look at some other maps for understanding abuse and consider the implications of some of their features.

Let us then begin our consideration of what we mean by abuse by looking in on the Johnsons.

> *For his third birthday, Jack got a tricycle. He loved it. The Johnson's house is on the corner, so Jack could go from property line at one end around the corner to the alley at the other end and then back. He would keep this up for hours while Joe worked in the garden.*

*Once Jack became really good at pedaling and steering he began to long for new places to ride. On the corner is a handicap access cut that is an attractive ramp. He rode his trike down the ramp and into the street.*

*Joe was on his feet and coming at a run as Jack turned around in the middle of the street.*

*"You may not ride your tricycle in the street!" yelled Joe.*

*Jack looked perplexed and Joe added, "You might get hit by a car."*

*Jack looked around and saw only parked cars and Joe realized that logic wasn't going to work with a three year old. "If you ride your tricycle in the street you are going to your room for 15 minutes," declared Joe.*

Consider your own understanding of abuse and see if you think Joe's behavior qualifies as abuse.

Some definitions of abuse include making threats or scaring others. Some parenting experts suggest that a "time out" should not last longer that one minute for each year of age for the child. Some parenting experts caution against punishing children by sending them to their rooms as that will associate the room with punishment.

*Jack indicated to Joe that he understood what the boundaries were and what the consequences would be. They went back to their activities.*

*Joe discovered that his yard work called for some supplies he didn't have and he needed to take a trip to the store. He let Jane know that he would be running an errand and to keep and eye on Jack.*

*As Joe returned from the store and came driving up the street he saw Jack ride down the ramp and into the street. Jack saw him and immediately got back up on the sidewalk. Joe knew that Jack understood what he had done wrong and decided to let it go this time. He got to work unloading the car saying nothing to Jack.*

*Abuse and Systems of Oppression*

So, what do you think? Is it abuse for Joe to fail to implement the consequences that he set for Jack?

Once having set a rule, it is important for parents to be consistent with their children. Jack won't be able to tell when a rule is to be followed, and when it isn't, if rules are not consistently applied. It is more work for Joe, at this point, to invoke the consequences, but it is better for Jack if he does. It is important for Jack to know that what his dad says goes. It may not be abuse for Joe to ignore the infraction, but it is certainly neglect.

> Or suppose instead that when Joe returns he finds that Jack has gotten tired of riding his tricycle, has put it away, and has gone into his room to start playing with his Legos. Joe finishes unloading the car and picks up the gardening tools. He goes in the house, washes his hands, grabs a beer out of the fridge, and sits down in the living room to read the paper.

> Jack comes bounding into the room with something he has just made out of Legos. "Daddy, Daddy, look what I made," he says as he tries to climb into Joe's lap. Joe pushes him away and says, "Give me a break, I'm tired. Go to your room for fifteen minutes."

So what do you say? Is this abuse? Some of you may say that it depends on Joe's tone of voice. Some may say it depends on whether this is the way Joe always treats Jack or if this is the first time. Most agree that this is not good parenting, but we may not see this as rising to the level of what we would call abuse.

Nearly everyone agrees that abuse is behavior that causes harm. If we are hurting people we are abusing them. Most folks are aware that there are many ways we can abuse. There is physical abuse, of course, but there is also emotional abuse, sexual abuse, verbal abuse, even spiritual abuse. But what if the action was accidental or, at least, that the harm was unintended? What if it wasn't very harmful? What if this is the first time it ever happened? What if the person harmed doesn't think it was abuse...or believes it was? What about the power the action has to control another? Does that make it abuse? Let's look at each of these and see if they help build our map for making sense of abuse.

I want to be clear about the purpose of this map. It is to help transform our own behavior such that we can build healthier relationships. This is not about deciding who should be punished; who should go to jail. That is an important map, but it is a different one. That is the map built by our criminal justice system.

It is hard to conceive of a definition of abuse that isn't about harmful behavior. But we want to make a distinction between hurting someone and doing harm to them.

> My friend, Bob, is a salesman. He makes his living meeting and greeting. But he doesn't have good oral hygiene. His breath is bad. If I tell him his breath stinks, it will hurt his feelings. If I don't tell him, it will hurt his business. So if I don't hurt him, it will harm him.

Let's make a distinction between *hurt* and *harm* and shape our behavior such that we are acting genuinely in each other's behalf, even if it is not what others may feel good about. We make our kids go to bed even when they don't want to and are hurt that we won't let them stay up and watch TV because we want what is best for them more than we want what pleases them.

There are many ways we have power over each other. Each mode can be an avenue for abuse. We have physical power and we can use it to harm others. We have economic, sexual, emotional, and social power. We can construct acts of abuse using any of the forms of power we have. Just because there are no bruises doesn't mean there has not been abuse.

What if the harm isn't very big? Maybe anything under a certain threshold shouldn't be considered abuse. Wouldn't it be better to reserve the term *abuse* to refer just to the big things?

We live in a society defined by certain limits. We have limits to personal behavior and corporate behavior which are defined by our laws and customs. Sometimes these limits are violated. We preserve our social fabric by constructing and maintaining ways of identifying when boundaries are transgressed and having consequences for those transgressions.

If we are looking for a definition about who we are going to send to prison, then we certainly don't want to have to address the little things. Intervention costs too much to do it when the harm is small. But since we are looking to transform our own behavior and, thus, the relationships we build with others, why not include the smaller things. **Let's** address all of it.

Also, sometimes we may **think that some** event is not that big a deal and we discover that it really is more **harmful than** we first suspected. We explore this circumstance more in Chapter Nine.

What if the action caused **harm, but it** wasn't the intention of the perpetrator to do harm? What if the actor just didn't know any better? Should we label behavior as abuse if it was just a lapse of judgment... or even an accident? Does this mistake make someone an abuser?

If we are concerned that we not label the behavior abuse because we don't want to label the perpetrators as abusers, then we are using a 2° map. At 2° there is no distinction between the one who acts and the action. Anyone who commits abuse is an abuser. Someone who commits a crime is a criminal.

But if we are going to construct a 4° order map, we want to begin to make that distinction. We are not vilifying someone. We are simply getting clear about the qualities of certain choices.

Some readers may begin to get uncomfortable at this point. If we are going to include even accidentally harmful behavior, we might come to include even the choices that we ourselves make. We are mostly pretty keen to protect ourselves from being seen as bad people, so we wouldn't want anyone to think of us as an abuser. Then again, we certainly have made choices from time to time which are harmful to others. Was that abuse?

It is important to pay attention to how our behavior affects others and especially if it causes them to feel abused. If they are feeling abused by us, the relationship is getting damaged. Still, we can be making perfectly appropriate choices but others may not like our choices so much that they allege abuse.

If I am sending my seven year old daughter off to bed and she throws a fit because she wants to see the end of the TV show and I hold my ground and she says she is being abused and is going to call the child abuse hotline on me I am likely to say, "That is fine, but you will have to do it tomorrow because right now you are going to bed."

Labeling another's behavior is a form of power. When my daughter claims to be abused by me she is looking for a power to counter my power to send her to bed. There is a certain power in being a victim. Any power can be used to abuse another. She can abuse me by claiming to be abused by me.

But, ultimately, I have more power. I can make her go to bed. I can control her. As much as she may not like it, it is still in her best interests. On the other hand there are circumstances in which it is not appropriate for me to control another. I have the right to control my daughter at bedtime because as her parent I have a fiduciary responsibility for her welfare. I do not have a right to control my partner as we have a mutual relationship. While exerting control in a mutual relationship is a kind of abuse, it is a bit different from the kind we are talking about at the moment.

## A Definition of Abuse

Given these considerations I suggest that we understand abuse to be any action by which one exerts power over another in which the intent is to get what one needs and in which the effect is to harm another.

We all have power over each other. We all make choices which affect those around us. Sometimes those choices can harm others. We can also make choices which are harmful to ourselves. Harming ourselves is not what we generally mean by being empowered. For the most part, we don't commit abuse by actions which are characterized by *power with* or *empowerment*. We abuse with *power over*.

Any choice we make is motivated by self interest. We do what we do to get what we need. It is entirely appropriate for us to use the power we have to construct circumstances in which we get what we need. Indeed, not acting to construct what we need is neglectful of ourselves.

The problem is not that we are powerful or that we act to get what we need but that we use that power to meet our needs at the expense of another. When we take from others what is rightfully theirs or hinder them from getting what they need or acting on their own behalf, we are abusing them.

## Reservations about This Way of Defining Abuse

I have been promoting this definition of abuse for many years now. While this definition is often well accepted, just as often it is met by startled resistance. The concern is that it is too broad. "By this definition everyone is abusive." There are some things we lose when we adopt a map that includes so much of what we all do and doesn't focus more on those actions which are more dramatically harmful. And there are things we lose when we define abuse as only something others do.

This brings us back to the question of whether abuse can be understood as a kind of "going too far." We may say about someone that we know he was just teasing, "But he took it too far." By this we are saying that this instance seems to have risen to the level of abuse.

When Child Protective Services visits a home following allegations of child abuse the workers are assessing the degree to which the conditions of the home are harmful to the children. Is the home clean? Is there food available? Are there marks on the children? Do they get to school? These are among the questions the evaluators answer in an attempt to come to a decision about whether to "substantiate abuse." If they come to a finding of abuse, there may be a range of interventions from getting the assistance of Intensive In-home Services to placing the children in foster care.

But how do we draw the line? In the case of Child Protective Services, the line may move depending on the availability of funding for services. Who gets to decide when someone has "gone too far?"

In the case of speed limits, they are all clearly posted. So if the speed limit is 55, how fast can you drive? If you are only going the speed limit during rush hour you have people on your bumper and on their horn. The police don't usually intervene unless you are going 10 mph over. So the effective speed limit when 55 is posted seems to be 64.

How about in the ways we address conflicts with our significant others? What is the line when our speech or behavior becomes abuse? I often have guys in my program for men who batter tell me that they never abused their partners. That is, what they have observed themselves doing during fights did not rise to the level of what they consider to be abuse. A couple of times I have even heard men say, "I never abused my wife. I always hit her with an open hand. Abuse is when you use your fist."

So, yes, we need a system which defines clear limits around harmful behavior and intervenes when those lines are crossed. This is the criminal justice system which interprets and applies the law to protect people from actions we have determined to be crimes. There is an awful lot of harmful behavior which is not criminal.

So, then, what if abuse is something everyone does? Doesn't that mean that everyone is an abuser?  Doesn't that trivialize abuse?  Doesn't that let abusers off the hook, allowing them to say, "What's the big deal?  Everyone does it!"  We do seem to need to say that there are some who are abusers and some who are not and that "I am not an abuser."

One of the things that almost always comes up in my program for men who have committed an assault in the context of an intimate relationship is their wish to appropriate this definition to justify themselves.

*"Well, given this definition," he says, "I am getting abused by my girlfriend."*

*"Yes," I reply, " so what will you do with that information?"*

*"Well, I'm going to tell her that she is abusing me."*

*"Yes, and that would be abuse."*

*"What?  It is abuse for me to tell her that she is abusing me?"*

*"Yes, exactly!  When you use the power you have over her to label her behavior, in a manner that gets you what you want (to be shown to be right and righteous) in a way that makes her lose (makes her the abuser) you are abusing her."*

*"So, it is abuse to tell someone they are abusing you?"*

*"Yes!  So are you going to use her abuse of you to give yourself permission to abuse her?"*

If everyone is abusive from time to time, what would it take for us to end the abuse in our lives?

## What Allows For Abuse?

Given this definition of abuse, abuse is something we all do.  It is something we do in relationships with others and it is something they do to us.  It is even something we do to ourselves.  Our goal here is to end the abuse we do to

*Abuse and Systems of Oppression*

others, the abuse others do to us, and the abuse we do to ourselves.

Some of you may wonder how we can end the abuse that others do to us. We cannot change others and we are not responsible for their choices. If others choose to meet their needs at our expense, we cannot stop them. Nevertheless, when we notice there is a pattern of these events happening in a given relationship, we can act to change the nature of that relationship.

If we are to change our relationships such that abuse is less likely, we have to identify the characteristics of a relationship which allow for abuse. What must be present for abuse to occur?

In some ways perpetrating abuse is a bit like starting a fire. There are three essential elements which all have to be present for the phenomenon to arise. If we are going to start a fire we need to have fuel, air, and heat. We have to have something to burn, the oxygen to support combustion, and the energy to kick off the chemical reaction that is fire. If we have fuel, oxygen, and heat, we have a fire.

If we want to put out a fire we need only take away one of these three. Without all three, the fire stops. We intervene with fires in different ways depending on the nature of the fire. If we are around the campfire and a spark sets someone's clothes on fire, we can roll them on the ground to smother the fire. This takes the oxygen away. If we are leaving the campfire we are sure to put it out by pouring water on it. The evaporation of the water removes the heat and makes the wood too cold to burn. But, when I am finished cooking on the gas range, I don't put the fire out by trying to smother it or pouring water on it. I just turn off the gas. I take away the fuel.

So if we have all three elements we have a fire, and we can put out a fire by taking away any one of the three, and which method of fire suppression we choose will be determined by the kind of fire we are addressing. It is just so with abuse.

For me to perpetrate abuse on another I need the opportunity to abuse them, permission to act as I do, and a sense that this will get me what I need. Without all three, there is no abuse. And I can stop abuse by taking away any one of the three.

Let us recall our scenario at the beginning of this chapter in which Joe is interacting with a three year old Jack over Jack's wish to climb into his daddy's lap and show him what he has made. A frustrated and tired Joe sends Jack to him room for fifteen minutes.

Is this abuse?  Is Joe exercising power over Jack?  Is this something which is designed to meet Joe's needs?  Is it harmful to Jack?

However much we may identify with Joe and understand his choices, this is not the sort of behavior which builds a healthy relationship between father and son, or, for that matter, get either what they really need.  This is not to say that Joe has to be available to Jack at all times.  But when Joe can't be there for Jack, he can send himself to his room until he can be more present.

The choice Joe makes harms Jack in that it confuses him about his relationship with his dad.  Jack's needs for attention and approval are things which have been met previously in his relationship with his dad.  Suddenly they are not forthcoming.  He knows he is being punished but he can't figure out what he did wrong—what he did to make his dad treat him differently.

## Opportunity

In order to abuse someone we need the opportunity to do so.  Opportunity to abuse is comprised of both power over the other and proximity to them.  When Jack came into the living room where his dad was reading the paper he created the proximity which allowed him to be abused.  This is not the same as saying that he is responsible for the abuse; his choices, however, created a context in which the abuse could occur.

When we are in chronically abusive relationships we can seek to end the abuse by removing proximity and power over.  We can remove proximity by getting away from people who treat us badly.  But how might we take away power over?

The only proposal I am aware of which would address ending abuse by taking away power over is the notion that everyone carry a concealed firearm and be trained and ready to use it.  The premise is that, if everyone has lethal power in relationship to everyone else, that is, all have the ultimate power, then no one could have power over another.  While I understand the logic of this position it only works in a society in which everyone knows that everyone else is willing to blow others away.  I am certain I would not want to live in such a society.

So we are left with removing proximity.  There are many ways we can do this.  We create prisons for people who can't seem to stop knocking off liquor stores and shelters for women who are battered by their partners. Prisons and shelters are ways of ending abuse by removing proximity.

The primary advantage of ending abuse by removing proximity is that it is quick and certain. The primary disadvantage is that it is really expensive. It is financially very costly to keep people in prison. Not only are those who are incarcerated no longer supporting the economy, they are sucking huge sums out of the collective coffers to keep them housed and us safe.

Divorces remove proximity but it is really expensive to get a divorce. Not only do we have to pay the attorneys, we have to divide the assets, pay for two homes, and lose some tax advantages. Even more, divorces are emotionally expensive for everyone.

We can end abuse by removing proximity but, as much as possible, we want to have that as a last resort or a short term option until we can find something better. We can end abuse by not being around those who treat us badly, or we can isolate ourselves from those we are prone to abuse, but as this solution is so expensive, we need some other ways to end abuse as well.

## Permission

In order to abuse someone we need permission to do so. When Joe sent Jack to his room for trying to show him what he had made, Joe felt as though he was fully within his rights as a parent. "Children should do what their parents tell them to do," he thought. "Besides, I am tired and crabby."

In fact, we do not have permission to abuse each other. In order to give ourselves permission we have to get altered in some way. There are two broad ways that we do this. One is that we can alter our mood, and the other is that we can alter our thinking.

### Altered mood

We alter our mood in many ways. We can engage in any number of 2° behaviors which are designed to change our experience. If we are tired we can rest. If we are lonely we can seek company. If we are anxious we can get drunk. If we feel aimless we can smoke crack. If we feel poor we can go shopping. These choices alter our mood but not the reality which causes those feelings to arise for us.

It is common for people who are normally considerate of others to become abusive when they are drunk or otherwise acting out. The alteration of mood gives some people permission to say or do things they would not otherwise be likely to say or do.

## Altered thinking

Similarly, we can alter our thinking in ways which give us permission to abuse with a cognitive distortion. In Joe's case we can find a couple of them. Most apparent is the notion that he has a right to send Jack to his room because "children should do what their parents tell them to do."

He may also remember that he failed to send Jack to his room for riding in the street. Having failed to follow through then he may think, "Jack should be taught a lesson for interrupting adults when they are reading."

Of course, this is not consciously available to Joe. If he really thinks about it, he can easily see that this is a very different context. In the first instance Jack was told about the forbidden behavior and what the consequences would be if he transgressed. In this instance Jack doesn't know what he has done wrong and the consequences were unexpected. But Joe may decide that he has a right, and perhaps even an obligation, to act this way toward Jack.

Permission is slippery. It can be very hard to see when we are giving ourselves permission to abuse others. It is important that we do everything we can to address the circumstances which allow for abuse, but it is hard to remove something we can't see.

There are certain circumstances in which we are more likely to give ourselves permission to abuse others. While some of these are unique to each of us, one very common circumstance we all experience as an invitation to abuse others is when we are ourselves feeling abused. When we have had a bad day at work we are much more likely to kick the dog as we come in the front door. If we want to avoid abusing others, we can pay close attention to when we are feeling abused.

As hard as it is to see when we are giving ourselves permission to abuse others, it is often even more difficult to see when we give others permission to abuse us. We often minimize the harm that we experience from the choices of others and make excuses for how they treat us. There are many ways we do this. Al-Anon groups help those who are "co-dependant" come to see how they have been colluding with the harmful behavior of their loved ones in ways which are not only harmful to themselves but ultimately delay the recovery of those whose behavior they are enabling.

## Motivation

In order to abuse someone we have to believe the action we are taking is in some sense getting us what we need. When Joe orders Jack to his room he is constructing a context in which he is getting peace and quiet and the capacity to focus more fully on the newspaper. If the only needs Joe has are those which are met for him in the context of his relationship with the newspaper, then this might work. But it is not that simple. There are also needs which Joe has in his relationship with his son, and with his wife, and even with himself. Jane is not likely to approve of this choice and, ultimately, Joe isn't going to feel too good about it either.

More than simply getting peace and quiet, Joe probably needs a sense of having control over his own life. He wants to know that he matters and that he is competent to make a world in which his needs are met. Instead of getting a sense of mastery, however, he discovers he can bully his three year old son. Abuse doesn't work. It doesn't get us what we need. However much it may appear to work in the short run, it doesn't actually construct the qualities we need in the long run.

If we are looking to end abuse, we can take away opportunity by removing proximity, but this solution is costly. We can remove permission by setting up clear rules, but applying the rules can be confusing. Or we can act in ways which actually construct what we need. This is not expensive; indeed, it pays big dividends. It is not slippery; indeed, it is by knowing what we need that our lives begin to get real traction. It is very hard to do only because it requires a depth of self-knowledge to discover what it is we actually need and distinguish it from what we want.

Because this is so hard to do, it is work we generally leave undone unless we are highly motivated to get to the bottom of the problem. We won't generally move above the cultural center of gravity and explore our interior awareness about those circumstances in which abuse occurs unless we have a lot to gain by doing so, or a lot to lose by failing to do so.

When we are the ones who are being hurt by the abuse, we have greater motivation to address the situation than when we are the perpetrators of abuse. This doesn't mean that perpetrators don't have something to gain by discovering their true needs, but simply that they are much less likely see the need to do the work. It typically falls to the victims of abuse to initiate the process of discovery.

Even so it can be hard for us as victims to see ourselves as being harmed by the choices of others. In many cases, these are simply the choices we have come to expect from others. This may be normal within our expectations. We may have a map that predicts this treatment.

As long as the only map we have is one that normalizes our experience, we tolerate it for a very long time. It is only when we get a glimpse of someone else's map, a map which suggests that another reality is possible, that we begin to see the injustice of what we are experiencing.

Thus, being in a community with others who are committed to ending the abuse in our lives becomes crucial for our growing capacity to transform our own lives. This is not work we can do easily or well if we do it in isolation from others. When we are connected to a community of recovery and restoration, we support the healing of ourselves and others.

In the context of a community of mutual support we become aware of the patterns of abuse which are present in everyone's life. These patterns reflect an undercurrent of abuse which we come to see as oppressive.

## Oppression as a Quality of a Relationship

Built into the very fabric of our society are cultural values and habits which support the oppression of some persons and groups of people by other persons and groups. These systems take on many forms but they all have essentially the same structure. If we are to effectively end the oppression, we have to understand the factors which maintain the systems themselves and address the things we do to support the maintenance of those systems.

The largest most oppressive legal structure in American history was the institution of slavery. The proposition that one person could own another was limited first by the Emancipation Proclamation and then rendered illegal by the Thirteenth Amendment. Those actions came less than 150 years ago.

While slavery was not only about whites' oppression of blacks (there were some blacks who owned slaves), the oppressive system continues in the form of racism. While all cultures have their own variations to the theme of oppression based on race, the general idea is that the darker one's skin, the less social value and power one has. Those with the lightest skin color have a right to dominate those who are dark.

Our culture tends to value males above females. While the culture is rapidly changing in the ways men are favored over women, especially in the developed world, there is still widespread physical abuse of women by men in some settings and very few places in which men and women have equal power. This attribution of rights and responsibilities based on sex is known as sexism.

Less visually obvious, but perhaps more pervasive, is the practice of extending to those with money and influence a level of privilege and protection which is not extended to all. We call this classism.

When a group of people who all identify as being members of a single nation claim a right to dominance over people they see as members of a different nation, we refer to this as nationalism.

When the members of a sect who hold a particular set of beliefs claim they have a right to dominate or otherwise disenfranchise others on behalf of their god, they are understood to be practicing sectarianism.

When people who identify a heterosexual orientation as the only correct one claim a right to limit the rights of those who are gay, they are practicing heterosexism.

There are many ways we can identify people as members of a particular group and, on the basis of that identification, deny them rights. Some are too young or to old (ageism), some have disabilities (ableism), and the list goes on and on.

Each of these "isms" has certain common characteristics. These fall within four key areas.

**Patterns of Abuse:** Systems of oppression are created by a series of acts of abuse which establish and maintain dominance. (Racism is not created by a single redlining, but by years of lynching and discriminatory laws and unfair labor practices.)

**Social Justification:** These acts are justified by the dominant group in the dominant culture as being ways to maintain the "appropriate social order." (The Bible says that there shall be slaves and that they shall come from the descendants of Abraham's servant girl.)

**Secrecy:** Nevertheless, the specific acts of abuse themselves are hidden in some sense from public view. They are not to be witnessed. (When the Klan rides out, they wear hoods.)

**Internal distress:** And the conflicts that appear to be between the oppressor and the oppressed are actually conflicts that are interior to the oppressor but acted out in relationship to the oppressed. (Anti-Semitism in Nazi Germany was not about the behavior of Jews but about the anxiety of Aryans who couldn't tolerate the humiliation of World War I.)

These systems are not simply the construction of those at the "top." There are women who teach their sons the lessons of patriarchy. Some light skinned Blacks lord it over darker skinned. And some who have a little look down on those with less and the whole system seems to conspire to keep the oppression going. At every level there are those who give themselves the right to be better than someone else.

Let's take a look at how these four features are present in a variety of oppressive scenarios.

*A group of urban young men are standing on a street corner on a hot summer night. They all know each other; all went to high school together, some of them worked with each other until a couple of weeks ago when the plant closed. They have already collected the last check and none of those who just lost their job has found another one. The men had been at the top of the order because they had the best jobs around ...but now those jobs are gone and their place is no longer secure.*

*They get to talking about how the good jobs are all gone and the problem is those immigrants who are coming in and taking the jobs. They remember when life was good and all their dads were working and how that was before all the Asians started arriving.*

*Abuse and Systems of Oppression*

*There is a convenience store on the corner that is owned by a Korean family. Someone throws a brick. Before anyone quite knows how, the shop is in flames.*

This becomes one of a series of events that cause Asian families to feel at risk in that town (pattern of abuse). The men who started it are clear that they are just trying to reassert the natural order of things (social justification). They won't say anything to the cops about how it started (secrecy). They don't have a problem with that Korean family; the problem is with their own confidence about supporting their own families (internal distress).

*A small not-for-profit company is starting to make some very positive turns in their public presence with a new logo and a new Executive Director when the Administrative Assistant - who has almost single handedly kept things going during some rough times in the past - develops carpal tunnel syndrome. Disability insurance covers some of the costs and she has medical insurance through her husband, but she can't work and continuing to pay her is getting very expensive for the company. Some members of the Board begin to fear that her illness will drag the company down just when things are starting to look up.*

*She would never resign; she loves the work and the people it serves. She could never be fired; she is far too beloved. The Personnel Committee, feeling the panic of the Executive Committee, sets up a meeting with her in which she is grilled about any financial irregularity they can find over the past couple of years. She is horrified about the implications of the questions, baffled at how they can be suspicious of her and, finally, furious at the idea that they believe she would do anything to hurt the mission of the organization. When, in the end, she is asked for her resignation, she gives it, goes out to her car and sobs for half an hour until she can pull it together to drive home.*

There are many examples of people losing employment over physical disabilities (pattern of abuse). The mission of the agency cannot be compromised simply for the welfare of a single employee (social justification). The minutes of the Personnel Committee where the strategy was discussed are, of course, sealed (secrecy). The Executive Committee is afraid that it cannot keep the operation afloat with a disabled Administrative Assistant (internal distress).

*A wife gets a call from her businessman husband to say that he will be late getting home. She can hear the stress in his voice. She knows whenever he has a hard day at work he is easily upset when he gets home. He is very intolerant of any sort of disorder and sometimes he rages at her when the dishes aren't done or toys aren't put away. She gets all the kids busy cleaning and the house is spotless when he arrives.*

*She greets him cheerfully and has all the smiling children with her. He scowls and looks around the home for something out of place. The fact that all is in order doesn't seem to please him and he continues to scan for some disarray. Finally he confronts the nine-year old boy, "Aaron, do you have a handkerchief?" When it becomes clear that the boy does not have a handkerchief in his pocket, he finally erupts and tells his wife, "This is why things are such a mess in our life. I don't understand why you can't maintain a little order in this home!"[16]*

This is a scenario which happens whenever he is stressed by work (pattern of abuse). He is the one who gets to decide who is and who is not doing their job because he is the "head of the household" (social justification). When he pushes her down the stairs and the neighbors call the police they are told that she slipped (secrecy). There is nothing she can do that will stop his outbursts because they are not about her. Indeed, the more she makes it hard for him to blame her, the more violent his outbursts are likely to become. He is getting relief by finding things in the home to be out of place as a projection of his own sense of things being out of place within himself (internal distress).

We are all profoundly impacted by the systems of oppression in the cultures in which we live. When someone stands up and proudly proclaims their privilege on the basis of their white skin, we don't have any trouble giving them the label *racist*. Even if people are not so overt, this doesn't mean they aren't influenced by a culture of racism to value people of color differently. Even people of color are influenced to value themselves differently on the basis of skin color. Saying we are not influenced by systems of oppression doesn't make it so. We swim in the cultural soup of oppression and we internalize the maps which lead us to expect either entitlement or that we will not have our rights recognized.

The only way to get free of the influence of such powerful cultural systems

---

16   This vignette is adapted from a story from the video, "Broken Vows" by FaithTrust.

of meaning-making is to act out of the assumption that we are held in their sway. Trusting that it is true for us in ways to which we are blind, our task becomes finding out how, and to address these issues as they arise in our experience. Non-cooperation with systems of oppression is only going to happen if we make a conscious effort to identify, in our own lives, how oppression is constructed and to work to deconstruct it in our own choices.

As the systems of oppression are constructed by these four aspects, we use the four to help us discover how we are co-constructing the oppression in our own lives.

**Patterns of Abuse:** I can notice the patterns of abuse in my relationships with others that create and maintain dominance. There are patterns of conflict in all of our relationships. Some of those conflicts evoke behaviors that are abusive as a tactic for addressing the conflict. But some of those tactics establish and maintain dominance, even in very subtle ways, and that is evidence of oppression.

**Social Justification:** I can notice the ways in which such dominance is explained or excused. This can be because of personal, familial or cultural history. It can be because of widely shared values, even religious values. It can even be the law. But, if it sustains oppression, it is unjust.

**Secrecy:** I can notice the ways in which I or others in the system work to maintain secrets. There is an important distinction to be made between secrecy and privacy. Secrecy is about keeping others from finding out what they have a right to know. Privacy is keeping others from finding out what they have no right to know.

**Internal Distress:** I can notice how my own internal conflicts get acted out in my relationships with others, especially with those I am closest to, and how the other's internal conflicts get acted out in relationship to me. If I am anxious and I don't know what it is about, I am almost certainly going to express that anxiety in a manner that tries to get someone else to take care of me. That is oppressive to them (unless I am a child and they are my caregiver, an exception we will look at in more depth later).

So, whenever I feel as though I have a right to dominate another, by whatever reason I might construct, and then act towards the other in ways I want to keep secret to soothe my own anxiety, I am constructing a system of oppression. Such behavior is unhealthy for the relationship and is harmful to me. This is nowhere more a concern than in our most intimate relationships.

The oppression that is domestic violence or battering is truly horrific in some relationships. We like to see it as a social anomaly that is present in some relationships but not in others. We especially like to believe it is not present in our own relationships. But oppression is so pervasive in our society that it is hard to imagine that there might be any culture, even the ones we create with our own significant others, which are not, in powerful ways, shaped (or misshaped) by these systems.

## A Second Form of Abuse

*Esuba* arises as a quality in a relationship whenever a party to the relationship makes a choice with the quality of *abuse*. The choice is one in which we

- use the power we have over others to
- act in ways that create what we want
- at the expense of what others need.

We do this in obvious ways which are clear violations of social and cultural norms, and we do it in subtle ways which are expressions of what we have come to believe we have a right to do.

Our rights come from our ability to be responsible. When we assume the responsibility for the welfare of another in a fiduciary relationship, we gain the right to make decisions on the other's behalf. But when we claim the rights without exercising the responsibility we are abusing the other's rights. We are engaging in a form of abuse of the other. So there are actually two kinds of abuse. One is a quality of a given choice creating a specific event. The other is a quality of a given relationship which then creates a pattern of events in that relationship.

Political corruption is a form of this second type of abuse. When a government official uses the power of his office to gain privileges for his own personal benefit this is an abuse of power and a violation of the public trust.

Parents may assume they have a right to tell their children what to do. And they do, insofar as they are exercising that right on behalf of their children. When parents structure their relationships with their children such that it becomes the child's responsibility to take care of the parent, the parent is perpetrating a form of abuse.

Sometimes we may assume that another will exercise power on our behalf but they have no sense that their power comes from a responsibility for our welfare. For example, workers in a factory may believe that the rights of management come from their responsibility to preserve the jobs of the workers. Management may believe their rights come from their responsibility to the share holders. Thus when they close the plant and move to another country, management is making what it sees as a responsible decision and the workers feel abused.

When a state has a vacancy in one of their Congressional Senate seats, the governor may be empowered to fill that seat until the next general election. This is a right which falls to the governor because the governor is assumed to be acting on behalf of the people of the state. When the governor instead claims this right as a power which he can exploit for his own benefit, he is abusing his power, may be said to be corrupt, and may be impeached and convicted[17].

As abuse can occur in a fiduciary relationship when the lines of accountability are not clear, so can it also arise in a mutual relationship. Remember that a mutual relationship is one in which all parties enjoy the same rights and responsibilities. Still, not everyone does the same task. Both parents are responsible for feeding the children but only one is expected to pick up milk on the way home. When there is not a clear understanding of who is responsible for which task, each may feel abused by the other and use that occasion as an opportunity to return the abuse. Feeling abused, they may give themselves permission to abuse each other.

So *abuse* is a quality of a choice we may make and *esuba* is a quality of relationships in which abuse occurs. One form of abuse is when one person makes a choice which harms another and another form of abuse is when one person makes a choice which harms a relationship. In general, when we are in a mutual relationship and act as though we have the rights which come from

---

17    as with Rod Blagojevich in Illinois

a fiduciary relationship, we are abusing the relationship. Conversely when we are in a fiduciary relationship and we act as though we are in a mutual relationship, we are also committing abuse.

A primary example of this kind of abuse is when people with fiduciary responsibility for the welfare of others begin to use their power in the relationship as a way to meet their own intimacy needs. This happens in a very overt form when a parent or family member initiates a sexual relationship with the child. It happens when a boss approaches an underling for sexual favors. It happens when a therapist allows sexual contact with a client. It can happen between pastors and parishioners or between teachers and students. It can even happen when parents value being friends with their children above being their parents.

When we act to meet our intimacy needs in the context of a fiduciary relationship it is a form of abuse. When we act as though we have a right to control the relationship in a mutual relationship it is a form of abuse.

## Two Kinds of Accountability

While we are acknowledging abuse as the source of esuba in relationships, we also want to appreciate the power that accountability has to form a foundation upon which to build or rebuild healthy relationships. Accountability is the ability to give an accounting of the choices which are shaping the relationship. As we have two fundamentally different forms of relationship—fiduciary and mutual—we have two very different forms of accountability.

In a fiduciary relationship (or in a reciprocal relationship which is essentially a bilaterally balanced fiduciary relationship) the right that one has to make a decision rests on the capacity one has to be responsible to the other. Thus accountability is the ability to give an account of one's responsibility to the other. At Henry's job at Universal Widget where Frank is his boss, Henry is accountable to Frank when he gives an account of his hours by filling out the time sheet, when he gives an account of how the widget machine is working by making an equipment report, and by telling him how many widgets he made on a given shift. Frank, in return, is accountable to Henry by giving him a paycheck and a performance review. They are each accountable to the other.

By contrast in a mutual relationship we are not accountable *to* each other, but accountable *with* each other.

*In Jane and Joe's marriage, as they have decided to have a mutual relationship, neither has the right to make a decision unilaterally except as they have decided together that the other will take on that responsibility. Thus Jane pays the bills because Joe and Jane have decided that they don't both want to have that responsibility and Jane is better with details than is Joe. Still, they are both earning income and both making financial choices. Jane doesn't have to clear it with Joe when she buys shoes and Joe doesn't have to clear it with Jane when he buys a new tool.*

*But when Joe pulls into the driveway towing a boat, Jane is outraged. This is not something they had discussed. This was not a mutual decision.*

*Joe responds, "But you don't have to get my permission to buy all of your shoes. What makes you think I should have to get your permission to buy something? I thought we had a mutual relationship."*

Joe is confusing *mutual* with *equal*. Just because the structure of the relationship is mutual doesn't mean that all choices we make are equal. The dollar difference between shoes and a boat puts this decision into a different class. And the issue here is not whether either needs the other's permission to act. Clearly Joe was able to buy the boat without consulting Jane.

The issue has to do with the degree to which they are each acting in accord with an agreement made with the other. When Jane buys shoes or Joe buys a shovel they are acting within the parameters of an agreement they have made with each other. Jane thinks buying a boat is outside the scope of their agreement. She wished that she had been consulted before Joe made this purchase. It is her sense that he is not being accountable with her as he did not take into account how his decision was likely to affect her.

In a fiduciary relationship we are accountable when we give an account to the other. In a mutual relationship we are accountable when we take into account two things: how our choices affect the other and how the other's choices affect us.

# Victims, Perpetrators, and Bystanders

We encounter abuse and oppression in our lives everyday. Sometimes we are just a bystander observing abuse done to someone else, but from time to time we are the victim and from time to time we are the perpetrator.

Some people are quite comfortable being tough but bristle at the notion that they may be or may have been a victim. Others freely acknowledge that they are victims but are horrified if someone suggests that they may be a perpetrator or have any responsibility for the abuse occurring in their relationships with others.

Remember that we have two meanings for the word *abuse* depending on the context. In one context *abuse* is a quality of an event. Abuse is harm done when one acts to meet ones own needs at another's expense. In the other context abuse is a quality of the relationship which two people create together. Abuse is a violation of the fundamental nature of the structure of a relationship to meet one person's needs. It is manifest in a pattern of choices, not simply a single event. While such a distortion of the relationship can sometimes be a shared choice by both parties (as in fraternization), usually there is a perpetrator and a victim for either kind of abuse.

We then have two kinds of victims and perpetrators. The first kind of victim is someone who is harmed by a discrete event in the personal realm. I may be the victim of a car crash or my family may be the victim of a tornado. When I make a choice which results in harm to another, I am the perpetrator of the abuse. The second kind of victim is someone who is in a relationship in which the other, the perpetrator, routinely and systematically distorts the fundamental nature of the relationship.

In the Personal realm a victim is harmed by an event. In the Interpersonal realm the relationship is harmed, thus doing harm to the persons in the relationship. What then might be a victim or perpetrator in the Intrapersonal or Transpersonal realms?

Most of us have a part of ourselves which is a critic, sometimes a harsh critic, and that critic may focus its attention on others or it may focus on another part of ourselves. Some of us have been so routinely harmed in the Personal realm and have constructed or had constructed for us such oppressive relationships in the Interpersonal realm that we have a part of us which is merciless in its critique of our own behavior and/or the behavior of others, thus crippling ourselves personally and socially.

When we are harmed in our Personal, Interpersonal, and Intrapersonal realms we carry that expectation into the Transpersonal realm. We see ourselves as someone that God doesn't love and perhaps even hates. God toys with us and it is our lot in life to be harmed. Being a victim is no longer a quality of an event or a relationship but a quality of our very being.

When we come to see ourselves as Victims in this spiritual sense we then either expect to be harmed or choose to protect ourselves by controlling everyone around us. Our map for who we are constructs behavior which gets us the very thing we don't want, indeed it creates the opposite of what we need.

The truth is we are all victims and we are all perpetrators of abuse. When we find it hard to see how we are both victims and perpetrators we may be experiencing identification with one or the other life stance. When we can't see that we are doing things which are harmful to others to meet our own needs, or when we can't see how our own needs are being compromised by the choices of those around us, we may have adopted a sense of ourselves which says, "I am tough," or "I am a victim." When we do this we are coming from a place which, while intended to protect us, actually deeply hinders our ability to construct healthy relationships.

And, as we have said, we are also bystanders. We see others around us making choices which are harmful to others. When those choosing and those being harmed are people we care about, we feel compelled to intervene to confront and protect. This is both a very generous and courageous impulse and one which can do as much harm as good. For that reason we want to be very careful about how we intervene. We look more closely at how we might appropriately intervene in Chapter Twelve.

## Summary

Addressing creatively the conflicts which arise in our most significant relationships depends upon our ability to understand the nature of the relationship in which the conflict appears. From time to time we each act in ways which harm the other. Whether by conscious choice or by inadvertent slip, we make choices which harm others even as we are just trying to get what we need. As we or those around us make these choices, esuba is generated in the relationship.

If we are to build healthier relationships we first have to stop doing the things which harm the relationship. We have to end the abuse. We have to put out the fire. Ending abuse can be done by taking away any of the three components of the abuse. We can take away opportunity by removing proximity. We can take away permission by addressing our anxieties in a more effective manner and by confronting our cognitive distortions. We can shift our motivation so that, rather than trying to change others to get what we want, we can change ourselves to construct what we need.

Removing proximity is quick but expensive. It is the first option we are likely to choose but it should be the last one upon which we rely. Removing permission is slippery. It is worth exploring how we give ourselves permission to abuse others and how we give them permission to abuse us, but even when we know, we may not get a grip on the causes and thus on a solution. Removing the motivation to abuse requires that we find a better way to get what we need. What we discover is that abuse is not actually constructing what we need. When we find what we need and how to get it, we have found a way of being which is durable and satisfying and we find less and less reason to abuse or to tolerate the abuse of others.

The abuse we do or have done to us may arise as an isolated event or it may be a part of a pattern of circumstances which construct a system of oppression. There are many systems of oppression with which we are complicit without ever really knowing that we are a part of the problem. It takes a conscious effort on our part to remove ourselves from participation in the oppressive structures.

This structure of oppression may even be expressed within our most intimate relationships. Thus, there are events which are expressions of abuse, but there are also ways in which relationships may be constructed which institutionalize the harm. When we unilaterally claim the right to make choices which meet our needs at the expense of others, no matter how we justify it, we are being oppressive to them and we are not actually constructing what we need.

Being accountable is a way of clearing away the rubble from a damaged relationship and building a firmer foundation to build on anew. Accountability is the ability to share an accounting of what is actually happening in the relationship. This is somewhat different in a fiduciary relationship than in a mutual one. In a fiduciary or reciprocal relationship we are accountable to each other. In a mutual relationship we are accountable with each other.

Just as we benefit from seeing the other's perspective, we benefit from fully understanding our own perspective. Am I looking at my experience from the perspective of a victim, or as one who is tough and won't let myself be hurt? Can I see how others are being affected by these events and respond in ways that genuinely help improve the qualities in the relationship? Or am I actually making things worse?

Being accountable depends upon seeing what actually is going on. We only see from our own perspective. To gather more data we are going to need to see from the other's perspective and to see particularly what they may be seeing about us. We benefit from being open to critical feedback from others, recognizing that not all feedback is of equal value and just because it is describing a different perspective from our own doesn't mean it is wrong or that our own perspective is wrong. They are not right and wrong, just different.

# 7

# Becoming Assertive

One of the essential distinctions we have to make if we are to address the conflicts which arise is to notice that *whether* we address the conflict is not the same as *how* we address the conflict.

Often we find ourselves wanting a closer relationship with another even as we discover ways in which we are different that we don't like. But we fear harming the relationship so we just don't say anything. "After all," we say to ourselves, "I don't want to start a fight."

## Fighting without Fighting

There are many strategies we can invoke to address and hopefully resolve conflicts. Among these strategies are a whole range of techniques and tactics which have in common that they are designed to make the other lose. We can try to make the other lose by ignoring the other, or belittling the other, or even physically assaulting the other. To the degree that these strategies work, they do so by making the other lose.

Most typically, when we are in a relationship with someone who is approaching us in a manner that is designed to make us lose, we respond by trying to make them lose. We enter into a full fledged fight. When we do this we generally succeed in making each other lose.

Since we don't want to lose—and we don't want to turn our beloved into a loser—we try to avoid getting into fights. But, if that means we don't address the conflict at all, we most likely will not resolve it. Our goal then is to be able to easily and confidently address the conflicts which arise in all of our relationships in a manner which creates safety and intimacy. That is, we want to fight without fighting.

Dr. Harville Hendrix, in his immensely popular book, *Getting the Love you Want*, introduces the notion of an *Imago*. The perspective he offers is that we each have unconsciously formed out of the experiences of our childhood an image of "the other we desire to be with." This *Imago* is in some respects a counterpoint to the *Ego*. My ego is an image of who I understand myself to be, or at least who I want to be. My imago is who I want my beloved to be.

When we are without a partner but are hoping to find someone special in our lives it is a bit like walking around with a map or template in hand comparing the image on the paper with the people we meet. "Hmm, does she fit? Does he fit?" Of course, we are not doing this consciously. We may even have a conscious image of the sort of person we are looking for and then discover feelings of attraction to someone very different from whom we thought we wanted to be with.

> *When Joe met Jamie at that wedding reception [back in Chapter Two] he felt immediately drawn to her. She felt safe. She was someone he could talk to. He believed he could depend on her.*

When we enter into relationships with others it is because of the things we have in common. We have to be in the same place—if only in the same chat room—and be speaking the same language. We have aspects of our life in common.

But we are also different. If we were just the same we probably wouldn't be so interested in each other. There are ways in which we are looking for others to be different from who we understand ourselves to be.

> *Joe knew that he was not good at naming and expressing his feelings. But Jamie seemed to know just what was going on with him and could help him understand and express himself.*

There are aspects of who we are that we share—that we have in common—and there are ways in which we are different. Some of those differences are just the things which attract us to the other. But some of those differences are ones we don't like. They don't fit with our imago and they don't satisfy what we need.

*When Joe and Jamie had been dating for several months and went to the wedding of some of her close friends, Jamie was so excited to reconnect with some of her old friends she neglected Joe. Joe was expecting her to be close to him and to assuage his anxiety of being out of place. Instead Jamie left him alone and he became more upset.*

So there are differences we like and differences we don't like. The differences we like draw us toward the other while the differences we don't like tend to move us to greater distance. We get to decide for ourselves which differences we like or don't like and what we will do about them when they arise in our relationships.

A graphic depiction of this dynamic is what I call the Cycle of Intimacy. Starting from the top center we move into relationships because of having a setting in common but we stay or leave because of the differences we discover.

When we are attracted to those differences we take the risk of being *open* to the relationship. This is a risk because, while this is a difference that we are attracted to, it may well be a difference the other doesn't like. We may be setting ourselves up for rejection. Thus we have to be *vulnerable* and discover that it is *safe* to do so if we are to build *intimacy* with the other. This experience of intimacy creates a new ground of commonality from which we discover new differences and the cycle repeats.

## Cycle of Intimacy

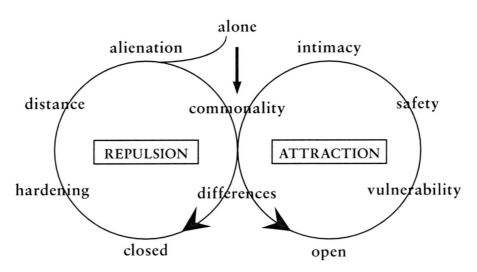

*Becoming Assertive*

When, however, we discover a difference we don't like, we feel repulsed and find ourselves *closing* up and backing away. We toughen or *harden* our stance toward the other and we seek the safety of *distance* (we remove proximity) and become *alienated*. This alienation may invite us to assert how we want things to be or how we want the other to be, or we may continue to move away and find ourselves *alone*.

I hope this map enables you see your own experience in a way that helps you to negotiate your circumstances better. For the purposes of our discussion here I just want to make two central points.

1.  At its most basic a conflict is simply "a difference I don't like." Things are not as I want them to be. All relationships have conflict. The inherent momentum of conflict is that it moves us away from intimacy.

2.  If we want to build intimacy we have to address these conflicts in a way that takes seriously our own vulnerability as well as that of our partner and creates safety for both of us. Whenever we act to compromise our own or the other's safety, we move to the left hand side of the cycle and thus toward alienation and aloneness.

## Aspects of All Conflict: Resource, Identity, and Process

If we are to become confident in our ability to address and resolve whatever conflicts arise for us, we have to discern the complexity of the conflicts themselves. Sometimes a conflict seems deceptively simple and yet proves devilishly difficult to resolve.

> *On a Sunday afternoon in late autumn Joe is in the living room watching the game as Jane comes in to speak to him.*
>
> *"Your dirty clothes are still on the bedroom floor."*
>
> *"Oh yeah, I'll get them."*

*Jane stands there waiting as Joe's attention returns to the screen. "When?"*

*"Huh? Oh, I'll get them at the half."*

*"Which half? This is the second game you've seen today and you promised me yesterday you would take care of this."*

*"Yeah, yeah, I said I will get to it. Sheesh!"*

At one level this is a simple matter of dirty clothes being on the bedroom floor instead of in the dirty clothes hamper or the washing machine. At the most basic level all conflicts are about resources. Resources are finite and thus to some degree scarce. There is not enough time, or money, or attention, or respect to go around. We want more.

At the most obvious level then this conflict between Jane and Joe is about where the clothes are. As long as Jane wants them dealt with and Joe hasn't addressed them, she is losing. She can only win by getting him to do what he promised to do...or was his promise actually just compliance with her demand?

If that were all that was going on here this would be much ado about very little. If this is such a problem for Jane, she can just pick the clothes up and put them where she wants them. It is much easier for her to pick up the clothes than it is for her to get Joe to do it.

No, this is about more than just where the clothes are. This is about who Joe and Jane are to each other. This is not just a conflict about resources; it is a conflict about identity. What is the nature of their relationship and how do they see each other?

Jane doesn't want to be Joe's maid. If she does what he promised to do and what she believes she has a right to expect him to do in the relationship—if she picks up after him—she is creating a relationship which is not as she wants it to be. She is complicit in constructing qualities which are contrary to her needs.

Joe works hard all week and is an avid football fan. He looks forward to Sundays in the fall as his time to enjoy a game he loves and it gives him content for his conversation with the other guys on his crew. If he misses the game he is left out of the conversation. He knows that Jane knows it and it feels really inconsiderate of her to insist that picking up clothes is something which has to be done right now. If he leaves the game and misses a big play just so she will shut up, he will feel like a wimp.

The resource basis of this conflict is actually not very important. Whether the clothes remain on the floor for another couple of hours won't determine the fate of the world. The heat comes from what it means to each of them about who they each are in the relationship and even the nature of the relationship itself. This is the identity basis of the conflict.

But there is a third level. Jane has spoken to Joe about her expectation that he pick up after himself and he has indicated that he is someone who is responsible for his own mess. Jane initiated a process for addressing her part of this issue and thought they had come to an agreement and now Joe is not keeping that agreement. There is something that isn't working in the process. This is the process basis of the conflict.

All conflicts have a *resource* basis, an *identity* basis, and a *process* basis. To resolve the conflict, all three must be addressed and resolved.

In the ongoing conflicts between the Israelis and the Palestinians there are huge resource concerns. Who owns which land? What rights do Palestinians have to return to their property? Who gets citizenship? Who controls Jerusalem? The fight over rights and property is hugely important.

But there is also an identity basis for the conflict. How are Israelis seen by Palestinians and vice versa? Does Israel have a right to exist? Is the ghettoization of the West Bank and Gaza justified by the Holocaust?

And perhaps the most difficult of all is the question of the process basis of the conflict. How did the current circumstances come to pass and by what authority can a resolution be fashioned? Is there sufficient trust that any agreement which could be developed might be found to have the durability to support peace?

It may seem that the situation is hopelessly complex. And truly it is complex. But it is not infinite. All conflicts can be resolved. We just have to name all of the aspects of the conflict, address each part of it, and fashion a resolution which creates what all of the parties need.

# Conflict Intensity

As a snowflake forms as water molecules coalesce around a dust particle, so do conflicts arise as emotion gathers around an event or circumstance or issue. The context of the conflict is the particle around which it forms. The intensity of a conflict is a measure of the emotion attracted by the context. An emotion is both data and energy. When two parties attracted by the same context have the same emotional valance - that is, they have similar feelings toward the context - then the charge between the parties takes on a positive quality. They enjoy a kind of intimacy.

If, on the other hand, the parties are attracted to the same context but have very different perspectives on the issues and circumstances, then the charge between them takes on a negative quality. They experience greater intensity in the conflict. There is a higher level of discord.

There are thus two kinds of variables in the formation of a conflict. One is the level of attraction or commitment to a given context for each of the parties. The other is the harmony or discord between the perspectives the parties bring to the context. Let's look at some examples of this.

> Joe loves to garden. The smell of the dirt, the fact that something beautiful or delicious comes from a tiny seed is a miracle Joe never tires of. Jane hates what gardening does to her nails.

> Jane loves Pilates. She feels invigorated by the workout and over the long run it gives her more energy and confidence. Joe finds that doing Pilates makes him nauseous.

> Joe and Jane love to cook. They delight in having friends over for dinner and they do an elegant tag team when the guests arrive greeting their friends and attending to dishes that are just about ready.

> Joe and Jane love their boys. They are the light of their lives. But Joe thinks Jane is too hard on them about keeping their rooms clean. They are just kids. Jane thinks Joe is coddling the boys. Her dad was way more strict with her than she is with them and she is proud of her ability to keep things orderly. She wants them to grow up knowing how to take care of their things.

Joe has an attraction to gardening that isn't shared by Jane. Jane is into Pilates and Joe isn't. Unless one of them thinks the other should like what they like, there isn't going to be much conflict here, but not much harmony either. These are just interests in their lives which they don't share.

They both have a high attraction to cooking and parenting. They approach cooking from the same, or at least a similar, perspective and it creates harmony and delight for them both. But the high level of concern they each have about parenting and the welfare of their boys, together with very different perspectives about what is in their sons' best interest, results in a relatively high level of conflict between them.

The intensity of a conflict between two parties can be seen as a function of both the level of attraction each of the parties have toward a given issue or context, and the level of agreement the parties have about how to look at and make meaning about the issue or event[18]. The emotional valance in a given relationship around a given issue or context can be seen as positive or negative in varying degrees depending on how much each party cares about the issue and how much harmony there appears to be between the perspectives each party takes toward the issue.

If we are to build effective strategies to resolve conflict it becomes important that we notice what it is that constructs the sense of discord or harmony in the relationship. For example:

Lets look at the issue of women choosing to end pregnancies through abortion: If a man adopts a posture that abortion is murder and the emotion he brings to the issue is heightened by a strong sense that he is acting on behalf of God and a belief that his mother would have terminated her pregnancy when she was carrying him had she had that option; then he is going to have a very strong emotional valance and a very clearly defined perspective.

If then in his community a group of people who very strongly value a woman's right to choose decide they will open an abortion clinic, they find themselves in an intense conflict with the man. Both parties have a high level of commitment to the issue and very different perspectives on how to address it. In the absence of other ways to address the high level of discord, the man may decide to picket the clinic.

---

18  I have given some thought to how to write this function mathematically, but I don't remember enough about trigonometry to know quite how to do it.

We are going to come back to this concern about how we might lower the intensity of a conflict but for the moment we want to look at how we already address the conflicts which arise for us. There are two sets of issues which correspond to the two variables which construct conflict intensity.

One has to do with the degree to which we are connected to a given circumstance or issue. We are going to call this variable *ownership*. To what degree is each party claiming a connection to what has happened or may happen in regard to the given context?

The second has to do with the degree to which we are insistent that our own perspective carry the day with regard to how we and others respond to the given context. We are going to call this variable *control*. To what degree does each party insist on things being seen from their perspective or that others respond to the context in the ways prescribed by their sense of what is right?

## Regaining Our Center: Being Assertive

When at times we begin to get overwhelmed by the enormity of the task of conflict resolution and become uncertain about our ability to actually know how to make things work, it is helpful to remember that we do actually resolve conflicts all the time. We are not as others want us to be or they are not doing what we expect of them and we address the issue and work it out and we restore harmony and build the relationship.

> *Mid-afternoon Joe and Jane talk by phone about their plans for dinner. It will be a busy evening with the boy's having commitments with their indoor soccer league and Jane having a meeting at church. They decide on what they will have for dinner but acknowledge they are out of milk and it would be good to get a head of lettuce as well. Jane will pick up the boys from the sitter.*

> *When Joe gets home Jane wonders where the milk and lettuce are. Joe says he thought she was going to stop at the store after she got the boys. Jane says she thought Joe was shopping. Joe says, "I'll be right back," and heads to the store.*

They get clear about what is going on, they each have a sense of how the current circumstances affect their family, and they come to a plan for how to proceed without really ever talking about it. They are working as a team to create what they both need.

When we are able to do this we probably don't even name the event a *conflict*. Usually we don't see an event arising as a conflict unless we don't know how to resolve it in a mutually agreeable way. When we only call events a *conflict* when we don't already know how to resolve them, we create the illusion that we don't know how to resolve conflicts. If we recognize that we have conflicts arising all the time, and that most of them we know how to resolve, we become more confident about our competence. We can't always resolve them, but most of the time we invoke strategies which work.

Let's start with what we already know how to do. Joe and Jane are clear that they are responsible for feeding their family and they know that have the power to make that happen. They possess both a sense of ownership of the problem and the power to create the desired outcome. They have control.

Whenever a conflict arises we respond to it out of our sense of ownership and our need for control. The trip Joe took to the store for milk and lettuce showed that he was both responsible and in control. Some events are more complicated, however.

> When Jack was in the third grade he brought home a note from his teacher that he hadn't been handing in his homework. Jane decided that she would make sure that he got his homework done and handed in. Jack didn't like this. He wanted his mom to just leave him alone and let him take care of it. But Jane decided that she was responsible for Jack's homework and would exercise control over him and the homework to ensure that it made it to the teacher.

In this circumstance Jane is framing her response to a conflict—she wants Jack to be someone who hands in his homework—by a set of decisions about her ownership and her need for control. She could say, "this is between him and his teacher. If is teacher can't get him to do his homework this is on her." Jane could deny her responsibility. Or she could say, "that homework is going to get done if I have to do it myself." She could take on responsibility for things she is not responsible for.

Consider, then, that there is a continuum of ownership from denial (I have no responsibility) to over-functioning or worry (I have to get everything done). The trick here is for Jane to figure out what she is responsible for and what she is not. There is a mid-point on this continuum where we are fully responsible for those things which are ours but we are not responsible for those which are not ours. If Jane says this is between Jack and his teacher she is denying her responsibility as his mother. But if she does his homework for him, she over-functioning and taking on responsibilities which are not hers (and, of course, not really helping Jack get what he needs).

This is such a common and problematic issue for so many of us that it has made very popular the Serenity Prayer. I have mentioned this earlier but let me repeat it here;

*God, grant me the serenity to accept the things I cannot change,*

Jane can recognize that she can't make Jack want to do his homework and she shouldn't do it for him.

*The courage to change the things I can,*

But she can make sure that he knows what is expected of him, has a place to work with good light and few distractions.

*and the wisdom to know the difference.*

And then let him do his work and ask for help if he needs it.

In a similar manner Jane has choices to make about whether and what she will try to control. She can listen to Jack's complaints about having to do his homework and decide that if he wants her to leave him alone about this, she will comply with his wishes. She will be who he wants her to be. Or she may decide that he isn't going to get off that chair at the dining room table until all of his homework is finished. She can insist that he is going to be who she demands that he be. She can be aggressive toward him.

# Assertiveness: What It Is Not...

So we have two continua, ownership and control, and we have two ends to each of them. The place we have the greatest power to affect a resolution to the conflict is at the mid-point of each of these lines. The extremities of each line move to a less and less powerful position.

## A Framework for understanding our patterns of dealing with conflict

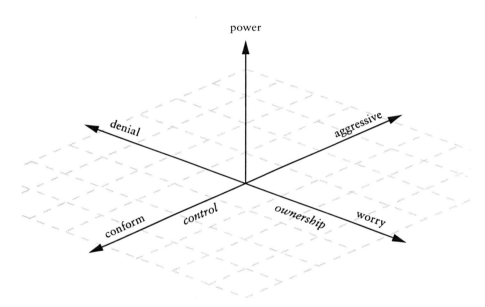

If we decide we have no ownership, we are in *denial*. We all have the power to make choices which affect outcomes. But if I say I am not responsible, I am not response-able. I claim a perspective which makes my own choices irrelevant. This is a cognitive distortion—a map which doesn't fit the territory—and a stance which does not support getting what we need.

If we decide we are responsible for choices we didn't make and outcomes we can't create, we become overwhelmed with *worry* and anxiety and we are powerless to create the outcomes which are open to us. This is also a cognitive distortion which hobbles our capacity to create what we need.

If we decide to control the situation by controlling the other, we become *aggressive.* We make others be who we want them to be, or we at least try. We may succeed in getting them, for the moment, to act as we want them to act, but they will revert to their more usual way of being as soon as our backs are turned. We can't actually get others to be who we want them to be. We can't change others.

If we decide to be whoever others want us to be, we *conform*, we immediately reduce tension in the relationship and appear to resolve the conflict. In fact, we have simply eaten the conflict and have now taken it within ourselves. The conflict is no longer between ourselves and the other who wants us to be different. Now it is between who we authentically are and who we are pretending to be to placate the other. We have created the appearance of harmony at the expense of our integrity by becoming compliant.

So it is the mid-point of the continuum of responsibility and the continuum of control which holds the greatest power. That is the stance we call *assertiveness*. We can use this model to help us identify when we are not being assertive.

If I find myself saying, "There is nothing I can do about this," I am not being assertive.

If I find myself saying, "Well, this really isn't my job, but I'll take it on anyway," then I am not being assertive.

If I find myself saying, "You are going to do it my way or else," I may have a brief rush of feeling powerful, but I am not going to create what I need and I am being aggressive. I am not being assertive.

If I find myself saying, "Whatever, I don't care, I will just be the way others want me to be," I am abandoning my own integrity and my own welfare and I am not being assertive.

We want to address the conflicts which arise in a manner which gives us the greatest possible power to create what we need. This is what we mean by being assertive. But there are a great many ways we can react which get us the opposite of what we need. This is not being assertive. It is very helpful then to notice how we are reacting and shift to a more satisfying way of being.

As we look for the patterns in our own behavior, we discover that we tend to react to the same or similar circumstances in the same ways over and over again. Some of us tend to deny our responsibility and some tend to take on too much responsibility. Some people tend to try to bully others and some are easily compliant.

Consider for a moment what you notice about your own behavior. Do you tend to hear yourself saying to yourself that you are powerless, that you are not response-able? Do you tend to go along with what others want and don't speak up for yourself? We tend to adopt a set stance in a given relationship but we may be very different in different relationships. We may be very compliant at work and then get home and dominate our children.

Using the chart, see if you can identify which quadrant you typically find yourself in. Are you an aggressive denier... or perhaps a compliant over-functioner? One common relationship between someone who is chemically dependant and someone who is codependent with them is just such a relationship. The disease of chemical dependency tends to breed a stance in which one denies responsibility for what is happening and insists that others be as they want them to be. Co-dependents, on the other hand, tend to comply with the demands of the chemically dependent and do whatever they can to clean up the mess the addict has made.

People who have adopted a life-stance as a *victim* tend to be compliant and to deny responsibility. Those who see themselves as *tough* tend to be over-functioning and willing to be aggressive to get things done.

Often people in a relationship with each other tend toward opposing quadrants in the chart. This is much like two people in a canoe where, when one leans left, the other leans rights just to keep the balance. This leads the first person to lean further left and pretty soon they are each stretched out over the water in a very unstable canoe. It is hard to move towards the middle because that seems to cause the canoe to tip.

## ...And What It Is

So we see that assertiveness is not being in denial, being aggressive, over-functioning or compliant. What then does assertiveness look like? We are looking for a way of being which actually leads to the resolution of conflict. Conflict arises for us a consequence of a real event. We start with that event. What actually happened?

Getting clear about what happened can actually be pretty difficult. Not only weren't we paying enough attention, but some of the relevant events happened out of our sight. The largest part of the problem, however, is that we have trouble seeing the distinction between what actually happened and what it means to us that it happened. We have to find an agreement about what happened. If we don't start from the same beginning point in our effort to resolve the conflict we never come to resolution.

Sometimes the best we can do is to agree that we don't agree. Then the issue we are attempting to resolve is that we aren't able to agree on what happened. This is not just agreeing to disagree. This is agreeing that we are not able to agree. The question then arises, would we like to agree? Sometimes we find others are actually invested in not finding agreement. So then the starting point is, "When we can't agree on whether to seek agreement..."

Whatever the starting place, the next step is to gain clarity about how we are affected by the event we are responding to. We know we didn't like it. If we liked it, it would not have caused esuba and we would not have recognized it as a conflict. But what, specifically, was the effect on us?

Knowing how we are affected begins to give us some very important clues about what it is we need. There are qualities we need which this event either demonstrated are absent from the relationship or which we are removed from the relationship. In order to know what they are, we have to pay attention to how we are affected. What sensations, emotions, thoughts and wishes came up for us as the event unfolded? What were we reminded of and what patterns in our past does this event connect us with?

How does this effect lead us to greater clarity about what we need? Not what we want... we want others to be as we want them to be. But what do we need? What are the qualities which would be optimal for us in the context of this relationship?

**Event:** If we are assertive, we become clear about what is happening which is a problem for us and name what is happening in such a way that others can see what we are talking about.

**Effect:** If we are assertive, we become clear about the effect that this event –or pattern of events—has on us and fully appreciate how and why we are so affected.

**Need:** If we are assertive, we become clear about the qualities which are missing from the relationship when events like this happen and we name the qualities we need.

## The Creative Power of Conflict: Finding Patterns

When I am sitting at my desk typing and I notice that I am cold, the world around me is not as I would like it to be; I am in conflict with my surroundings. When I get up and put on a sweater, I change myself in a way that more fully meets my needs. I create a solution to my problem. Conflict is the mother of creativity.

Larry Page and Sergey Brin were trying to sort through a mountain of data and found that it was hard to find just what they were looking for; they were having a conflict with the search engine tools that were available to them. They recognized that they could use the information from the back links that other Internet users had found for themselves. This allowed them to harvest the work that others had already done in finding relevant answers to their search questions. Google was born.

At the core a conflict is simply the tension that exists between the *what is* and the *what might be*. This is the creative tension out of which our experience arises. When we begin to see conflict as a creative opportunity that is present at all times in all relationships, we dramatically shift our stance toward conflict. Instead of it being something to be feared or avoided, it becomes something to be sought after and embraced.

But with this shift in perspective comes the awareness that we are awash in conflict. In every moment and in every relationship there are ways in which the experience we are having is not as we would have it be. Others are not who we want them to be. We are not who they want us to be. We are not even as we want ourselves to be. This may offer opportunities for creative transformation, but it is too much. We can't take it all in.

We have to limit the scope of our inquiry. We can't pay attention equally to all things all the time. We must focus on those things that are most important. We must look most closely at the places where we can make the biggest difference in our safety and our satisfaction. We must do that which will most get us what we need. Therefore we want to pay special attention to the patterns of conflict that arise in our most significant relationships.

You have probably had times in your most significant relationships when a familiar conflict recurs and you think to yourself, "Here we go again." The shoes are in the middle of the floor again. The toilet seat is up again. The car is on empty, the trash is overflowing, and the refrigerator door is open...again.

Conflicts arise in every relationship and they matter the most in our most significant relationships. Events we would hardly even notice in a relationship with someone who is not important to us become monumental when they arise over and over again in the context of relationships with people who matter to us. While these conflicts can be very aggravating, they are also rich opportunities for creativity and transformation.

As you spend five minutes every day doing the Bothers Me Log (you have started that haven't you?), you begin to notice how the same things arise day after day. The best issues to work on tend to be the little things that happen over and over again. We can also get great satisfaction from addressing the really big events that happen only occasionally, but those tend to be more difficult to address so it helps to start with small things that happen often. That way we get more chances to practice.

I want to give an example of how this can work, but let me first offer a very helpful turn of phrase and a shift in perspective that is given to us by Robert Kegan and Lisa Laskow Lahey in their book, *How the Way we Talk can Change the Way we Work*. They invite their readers to develop an awareness of the *language of complaint*. They invite readers to notice what is bothersome in the ways they function with others as a group. They lead the readers through a process of looking at the values they hold and the behaviors they choose and urge them to sit with the tension of the competing commitments and to resist the urge to solve the conflict. Instead they invite us to "let the conflicts solve us."

Rather than solving the conflict, instead of trying to get others or the system to change, can we let the conflict solve us? Can we see how the conflict invites us to know ourselves better, to identify what it is we are actually committed to, to see the assumptions we are making that may be constructing the problem we are having, and then to alter ourselves, rather than insisting that those around us change.

> *Eddie is a guy who was in one of my groups many years ago. He had been ordered out of his own home as a consequence of his abuse of his daughter, but he was steadfast in his wish to restore his marriage and his family. In order*

to minimize his own expenses so as to continue to financially support his wife and children, he moved back in with his parents.

Eddie was earnest and honest and hard working, but not very psychologically minded. He had no sense of what was going on with him when he sexually abused his daughter. He insisted that he had not been abused himself as a child. He was able to recover a memory of feeling abused by the school system when they put him into a program with mentally retarded kids when he was found to be severely dyslexic. He did remember when he was about three and the emergency room nurse asked him if the gash on his head was from falling down the stairs as his father had said. Not realizing that he was supposed to lie, he corrected the report explaining that his dad had thrown him against a radiator. But he was quite certain that he had never been sexually abused. He had seen his dad sexually abuse his mother and his sister, but he had never been sexually abused himself.

Eddie had a difficult time identifying any of his feelings. This was most evident around his anger. Many people suffer from being too angry, that is they tend to act out anger over even small things that happen. Eddie was one of those people who don't have enough access to their anger. Some people are so unaware of anger that they are easily taken advantage of. This was a problem for Eddie.

Thus it was quite a breakthrough when Eddie came to his Monday evening group and announced that he was angry. I was delighted. "So, Eddie, what are you angry about?"

"It is my dad. He just doesn't treat me right."

"What happened?"

"It was yesterday morning, Sunday morning, and I was in the kitchen fixing my breakfast, I was frying some eggs, and just as I was about to use the spatula to get the eggs out of the pan, my dad comes in, it is a small kitchen, and as I get *the spatula under the eggs, he pushes me to the side to get to the coffee pot and the eggs fly across the room and onto the floor."*

*"Wow, so what happened?"*

*"He poured his coffee and went into the breakfast nook to read the paper."*

*"No, I mean what did you do?"*

*"I cleaned up the eggs."*

*"Did you say anything to him?"*

*"No, that wouldn't do any good. He isn't going to change."*

*"Right, well, whether he changes or not, you can't change him... but didn't you feel like telling him off or anything?"*

*"No, that wouldn't do any good, he isn't going to change."*

In the discussion that followed we affirmed that we were not going to change his dad but that there are things that Eddie needs that he isn't getting when these things happen. Eddie was easily able to see that his dad always treats him this way and that it hurts his self-esteem. He was able to frame the issue in terms of self-respect. He was not getting the respect that he wanted from his dad. What might he do that would create for himself the respect that he needed. What could he do which would create a greater sense of self-respect?

We discussed what he might do differently whenever these events come up and set up a three part response to these events in his relationship with his dad. They were:

1. "Dad, when you (in this case) push me and my breakfast ends up on the floor and you don't acknowledge responsibility for what you have done, [event]

2.  I feel as though you don't have respect for me and are not interested in being accountable for how you affect me, [effect] and

3.  I wish we had a relationship in which we treated each other respectfully." [need]

Eddie agreed that it might feel good to say this to his dad, but he had to remind us again that his dad wasn't going to change. I assured Eddie that we weren't trying to change his dad but were supporting Eddie in being different in a way that created the respect that he was missing. He agreed to try this different way of being in the coming week whenever his dad treated him in a manner that didn't feel respectful. He allowed as how that was just about any time he and his dad were in the same room.

The next week when Eddie checked in at the group session he reported the following:

> "It didn't work."

> "How do you know it didn't work?" I asked.

> "My dad isn't going to change."

> "No, he isn't going to change and we aren't going to change him. What happened?"

> "I was sitting in the living room reading the newspaper and he came in and took it right out of my hands. I said to him, 'When I am reading the newspaper and you take it from me without saying anything to me it feels like you don't have any respect for me and I want to have a relationship where we treat each other with respect.'"

> "Excellent! So what happened?"

> "He looked at me like I had two heads and then sat down and read the newspaper."

> "Okay, but what happened with you?"

*Eddie had to stop and think about this for a minute. He was not yet accustomed to paying attention to his own feelings at this point and he had to do make some space in his awareness.*

*"Well, actually, now that I think about it, it felt kind of good. Even though my dad looked at me like I had two heads, he looked at me. He doesn't normally do that. And another thing, it felt good to hear myself stand up to him."*

We talked some more about how it felt to him and then he committed to continue to respond to his dad this way.

Here was a pattern of conflict—Dad treating him disrespectfully—in a significant relationship with which Eddie had sat long enough that it had begun to solve him. He had a new way of being in the relationship which could begin to construct what he needed without depending on or insisting that the other change.

Over the course of the next several months Eddie continued to practice this speech to his dad whenever his dad treated him in a manner that did not feel respectful. Over the months Eddie got better and better at delivering the speech and felt stronger about himself for being able to present his wishes clearly. But he also began to notice a shift in his dad. From time to time his dad would start to do something disrespectful and then stop himself, as if he didn't want to hear the speech. His dad's behavior was changing, not because he changed his dad, but because he changed his relationship to his dad and his dad had to adjust to the change.

Eddie was able to identify a pattern of conflict in a significant relationship and to fashion a plan for how he wanted to be different whenever the pattern emerged. The goal of the plan was to change the way Eddie acted such that he would be responsible for creating what he needed without expecting or depending upon the other to change.

## Discipline #9: A Framework for Creative Conflict Resolution

We are ready now to look at the central discipline of Creative Conflict Resolution. This is essentially a map of what Eddie was able to do with his dad. It is also the ninth discipline. I know, I am introducing it out of order here, but I want you to understand the purpose of the next few chapters in the task of becoming masterful at conflict resolution. This discipline is so central to that mastery that we want to have it in front of us as we consider the next components of Creative Conflict Resolution.

## Significant Relationships

As we have already mentioned, we are awash in conflict. We have far too many conflicts to respond to all of them with the care that assertiveness demands. We have to limit our field just a bit. So we focus especially on those relationships which are most significant

## Pattern of Conflict

Still, within our most significant relationships there are very many conflicts. As we do the Bothers Me Log we discover the degree to which it is the same conflict over and over, though perhaps in somewhat different forms.

## Event

We must name the event in such a way that everyone who is a party to it can agree that this is happening. This step is so important to resolution that often simply doing it well results in clarity and an end to confusion. If we can't agree on what happened we are certainly not going to agree on what to do about it.

## Effect

We must to be as clear as possible how this event, and the pattern of events of which it is a part, affects us. We pursue this task more deeply in the next two chapters.

## Need

We must identify the quality which is missing when this pattern of events occurs. This is the focus of Chapter Ten.

[You of course recognize these three items (event, effect, and need) as the steps to being assertive.]

## Action

And then, and only then, we must act in a manner which moves us toward what we need without expecting or depending on the other to change.

As Eddie was able to discover with his dad, when he isolated a particular pattern of conflict, he was able to design a specific intervention which he could use every time it came up. Sure, there were minor modifications for each event, but the heavy lifting of figuring out what to do to be assertive was already in place. That is, all he had to do was to name the event, know how it affected him, know what he needed, and then act in a manner which moved him toward what he needed. We will expand on this through the practical disciplines we explore in Chapter Eleven.

## Reacting or Responding

Whatever insight or awareness we may come to about what is bothering us, how we would like things to be, or how we might like to act in our relationships with others, nothing will change until we change our behavior—until we change what we do. So this final step in the Framework—that of taking action—is clearly the most crucial. The urgency we feel about being able to act to create what we need is so great that we often rush to discover a strategy before we know what it is we need. This can be disastrous.

> Larry had been in the program for a couple of months when, in the second week of October, he came to group angry. He had just had a birthday, but it was not a happy one.
>
> "I am just so angry at my mom. I had a birthday this past week and she didn't even acknowledge it. It's not just that she didn't get me anything, she didn't even call me. That's the way she is. She won't be doing anything for Christmas either. I am just so fed up. I am cutting her off. I just won't have anything to do with her."

Let's look at the conflict Larry is having with his mom from the lens of the Framework for Creative Conflict Resolution.

Is this a significant relationship? Sure, this is his mom. We all have significant relationships with our mothers.

Is this a pattern of conflict? Sure. This has happened before and he fully expects it will happen again at Christmas in a couple of months.

So what was the event? Larry had a birthday and had no contact with his mother on his birthday and no acknowledgment that it was his birthday.

And how did this affect him? He felt empty, unloved, hurt, sad and angry. He believes his mom doesn't care about him. He knows she knows when his birthday is. She was there. It was a big day for her, too. She knows when his birthday is so it must be her choice to disregard and disrespect him. He would like her to be someone who cares about him and honors him on his special day.

And what does he need? He needs the qualities of care and consideration in the relationship. He would be more satisfied in the relationship if they were able to show their appreciation and love for each other, to let each other know they are important.

And what will he do? He will cut her off and have nothing to do with her.

Huh? How does that move him toward what he needs? It won't. In fact, it moves him away from what he needs.

We often make choices which construct the opposite of what we need. We act in ways which create what we are afraid we are going to get, rather than creating what we need.

Larry is *reacting* to the event by making a choice that doesn't consider what he needs. Indeed, he has no idea what he needs when he makes that choice, he only knows what he expects to get and, if he chooses in a manner which assures him of that outcome, at least he doesn't feel powerless. But he doesn't get what he needs.

When, instead, we *respond* to the event by acting in a manner which moves us toward what we need we at least get some part of the qualities which support us. So what might Larry have done to respond to the event in a manner which created what he needed?

Remember that what Larry needs is a relationship with his mom which is characterized by appreciation and respect. So how might Larry create that with him mom?

As the group discussed his situation and thought and talked about what ideas for action would create what Larry needed, a plan emerged. What would it be like for Larry if he were to contact him mom, either by phone or by mail and tell her something like the following.

> *"Mom, it was my birthday last week and we didn't get together or speak. I have been thinking about how it felt to have a birthday without talking to you and I don't like it. I was waiting for you to contact me, but it occurs to me now that I could have called you. I am very grateful for the life you gave me by giving birth to me and I regret that I didn't call to thank you. I hope we can build a relationship in which we can remember to appreciate each other."*

Larry considered what it would be like if he were to say something like that to his mom. He admitted it would be true. Still, he didn't think he could actually say that. He was too hurt and angry. He knew he couldn't get the words out.

While our feelings often help us know what we need, they can, in their expression, get in the way of our ability to act constructively. Larry's feelings are so intense that they hinder his ability to calmly follow through on a plan to rebuild his relationship with his mom. We turn in the next chapter to a consideration of what feelings are, what they are for, and how we can best use them, but first we look at a couple of other barriers to Larry doing what would heal his relationship with his mom. Firstly, he needs to have a plan for giving and receiving critical feedback that would be easy and safe for both him and his mom. And secondly, he needs to move from a 2° to a 4° strategy for addressing this conflict. This requires that he let go of trying to change his mother.

## The Language of Complaint

Larry has had conversations in the past with his mother about how they are each not as the other wants them to be. These have not gone well. He doesn't want to revisit those ugly times.

Critical feedback can come in different forms. When we give feedback we can be offering a concern, criticism, contempt, or control. When we receive feedback we can hear is as an expression of domination, contempt, criticism of our choices, or a comment on the quality of our relationship.

*Concerns* are statements that focus on the *qualities which are arising in the relationship* which we don't like or find harmful. "When you promise to take out the trash and then don't do so, it makes it hard for me to trust you and I don't feel supported in caring for this household."

*Criticisms* are statements that focus on the *choices the other is making* which we don't like. "When you don't take out the trash as you said you would you are being immature, selfish, and lazy."

*Contempt* shows up when our statements are focused on who the other is, on the *nature of their being*. "You are a selfish, lazy bum who won't even take out the trash."

*Control* may come through what we say to others which indicates that we believe we have the right to control their actions but it may also be expressed through our physical reactions to them through pushing, pulling, or even striking them. Our focus is on *what the other must do to meet our demands*. "Take this out now," we growl, as we thrust the trash into the other's face.

It is most helpful when others offer us critical feedback in the form of concerns which focus on the qualities in the relationship while letting us know specifically what we are doing they don't like, but sometimes their anger gets the best of them. When it does, we may hear them speaking to us with contempt or attempting to control us. Rather than react back and enter into a fight, we are more likely to construct what we need if we can translate the feedback into a concern before we respond. I suspect this is something we can all use some work on.[19]

If Larry can express his concern that he and his mom don't have more connection to each other, she will probably be able to hear him fairly easily and may even confirm whether that is what she wants.

---

19   These distinctions are derived from the work of Dr. John Gottman. I have taken his work as a starting place and expanded and refined it for the purposes of Creative Conflict Resolution.

If Larry chooses to state his criticism of her for not calling him on his birthday, she is likely to respond with things he does or fails to do about which she is critical.

If Larry chooses to belittle her mothering because she is so indifferent to her child that she doesn't even consider his birthday, she is likely to pull out a list of all of the defects she sees in him.

And if he chooses to control their conversation by having nothing to do with her, she isn't likely to respond by calling him. They will continue to have no contact.

If Larry can focus on addressing his concerns he may have a conversation with his mom which moves them to having a better connection. He also has to let go of the expectation that the conversation will get his mom to treat him differently. This requires the transformation of his map of what conflict resolution looks like.

## Stages in the Development of Our Capacity to Resolve Conflict

As we have already pointed out several times, anything which grows, grows through stages of development. One of the things which develops is our capacity to address and resolve conflict. We get better and better at it the more we practice our skills and the better we become at selecting the most helpful maps. With that in mind, let's see what the map of the Orders of Self can show us about stages in the development of our capacity to resolve conflicts.

To start with we have to notice the conflict. I have to know there is a rock in my shoe before I take it out. This is a 1° [Personal-material: perception] capacity to know what my current experience is. Then, should I choose to remove the rock, I will invoke the 2° [Personal-material: choice] skill of removing my shoe, emptying it, and restoring the shoe to my foot. At the most basic level, conflict resolution strategies are 2° ways of doing which transform our experience at 1°.

[Remember that the odd numbered orders are levels at which we are constructed by the experience of being, that is, by the awareness and acceptance of *what is*; and the even numbered orders are levels at which we have mastery over our experience. They are ways of doing which create *what might be*.]

Some strategies are about gaining mastery over my 1° experience. I may, for example, decide to put on a sweater. But some strategies are about gaining mastery over my 3° [Interpersonal-relational: perception] experience. I may want my mom to be pleased with me. I may want to get into the college of my choice. These problems require that I know how to function at 2° in a way that resolves problems at 3°. So there are 2° strategies which address problems which arise from a 1° awareness or from a 3° awareness.

At some point we may find we are not going to resolve a conflict from a 2° level of understanding. We may find a conflict which is of such intensity that we are only going to resolve it from a 4° understanding. This is just what is being required of Larry in this potential response to his mom when she "forgot" his birthday.

Our goal is to use the conflicts which arise in our most intimate relationships to spur us to move from a 2° perspective on the nature of the problem and on what we can do to address and resolve it, to a 4° perspective thus transforming ourselves and our relationships.

## Styles of Conflict Resolution

We do not address every conflict in the same way. We have many different parts or perspectives from which to see and respond when conflicts arise in our awareness.

Most of us have a part of us which is easy-going and not easily troubled. That part addresses conflicts by not letting others bother us.

We also have a part which is anxious to get along with others, which tries to please others and to do as they want. This part hopes that, if we are pleasing to others, others will respond by trying to please us as well.

And we have a part which is clear about how we want others to be and is willing to be forceful in expressing our wishes and may even insist that others do what we want them to do. These may seem to be developmental stages as they may arise sequentially as we try to address a given situation, but they are all 2° strategies.

Recall that we choose a *strategy* to create an *event* which we expect will create the *qualities* we need. We can assess the level of a strategy by the characteristics of the event we intend to create. Each of these strategies has in common that it creates what we want by getting the other to change. These strategies only work in fairly low intensity conflicts. These three styles are displayed in the chart on the bottom row. [A color version of this chart is available at JustConflict.com.]

What they all have in common is that the event they are intending to create is one in which the success of the strategy is determined by getting the other to change. We each have these parts because these strategies sometimes work to get us what we need. As long as the intensity of the conflict is fairly low, we have a good chance of creating what we need by one of these approaches. But when the intensity is high, they don't work as well.

Remember that the intensity of a conflict is a function of how attached the parties are to a particular issue, circumstance, or outcome, and the degree to which they see things from a different perspective or point of view. As long as the issue is one I don't care much about, I can comfortably come from that part of me which is not easily bothered [2° stillness]. If it is something I have a bit more attachment to but we are seeing it from a similar vantage point, I may use the approach of being more conciliatory and placating [2° yin][20]. If I really care about this and the other is not seeing it my way, I may become more insistent and urgent and even demanding [2° yang]. But if the other is equally attached to the issue and to the other's perspective we are just going to get more and more entrenched in our separate ways of doing and seeing.

## Conflict Resolution Styles

| Orders of Self | types of energy used in addressing conflict | | | |
| --- | --- | --- | --- | --- |
| | yin | stillness | yang | goal |
| 4° | I am willing to change myself in order to move toward the relationship that I want. | | I know that I can powerfully transform the relationship by being who I choose to be. | changing the *relationship* |
| 3° | | I feel dispair at changing the other. There is nothing I can do. Hopelessness. | | |
| 2° | I will try to be who others want me to be to minimize tension and get them to take care of me. | | I will get the other to change by telling them how to be, blaming, forcing, violence. | changing the *other* |
| 1° | | This doesn't bother me. There is no conflict. Denial. | | |

---

20 The terms "yin" and "yang" are from Chinese philosophy and refer loosely to qualities which are more open and passive, and more rigid and active. They are used here with the term "stillness" to simply note that different strategies may be of different types without being on a different developmental level.

While we may see this entrenchment as a problem in the short run, in the long run it actually presents a wonderful opportunity for transformation. This may be an issue which allows us to transform our own way of approaching the problem such that we can move to a 4° [Interpersonal-relational: choice] perspective. At this level we have abandoned trying to get the other to change and are instead looking simply to transform the relationship by changing how we act. This may mean that we act in ways which appear very similar to the ways we acted at 2°, but the strategies have a very different quality to them.

We may despair of changing the other and simply remain present to them as they continue to do what they do. This is not abandoning concern for the other, but it is a stance of *caring for* without *taking care of*. This is 4° stillness.

We may find that we can be present in the ways the other wants, not because it pleases the other, but because it creates the qualities in the relationship which we desire [4° yin].

Or we may find that we are not fettered by the wishes of the other and are free to show up just as we want to be. This is not the same as not caring what others think. This is being fully aware of what others expect and being able to freely choose a way of being which is creative in the midst of conflicting expectations. This is just what Anne was doing when she responded to her daughter Christy about her own sexual behavior when they were talking in the grocery store [4° yang]. (See page **100**.)

The possibility exists for Larry then that he is so attached to his relationship with his mother that he does not blow off this opportunity for transformation. He cares about the rift between them and is compelled to move to a 4° perspective from which he can be more of who he chooses to be in a way that heals the relationship with his mom. He can use this conflict as an opportunity for self-transformation.

## Non-violence

Nonviolence is a philosophy (and the strategies that derive from that philosophy) that exists as a distinction from both violence and passivity. It observes the destruction that comes from violent and passive strategies and rejects them both.

Nonviolence acknowledges the presence of oppression and the structures by which the oppression is created and maintained. It seeks to dismantle systems of oppression. It assumes that the oppressed are far more interested in working to dismantle the structures of oppression and so tends to be more easily allied with the oppressed, but it also sees the oppressor as one who is harmed by the oppressive systems. This harm is much less evident, therefore oppressors are not likely to be interested in changing the system, but rather work very hard to sustain the system.

Nonviolence sees the system as the problem, not the people in it. It seeks to transform the system. It does so by recognizing that the system exists only because the people continue to serve it. The system collapses, or at least changes, when those supporting it decide together to transform it.

For people to be willing to experience the stress of change, they have to hold to a vision of a way of being that is clearly better than the current system. Their perspective has to be rooted in a developmental level above the current one for it to be seen as more effective (though those who are entitled or privileged by the current system won't like it in any case.)

The nature of nonviolent resistance is to organize those who are oppressed by a system to act in a manner that is both non-cooperation with the assumptions and activities of the oppressive system, and which embodies a vision of community that is more developed and, thus, more complex than the oppressive one.

Nonviolence is about recognizing that the "logic" of the oppressive system is actually not what it appears to be. The glass which has the juice rising higher is not actually the glass with the most juice. There is another choice that works better for everyone. Having recognized a better way, nonviolence then engages many people in taking a small step, a step that can easily be taken, but one which challenges the logic of the dominant system. The Montgomery bus boycott was about simply not taking the bus: a simple step that worked only because so many were willing to take it.

Nonviolence is not immediately effective in a 1° [Personal-material: perception] sense. If I refuse to get on the bus I am not going to be able to get to work.

Nonviolence is not effective as a 2° [Personal-material: choice] intervention. They have more power and I am not going to change them. I just have to walk to work.

Nonviolence says to the 3° [Interpersonal-relational: perception] forces that tell me who and how I am to be that I am not going to be their way. That makes me appear to defy convention to those who are operating at 3°. That allows them to demean and dismiss me.

It is not until we get to 4° [Interpersonal-relational: choice] that nonviolence begins to appear as effective. Nonviolence depends on finding others who are observing from a 4° perspective that there is another way of structuring relationships and society. This new way is going to work better for all. And these others, these comrades, share a faith in that vision such that they are willing to live into it in a manner that challenges the 3° assumptions. These are those we join with to live in the realm that is "already but not yet."

To act in concert with others in a nonviolent way, we must address our 5° [Intrapersonal-internal: perception] multiplicity and to know our parts that would seek to impose our 2° will on others and have those aspects of who we are recede. We have to let go of the parts that want to be right and the parts that want to get even and just rest in the knowledge of our own complexity and complicity and be accepting.

When we can see from 6° [Intrapersonal-internal: choice] a way that all may be together in a manner that is best for all, with a 7° [Transpersonal-spiritual: perception] compassion and perhaps even an 8° [Transpersonal-spiritual: choice] capacity to identify with those who see us as enemies; then we can reliably let go of any attachment to the outcome and simply trust in the manifestation of Truth, or Soul-force, or satyagraha[21] in our lives.

## Summary

If we are to resolve conflicts we have to address them. We are shy about this because much of what we have tried only seems to make things worse. If we are to address a conflict we have to know its name. We have to know what to call it. A common name for a conflict is that it is *a difference we don't like.* When others are not as we want them to be or we are not as they want us to be, we experience a conflict.

As we have noted, conflicts can be complex. A part of the complexity is

---

21    Satyagraha is a synthesis of the Sanskrit words *satya* (thruth) and *agraha* (holding firmly to). For Gandhi, satyagraha went far beyond mere "passive resistance" and became strength in practicing non-violent methods.

that, when the other is not as I want the other to be, there is always a resource based component to the conflict (not enough time, or money, or attention), an identity based component (who are we to each other) and a process based component (how will we deal with this).

Some conflicts are more intense than others. Low intensity conflicts are easy. It is the high intensity conflicts which are hard to resolve. The intensity is a function of both how attached the parties are to the issues or circumstances and how well aligned or divergent the perspectives are that the parties bring to the event. The more attached and divergent, the more intensity the conflict holds.

It is fairly easy to hold to our center when the intensity of the conflict is low. The more stressed we are by the conflict the harder it becomes to act in a manner that is calm and creative. It helps to have a clear sense of what we are trying to do and what we are trying to avoid. It helps if we have the intention of being assertive and have a clear sense of what that looks like, and what it doesn't look like.

We tend to approach conflicts the same way in the same relationships. We tend to either deny our responsibility, or we tend to take on responsibility for things we cannot change. We tend either to try to get others to do what we want, or we tend to abandon our own interests and just comply with the other's wishes. Assertiveness is none of these.

Being assertive means identifying the event to which we are responding, how we are being affected, and what qualities would be better for us when this event happens. This sounds very simple, and indeed it is, but it is not easy. When we can do this we discover how very powerful we are in constructing what we need. But it takes many repetitions to master this. Fortunately we have lots of opportunities to practice.

These problematic events tend to happen over and over again in our most significant relationships. When we can identify the pattern and get very clear about how we would like to address the pattern, then we can practice every time it arises. This requires that we become able to master a set of skills. When we put these together we get the Framework for Creative Conflict Resolution, which is Discipline #9. This discipline is built upon a series of skills which will be introduced in the next few chapters.

As we master these skills we become less and less reactive to the conflicts and more and more responsive to them. We become more likely to do the things that move us more toward what we need, and less likely to do the things that get us the opposite of what we need.

In nearly every case, though, we have to speak to the other about what is arising in our relationship. We have to say that we don't like what is happening and to do so in a way such that the other can hear our concern. This is an essential part of being assertive. But often when we complain we either do it badly or the other doesn't listen or both. For that reason we want to be careful about how we use the language of complaint. We want to try to reflect on the qualities of the relationship (concern) rather than the qualities of the other's choices (criticism), the nature of who they are (contempt), or to say that they have no intrinsic worth (control).

As we practice the skills we discover that we are developing a more complex but more effective way of addressing conflicts. We become less reliant on 2° [Personal-material: choice] strategies and more on 4° [Interpersonal-relational: choice] strategies. We become less concerned with changing the other and more with changing the relationship by changing our own choices. We discover that while this is more difficult, it is also more effective.

It is just this shift which is at the heart of the conflict resolution strategy known as non-violence. While we tend to think of the tools of non-violence being used in addressing problems of social oppression, as we have seen, we also experience oppression in our most intimate relationships and the approach is equally valid and effective there. Through such an approach we develop the capacity to see the conflict from a more complex perspective and then act from that perspective in a manner which is more effective at creating what everyone needs.

# 8

# Interior Awareness:
# Anxiety, Anger, and Desire

## Anxiety

We all experience anxiety. For some people at some times the anxiety they experience becomes so extreme that they require professional help to manage it, but all of us have some level of anxiety all the time. At its simplest, anxiety is the feeling which arises for us when we want two mutually exclusive things at the same time.

> Joe has started a new job that he really likes but he is afraid that he is not making a very good impression with the boss. He has been a few minutes late every day this week. Getting the boys up and dressed and fed and off to school just takes more time than it should.

> But Joe is feeling hopeful this morning. He is out of the house on time and traffic looks good. Barring a major problem he should make it just on time. As the thought "major problem" goes through Joe's mind, he looks at the instruments on the dash to assess the condition of his car and the gas gauge catches his eye. It is on empty.

So Joe experiences anxiety. He wants to be at work on time and he wants to get gas. If he doesn't stop and get gas he might be very late to work. Or he may not get to a gas station after work. He wants two apparently opposite things at the same time.

We want to just note here that if Joe had the foresight to notice he was low on gas yesterday evening on the way home, he could have stopped then or at least been aware that he would have to stop this morning. When we anticipate and address these apparent conflicts they go away without causing discernable anxiety.

As we don't address the conflicts the anxiety grows in intensity until we notice and address it. This is what anxiety is for: to bring our attention to problems so we can give them our full attention.

## Problem Solving: The Doing Cycle

You may recall back in chapter three as we looked at how we build our perceptual maps we introduced the observation that we are engaged always in three interrelated activities: we are assessing the current situation, we are deciding how we want things to be different, and we are selecting and implementing a strategy to create change.

> Joe looks at the clock on the dash and the gas gauge and tries to determine how much time he has and how much gas is in the tank while he estimates the miles to work and the fuel efficiency of his car. He adds to the mix his awareness of where there are gas stations and how long the lines are likely to be at each one and the time to get in and out. He checks to make sure he has his wallet hoping the credit card is in it. He tries to remember if he has his boss' phone number with him so he can call if he runs out of gas and then decides that is not a good plan. He pulls into a convenient gas station.

Joe is rapidly cycling through a series of steps in problem solving. He is gathering information about his current situation. He is clarifying his goals. And he is selecting strategies which move him toward his goals. He is developing a strategy for resolving a conflict. We all do this all the time.

As you read this you are noticing what time it is and you wonder if you will finish this section before you put the book down and get to sleep or do the dishes or whatever else is on your task list for the moment. You have things to do. You know what many of your goals are and you have a sense of the strategies you have to invoke to create what you need. You are doing all of this with very little conscious awareness most of the time.

But, from time to time, we find that we don't know what is going on. We are paying attention—sometimes close attention—but we can't figure out the current condition. We become anxious.

Or, perhaps we know what is going on but we can't figure out what it is we want to have happen. There are a number of possible, and even desirable, outcomes available but they are not all possible so we can't figure out what we want. We become anxious.

Or perhaps we are clear about what is going on and resolute about what we want to have happen but we can't seem to settle on a strategy for creating what we need. We have several options open to us but each has shortcomings and may not work or may cost too much so we aren't sure what to do. Perhaps we feel as though we have tried everything and nothing seems to work. We become anxious.

Anxiety is the feeling we have whenever the "doing cycle" gets stuck. It is the natural and normal response to a restriction in our ability to get things done and it draws our attention to problems so we can use the light of our awareness to illuminate and resolve them.

As long as we are functioning optimally this process works well and smoothly. But sometimes we get overloaded with anxiety. Sometimes a problem arises and our attention is brought to it by our anxiety and we begin to address it but, before we resolve it, another problem arises...and then another... and another... and pretty soon we find ourselves flooded with anxiety.

So, the current condition is that we are overwhelmed by anxiety. The target condition is that we be anxiety free. The strategy is... to go shopping, or have a drink, or smoke some pot, or maybe some crack.

When the anxiety is no longer a way of bringing attention to a problem but becomes a problem itself, we look for ways to soothe ourselves. And there are many ways we can do this. We can listen to music, take a walk, go fishing, meditate, pray...

# Ways of Being

The *cycle of doing* has as its goal to create an event in which a specific problem is solved. *Ways of being* also create events but they are ones in which certain qualities can be nurtured.

Some people go fishing to catch fish. But many go fishing to *be* fishing. There is a quality which arises in their awareness when they are on the banks of the river or lake or ocean and they watch the line and feel the tension and just wait.

Some beginning meditators get anxious about whether they are meditating *right*. This is normal. But meditation is not a way of *doing*; rather, it is a way of *being*. Whatever arises is what arises. Meditation is simply observing in an attentive way whatever it is that arises in our awareness and, then, letting it go. It is not a process of trying to fix, solve, or understand anything. It is a process of observing, letting go, and seeing whatever arises next.

There are many schools and forms of meditation and there are many things we do which are meditative which may not ever be identified as such. What they all have in common is that they provide an opportunity for us to step back and observe. We move to a location in our own interior from which we become a witness to our own experience.

We function best when we have a balance between our *doing* and our *being*. If we spend all of our attention on *doing* we get a lot done, but we can be overwhelmed by anxiety. If we spend all of our attention on *being* we are able to be at peace... but we never seem to get anything done. The trick is to find an appropriate balance.

The pace of contemporary culture in the developed world is one in which everyone is very busy *doing*. This is a shift from what we most often think of as "primitive" cultures in which much time and attention goes to simply *being*. In today's world we don't have time to just *be*.

It is possible that the now ancient notion of keeping a Sabbath—setting aside a day each week to just be—came from the observation of how human relationships are damaged by a move to a more work intensive society from a more laid back existence of hunter-gatherer bands.

We are out of balance and we are so busy doing and have so little time to just be that we get more and more stressed and become more and more anxious. So, instead of addressing our anxiety by being, we find ways of doing which soothe the anxiety... at least in the short run.

> Joe was late getting to work and he got a warning from his boss about his tardiness. That was just the start to an overall bad day, so after work he decided to stop into the bar for a couple of drinks. It was after 7:00 when he finally got home and he and Jane got into a huge fight so he slept on the couch. In the morning he had a hangover. The only time he really felt good all day was while he was at the bar, so he will plan to go out drinking again tonight.

The problem with using mood altering chemicals to soothe our anxiety is that they work... in the short run. When we use something to soothe anxiety which works we tend to use it again, and again, and again. We become addicted.

We will not go into a deep analysis of addiction here but it helps us to notice that the addictive behavior, whether to chemicals or to behaviors like shopping, biting fingernails, food, sex, or video games, is a reaction to the anxiety which we all experience. We are not able to durably change the addictive behavior without addressing the anxiety which gives rise to it. We all feel anxiety. We all get overwhelmed. We all self-soothe.

Some of us limit our self-soothing behavior to *ways of being*, but most of us also *act out*. We act on the anxiety in a way which projects it out into our behavior and into the larger world we inhabit. We eat when we aren't hungry. We watch TV when it bores us. We smoke cigarettes in spite of knowing they are killing us.

The acting out is an effort to soothe the anxiety we are feeling and it works. But it doesn't actually address the cause of the anxiety, only the experience of it. For us to stop the acting out we have to know what is causing the anxiety which spawns it. But as long as we do the acting out the anxiety is soothed so we don't feel it. How might we know what it is we are actually anxious about so we can address and resolve the conflicts we are having with ourselves?

To address the core issue we have to feel the anxiety. To feel the anxiety we have to stop the acting out. We act out to not feel anxious. We stop the acting out in order to feel anxious. We feel anxious in order to discover the unresolved internal conflict which is separating us from our best selves.

# Discipline #4: Suspending Self-Soothing

In order to address and resolve a conflict we first start with an awareness of the conflict. Our biggest conflicts with others are rooted in the conflicts we have with ourselves. The conflicts we have with ourselves are accompanied by anxiety but we typically don't know what is causing the anxiety. The fourth discipline is designed to help us clarify the source of the anxiety within the realm of our 5° [Intrapersonal-internal: perception] awareness of Self.

The first step is to notice what it is we do to make ourselves feel better when we are anxious. Some of these are more *ways of being* and some more *ways of doing*. There are few things that are clearly one or the other. As noted, we can even make meditation into a way of doing.

But watch what you do when you are anxious or bored. Boredom is what we call the feeling which arises for us when what we have been doing to soothe our anxiety isn't working any more. For example, do you ever get bored watching TV? How is that possible with hundreds of channels and corporations spending millions to keep us engaged and entertained?

If I am anxious about something and don't want to feel it I can focus on the TV screen and surf the channels looking for something which keeps me so engaged that I don't notice the anxiety. But when that stops working I find myself feeling bored with the TV. It isn't working anymore. I need a stronger drug.

I have never personally been able to get into playing video games. They take so much attention and time that I haven't had the patience to learn them. So, I was very surprised to hear a young client of mine explain that he was getting bored with his video games. He had become so adept at playing them that he could play a game without it actually being the focus of his attention.

What do you do to self-soothe when you are anxious? Make a list of what you observe yourself doing.

Now quit doing them. Just suspend those activities for a while. This should make you anxious. Notice what you become anxious about.

If you become too anxious you can always resume the behavior. You don't have to torture yourself. But, more and more, as you pay attention you find yourself discovering the sources of your anxiety. And once you know, you become better able to address the causes.

Let me insert here that while we all self-soothe and can benefit from watching for those behaviors, this is not something we are going to do on our own, especially when they have risen to the level of an addiction. It is unlikely that we can fully address any acting out on our own. This is what self-help programs and therapy are for. And the reason to get help is not because you are bad or incompetent, but because you are precious and deserve the healing presence of others.

## Discipline #5: Self-care Routine

The fifth and the last of the mindfulness disciplines provides a good segue into the material in Chapter Nine.

We all *care about* ourselves and we *take care of* ourselves. And none of us does as good a job of self-care as we could or as we would like. In this way we are all at odds with ourselves around a very important matter. We are in conflict about how much time and attention we put to our own wellbeing.

Consider whether you have anything to do that is more important than taking care of yourself. As you do this you will likely immediately notice a tension. On the one hand we all know we have to take care of ourselves if we are to function in the world. We have to get enough sleep, eat good food, exercise, and attend to our hygiene. If we do not, we are not much use to ourselves or anyone else. On the other hand we have responsibilities we have to attend to before we can indulge our own wishes. If all we are doing is caring for ourselves we are not acting to meet those responsibilities and we are being selfish. It is just this tension we want to mine to create greater mindfulness.

Start by making three lists. Include on the first list all of the things you do everyday to care for yourself. You sleep. You eat. You probably brush your teeth. Put on this list everything you do everyday for which you are the primary beneficiary.

On the second list enter all of the things you have done in the past which are good for you and which you wish you were continuing to do but which you are not as consistent about as you would like. You might include here things like taking a yoga class.

On the third list enter all of the things you hope to get around to someday. These are things you are quite certain would be good for you if you were to do them but you have never been able to muster the discipline to actually give them a try.

Now take lists #2 and #3 and set them aside. We are only going to work with the first list, the things you already do everyday to care for yourself. Make this list into a schedule. You sleep. When do you go to bed and when do you get up? You eat. When do you eat and what do you eat and what don't you eat? Add all of the things you do everyday to care for yourself and enter a time at which you will either do this self-care activity or you will notice whether you have done it or are going to do it.

Once you have completed the schedule review it to make sure it is actually what you believe is a good schedule for you. If it isn't, change it. Make sure it is what you alone believe is in your best interest. Don't make it what you think someone else would say is good for you. This has to be your own conviction about what you do when you are taking good care of yourself.

Now begin to notice each day when you keep to the schedule and when you depart from it. You may have decided that you would be in bed by 10:00 and here it is 1:00 and you are watching a movie you have seen three times. You may have decided you are going to eat healthy food and here you are with a donut in your mouth.

The goal here is not to give that critic we all have inside us some material with which to shame us, but to notice how we decided not to do what we believe is good for us. We want to exploit that tension to discover more clearly our own complexity and conflicts.

We want to look more closely at what is going on with us when we have an impulse to do things which are not in our long term best interest and we can't seem to stem the self harming behavior. While this may apply to dramatically self-harming behavior like cutting, it is true for all of us that there are things we do that we wish we didn't and things we don't do that we wish we did. These can be things like;

- I eat when I'm not hungry.
- I smoke cigarettes even when I know how harmful they are to me.
- I criticize myself mercilessly when I make small and insignificant mistakes.
- I don't check my bank balance when I am afraid I may bounce a check.

The typical pattern is:

1.  I observe that I am failing to act in a way that is in my best interest,

2.  I determine for myself what a better course of action would be and resolve to behave that way,

3.  And then I don't.

What we typically do then is to try to summon enough "will power" to make ourselves do what we resist doing, or to stop ourselves from being so "impulsive." This sometimes works, but typically it is not effective for the biggest issues in our lives. So let's look more closely at how we might map this out with the use of a 5° [Intrapersonal-internal: perception] perspective of Self.

One part of me is the part which observes the behavior which it labels as impulsive and harmful and resolves to stop that behavior. This part is a manager which is trying to do what it believes is in my best interest. This part notices when I am about to eat something which is not nutritious or I am about to eat at a time when I am already well fed. It sees me reaching for a cigarette. It hears me criticizing myself. It wonders about my bank balance and resolves to check it. This is a part that easily comes into my conscious awareness.

But there is another part of me which is eating junk food when I am already full, lighting cigarettes, belittling me, or "forgetting" to check my bank balance. This aspect of my interior being is much harder to find, but at least I know when to find it. It shows up when I am around food, cigarettes, mistakes, and whenever I resolve to call the bank. So, I can wait to ambush it.

But, even if I can get hold of that part, what do I do with it? I had a client many years ago who shared a series of sayings about relating to pigs. One I remember well was, "Never try to wrestle with a pig. You will both get dirty... and the pig will enjoy it." I have come to think of the activity of finding the impulsive part and wrestling it into submission as a kind of pig wrestling. I may dominate the pig in the short run, but it will come to the fore sooner or later. These impulsive parts can, paradoxically, be very patient.

But there is another part, a third part of us, which is often very subtle, almost as though it were hiding in the shadows, which plays an important role

*Interior Awareness: Anxiety and Emotion*

in this internal drama. It is the part which gives permission and encouragement to the impulsive part.

As we get more and more parts into play here it helps to give them names so we can keep straight which one we are talking about. It is always a bit problematic to name parts which are conflicted because the names they give themselves are often very different from the names the other parts give them. So let's try not to be too distracted by the names I give them. I will refer to the part which sees the behavior as harmful and tries to alter it as Manager. I will call the impulsive part Pig. And I will refer to the one who gives encouragement and permission to Pig as Coach.

When we first get a sense of Coach it may appear just to be an aspect of Pig, but as we watch for it we generally discover that Pig is just an appetite of some kind, not generally very mature. Coach, on the other hand, can be quite alert and even compassionate. Coach may say, "Wow, you are really stressed! You should take care of yourself. How about a cigarette?" Or it may say, "If you check your bank balance you are just going to get alarmed and it isn't like there is anything you can do about it. Just forget it."

Coach is aware of things we need which are not so immediately apparent. If we could be more conscious of those needs we could then find ways to act to meet those needs in a more robust way. Cigarettes may ease the symptoms of the stress, but if we knew what was causing the stress, and put the energy into addressing the stressors, then we wouldn't feel the need to smoke. So we would do well to hear from Coach what Coach knows about our more subtle needs.

But Coach stays in the shadows. Coach is not likely to just come forward and tell all. Coach has seen the way Manager relates to Pig and, while Pig is resilient and even enjoys a good fight, Coach doesn't want to be vulnerable to getting pummeled by Manager. Coach would have to know that Manager was genuinely curious about what Coach knows and would respect that Coach is also trying to act in a manner that is best for the whole system.

But to Manager, Coach is a shadowy figure that is inciting harmful behavior. Coach is responsible for great harm and must be rooted out and exiled from the system. Manager isn't likely to sit down for tea with Coach. Manager has to see that Coach is actually a potential ally and that, if they can learn to work together, they can both promote the wellbeing of the whole internal system.

So Manager is trying to stop Pig from digging up the vegetable garden and sees Coach as opening the gate. Coach sees Manager as trying to starve Pig and is just trying to get Pig what it needs. The wellbeing of the whole garden depends on Manager and Coach working together to protect the plants while keeping Pig fed. Who can help Manager and Coach learn to work together? That would be the Self at 6° [Intrapersonal-internal: choice]

The 6° Self is able to step back from all of the parts and observe them as equal partners in constructing our awareness and our capacities to respond to various circumstances. Indeed, it is this stepping back and observing which constructs the 6° awareness. And it is from this perspective that healing can occur.

So when we use Discipline #5 to address our needs for Self-Care, it is essential that we let the 6° Self hold the tool and not let Manager have control of it. Manager is tempted to use it to put a harness on Pig and drive Coach further into the shadows. But Self uses Discipline #5 to acknowledge Manager and appreciate Manager's wisdom and care for the system. Self observes Pig's appetites and is curious with Coach about what it is that Coach sees as the deeper needs which must be addressed to find a fuller sense of wellbeing.

## Feelings

Health is about getting what we need.

- From the lens of diet: health comes from eating that which is nutritious and avoiding or cleansing that which is toxic.
- From the lens of exercise: health comes from building a physical frame that is strong and flexible.
- From the lens of relationships: health comes from building relationships which are strong and flexible and in which we attract and create that which nurtures us and in which we can expel or cleanse that which is toxic.

Are you getting what you need? If you just ponder this for a moment, would you say that you are mostly getting what you need, or are you mostly not getting what you need? However you first answer the question, try on the opposite response and see what comes up for you.

When I ask this question in a large enough audience, those who say "I am mostly getting what I need," and those who say, "I am mostly not getting what I need," tend to be about equal in number. Even when we have most of our needs met, we can still find things we need that we don't have. Even when we have huge unmet needs in our lives, we can still find areas in which we are getting what we need. Whether our glass is half empty or half full, it is still fairly close to the half-way mark. We seem to have an innate need to preserve both a sense of what we have for which we are grateful, and a sense of what we don't have for which we strive.

But now let me ask another question, "How do you know?" When I asked whether you were mostly getting what you need or were mostly not getting what you need, to what did you look to answer the question? There are two places we look for answers to this question. We look out, and we look in.

Looking to the outside into the world of our *perception* we notice whether we have a place to sleep tonight, whether we have food to eat, a job to which we go, and friends that look out for us. To answer whether we are getting what we need, we look to the world around us to see if it is as we would have it be. If things are the way we want them to be, then we must be getting what we need. "God's in his heaven—all's right with the world."[22]

Looking inside into the interior world of *interoception*,[23] we notice what feelings arise in us and whether those feelings are good ones (ones we like) or bad ones (ones we don't like). We check and see if we are anxious, or afraid, or satisfied, or scared, or safe, or content, or guilty. If we are having what we consider to be good feelings, then we are generally feeling safe and satisfied and so we assume that we are getting what we need. If we are having what we consider to be bad feelings, then we are experiencing some sort of hurt and we assume that we are not getting what we need.

If we want to know what we need, we have to be exquisitely sensitive to what is going on around us and within us. And why would we want to pay attention to what we need? Because the chances of my getting what I need rise dramatically the more I know about what I need... and the more I create what I need, the healthier I become.

---

22   A line sung by a little Italian girl, Pippa, in the poem "Pippa Passes," by Robert Browning.

23   This is a term I was introduced to at the IFS Annual Conference in October of 2007 during a plenary address by Bessel van der Kolk. Interoception refers to the process of looking inward and is thus in a sense the opposite of perception.

In the exterior we focus on attending to the conflicts that arise in our relationships with those around us. We notice that they are not as we would have them be and we are not as they want us to be. These conflicts are windows into what we need—especially the ones about which we have strong feelings and which happen over and over again. In fact, simply by resolving these conflicts we create what we need.

In the interior we focus on attending to the feelings that arise in ourselves in the context of our relationships with others, especially those with whom we are closest. We notice that our interior world is easily as varied and diverse and complicated as the world around us. For most of us this is an exploration of uncharted territory because we live in a culture that does not encourage this sort of exploration. Indeed, we sometimes refer to this sort of inquiry as "navel gazing."

We disparage explorations of our feelings because we imagine that emotions are less valuable than reason, and we may even believe that emotion can corrupt the pure light of reason which can illuminate the solution to all of our problems. If we allow ourselves to be too conscious of our emotions, we fear, those feelings will hide the salvation that reason can provide.

In fact, as we will see, while emotions and thoughts are different, and it is true that there is a sense in which thoughts are above emotions because our thinking, judging, reasoning rests on the rock of our emotional connection to our experience; nevertheless, if we are not fully aware of and appreciative of our emotions, then our judgments have a weak foundation. The denial of our emotions weakens our capacity to make sound judgments.

However much Larry (from Chapter Seven) would like to be someone who can rise to a 4° [Interpersonal-relational: choice] way of being to address his relationship with his mother when he has an unacknowledged birthday, he can't actually do what he wants to do. He is too angry. His feelings are too strong to let him act creatively.

## What Feelings Are: Data and Energy

These are all concepts to which we will return but, for the moment, let's look at the relationship between knowing what we need and our familiarity with our feelings. How does knowing how I feel help me know what I need and help me act in ways that create what I need?

As I write these words it is winter, a blustery day in February. It is cold and I notice that I am cold. I have a feeling, in this case a sensation of cold. Feelings are data. They are data about the qualities in the relationship between my "I am," the core sense of my identity, and the world around me. In the case of sensations, these are data about the relationship between "I am" and the physical world in which I find myself. Because "I am cold," I will now act in ways that create what I need. I can identify that cold doesn't satisfy me. What I need is warmth. I identify that there are at least two immediate options I can follow. I can flip on the space heater or I can put on a sweater. I make a choice and see if my actions create what I need by continuing to monitor my sensations. This is what feelings are for: to give us the data about what we need, or that we don't have what we need, so that we can act in ways to create what we need.

"Sensation" is one category of internal experience. There are many different ways to construct a typology of interior experience. Deepak Chopra in one of his books lists ten domains of consciousness. For our current purposes, that is a bit too complicated. Ten are more than we need for now. We start with just four. Later we add another two. We use the acronym STEW to remind us of the four primary interior domains. Hopefully this is a helpful mnemonic as we often say we are stewing about something when we are stirred up.

**Sensation:** I feel cold.
**Thought:** I feel like I am being mistreated.
**Emotion:** I feel hurt and angry.
**Wish:** I feel like taking a walk.

Whenever you are stewing about something, remind yourself to identify each of the four domains in what you are worrying about. What are your Sensations, Thoughts, Emotions and Wishes? Notice that each of the four interior domains is a feeling, or at least we can speak of it as such, but each is distinctly different. A *wish* is very different from a *sensation*. A *thought* is very different from an *emotion*.

If something upsetting happens I am likely to feel bad. But is this a sensation, a thought, an emotion, or a wish? It can easily be all four.

Suppose I finally get around to registering for the semester and find out that the last class I need to take to finish my degree is already filled. There is a sinking feeling in the pit of my stomach. I feel nauseous (sensation). I know that if I can't find a way to get into that class, I will be delayed six months in graduating (thought). I am furious at myself for not getting around to registering sooner (emotion). I wish I weren't such a procrastinator (wish).

The strength of the sensations and the emotions help me gauge the urgency of this issue and motivate me to act. The thought about delaying graduation six months reminds me that the need is not just about this class, but about the degree and the employment opportunities that I believe will open up once I have it. And the wish reminds me that there are certain qualities of self care that I can address where I pay more attention to what I need and I don't put off acting in ways that get me what I need.

The creation of this internal awareness we call *feelings* is something which develops as we mature. We have placed these in an order which spells STEW and thus makes it an acronym which is easier to remember, but the developmental sequence is actually from *sensation* to *emotion* to *thought* to *wish*.

- Even before we are born we have *sensations*. Though we don't have a conscious memory of our awareness before birth, we hear what music Mom is dancing to and the voice of Dad as they talk in bed.
- Once we are born we now have a relationship and that relationship has qualities which cause *emotions* to arise within us. We come to recognize mom's face and we feel joy. We have a pain in our stomach and we feel fear. We hear footsteps outside our bedroom door at night when we cry and we feel hope.
- We come to associate the sound with the presence of someone in the hall. We have built a cognitive correlation between the sound and the person coming into the room. We observe events and ascribe meaning to them. We become able to *think*.
- And, having thoughts, we begin to anticipate what might happen and even to consider what we might *want* to have happen. We become aware of desires and *wishes*.

So we develop from *sensations* to *emotions* to *thoughts* to *wishes*. Each stage of awareness depends on the one below it. My wish that someone would care for me in the middle of the night depends upon my thought that there are parents nearby who can hear my cry and my hope that they will respond to me; all of this is supported by my sensation of hearing footsteps in the hallway.

In the 70's a friend of mine lived in a cooperative house in which there was a sensory deprivation tank. It was a big tub in a dark and quiet basement filled with salt water heated to 95°. When one would lie in the water in the dark and the quiet with no sensory input for a period of time, images would begin to appear in one's awareness. It was a sort of acid trip without the acid.

It seems that, without sensory input, we begin to lose our upper level cognitive functions. The sensory deprivation tank was intended in that setting to be recreational or even spiritually enlightening. But sensory deprivation is also a form of torture called solitary confinement. We need sensory stimulation to have emotional awareness to have cognitive functioning to know what we need.

So, if I want to get what I need, I have to know what I need and, thus, notice when I am not getting what I need. I know I am not getting what I need (or perhaps I am getting what I don't need) whenever I have a "bad" feeling. I put bad in quotes here because the feeling itself isn't bad. It is good data. It is just a feeling I don't like having. If I step into the street and look up and see a bus barreling down on me, I feel fear, I step back out of the street. I don't like being afraid, but I like getting squashed by busses even less. The fear is my friend.

"Good" feelings also give me information about what I need. When I feel safe or satisfied I am getting feedback that the current situation is healthy for me. If I can figure out what is working and what I did to create it, I can recreate the situation in the future.

Knowing how I feel helps me know what I need. Ideally, once I know what I need, I know what to do to create what I need. But I am not likely to create what I need without knowing what that is and I won't know the need unless I know what I feel.

So feelings in general and emotions in particular are information about the qualities in our relationships. They help us know what is currently going on and can guide us in determining what we need. They are also a source of energy. The fear gives me the strength to step out of the street.

**Emotional Energy**

The energy that emotions carry is not the same kind of energy we get from filling our gas tanks or having a good meal and a good night's sleep. When I am low on gas I know that my car is about to run out of energy and I need to stop and get gas. When I have had a long hard day I am tired and hungry and I need to eat and sleep. Physical energy is finite. When we run low, we have to fill up.

Emotional energy is infinite. We don't run out of love if we love too much. We cannot hate someone so much that we quit hating them. I may become accustomed to being afraid of someone, but I don't stop being afraid. Emotional energy is an eternal resource. It is *prana* in Sanskrit and *chi* or *qi* in Chinese. It is the force of the universe present in all things and flowing through everything, most especially through us.

One way I sometimes think about this energy is that it is like the vision that Neo had at the end of the *Matrix* when he became able to see the foundation of the material world as a flow of 1's and 0's coming down through the walls with an eerie green glow. All matter is energy.

When we are in a harmonious relationship to everything which arises around us we can be open and relaxed and can allow the energy to flow fully and freely. We have an experience of shalom. But when something happens which invokes esuba we feel fear or anger or sadness and we constrict around the flow of energy. This constriction impedes the flow of energy. Just as when there is resistance in a wire which is conducting electricity, we start to get hot. The constriction causes a change in the quality of the energy which can both draw our attention to the problem and can be a source of energy for addressing it.

## Complex Feelings

Feelings are an internal awareness which gives us information about our relationships and which prompts us to act on our own behalf. They are data and they are energy.

There are many typologies of feelings. We have already suggested that when we are stewing about our experience we might remember to attend to our sensations, thoughts, emotions and wishes. But especially as we look at becoming aware of our emotions, we need a bit more help.

As a culture we are generally aware of what we want. We have a lot of permission to be conscious of our desires. If you don't know what you want, simply turn on the TV and you will find lots of advertisers telling what you should want.

We are also aware of what we think. Most of what we do in formal education is about learning how to think. We learn what symbols mean and how to manipulate them to create meaning. Reading, writing and arithmetic are all about symbol manipulation for the creation of meaning.

When we get down to emotions we start having more trouble. While there have been some efforts to teach emotional awareness as a part of our schools (as with the Magic Circle[24]) for the most part we are dismissive of the value of emotion. After all, it is not rational. And rational is good.

And when we get to the level of sensations we tend to be dismissive of our more subtle sensations. We allow these subtle sensations to inform our speech from time to time, as in when we say things like, "that guy is a real pain in the neck," but we don't generally feel the pain that is appearing in our neck as a source of information about how we are being informed by our surroundings. More often we dismiss such sensations as though they are not genuine. We trivialize what are known as psycho-somatic complaints by telling ourselves they are not real; they are all in our heads.

Some people allow themselves to be aware of these subtle sensations and to value and appreciate them and to expand their capacity to experience them. We sometimes refer to these people as Intuitives. They know without clearly knowing how they know or, at least, it is not a cognitive knowing. They just have a feeling, a sensation. When we allow ourselves to attend more fully to the subtle sensations and emotions which come to us we become more and more intuitive.

In the same way as we allow our thoughts and our wishes to create a fuller vision for how we want things to be, we become more imaginative. We now have six kinds of internal awareness: *sensations* and *emotions* which support *intuition*, and *thoughts* and *wishes* which support *imagination*.

---

24    Magic Circle is a process developed 40 years ago for teaching young children how to identify and name their emotions.

| Wishes Thoughts | Imagination |
|---|---|
| Emotions Sensations | Intuition |

If we are to develop a greater capacity to create what we need and what the rest of the planet needs, we have to nurture a greater capacity to know our feelings. The place we have the greatest difficulty is with our emotions. We live in a culture which is very disparaging of emotions. This is especially true for men, but we can also be cruel to women's emotional expression as when we label them hysterical.

It helps if we use our capacity to think to support our awareness of our emotions. To that end I suggest a cognitive map for helping us know what emotions we are having.

As we have already noted, there are really no bad feelings; there are just feelings we don't like having. Some emotions arise from events in which we get what we need and some from events in which we don't get what we need. Some emotions arise from events in which we get what we don't need and some from events in which we don't get what we don't need. This is confusing so let's create a chart.

| **Do** get what we **do** need = | Satisfaction |
|---|---|
| **Don't** get what we **don't** need = | Safety |
| **Don't** get what we **do** need = | Hurt |
| **Do** get what we *don't* need = | Hurt |

We therefore have the good feelings of safety and satisfaction and the bad feeling of hurt. This is our fundamental distinction between emotions. When we don't get what we need we are hurt and, when we do, we are safe and satisfied.

Remembering that our goal is to identify what we need by attending to what we are feeling when we are not getting it, we want to give special attention to the bad feelings… to hurt. As we do this we notice that hurt can happen in the past, the present, or the future. Hurt can be something done to us or something we do to others. So we can identify five distinct "bad" feelings.

When we have a present experience of getting what we don't need or not getting what we do need we feel *hurt*.

When we have an experience of anticipating that in the future we will be hurt we feel *fear*.

When we remember a time in the past when we lost something which was precious to us or didn't get something we needed we feel *sadness*.

When we are hurt by what we experience as the result of the choice of another we feel *anger*.

When we cause hurt in another by a choice we have made we feel *guilt*.

Let's make another chart just so we have these five feelings in front of us.

Fear

Anger     Hurt     Guilt

Sadness

Each of these words for an emotion is but the title of a category of feelings. Under *fear* we find worry, alarm, terror... Under *anger* we find peeved, mad, furious... and so on. Each of these other feelings are derivatives of the larger feeling, variations that are more or less intense or otherwise showing a gradation of color. We may think of emotions as colors on a painter's pallet. Each of them may blend with others to create new shades and gradations of emotion.

When we feel "bad," it is because we are feeling one or more of these feelings or their derivatives. In fact, we are probably feeling many of these feelings at the same time.

> *After Joe was late to work, having stopped to get gas, he decided that, instead of brooding and blaming, he would actually use the feelings coming up in him to get to know his interior better.*

> *He knew he was mad. He was angry that the boys were so hard to get going in the morning and he was mad at himself for not having noticed that the car was almost out of gas and he was mad at his boss for being so rigid about the starting time.*

> *He was afraid that he was not going to get a handle on the morning routine and he would continue to be late and that might result in him losing this job or at least not getting a raise.*

*He was hurt that Jane didn't seem to appreciate how hard this was for him in the morning and that his efforts to be a better dad to his boys than his own father had been for him were not being appreciated.*

*He was sad that his relationship with Jane had become strained by her having to get to work so early that she couldn't be there to help and he missed the close time they used to have in the morning.*

*And he felt guilty that he was so short with the boys and didn't give Jane appreciation for how hard she was working.*

When Joe sits with his "bad" feelings he discovers rich and vivid information about how the qualities in his relationships are not as he would have them be. He can respond differently in ways which create more of what he needs by attending to each of these emotions. If he doesn't know what he is feeling he doesn't know what he needs and he can't do anything to address them short of going out with his buddies and getting drunk.

Our "bad" feelings, when they are not named and addressed, can be the stimulus for bad behavior. When we feel bad we have a tendency to do bad things. Consider for a moment a time when you acted in a manner you regret which resulted in harm to someone you care about.

Now, try to remember what you were feeling just before you made the choice you regret. This feeling is different for different people, but in the years I have been posing this question I would guess that about 90% of the time the answer is anger.

## Working with the Passions: Anger and Desire

Even the most casual observer will notice that the way we relate to our own anger can be seriously destructive. High school students arm themselves and then attack the sources of their humiliation like commandos on a raid against a military stronghold. Drivers force each other off the road to pummel each other in fits of road rage. Husbands murder their wives and children and then turn the weapon on themselves. Each of these actions is an expression of futility and fury.

In the self-help section of the local bookstore one can find shelf upon shelf of books which purport to offer expert guidance on how to manage one's anger. I have surveyed a good many of these and, while many of them are excellent, nearly all of them miss a really important distinction that is central to being able to manage our behavior when we are angry. The *emotion* of anger is not the same as the *behavior* of anger.

This distinction is partially obscured by the fact that we use the same word (anger) to refer to both phenomenon and partially by the fact that both so often appear together. It is not a surprise that most people don't see the difference. But it becomes an essential distinction if we are to have a healthy relationship with our anger.

Everyone is angry from time to time. Indeed, everyone has anger all the time. This is a distinction I learned from some very angry men in my years working with aggressive offenders. Try this exploration for yourself.

> *Think of a time when you were angry. Try to remember the time when you were the most angry you have ever been. Bring to mind as clearly as you can the sensations you had when you were so angry.*

You are probably not so angry now about whatever invoked your rage then, but you may well recover a part of the feeling you had then. You may even find that you still have some anger about that or other events. So even though you no longer *are* angry, you still *have* anger. This recognition that we are not always angry but we always have anger is very important. It is the difference between *being angry* and *having anger*.

Some of you are at this point saying to yourselves, "No, I don't have any anger. Yes, I remember when I was angry but it is completely gone and not a shred of it remains." I know that many have this response and we will come back to address this in a moment. But for now, let me just ask you to remain curious about where your anger goes when it goes away.

We are very uncomfortable with anger. We have been angry and we have acted on the anger in ways we regret. We don't want to be angry because we don't want to do those angry things. We are also uncomfortable with other people's anger.  We have been around folks who were angry and their behavior was scary and harmful and the trauma of that angry behavior keeps coming back to us in distressing ways.  And we are uncomfortable with the ways others treat us when we are angry.  They criticize or shun us when they see that we are angry so we want to protect ourselves by not being angry.  So, no, we are not angry.

*I am someone who grew up in a family where anger was forbidden.  I used to say that I could count on one hand the number of times I saw my dad get angry, but I can't even think of five events.  So I was proud of the fact that I never got angry.*

*One summer when I was in seminary in my early 20's I was a leader for a group of teens who were working in a poor community in the Bootheel of Missouri.  There were a great many things about the experience which were stressful for me but the largest was that I felt such a great responsibility for the welfare of the kids and the project and I had so little power to make things go well.*

*One day during the lunch break all of the kids and leaders were in the community center eating and planning for the work we would do that afternoon.  Out on the porch of the building a nine year old kid was walking up and down with a foot long piece of pipe running it along the slats of the railing and making a loud tatatatata.  I went out to him to ask respectfully that he not do this as it made it impossible for us to hear.  He looked at me and stopped but didn't say anything.*

*This kid was very curious about our presence in his community and was generally friendly and helpful.  I had no sense that he was trying to cause trouble, he was hoping to get attention.  I went back inside.*

*Not two minutes later the noise resumed. Tatatatatat.  I went back out and raised my voice to him.  "Look, we are trying to meet in here and we can't do it with you making such a racket out here."*

*He stepped toward me with a defiant shrug and waived the pipe at me.*

*I snatched it out of his hand and fiercely hissed at him, "If you don't keep it quiet out here I am going to wrap this around your neck."*

*I turned and went inside. He remained quiet.*

*I was appalled. I couldn't believe what I had just done. I didn't know who I was. I felt horribly guilty and terrified about the harm I must have just done to this kid because I lost it. I wasn't sure I could face him but I suspected I would never see him again.*

*But when we went out to get back to work after lunch he was there. He was cheerful and helpful as always. It seemed my outburst had had no effect on him. If anything, he seemed more at ease.*

This event occurred nearly forty years ago but I remember it vividly. I suspect the kid didn't remember it a day later. I suspect this was not at all unusual for him. He was quite accustomed to adults being angry and threatening to him. I imagine my anger was pretty tame to him. I was just some adult letting him know where the boundaries were.

But for me the event was staggering. I had been more visibly angry than I could ever remember having been. I knew that my anger was not primarily at him. He was just a kid being a kid. I was angry about a whole host of other things and I had taken it out on him. I was mortified. And, it seemed that what I had done was not only not harmful to the kid, it actually seemed to reassure him. This did not fit the perceptual map I grew up with. This didn't make sense.

Anger is a natural and normal human emotion that arises whenever we experience some sort of hurt as a consequence of what we perceive to be a choice by another. Anger is a cue that we should protect ourselves from harm and we should clarify the choices that others are making so that we might determine if we can be safe in relationship to them. If we can be aware of the emotion, decode the data it contains, and then use the energy contained in the emotion to propel us to act in creative ways, we can restore safety and satisfaction. We can address the esuba and restore shalom.

But that is not what we have learned to do with the emotion. Instead, we are so alienated from our emotions that when anger arises we get scared. We are not only afraid of the event which has brought forth the emotion, we are afraid of the emotion itself. We are afraid of what we will do when we allow ourselves to feel fully the feeling.

So we stuff it. We have a kind of emotional stuff sack into which we put all sorts of unwanted feelings. Typically most of the feelings in the sack are anger and its derivatives.

*It had already been a rough day, but Joe's boss pulled him aside as he was leaving work to tell him that his performance that day was not up to company standards. Joe muttered under his breath as he went out to his car, "He's just an asshole."*

*Joe put the key in and turned it over and the car cranked but wouldn't fire. He knew it was overdue for a tune up but he just hadn't found the time. When it finally started there was a cloud of smoke and Joe suspected everyone was looking at him.*

*Traffic was typically bad on the way home and when he pulled into the driveway, there was Jack's tricycle sitting blocking the way. He had told him time and again to put that damn thing away. After a vivid fantasy of just pushing it out of the way with the car, he got out to move it up by the house. Once he got the car parked, he turned it off but it wouldn't quit. It dieseled on for a couple of seconds making a foul smell.*

*He grabbed a beer out of the box in the kitchen and plopped down into the easy chair in the living room to watch the Channel 5 news.*

*Jane had an early day and had picked up the boys and had heard a promo for a segment on the Channel 2 news she really wanted to see. She rushed into the room and picked up the remote. When she switched the channel, Joe exploded. He was not able to control his boss, his car, or his kids, but he could for sure control what TV show he was watching.*

Joe had taken all of the feelings of anger from each of these events and crammed them into his emotional stuff sack, but when Jane changed the channel some part of him said, "This is something I can be angry about." He reached into the sack for a pinch of anger but came out with a fistful. Joe overreacted.

## Anger Management

In 2003, a movie starring Adam Sandler and Jack Nicholson tried to make the business of anger management into a comedy. To the extent to which it succeeded, it did not accurately portray what happens in a typical anger management program. Nearly every major city has some sort of anger management program available for people who have allowed their anger to get them into trouble because of bar fights, road rage, altercations at work, and domestic disturbances. These programs offer a set curriculum in a group or class setting.

Most of these programs approach the mismanagement of anger as an impulse control problem and teach a set of techniques for building greater self-control. They can be as brief as a one day workshop to a series of meetings spanning many weeks. Domestic violence intervention programs tend to be much longer, typically lasting six months to a year; these programs also understand that the dynamics of intimate partner abuse are about much more than anger out of control.

There is some controversy within the anger management industry about how best to intervene and what techniques help and which actually make things worse. These disagreements come from different perspectives on the "problem" of anger and what causes it and what we can do about it. Because anger is so often a consequence of conflict, and can be such an impediment to addressing conflict creatively, we improve our chances of acting assertively if we can appropriately manage our behavior when we are angry.

Since we are looking to exercise better self-control, let us begin by noticing what is and is not within our control. We can control whether we pay attention to what we are feeling. We cannot control what we are feeling. We can control what we do. We cannot control what others choose to do.

Joe could not control whether his boss chose to give him critical feedback as he was leaving work. He could control how he responded to that feedback. He couldn't control whether he was hurt or scared or angry about the feedback. He could control whether he noticed his feelings.

Joe tried to get the car to start and found that hard to do. He knows the problems with the car's performance are a consequence of needing a tune up. He could decide to work on the car instead of drinking beer and watching TV. Joe cannot control whether Jack leaves his tricycle in the driveway or whether Jane changes the channel, but he can decide to move the trike without driving the car over it and he can talk to Jane about his feelings.

Still, to do so requires that Joe know what he is feeling and believe that talking with Jane about them would be beneficial; he also needs to trust that he can talk about his feelings without acting them out. How can Joe grow to a place where he can do this? What techniques can help him become the person he wants to be?

## Two Schools of Thought: Vent it or Soothe It

We all know the pent up feeling we get when we are very angry. Many of us have let it out by slamming doors, yelling, pounding our fists, and even punching walls. When we take the energy of the emotion of anger and express it physically we find that we get some sense of release and relief.

We also know, not only from our own experience but from extensive research, that when we keep our anger bottled up it can be very harmful to our health causing high blood pressure, back problems, irritable bowel syndrome, and increased risk of heart attack. Keeping our anger contained is toxic to us.

There are many techniques for letting the energy out through yelling, punching a bag, or exercising in a controlled way. The goal is to channel the energy safely. But how safe is it? Some studies indicate that such practices actually increase the prevalence of aggressive behavior. It seems that the more we practice being angry, the angrier we get.

Instead we can practice letting it go through breathing exercises, listening to our hearts, and meditating. This school of thought builds upon the observation that we construct our experience by choosing that to which we pay attention. By learning to consciously direct our attention we can attract the positive qualities we need and avoid those which are toxic to us.

If we focus our attention on the things we cannot change, we begin to feel helpless and hopeless. If we focus on the things which are harming us and those who are causing those events, we become hurt and angry. If we focus on all of the ways our needs are being satisfied we become grateful and at peace. Our interior choices construct our relationship to the world around us.

So it seems that both schools of thought have something to offer, but each has concerns about the other. The *vent it* school argues that not noticing what is bothering us doesn't make the problem go away. Denial is not a durable solution. The *soothe it* school argues that acting out the anger actually creates many of the problems it is designed to address. We drive up our blood pressure and become more aggressive when we focus on our anger. So what might we do to draw from the strengths of both perspectives?

Let us remember that anger is a natural, normal, and healthy emotion which arises in all of us. It is the awareness that we are being hurt by someone's choices. From time to time we become angry, which is to say that some event happens which raises the awareness of our anger and it becomes foremost in our attention. But even when we are not angry, we still have anger. Indeed, we have all of our feelings all the time. They are just not all arising for us at any given moment such that they are all at the top of our awareness.

Let us also remember that our emotions are both information and energy. Emotions are data about the relationship between the locus of our identity— the place from which our awareness of Self is currently residing—and the rest of the world—whatever we are experiencing as not-Self. And emotions are energy which we can harness to address the qualities in the relationship.

When we are aware of our emotions and the circumstances which give rise to them we can act in ways which construct what we need while also creating the circumstances which are best for others. When we don't acknowledge our feelings they continue to have an effect on us, but we are not free to respond creatively to that effect. We are likely to behave in ways which are harmful.

Some of us *act out*. We take the energy we have stored in the emotional stuff sack and we shower others with it when they do something which breaks the threshold of our anger. We stuff it and stuff it and stuff it and then, when someone does something which is either big enough that we allow ourselves to feel our anger, or safe enough that we allow ourselves to feel our anger, we reach into the sack for a pinch of anger and come out with a fistful.

Or, when we decide it is not safe for us to be aware of our anger, we may become passive-aggressive. We don't allow ourselves to be aware that we are angry but we make unintended choices which make others angry with us. We take our anger and give it to others so they can express it for us.

Some of us *act in*. We take the energy we have stored in the emotional stuff sack and we keep it in so tight for so long that is starts to eat its way through the sack. The sack becomes porous and it leaks into our unconscious in toxic persistent ways. We become harshly critical of ourselves and others, we develop physical ailments—often in our bowels or our back or with migraines, and we become depressed. Sometimes we may even actively harm ourselves through cutting, eating disorders, use of drugs, or other forms of self-harm.

Instead, if we have a healthy relationship with our anger, we can notice whenever anger arises and be grateful that it is informing us about some quality of harm which is occurring to us. We can fully feel the feelings, know what is causing them, know what we need, and act creatively to evoke those qualities.

## The Anger Workout

We introduced the Anger Workout as our second discipline back in Chapter One. If you have been doing it ever since, great! But you probably haven't been. My experience is that most folks have to be confronted several times by how beneficial the Anger Workout is before they begin to take it on. So let's explore this discipline a bit more deeply now that we have some new perspectives through which to look at it.

First of all, the purpose of the Anger Workout is not to be less angry. There is nothing wrong with any of our feelings, including anger. Anger is a necessary and helpful emotion. Doing the Anger Workout consistently does not make you less angry, but it does make you more comfortable with your anger and more likely to act creatively when you are most angry.

Quite often in the Building Healthy Relationships program participants identify patterns of conflict in significant relationships, are able to describe clearly what it is that is happening and how it affects her or him, and have a clear idea of how he or she would like to act to create what they need. They then find they are not able to do what they decided to do. Their anger is in the way. (This is just what happened to Larry in the previous chapter.) For all the ability some calm and rational part of them has to envision a creative intervention, there is another part which takes over and trashes the calm and the creative.

As much as we may be able to pay attention to whatever is arising in our 1° awareness, and make 2° choices to move us to a more satisfying experience, fully attending to the 3° expectations built into our relationships, and deciding how and who we want to be at 4°, we may find that we can't do what we have decided to do. We may be ambushed by a conflict between parts of ourselves we can only become aware of at 5°.

While it is certainly true that some of us tend to *act out* aggressively or passive-aggressively, and some of us tend to *act in* in ways that are self-harming, it is also true that most of us have parts of ourselves who have each of these responses to anger. From time to time in different relationships under different circumstances we may be very timid or very much up in the face of the other. Joe may scream at Jane when she changes the channel he is watching but not be able to find his voice when his boss is criticizing him.

The purpose of the Anger Workout is to identify and address those parts which are most likely to sabotage our most creative efforts at conflict resolution. Vowing to not let that part of ourselves act out only works in the short run if it works at all. And keeping it in the bag takes a lot of emotional energy which could be better used on other things.

One very common anger management technique is to count to ten. The idea is that as we become aware of being angry, we slow things down by counting to ten before we act. We do this to interrupt the impulsivity of the angry part. Some people have what is known as a "short temper." By this we mean that the time between their awareness that they are angry and the time they act on the anger is short. They are impulsive. Counting to ten stretches out the time so they are less impulsive.

There is another way to address having a short temper. Rather than setting back the time at which we act on the anger, we can set forward the awareness of the anger. How would it be to be more aware of the anger sooner?

Most people respond to this question out of the learned response that we don't want to be angry. Remember, anger is an emotion that naturally arises whenever we are hurt by the choices of others. Do you ever get hurt by others? Of course. Do you want to take care of yourself when that happens? I hope so. To do that we must notice when we are angry.

Anger is something that comes in varying intensity. The more we are hurt, the more angry we are. The more we perceive the hurt to be the conscious choice of another, the more angry we are. If someone hurts us accidentally we are not typically nearly as angry as if they are doing so intentionally.

So some events just bother us, some irritate us, some get us peeved, others piss us off; they may make us mad, furious, or enraged. Anger comes in many intensities. Most of us find it easier to be creative when we are bothered than when we are furious. So the more quickly we can identify the anger and catch it before it gets too big, the more easily we are able to respond instead of react.

This is all part of what doing the Anger Workout routinely does for us. Are you interested? Then let's look at what it would take for you to begin to include this discipline in your life.

An Anger Workout is a physical activity done everyday for at least five minutes at a time. It is something which is safe for you and others during which you are as keenly aware of your anger as possible. Let's tease this apart.

*Fully Aware*

Think of a time when you were as angry as you ever remember being. Try to bring to mind your most furious moment. As you remember it, allow yourself to remember your STEW: sensations, thoughts, emotions and wishes.

Let's look at this in reverse order of the development of our feelings.

You certainly can remember for what you were wishing. Whatever was happening was not what you wanted and you probably have a clear idea of how you wanted things to be different.

You had some thoughts about what was happening. You looked at what was happening and what it meant and you may have had some confusion, but you knew that what was happening wasn't right.

When it came to your emotions, you were certainly angry, but at this point you most probably had some other emotions as well. Were you scared, or sad, or hurt?

What sensations were you having, not from the hurt the other caused, but from the anger itself? What is that like for you when you are very angry? Do you feel it in your chest, your head, your shoulders, your gut... Where do you carry your anger?

*When Joe settles in to watch the news and Jane comes in and changes the channel, he knows that he wants to watch the channel he chose and he wants the respect of his wife to honor his choices. He thinks that the one who is watching first should get priority and anyone who wants something different should ask. He thinks she is out of line. He feels angry, but he is also hurt that she doesn't consider him and is a bit afraid that he is going to get run over. But when it comes down to the sensations, he is stuck. He has to sit with it for a bit before he notices that it is a hollow feeling in his chest and that reminds him of the sensation he had when his dad yelled at him as a kid.*

So the intention of the Anger Workout is to get as far down the developmental ladder as possible and try to get to the sensation itself. This is not about solving a problem... it is about connecting to an experience. It is about getting grounded in our Selves.

## Safe

Doing the Anger Workout has to be safe, both for you and for those around you. This means it can't be something which puts you at risk for getting harmed by others but it also means it can't be something which increases the risk of harm to others.

If you are someone who hits people when you are angry, don't select punching a bag or hitting a wall as an activity for your Anger Workout. Don't rehearse violence. If you are someone who yells at people when you are angry, don't yell as an Anger Workout. On the other hand, if you are someone who clams up and can't speak when you are angry, then doing an Anger Workout in which you go to a small room in the basement and scream may be a very good thing.

Don't do something which invites others to criticize you or which may cause you to feel embarrassed. One participant in the Building Healthy Relationships group decided to take a walk as his Anger Workout but he had trouble connecting with his anger. He discovered that if he growled while he walked it made it much easier for him to get connected to his feelings. He had to be careful, however, not to growl when anyone else was around.

In general it is best to do the Anger Workout alone. Certainly don't do it around anyone you are angry with or anyone who fears your anger. That isn't fair to them and it harms your relationship to them. It is probably best to not even do the Anger Workout while you walk your dog. Pets, especially dogs, can be very sensitive to our emotions. It freaks out the dog and it distracts you from giving all of your attention to your anger.

## Routine

Do the Anger Workout with at least the same regularity as you brush your teeth. It helps if you can do the same thing at the same time for the same length of time but the most important thing is to do it every day.

Don't wait until you are angry. It may help to do something when you are angry to help you manage your behavior but that is not an Anger Workout. Do it everyday, at the same time each day, whether you are initially aware of the anger or not.

Some days you will have no trouble at all finding your anger. It will be in your face. Other days you will look and look and not find any. Do the Anger Workout anyway. The part that carries your anger is there somewhere and it may be hiding, but it is there. Let it know you are looking for it.

In the description of the Anger Workout in the Appendix (all of the Disciplines are listed in the Appendix) you will find a reference to the Anger Dog. It helps some people to think of the part which carries our anger as being like a big dog... a working dog. Its job is to protect us but sometimes it gets carried away and misbehaves. We have to train it to mind us. We do that by exercising it everyday. Exercise your Anger Dog by doing the Anger Workout. Some people do the Anger Workout as part of a physical workout. They call their anger to mind as they lift weights or ride a stationary bicycle. Some people run, some walk, some just sit and breathe. Breathe in anger... breathe out peace.

> One participant in the Building Healthy Relationships class decided to do a breathing Anger Workout for his road rage. He was almost always angry on the road but he had done some things he thought were stupid and was trying to get a handle on his anger. He would sit and follow his breath for five minutes a day, breathing in and feeling as furious as he could... and then he would breathe out and allow his body to be filled with peace.

*One evening he came to class very excited about his anger work. He had been on the highway and some guy pulled across his lane right in front of him to get to an exit. He caught his breath in surprise and then, as he let it out, he found himself filling with peace. He easily saw that his response to this guy was a choice and he didn't have to chase him down and beat in his windows with a baseball bat.*

His habit of flying into rage at others was broken by creating a link between the act of breathing and being in control of his behavior when angry. He felt the anger, but he didn't allow the anger to control him.

## Promises of the Anger Workout

If you do the Anger Workout consistently—and for most folks this means every day for at least two weeks—you will begin to see some changes in your relationship with your anger.

The first thing you notice is that you always have some anger. There is no time at which there is nothing happening in your life about which you feel some anger. But even as you become more aware of the anger, it gets harder to find. The huge things that used to get you so riled up begin to fade in intensity.

The second thing you notice is that when an event happens which triggers your anger you are only angry about that event. You do not find yourself piling on all of the other things you have been stuffing in your anger sack, because you are no longer stuffing the anger. You are much more "in the moment" with your anger.

And the third thing you will notice is that when you are angry, as you are addressing the cause of the anger, you are much more calm and creative. You may even choose to address the source of the anger without letting on to others that you are angry. Or perhaps you decide to let the other know. But it is your choice.

# Passion: The Energy of Emotion

Emotion contains both information and energy. The information communicated by an emotion is often easier to appreciate than is the energy which the emotions open up to us. In order to explore a bit more deeply the notion that emotion can give us energy, let's give some attention to this feature of our awareness in its most potent form; the passions.

All emotion potentially opens us to the energy of life… to prana or chi. But some emotions are particularly potent. Anger is one of these which, when very strong, can be termed a *passion*. Any strongly felt emotion is a passion.

Anger can be a particularly strong "negative" emotion in that it is the feeling we have when we are *hurt* as a consequence of the choices of another. As hurt is the central feature of what we call "bad" feelings, and safety and satisfaction are the central feature of what we call "good" feelings, what might we call the emotion which arises when we experience safety and satisfaction as a consequence of the choices of another? Most especially, how do we feel toward those whose choices evoke in us the feelings of safety and satisfaction?

We certainly like those people, we want to be around them, we feel attracted to them, we may even say that we love them. But we are going to be careful with the word "love" because its meanings are so numerous. Acknowledging there are many words we could choose here, we are selecting *desire* as the word for the emotion which arises for us when we experience safety and satisfaction as a result of what we believe to be the choices of another.

We may see anger and desire as polar opposites. They both arise from choices others make, but one comes from bad feelings and one from good feelings. Certainly they are not mutually exclusive. It is not as though we either feel anger or we feel desire. We can easily feel them in the context of the same relationship and we can even feel them both at the same time in the same relationship. When the other is very important to us… when this is a significant relationship (when we spend a lot of time together, have strong feelings about the other, and the other makes choices which have a big impact on us) then we are likely to have both anger and desire arise together.

Because of the co-occurrence of anger and desire in our most significant relationships and because of the impact of these passions on the ways conflicts appear to us and the ways we typically react to those conflicts, we are helped to explore more deeply the interplay between them.

As we use the word *anger* to describe both an emotion and the behavior we manifest when we feel that emotion, what might be some words which describe our behavior when what we feel is *desire*? When we desire someone we may show it by some gesture of affection. And if the affection is mutual and the sexual orientation is harmonious, we may even express the desire through sexual affection leading to intercourse.

We assume that a couple expressing mutual affection in sexual ways is feeling the emotion of desire. They want each other. We also assume that a couple expressing mutual depreciation by yelling insults at each other is feeling the emotion of anger. And we can easily imagine the same couple at different times doing both. Indeed, we may have been a part of such a couple.

But is it a part of your experience to have been in a couple in which both anger and desire were having passionate expression at the same time? It may not have been your personal experience to have been caught up in the throes of rage and desire at the same time, but there is little doubt that this happens and even happens often. We get the emotions of anger and desire all tangled up, and we especially get the behaviors of anger and sex tangled up.

If you have any doubt that anger and sex get all caught up in each other, simply consider what is both the most common and the most vile of all curse words, *fuck*. While the origins of the word point to sexual intercourse, when one person hisses at another, "I'm going to fuck you up," he isn't talking about making love.

As you consider your own awareness of how anger and desire arise for you and are expressed in your most significant relationships, I would urge you to look at how anger and sex fit for you. How do they arise together in your own experience?

For some, the idea of being physically intimate with someone with whom they are angry is just unthinkable. That is the last thing they would want.

For some, fighting and fucking are both forms of intimacy. They are expressions of passion in the context of their most significant relationship. The best sex is the make-up sex after a fight. Starting a fight can be seen as a form of foreplay.

But for some sex can be an expression of the anger, not a form of intimacy or a show of desire. Rape is not a crime of passion in the sense that it is not about desire. It is about anger. And for the rapist, the anger may not even be towards the victim but towards what the victim represents to him.

Whatever your relationship to anger and desire; how you relate to these passions and how you allow them to shape your behavior when you feel them have a huge impact on your most significant relationships. Watch for how they arise for you so that your choices are ones which use the energy creatively to generate what you and your partner both need.

## Restoring the Self to Our Center: Good Emotional Hygiene

Events happen in our awareness and the emotions which arise in us give us information about how we are being affected and supply us with the energy to respond in ways which move us toward what we need. Or at least, that is how it might be for us. But our training has not generally prepared us to be so creative. Instead we are either unaware or reactive and end up doing things which create the opposite of what we need. How might we begin to be as healthy as possible with the emotions which are so strong that they come into our conscious awareness?

To have good emotional hygiene (that is to practice principles which promote and preserve emotional health) there are three sets of skills we need to master. We have to know what we are feeling, we have to know what is causing the emotions to arise, and we have to act in ways which create the qualities we need when these feelings occur.

### Naming Feelings

When a conflict grows to sufficient intensity it will break through into our conscious awareness. We may discover it by noticing that others are not doing what we want or they are expressing discontent about our behavior. But if we are going to respond creatively we have to move into our own interior and discover what we are feeling. As we identify what we are STEWing about we gain greater and greater familiarity with what the event is teaching us.

When Joe looked down and saw that the gas gauge was on empty he was angry. When Joe saw Jane come into the living room and change the channel as he was watching TV, he was angry. But under the anger he found many other emotions. He was scared and hurt and sad and guilty, too. The more emotions we can discover, the more data we are getting by which to figure out how to respond creatively.

## Feeling Feelings

Whenever a feeling rises to conscious awareness we can gauge whether we are feeling the full feeling or whether part of it is going into the emotional stuff sack. Or perhaps some of what we are feeling is not about the current incident. Maybe we are pulling some feelings out of the sack.

When, for example, someone makes a choice which hurts us and we are not angry, where did the anger go? When someone doesn't generously let us into the line of traffic as we would like and we begin to yell at them, where is the anger coming from.

One of the men in the Building Healthy Relationships class that I'll call Ted, went into a tirade one night about his daughter's inattention to her driving. She had borrowed his new truck and as she was backing it out of the garage, caught the rear view mirror on the garage door jamb and ripped it off the truck. He was furious.

A couple of weeks later I asked if she had gotten the truck repaired as he insisted. "No," he laughed and shook his head. "She borrowed it again last weekend and drove it into a ditch and rolled it. She totaled it. At least she is okay."

He was so angry about the mirror that he didn't leave himself any headroom on his anger. When she destroyed the vehicle he couldn't possibly be angry in proportion. So he just stuffed it all.

Was the anger he felt when she damaged the mirror all about the mirror? Probably not. But he never really figured out what it was about. A part of it was that he didn't feel like she was careful with or appreciative of all the things he gave her. A part of it was probably his guilt at not being more available to her as a father. He knew he wasn't doing a very good job of raising her. Unfortunately those feelings never came to the surface in a way that could guide his choices.

## Using the Energy to Create What We Need

Once we know what we are feeling and where the feelings are coming from, we can act in ways that move us toward what we need. We can design actions or strategies which allow us to be in relation to others such that the qualities we need are created.

Joe can notice that he is angry at himself for not paying attention to the car and its care and set aside some time to give it a tune up. He can use the energy from his anger to get himself to do the work.

Joe can notice, when he snaps at Jane for changing the channel, that he is burnt out and can discover that he feels really distant from her so he can ask if they can just turn off the TV and talk.

Or Ted can let his daughter know that he doesn't have the relationship he wants with her and can can ask if they might plan to do some activity together every week.

Each of these is a strategy which moves them towards what they each need. But discovering how they feel, what they need, and what they can do to approach what they need is going to take a lot of work. Where are they going to find the energy to do all this work?

The energy lies in the emotion that arises out of the conflict.

In Appendix A of Daniel Goleman's book, *Emotional Intelligence*, he notes that many researchers in the field of emotion suggest that there are certain core or basic emotions upon which all of the other emotions are derived. He uses the analogy of colors or of vibrations as physical correlates of emotional energy. Just as different colors can be created from the basic colors of red, yellow, and blue, different emotions can be blended from the primary feelings. For example, jealousy is a mix of anger, fear, and sadness.

There are many consequences of not being sufficiently connected to and expressive of our emotional life. *Alexithymia* is the technical name for a condition in which one has difficulty naming one's own feelings. This can be the consequence of a neurological disability or past trauma or just from lack of training and support in knowing and expressing one's feelings. The consistent consequence of this disconnection with one's own interior awareness is a failure to create and sustain intimate relationships. Nearly all of the men I have worked with in my program for men who batter could claim a diagnosis of alexithymia.

The good news is that, except in the rare case of neurological deficits, almost everyone can increase their ability to know and name and express their emotions. It just takes practice. The bad news is that the emotions that are most helpful are the very ones we most don't want to feel.

For that reason we are not good about knowing what we feel. Even when we know we are feeling bad, we may have little idea what the source of the bad feeling may be. Isn't there an easier, perhaps more immediate way to know when we are not getting what we need? Yes, indeed. Instead of looking inward, we can look outward upon the many relationships in which we find ourselves. Whenever, in any of those relationships, we are not getting what we need, we experience conflict. The conflicts we have with others, especially with our most significant others, and most especially the ones which arise over and over, are always a reflection of the conflicts we have within ourselves.

## Summary

Anxiety is the sensation we have when we have mixed emotions about a confusing circumstance and can't settle on what we want. Sometimes we aggravate our own anxiety by trying too much *doing* and not enough *being*. In any case we are not going to resolve our anxiety until we know what is causing it. Discipline #4, Suspending Self-soothing, is designed to help us identify what we are anxious about so we can begin to address the anxiety.

Discipline #5, Self-Care Routine, helps us focus on the tension between how we want to care for ourselves and what we then actually do. Recognizing we have nothing more important to do than to care for ourselves and recognizing we routinely abandon our own wellbeing helps us discover our internal conflicts.

When we are getting what we need we are healthy. We monitor our wellbeing by paying attention to our feelings. We like the feelings we have when we are getting what we need. We don't like the feelings we have when we are not getting what we need. But those feelings we don't like are crucial to our wellbeing because they alert us to problems. If we don't know what we are feeling, we don't know when we are being harmed.

Feelings are data about what is happening to us and a source of energy for addressing those problems. The trick is to know what the feelings are telling us and harness the energy to act in our own behalf. The energy in our feelings is not like finite kinetic energy but is a manifestation of the boundless energy of creation.

As we enter our interior world and attend to our feelings we discover they can be quite complex. When we *stew* about something we can tease apart the sensations, thoughts, emotions, and wishes. As we become more aware of our sensations and emotions we build intuition. As we become more facile with our thoughts and wishes we foster our imagination.

While we would rather have the feelings which come from safety and satisfaction, we need the feelings which derive from hurt so that we can act to protect and heal ourselves. These "bad" feelings are crucial to restoring our wellbeing.

Some feelings are a complex mixture of sensations, emotions, thoughts, and wishes. When these complex feelings are infused with a high level of energy we refer to them as passions. We observe that anger and desire are in a sense opposites –we feel anger when we are hurt by another's choices and we feel desire when we are made safe and satisfied by the other's choices—but they can easily arise in the same relationship and even be present at the same time.

Anger is particularly problematic because we are so afraid of it that we often let it control us instead of being able to use its energy appropriately. The Anger Workout is designed to help us become so comfortable with our anger that it becomes a tool for creating what we need instead of an invitation to disaster.

Desire can also be a source for the creative impulse or it can be a passion which inspires destructive choices. Passions contain so much energy that we must be careful with them so that we use them well. In general, good emotional hygiene depends upon knowing what we are feeling, clearly identifying the source of the feelings, and being able then to act in ways that create what we need without doing so in a way that is at the expense of others or in anyway depends on them changing.

# 9

# Childhood Trauma and Adult Healing

From time to time as conflicts appear to us and we attempt to address them creatively we find ourselves stuck... trapped... unable to do what we believe would help to resolve the conflict. We may not be able to identify what we are feeling. Or knowing that we are having such feelings, we may be unable to admit to others the feelings we have. Or having made a plan for what we intend to do to construct what we need, we find ourselves unable to act on the plan.

When this happens to us we can usually look to some long past event as the source of this barrier to our own transformation. These events can be very old, even things that happened to us in early childhood.

While many people resist the notion that things which happened to us long ago can affect who we are and what we do as adults, I suspect that most readers of this book are more psychologically minded and respond more along the lines of, "Well, yes, of course." But even when we have a part of us who is well educated about developmental psychology and fully gets that childhood events affect our growth into maturity, we also have parts which insist, "But that was a long time ago and I am over it now. I have talked about it in therapy and have worked it through."

*Working through* is not about getting to a place where we are no longer impacted by prior events. Working through is about getting to a place where, when we are reminded of earlier events, we know quickly and easily what to do to care for ourselves.

# What is trauma?

Anything that causes our development to get stuck is a form of trauma. Usually we use the term to refer only to big events which would be upsetting or damaging to anyone, but this is a difference of degree, not of type. Anytime we find ourselves stuck, unable to move, whether it be physically or emotionally or cognitively such that we cannot move away from hurt and toward safety and satisfaction, we experience trauma.

Now, I know, this is not the way we normally think of trauma. Usually we limit our understanding of trauma to events that are either hugely disruptive natural disasters or are criminal. We acknowledge that surviving Hurricane Katrina or having loved ones die on 9/11 is traumatic. We know that being sexually abused as a child or battered by a spouse is traumatic. But I am suggesting that we all experience smaller traumas all the time. They are different only by degree and understanding how small traumas affect us can help us better appreciate and know how to respond to the large traumas.

Trauma is simply the experience of having something happen to us that we can't make sense of. We have an experience which doesn't fit on our perceptual map and we can't seem to find a way to make it fit. So we impose a meaning on it that is the best we can do but which is so far from the reality of the situation that we end up with a cognitive distortion which skews how we then act to create what we need.

> The sun was bright and the air warm as Jane headed north on the beltway on her way to her afternoon appointment. The winter had been hard on the roads and she dodged potholes and kept a safe distance behind a flatbed truck in front of her. The truck was loaded with large metal parts on the way to a metal recycling facility.
>
> The truck hit a pothole and a 35 lb. cast iron housing bounced off the truck, hit the pavement once and then came through Jane's windshield and embedded itself in the empty passenger seat next to her. She was able to get her car to the shoulder as the truck and rest of the traffic rumbled on. Her windshield was gone and she was littered with tiny pieces of glass, but otherwise she was fine. She dissolved into sobs.

*10 minutes later a police officer came to her car to see if she was alright. She was barely able to speak. It was two months before she was able to drive.*

Jane was physically fine. But she knew that if she had been driving a foot and a half to the right, she would be dead. Had anyone been riding with her, they would be dead. She thought she was safe. She was wrong. Her map was suddenly very out of date. It took her months to restructure her map so that, even though she was not safe, she could still choose to drive.

In this case at least there was a clear relationship between the triggering event and the emotional wound. The effect of the trauma was clear and there were some tangible markers for how well the healing was progressing. Jane will probably always have trouble on that stretch of highway or may even have a particular fear when driving in early spring, but she understands why those feelings arise. She knows where they come from and what she can do to heal.

## Healing the Past through Transformation in the Present

Many traumas are not so discrete or so recent. When something happened long ago and it stretched out over a period of time, the source of the barrier to development which the trauma created can be very hard to discover. Sometimes even very small events, when they happen in the context of a relationship which is with someone we spend a lot of time with, have strong feelings about, and whose decisions powerfully impact us—that is, they are significant to us—can have a huge impact.

> *Joe has been noticing that he is more and more bothered about the way a couple of his coworkers are sloughing of at work. He knows that they are harming the team and the company and that it harms him in the long run. He has repeatedly tried to talk to them but they just laugh at him for being such a "good boy."*
>
> *He has decided that he wants to say something to his boss but he is worried that his boss will be upset with him for "ratting on" his coworkers. Even though there is a part of Joe who is worried about what will happen if he speaks up, he*

*is clear that the best thing for him to do is to let his boss know what is going on. Still he can't seem to start the conversation.*

*Joe remembers the summer he turned seven. This was the first year he played real baseball, or at least, that he was going to play ball. He was a great sports fan and had wanted to play so much. The prior summer he played T-ball but this was to be his debut in the big leagues.*

*At the third or fourth practice of the season he came up behind his best friend Bobby as Bobby was taking a couple of warm up swings. The bat caught Joe in the shoulder and he felt something snap. He thought he was okay but it hurt really badly. After practice his dad took him to the emergency room and the X-ray confirmed a broken collar bone. He left with a sling for his arm and his baseball season over.*

*On the way home his dad tried to comfort him. "Oh, Joey, that is some really bad luck. You can't play baseball with your arm in a sling but I bet you can fish one handed. How 'bout you and me goin' fishing next weekend." As much as his shoulder hurt, Joe managed a smile. He loved to fish with his dad. His dad fished all the time but he rarely got to go. This would be great!*

*When he woke up the next Saturday morning he quietly got dressed so that he wouldn't wake his brother, Frank. Frank didn't like fishing anyway, but he hadn't said anything to Frank about getting to go because he knew it would start a fight and his dad might change his mind. He didn't want to do anything to spoil this trip.*

*But when Joe got down to the kitchen he knew something was wrong. Dad's tackle box wasn't in the corner of the kitchen and when he looked out the window he could see that the pickup was gone. Joe was stunned. He went back to bed but he couldn't sleep.*

*By Tuesday evening at dinner Joe screwed up his courage enough to say something to his dad about the trip. "Uh, Dad? I thought you were going to take me fishing?"*

*Childhood Trauma and Adult Healing*

*"Huh? Oh, yeah, that's right, I'm sorry, I completely forgot. Well, I can't go this weekend but the following weekend we can go, okay?"*

*"Sure, that'd be great!" Frank watched the exchange from his place at the table with a detached expression that said, "whatever."*

*Joe knew that it wasn't this coming weekend but the next one and he counted the days. He didn't say anything to Frank or to his dad but he day dreamed all the time about being out on the water with his dad.*

*When that Saturday morning arrived, Joe knew as soon as he woke that it happened again. It was light and his dad always wanted to be on the water when the sun came up. He later learned that Dad had gone with one of his buddies. He never brought it up again.*

*But he couldn't figure out what had happened. What had he done to make his dad decide not to take him? He thought back over the previous week. The only time there had been a problem was the Thursday evening before they were to go fishing. Joe was at the store with his dad when he saw a toy that had just been on TV and he started to plead with his dad to get it for him. "Please, oh please, dad, can I get that?"*

*"Oh, quit your whinin'," snapped his dad, "You sound just like a girl". Stung, Joe shut up and never mentioned it again.*

*If you were to ask Joe now about that summer when he turned seven he remembers how he didn't get to play ball because of his broken collar bone. He remembers how disappointed he was and how much his shoulder hurt. But he doesn't remember that he didn't get to go fishing and he can't figure out why he can't speak up at work.*

Joe has a young part of him that developed out of that experience of not going fishing. He struggled to figure out why he wasn't getting his wish, and, like all kids that age, he couldn't let himself believe that the dad he idealized was fallible. He couldn't let the answer be that his dad forgot. So it had to be something he had done.

What he was able to find as a reason was his having asked for what he wanted and been told that he could not have it and that asking made him like a girl and thus not fit for the world of men. If he was to act like a girl, he could not join the world of men on a fishing expedition. If he wants to be acceptable to the male fraternity, he cannot complain.

So now, many years later, he wants to tell his boss that the co-workers are not pulling their weight, but to do so would be to make a girly complaint. He is not consciously aware of this young part, but it shapes his behavior nonetheless.

The impact of this trauma would have been much less if it had happened in the context of a less significant relationship. Had the same thing happened to Frank, it would not have occurred as a trauma. Indeed, Frank didn't want to go fishing so if he had been forgotten it would have been a blessing. But in the interior world of Joe's effort to make meaning and get what he needs, this series of events established a pattern for his meaning making and thus his perceptual map which affects to this day the way Joe acts in the midst of conflict.

There is no one who is free of these wrinkles in our perceptual maps. We all have experienced times when we couldn't make sense of what was happening in our most significant relationships and constructed a way of making meaning which doesn't fully make sense, or at least doesn't accurately portray reality. We all have cognitive distortions.

These distortions affect every aspect of our lives, but they are the most apparent in the relationships which are most important. The context in which we can most easily and clearly discover our own issues is in the relationship we construct with a primary intimate partner. Since we are committed to our own personal transformation by identifying and addressing our own issues we look to our most significant relationships and the conflicts which arise for us there as the most fertile ground for our discovery.

## The Healing Potential of Intimate Relationships

Remembering that anything which grows does so through stages, and that each stage builds upon the ones before it, and that each stage is more complex than the ones which precede it but which make our circumstances simpler when we master them; let's look at a three-stage map of the development of primary intimate relationships.

*Childhood Trauma and Adult Healing*

# 1+1=1: Symbiosis

When we are seeking to build a primary intimate relationship we first have to identify someone to create it with us. We cannot do it alone. We have a map, a template, an imago, which guides our search. When we find someone who fits the imago, we hope that we are a good match for the other's imago too. We try to discover who the other is looking for and then try to be that person so the other will choose to be with us.

If we are a close enough match, we choose each other, and we try to construct a relationship in which we are each who the other wants us to be. We fall in love.

> When Jane's best friend from work invited her to a neighborhood picnic Jane hesitated knowing she wouldn't know anyone there but her friend. "Come on," her friend chided, "There will be a lot of cute guys there."
>
> Jane hadn't dated anyone steadily for months and she did want to find someone special but she really didn't have high hopes that this would be the place to find Mr. Right. But one of the guys playing softball caught her eye. He was vigorous in a way her dad never was. Her dad had been sick most of her life and she knew she wanted a partner who would be an active father.
>
> Joe was at the picnic at the request of a buddy of his who hoped they could gather enough interest in softball to field two teams. "Besides," he said, "there will be lots of good food."
>
> Joe noticed Jane. It wasn't until months later that he realized that her face was like his second grade teacher, the one who had been so gentle and kind to him when he told about the summer and how he couldn't play ball because of his broken collar bone.
>
> Jane and Joe happened to sit across a table from each other at the picnic and over potato salad got to talking about fishing and Joe mentioned how much he was looking forward to going fishing with his son. Jane was smitten.

Joe and Jane each have a mostly unconscious image of who they are looking to pair with to construct a primary intimate relationship. Over the weeks and months that follow they get to know each other better and test out more and more to see if the other is who they are looking for. But since they each want the other to want to be with them, they are trying to be who the other is looking for. They are each trying to match the other's map.

When we are able to do this with someone, we fall in love. We believe we have found our soul mate. This feeling of infatuation is intense and wonderful. It is better than the best drugs. But it is a fantasy. The other is not my imago. The other is a person in his or her own right, and not the perfect screen for my projections.

Sooner or later, I discover that the other is not who I want the other to be. Sooner or later, the ways my image of the other is not who the other really is become apparent. This may happen after a few minutes or a few hours or days or weeks or even years. I had a client who discovered he had kept this fantasy alive for the whole eight years of his marriage. When it collapsed, he was devastated. The notion that there is a perfect person out there somewhere, and when we meet we will be perfect for each other, and be in a profoundly intimate relationship which will be easy and fulfilling—the notion that we each have a soul mate—is a fantasy. And sooner or later we discover that.

## 1+1=2: Partnership

If the other is close enough to what we are looking for in a partner we begin to look to what the relationship is like that we create together. Having discovered that the other is "good enough" we consider whether the qualities of the relationship we are creating are what we are hoping for. We form a "we" that is a manifestation of what we each bring to the relationship.

> Joe and Jane dated for six months before they got engaged. They moved into an apartment together which they furnished from items they had each collected but they also began to buy together. They wanted to get a house as soon as they could because they didn't want to start a family in an apartment. They had a shared vision of the family and the life they were going to create together.

We can weather the disappointment that the other is not who I want the other to be as long as we can trust that we are together creating the relationship we each want. We become partners in the pursuit of a common dream. We divide up the responsibilities for creating our common life and as long as we each hold up our end we have a stable and durable relationship.

> Jane and Joe saved enough during the first two years of their marriage that they were able to make a substantial down payment on a three bedroom house in a good neighborhood. Joe set himself to creating the garden and doing some landscaping while Jane repainted one of the bedrooms as the baby's room.

> The plan was that they would wait another couple of years before starting a family so they could afford for Jane to stay home, but she went off the pill and one night in a moment of passion, Jack was conceived. Two years later Jesse was born and Jane was up to her elbows in diapers and Jack was working all the hours he could get just to keep up with the bills.

> While this felt a lot like what they said they wanted, Joe wasn't prepared for having so little time with Jane. He didn't think of himself as emotionally needy, but he found he was getting lost in the busyness of their lives. They would pour themselves into bed exhausted after getting the boys to sleep. Those days when they would make love for hours were long gone and Joe missed both the physical and the emotional intimacy.

While a $1+1=2$ Partnership can create a durable framework for a shared life and future, it may not sustain the kind of intense intimacy and passion that a $1+1=1$ Symbiosis generates. We thus may find ourselves longing for the old days or even for a new relationship.

> About this time Joe was assigned to a special project at work which was a collaboration between his department and another one. His counterpart was a perky young woman who was playful and quick with a smile and Joe could tell she liked him. He began to notice that he would think about her when they weren't together.

Joe might create those feelings in his relationship with the colleague at work, but they would last a few weeks or months at best and they would trash what he has created with Jane.

1+1=2: Partnerships can be very durable and can sustain a relationship well into a Fiftieth Wedding Anniversary. But it may not generate a deep level of intimacy. Even couples who remain sexually active may lose emotional intimacy. While having sex he may be thinking about the men's magazine he just bought and she may be lost in thoughts about the romance novel she has been reading. They may be physically together but emotionally in separate fantasies.

So how can we sustain a durable partnership and have a deep intimacy which doesn't deny who we really are in all the ways we are not who the other wants us to be... indeed, how we are not who we want ourselves to be?

## 1+1=3: Mutual intimacy

A mutual intimacy is constructed from three parts.

1.   I am a fully functioning autonomous individual. I can take care of myself. I am not looking for a relationship in which the other takes care of me. I am looking for a relationship in which the other joins me as a full partner.

2.   My partner is a fully functioning autonomous individual. He or she can take care of him or herself. She or he is not looking for a relationship in which the other takes care of her or him. He or she is looking for a relationship in which the other joins her or him as a full partner.

3.   We create together a relationship in which we both find a context for intimacy and growth. We are each fully responsible for deciding what the relationship is like and for doing what it takes to create the relationship.

No two people want exactly the same things. As we each describe what we want the relationship to be like we are going to discover differences. We are going to have conflicts. But we must have enough agreement about what we want that we both remain committed to creating this shared relationship.

*Childhood Trauma and Adult Healing*

To be able to do this there are some skills we both have to utilize. We have to discover what we want the relationship to be like, that is, we have to talk about the relationship. We have to manage our own anxiety when we see that the relationship is not what we expected. And we have to remain curious about what we are each doing to make the relationship be other than what we want and be willing to address and change our own behavior so that we are acting consistently with our own needs. Let's look more closely with each of these.

## Talking About the Relationship

Whenever we are approached by our partner who says, "Honey, I want to talk about our relationship," we typically go into a major flinch. We pull back from what we expect will be a complaint about what we are doing. It seems that the only time we talk about the relationship is when there is something wrong.

Be that as it may, we will not agree on what we want the relationship to be like if we don't talk about it. And this is hard not only because we typically do it when we are under duress. It is always hard. It was even hard to do when we first started talking about it.

> Once Joe and Jane started dating they spent nearly all of their time together. They would spend some nights at his place and some at hers but rarely apart. This went on for a couple of months before Joe decided to suggest that they get a place together. He was pretty sure he wanted to marry Jane, but he wasn't ready to have that conversation. But he thought he could suggest they live together.
>
> He didn't know why it was so hard for him to bring it up. They already pretty much lived together. And he was almost certain that Jane would choose to do that. She had already mentioned casually that her lease was almost up and she wasn't sure she wanted to extend it. Still, to bring it up was to make a commitment.

To be able to talk about any of our feelings—sensations, thoughts, emotions or wishes—we have to know what we are feeling, have words to express how we are feeling, and believe it is safe to say what we are feeling. Further, to talk about what I want for dinner is a 2° skill. To talk about what I want our relationship to be like is a 4° skill. Much more complicated.

## Managing Our Own Anxiety

Because this is so hard, we tend to pull back when we consider talking about something as important as our primary relationship. We put off talking about the relationship. Most often when we are having a conversation it is when something has happened which puts the stability of the relationship at risk. We are thus understandably anxious. We aren't sure what is going on. We don't know clearly what we want and we are afraid that our partner wants something different from what we have and perhaps different from what we want. This is a minefield.

To negotiate it we have to calm our own anxieties enough that we can actually hear what our partner is saying over the din of our fears. We have to calm ourselves enough that we can actually know what we want.

## Addressing Our Own Issues

Remembering that we all have issues and that they are most likely to surface in our relationships with those who are most significant to us, it is absolutely certain that our own issues will emerge in the context of the primary intimate relationship we construct with our beloved. Absolutely certain.

These patterns of conflict which arise again and again in the context of these most important relationships are always constructed by the issues we each bring to the relationship. Nothing is only the other's fault. We always have a role to play. But it can be very hard to see our own part. When we can see our own part and name it, address it, and resolve it, the conflict ceases to be a source of esuba for us. (This is not the same as saying we are able to get the other to change to be as we want them to be. If that is how we are constructing our map of the problem, then that is at least one of the issues we are bringing to the situation.) When we address and resolve our own issues, assuming we could ever fully do that, what remains is only what the other is bringing to the situation. By doing this we get our own junk out of the way and create an open space in the relationship in which they can do their own work.

Remember back to the vignette in Chapter Seven where Jane spoke to Joe about his dirty clothes on the bedroom floor as he was watching a football game? Let's look at what it might take to restore their relationship in the wake of such an event.

(I offer these scenarios with some hesitation because I don't want anyone to assume I am suggesting these are right things to do. There are many things they can do. I only want to offer that, among the very many things each might choose to do, here are a couple that suggest themselves to me.)

> Jane retreats from the living room as Joe returns to watching the game. She notices that she is really steamed about this event and decides to pay attention to what she is feeling.
>
> She notices that under her anger at Joe is a fear that their relationship will turn into one like her parents had in which her mom was always nagging her dad and her dad became more and more sullen and withdrawn.
>
> She also notices that Joe seems to feel entitled to just watch TV when there are so many things that need tending to around the house.
>
> She notices that the work is never done so she never gives herself permission to spend time doing what she enjoys and resents that Joe can give himself that permission. But she wants a relationship in which they each fulfill their promises to each other and, when Joe promises to pick up after himself and then doesn't, she feels underappreciated. She recognizes that she needs a relationship with Joe in which they honor each other by honoring their commitments to each other.
>
> She decides she wants to talk with Joe about this. As she comes to this, she also notices that the times she tries to talk with him are the very times he is least available. It is as though she sees football as her rival and she wants Joe to pick her over the game. So she tries to woo him away with her anger and that never works. So she decides to try to let Joe know about what she wants in their relationship at a time when he is fully available to hear her.

*She goes back into the living room and waits for a commercial and then says, "Joe, I know you are in the middle of the game now, but I would like a chance sometime today to talk about some things that are bothering me. I am wondering if we could get fifteen minutes to talk later. Would you let me know when a good time would be for us to do that?"*

Or another option might be:

*Joe watches Jane retreat from the living room and he is aware of her anger and his own, and notices that he resents that she resents his attachment to football. He likes the fact that he is a fan, and that he is willing to get into the game instead of having to be busy all the time the way Jane seems to. He notices that he is worried that she seems so driven.*

*He also notices that he is giving her more work to do when he doesn't take care of his own obligations and so recognizes that his own choices are creating the opposite of what he needs. He feels guilty and also notices that the distance between them scares him.*

*He notices that he may be giving Jane the sense that football is more important to him than she is. He realizes that is not the case and he gets up and goes into the bedroom and puts away his clean clothes and puts the dirty ones in the laundry.*

*Then he goes to find Jane and say, "I'm sorry honey, I do want to be responsible for my own things and not make more work for you. I wish you could slow down and relax more. Is there anything I can do to take some of the load so you can have some time to do what you want to do?"*

I want to stress here that either one of them can act in ways to heal their relationship in the midst of the conflict by acting in ways that move either of them toward what they need. When they each get what they need they both get what they need. They have the same needs and the more they each act to create those qualities in the relationship the more they both win.

Now you may be thinking to yourself, "people aren't really like that. No one is that introspective and gracious." If that is what you think, you are mistaken. I grant you that such people are rare, but they do exist. Do you want to be one of them?

To enact these skills in your own life there is a set of distinctions you need to make. We introduced these back in Chapter Three but let's review them.

# Five Crucial Distinctions

Remember, a distinction is simply the recognition that this is *different from* that, not that this is *better than* that. Corn is a great crop to grow but not in a soybean field. In a soybean field it is a weed. A measure of our intelligence is the capacity to make distinctions, especially in vocabulary. But this is more than an abstract measurement. How we speak shapes how we think. How we think shapes our understanding of the world we live in. Our understanding governs our choices. And our choices create our world.

## Event from Effect

The distinction we want to notice here is a bit more subtle than that of cause and effect. On the one hand there was an actual event which occurred in the shared space of the relationship. Everyone was affected by the shared event. But not everyone was affected the same and some of the difference comes from how meaning is made by each person about the event.

When Jane came into the living room and pointed out that Joe's dirty clothes were still on the bedroom floor [the event], Joe was irritated that she was interrupting the game and stung by the shame of not having done what he said he would do [the effect]. Jane was proud of herself for being able to speak up for herself [another effect].

Thus what this event means to Joe is that Jane is interrupting and shaming him and what it means to Jane is that she is an assertive woman.

## Feelings from Behavior

Jane and Joe are both angry about what happened in the living room as Joe was watching the game and Jane wanted him to clean the bedroom. In this scenario neither was really furious, but I did hear of a similar situation in which the wife tripped the circuit breaker and while her husband was looking for why the power was off, cut the plug off the power cord to the TV.

Jane and Joe feel their feelings but do not have to act them out in a manner that only increases the tension. They don't have to start a fight. They are not trying to make each other lose. They know that their emotions don't determine their choices.

## Effect from Cause

This then leads us to a still more subtle distinction between what we make this event mean about what is around us and what we discover that it means about what is happening within our own awareness. A part of the meaning comes to us from our apparent perception of what is happening in the world beyond our selves, and part of it comes from our interoception of what is happening within our selves.

Notice I said apparent perception. We are not only making meaning about what is happening to us, we are making meaning about why it is happening. We may decide that we know why others are making the choices they are making. Joe may say to himself, "Jane is just nagging me because she doesn't want me to have any fun." It may actually be true that Jane resents Joe sitting down and enjoying the game, but Joe doesn't know that for sure and, in any case, it is not the same as how *he feels* when she interrupts him. Jane may say to herself, "Joe just doesn't have any respect for me," when she finds his clothes still on the floor, and while it may be true that Joe doesn't honor her the way she would like, it is not the same as noticing that she feels disrespected and needs the quality of respect in her relationship with Joe.

## Need from Want

We can't discover what we need if we don't let go of holding only to our judgment about what it means about the other when we are in conflict with them and look instead to how we are being affected. When we stay in our projections about who they are and what they are doing wrong and how we would like them to do differently, we are remaining focused on what we want, not on what we need.

Jane needs a quality of respect in the relationship which is missing when Joe doesn't do his part. Well Joe needs a quality of respect which is missing when Jane interrupts the game. He also needs a quality of personal integrity which is missing when he doesn't follow through on his commitments. Jane also needs the integrity to notice her own needs and to act to care for herself. They each have the same needs and acting to create what they each need doesn't compromise the wellbeing of the other; indeed it promotes it.

This is a hugely important distinction to which we devote most of the next chapter. For now let us simply remember that, "You can't always get what you want, but if you try sometime you just might find you get what you need."[25]

## Can Do from Cannot Do

But finally and most importantly there are things we can change and things we can't. When we focus our attention on the things we cannot change we create for ourselves feelings of helplessness and hopelessness and we come to the conviction that there is nothing we can do. This is clearly a cognitive distortion. There are a theoretically infinite number of things we can do. But there are outcomes we cannot control. We cannot make things be as we want them to be. That is certainly true. But we can move things toward conditions which nurture the qualities we need. And in that regard we are immensely powerful.

Joe can pick up his clothes. He can offer his support to Jane. Jane can frame her requests to Joe at a time when he is most available. Jane can ask to speak to Joe when he is ready to connect with her. These are all things which are easily in their power to do and which construct what they need. These are choices which lead to addressing the issues which arise as they build a healthy relationship for which they are both responsible... one in which they are each supported in naming, addressing, and resolving the issues they bring to the relationship which arise for them as a consequence of unresolved past trauma.

❧

---

25   Yes, this is from the Rolling Stones. You didn't need to look here to know that but I still had to post it. First released as track 9 on "Let it Bleed" in 1969.

Back in Chapter Three we introduced the three pillars on which Creative Conflict Resolution stands as Awareness, Acting in our behalf, and Accountability. In Chapter Six we again referenced accountability as essential to dismantling abuse and challenging oppression and we introduced the idea that there are different kinds of accountability. As we are now looking at what a deeply healthy relationship might be like we return again to the notion of accountability.

## Radical Accountability

It is quite literally impossible to open the newspaper and not find a call for someone to be held accountable for some alleged wrongdoing. Whether it is a public official having failed to maintain ethical standards, a corporation which has allowed its product to harm someone, or a family member who has abused a child or spouse; calls for accountability are all around us. Less commonly heard are declarations by individuals and corporations of a desire to be accountable. We tend to think of accountability as something that is good for others but not for ourselves.

Accountability is an essential quality of healthy relationships. If we are to build healthy relationships, we have to learn to be accountable. To start with we have to be sure we know what accountability is and is not. One strategy for constructing accountability is so common and creates such problems in relationships that we identify and address it up front.

### Problems with Fault and Blame

One very common strategy for addressing conflict is to ascribe blame. If we can decide whose fault it is, the reasoning goes, then we have done something to solve the problem. There are several reasons why this doesn't work.

The primary one is that blame doesn't actually do anything to change the relationship or the choices that people are making to construct it. When we ascribe blame, we are determining that someone has the preponderance of responsibility for constructing an event with negative consequences. (When the event has what we consider to be positive consequences, we call it *credit* rather than *blame*.)

If my wife and I are having an argument about whether our teenage son's

*Childhood Trauma and Adult Healing*

misbehavior is my fault, I can either take the position that it is or that it is not. But neither position will affect our son's behavior. Even if we are arguing about some clear choice I made (I put the dishes in the dishwasher without rinsing them first) acknowledging that I did that (and that she thinks they should be rinsed) doesn't mean I won't do it again. We haven't actually solved the problem.

At a deeper level, the problem with blame is that it assumes that someone has the preponderance of responsibility for a given outcome. This is almost never true, though it is a way of thinking about a problem that is supported by the traditions of our culture. When a bad thing happens, find someone to blame.

> On February 3, 1998 an American EA-6B Prowler assigned to the base at
> Aviano, Italy, flying low over the Italian Alps, clipped a cable supporting a
> gondola full of skiers with its right wing and sent them falling to their death. In
> the military court of inquiry following the incident (Italian courts determined that
> they had no jurisdiction over a NATO action), all four Marines on board were
> charged with crimes. The two in the back of the plane (who couldn't even see
> out) immediately had charges against them dropped and it appears they were
> only charged in order to scare them into giving up any information they might
> have had about the accident.

So who is to blame for this tragedy? Of course it makes sense that the pilot is to blame.

No, as the pilot pointed out from the stand, he was simply flying the course set by the navigator. The pilot doesn't have time to look at a map. The pilot only does what he is told. It is the navigator who decides where the plane is to fly and he was following the instructions of the navigator.

The navigator took the stand to explain that he was simply following the flight plan he was ordered to plot by the base commander using maps supplied by the military. There was no gondola cable on his charts.

The inquiry continued with the testimony of the base commander and the team which compiled the maps. In the end a massive web of failures emerged which included the discovery that the Air Force pilots were not making information available to the Marines who sometimes used the base. The pilot and the navigator were charged with obstruction of justice (they did not disclose a video camera that was in the cockpit at the time of the accident even though the camera was not on), but no one was found guilty for the deaths of 20 people.

The Italian people were incensed. No one was "held accountable" for the tragedy. No one was found to have had the preponderance of responsibility for the deaths.

When we use blame as a strategy for addressing conflict we are engaged in a kind of fight. The person who is found to be to blame loses. Blame is a strategy which has broad social support but which doesn't create what we need and which is based on the clear distortion that only one person's choices matter in the creation of the negative outcome.

Still, it makes sense that we want to have relationships that create a kind of accountability. Blame is at least a kind of low level accountability. We need a more mature and robust perspective on accountability which fully takes into account the choices everyone is making in the construction of the relationship.

## Responsibility and Accountability

We often use the terms *responsibility* and *accountability* interchangeably. I have reviewed several dictionaries in an effort to discover differences between the terms and have found there is little distinction made between them. Indeed, they are often given as synonyms. For our purposes though it is helpful to define a difference.

When we use the term *responsibility* we are referring to what actually occurs out there in the realm of the physical world as we can observe it. If there is an *action* and it has an *effect*, the *action* is *responsible* for the *effect*. If I reach for the phone and spill my tea, I am responsible for spilling my tea. If I say, "I didn't spill the tea," I am refusing to be accountable.

*Accountability* is a condition that is created in the interior of our relationships. It is a quality of the intersubjective space constructed by the assumptions and agreements which build relationships. If I acknowledge that I spilled the tea, then I am being accountable.

This quality of being accountable arises differently in mutual relationships than it does in fiduciary or reciprocal relationships. In a reciprocal relationship, accountability is the ability to give an account. We are accountable to the other with whom we have constructed this relationship.

*When Henry hired on at Universal Widget, he agreed to be accountable to Frank. He gives Frank an account of when he shows up for work, how many widgets he has made, and how well the widget machine is working. And Frank agreed that he would give Henry an account of how much he had earned (in the form of a paycheck), how many sick days he had accrued, and whether he was meeting his quota.*

Accountability appears differently in mutual relationships. We are invited to *take into* account the other, not to *give them* an account. We are accountable *with* the other, not accountable *to* them.

*For many years I was a member of a men's support group that met every other Sunday evening. This group was a vital support for me during the collapse of my first marriage and I continued to meet with them well into my second one. Joan, the woman with whom I am now married, was very much aware of the importance of this group for me.*

*One Sunday evening as the group was breaking up, one of the members spoke up and said that he would not be able to meet with us in two weeks. Two other men quickly also stated that they wouldn't make it either. If three of the six men in the group were going to miss, we weren't going to have much of a group left. We began to look at alternatives and found that we would all be able to meet that weekend on Saturday instead of Sunday. It was agreed.*

*I went and told Joan that the men's group would be meeting on Saturday instead of Sunday in two weeks. She was clearly angry. I asked what the problem was. She stated that she wished I had spoken to her about it. I said, "I am talking to you about it."*

*"No, I mean before you made the decision."*

*"I don't see what the problem is. We can't meet on Sunday so we are meeting on Saturday. What is the big deal?"*

*"Because we always do things together on Saturday evening, and now you have decided that we won't and you didn't talk to me about it."*

*"Well, we can spend Sunday evening together."*

*"Sunday evening is not the same as Saturday evening. I have to teach Monday morning. You left me out of the decision-making process."*

*"Well, what was I supposed to do, tell the guys that I couldn't meet on Saturday without your permission?"*

*"No, it's not about my permission; it is about whether we consult with each other. You could tell them you will talk to me and let them know."*

I was seeing the relationship, and thus the problem, from a different perspective than was Joan and, thus, I was coming to a different way of handling things and constructing a different kind of accountability. I was looking at our relationship through the lens of a fiduciary relationship and saw no reason to have to get her permission. She isn't my mom after all.

Joan was seeing the relationship from the perspective of a mutual relationship in which we make decisions together. She wasn't expecting me to get her permission. She just wanted our relationship and the commitments we make to each other to be more important than my wish to be one of the guys. She wanted us to be accountable *with* each other by taking into account how our choices affect each other.

So accountability in a fiduciary or reciprocal relationship is created out of the ability to give an account; it is accountability *to*. But accountability in a mutual relationship is accountability *with*; it is created out of the ability to take into account two things:

- how are my choices affecting the other, and
- how are the other's choices affecting me.

This is being mutually accountable.

*Joe and Jane had a whirlwind romance and married 10 months after meeting at the picnic. When they had been married for a year, an incident arose which thrust them into the hard work of being in a durable intimate relationship.*

*Back then Jane would typically get home a bit earlier than Joe and she would usually start dinner. One evening as Jane was dicing the onions and listening to the news, Joe got home and came quietly into the kitchen. He came up behind Jane and grabbed her around the waist.*

*Jane shrieked and collapsed on the floor. She was wide-eyed and hyperventilating. Joe tried to hold her but she screamed, "Get away from me, just get away." The more he tried to comfort her, the more frantic she became until he finally left her on the kitchen floor and she just sobbed.*

What Joe didn't know is that Jane was raped five years before when she was walking home through the park. As she was dicing the onions she noticed the knife she was holding and she saw that it looked like the knife that her attacker was holding when he came up behind her and grabbed her around the waist and dragged her into the bushes.

*Once Jane's terror subsided it was replaced with rage. "How could you do that to me?" she challenged Joe.*

*"Do what?" he asked, "I was just giving my wife an affectionate squeeze when I got home."*

*"Just don't ever do that again," Jane demanded. "Just don't ever sneak up on me again."*

As Joe and Jane worked at repairing their relationship, they struggled with the way they understand both responsibility and accountability. Joe did walk into the kitchen and he did come up behind her without her knowing he was there and he did grab her. He intended to surprise her. He did not intend or expect to scare her. He didn't know about the rape and probably wouldn't have thought about it if he did.

Jane did collapse on the floor, rejected Joe's efforts to comfort her, and did imply that he intended to scare her. She had withheld from him information about her experience of being raped.

Each made choices that constructed an event that neither one wanted to have happen. Each shares a responsibility for what happened. What then might it look like for them to both be fully accountable for how they deal with their relationship into the future?

## Four Orders of Responsibility

Let's start with a fuller exploration of what we might mean by *responsibility* and allow it to lead us to as a fuller understanding of *accountability*. *Responsibility*, being out there in the physical world of (hopefully) consensual reality, is easier to identify than the more ethereal quality we call *accountability*. We use our understanding of responsibility to construct a deeper understanding of accountability.

As we do this we are going to observe that there are actually four different ways that we use the term *responsibility*. Much confusion results from speaking the term from one perspective and hearing it from another. Furthermore, we are going to see that these ways build on each other. There is a developmental sequence of growing responsibility.

You recall that any developmental sequence has certain characteristics. Insects develop from an egg to a larva to a pupa to an adult. Oak trees develop from acorn to seedling to sapling to adult tree. Each stage in a developmental sequence builds on the one before it. We may not skip a stage and we can't do them out of order. If an earlier stage is missing or damaged, the later stages cannot develop. These facts are true for all developmental sequences.

At 1°, responsibility is the relationship between a cause and an effect. When an infant is teething, the growing teeth pushing through the gums causes pain. The new teeth are responsible for the pain. When one sits out in the summer sun for a long time, one can get sunburned. The UV rays are responsible for sunburn.

At 2°, responsibility is a result of a choice. The choice is a cause that results in an effect. When the infant chooses to bite down on a teething ring, the biting relieves the pressure of the emerging teeth and causes the pain to subside. The infant is responsible for relieving her own pain. When the sunbather sits for hours in the sun, the sunbather is responsible for the sunburn.

At 3°, responsibility is a result of an agreement. When two or more persons make a choice to enter into an understanding with each other, they construct a set of rights and responsibilities as a product of the commitments they each make. If I contact the gas company to arrange for natural gas service to my apartment, I enter into an agreement with the utility in which they are responsible for providing me with gas and I am responsible for paying the bill. As the infant is nursing, her mother is responsible for nourishing her and she is responsible for suckling. When the infant is teething and bites the mother's nipple, the infant has reneged on an implied responsibility and the mother begins weaning the child.

At 4°, responsibility is a result of a way of being that one creates as a consequence of taking into account all of the relevant expectations of others, the choices that are available, and the desired effect that one wants to create. 4° responsibility is the ability to respond to the demands of the relationships in which one finds oneself in a manner that constructs conditions which meet ones own needs and ideally the needs of all. The mother, unwilling to experience the pain of being bit by her daughter, but still committed to nourishing her child, begins to express her milk with a breast pump and provides it through a bottle.

In our efforts to build healthy relationships we are looking to do so by being responsible at 4° [Interpersonal-relational: choice]. We recall that responsibility at each order is constructed on top of responsibility at the previous orders. The mother's ability to be responsible at 4° is dependent upon her ability to meet her 3° commitments by making a 2° choice to have a 1° effect which is to nourish her child.

By way of example, let's return to Joe and Jane and their responsibility for her panic when he grabbed her.

At 1°, Jane experiences a flashback and the associated emotions when she is looking at a knife and remembering the rape as Joe grabs her from behind. At 2°, Jane chose to have a knife in her presence to dice the onions and chose to remember her own experience. Joe chose to surprise Jane by coming up behind her and grabbing her around the waist.

At 3°, Jane asked for an agreement that Joe wouldn't do "that" again but Joe wasn't sure what it was that he had done and couldn't see how it had caused the outcome. Jane chose to construct a deeper understanding between them by telling Joe about her assault. They both came to understand how much the assault had affected her and how much she was still traumatized by it.

At 4°, Jane decided that she has more healing to do than she realized and found a support group for rape survivors. Joe supported Jane in her commitment and vowed on his part to not sneak up behind her and to generally be more cautious about surprising her.

## Four Orders of Accountability

While these events are happening out in the manifest world of the relationship between Joe and Jane, there is a parallel set of circumstances that are being created in the qualities of the subjective world they are creating with each other. It is this interior of the relationship that we want to explore with greater depth.

### 1° Accountability

At 1°, accountability is the ability to take into account the experience of the other. It is the ability to construct a quality of presence in the relationship. I am accountable to the degree to which I can be fully emotionally present to the feelings of the other. This capacity for presence has its own developmental sequence from *pity* to *sympathy* to *empathy* to *compassion*. It is hard to be fully emotionally present to others because their feelings can resonate with our own feelings and thus trigger a flood of emotion that we may not be prepared for. A deep compassion for others is thus only possible when we are fully comfortable with our own feelings.

Joe has done something to trigger panic in his beloved. She is clearly terrified and is reacting to him as the one who is the cause of the feelings. If Joe can fully experience her fear then he will likely get in touch with his own fear. He may be afraid of losing his relationship with Jane because he has harmed her. He may be angry that she has identified him as the assailant. He may be guilty about scaring her. He may even get in touch with guilt about times in his own past when he engaged in sex with a woman when he was more interested in the sex than in the woman.

Accountability at 1° is hard to do because of the emotional demands it places on us, but it becomes the essential building block for higher orders of accountability. We are never fully accountable at 1°. Even as we work on building accountability at the higher orders, we must continually return to go deeper at 1°.

## 2° Accountability

At 2°, accountability is the ability to take into account the choices we have made which construct the relationship. It is the ability to recognize the extent to which the *actions* we take which shape our relationships with others are actually a consequence of *choices* we make. Often the actions we take seem as though they just happen. They don't seem to be our choices. Accountability depends on being able to acknowledge the fact that we do what we do because we choose to.

Jane is not likely to find it easy to acknowledge that her reverie about the memory of her rape was a product of a choice she made. It just came up when she saw the knife. She will certainly not be immediately able to see that collapsing on the floor of the kitchen was a choice she made, though she may be able to come to see that her dropping down in that way may have been her body's strategy for protecting her. She will probably see that telling Joe to get away was her choice and she may even see that her identification of him as a threat was a choice.

Joe will have an easier time identifying his choices because he was less overwhelmed with feelings but he may still have difficulty admitting that he did choose to surprise her, that he did choose to grab her, that he did choose to try to hold her, and that he did then choose to leave the kitchen. But he may tend to minimize these as choices by asking the rhetorical question, "What should I have done?" The implication here would be that there was nothing else he could have done which is certainly not true.

The challenge of 2° accountability is, first of all, to see that our actions are the result of choices, and, as our choices construct actions, our actions are constructing consequences; and then to name this connection in our relationships with others.

## 3° Accountability

At 3°, accountability is the ability to take into account the understandings we have made which construct the relationship. It is the ability to recognize the set of expectations, agreements, understandings, and commitments that we have constructed or which have been constructed for us. Even if we don't end up doing what others expect us to do, accountability still demands that we maintain an awareness of those expectations. Further, accountability at 3° depends upon our capacity to clarify and repair those understandings when they are not being met.

Jane was under the impression that she could be in the kitchen of her home and be safe from assault. She thought she could count on Joe being sensitive to her space and emotions and would not terrify or harm her. She thought the rape, since it happened before she met Joe, was none of his business and was not something that she ever needed to talk about with him. She expected that if she told him not to touch her that he would respect her wishes.

Joe expected that he could come up behind Jane and surprise her and that she would be pleased by the surprise and happy to see him. He expected that he would be able to comfort her when she was emotionally distraught. He expected that she would see him as abandoning her if he left the room when she was upset even when she was asking him to leave her alone.

Recognizing that each of them was coming at the events from the perspective of their own expectations and that the differences between them were constructing a conflict, they could create a new set of expectations. Joe will not surprise Jane. Jane will talk about what happened to her and the feelings that arise for her now.

## 4° Accountability

At 4°, accountability is the ability to take into account the ways of being we have made which construct the relationship. It is the ability to see that how we enter into the relationships we build makes the relationships what they are, and that, when the relationships are not as we would have them be, we can heal them by adopting a new way of being.

This is a very difficult concept to take on. Even when we think we understand it, it remains a difficult thing to actually apply in our lives. A good part of the rest of this book is an exploration of what it looks and feels like to be accountable at 4°.

Jane has come to see that her way of being around the trauma of her rape five years ago is not only not working for her relationship with Joe; it is not working for her. She has decided that she wants to develop a new way of being in relationship to the rape. Rather than adopting a position that it was in the past and she is over it now, she has decided to be a rape survivor and to ally with other women who are surviving rape.

Joe has recognized that, whatever his intentions might be, they are not worth much when it comes to how he is actually affecting Jane. He has decided that he is not content to simply be someone who has good intentions; he wants to adopt a way of being that is attentive and responsive to whatever the actual effects of his behavior might be.

## Becoming Mutually Accountable

If we are to develop healthy relationships, we have to learn to be accountable, and to do it in the most complete ways. This means being able to be mutually accountable at all four orders.

- Be able to know when something is bothering us, and be able to know when the other is bothered.
- Be able to know what it is that others are doing and what choices they are making that we are finding bothersome, and be able to know what we are doing that they find bothersome and to recognize that our actions are the result of choices we are making.
- Be able to know what we can reasonably expect of the other and what they can expect of us and be able to clarify and repair the understandings that we have with others.
- Be able to allow the ways in which we are bothered and the ways in which others are bothered by us to inform us and to help us discover new ways of being that move us toward relationships in which we are more and more likely to create what we need.

# Summary

We often flinch in the face of conflict especially when we don't think we can respond to it creatively and most especially when we have tried to address it before and we feel stuck. This feeling of being stuck now is often connected to and, in some sense, caused by having been stuck in the past.

When we are stuck and can't move, either physically or emotionally or cognitively, we experience trauma. We are always trying to make sense of what is happening to us, to know how to feel about it, and what to do about it to create what we need. When we can't do any of these we are traumatized. This may not be something those around us can see when it is happening to us. We may be having these thoughts and emotions only within us and so others may not be able to validate our experience.

We all carry within us the effects of past trauma and we are all likely to re-experience the traumas when current circumstances arise which resonate with the traumas of our past. While this is disorienting and even painful when it happens to us, it is an opportunity for us to address a current difficulty and, in the process, heal a past wound.

This healing is available to us in all of our relationships but it is most available in the relationships we have with those we are closest to. Our most intimate relationships are a crucible for burning off the junk from our past but are, thus, also the context for our greatest turmoil. Our intimate partners can be mentors and they can be tor-mentors.

To use these relationships for healing we have to talk to each other about the relationship while we manage our own anxiety and address our own issues. For us to do this we each must have some skill at making each of the five crucial distinctions. As we make the distinctions we construct conversations in which we can each work toward our own healing as we identify and address our own responsibility for the problems which occur in our relationship.

As we construct the space in the relationship to do this work we are creating a radical mutual accountability. This is not about blame but about the ability to keenly know how we are affecting each other and how we are being affected and create a shared understanding of the relationship we both need and trust that we will both work to create it.

# 10

# Knowing What We Need

In 1943 Abraham Maslow published a paper on "A Theory of Human Motivation" in which he first proposed his now famous hierarchy of needs. While he has had his detractors, it is now pretty much universally accepted that 1) there are different kinds of needs we experience, 2) they arise for us in a universal sequence and, 3) when lower order needs are not met, they have priority over the higher order needs. Let's take these three points separately.

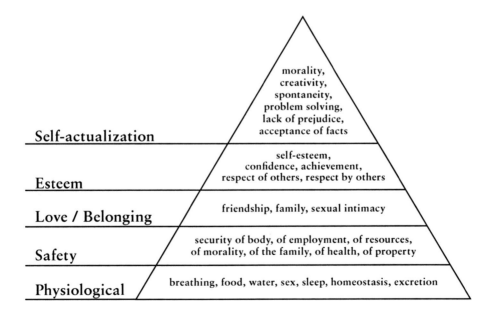

Maslow suggests that there are five categories of needs:

- Physiological needs: air, food, water, sleep, excretion, homeostasis
- Safety: security of one's own body, family, property, job, resources, community morals
- Love/Belonging: durable connection to friends, family, lover, community
- Esteem: being respected by others, having confidence and self respect, symbols of achievement
- Self-actualization: clarity of purpose, clear sense of one's own identity, creativity, acceptance of others

When we talk about needs we are talking about all five areas, though for the purposes of a conversation about healthy relationships, we are generally not focusing on physiological needs but those higher up.

Maslow's second point is that we are not motivated by symbols of achievement when we don't have a place to sleep tonight. It is only as the needs at a particular level are met that we begin to identify and work towards the needs at a higher level. It also suggests that whatever we may say we are about, what we are really trying to do is to meet the un-met lower order needs.

When members of a rival gang meet and are challenging each other under the rubric of *respect* (as when one confronts the other with, "Are you disrespecting me?") it is more likely that the issue at hand is one of establishing *security* or *belonging*. It may appear to be an esteem level need but it is more likely a way of backing the other off to create safety and to show off to members of one's own group to create a sense of belonging.

And the third basic point that Maslow is making with his hierarchy is that even as we are working at meeting the higher order needs, when we are under stress and the lower order needs are not met, they take priority for us. I can be addressing an issue with my son about his curfew, but if I have an asthma attack my only concern is being able to breathe. I really don't care when he gets home.

Sometimes, even as people experience setbacks which challenge their ability to meet lower order needs, they don't adjust. If a man loses his job but won't seek another one because that would require him to admit that he lost his former one, he is trying to maintain esteem but at the expense of security. This is an example of pathology. We have to meet the lower order needs in order to address the higher order needs.

One other thing Maslow pointed out in that paper from 1943–indeed, this was a central point he was making–was that whenever we act we do so because of a complex web of needs we are trying to meet. Rarely is there is a single need that motivates our actions. We do what we do for very complex reasons connected to what we need but in ways that may be not available to us consciously.

The more conscious we are of what we need, the more effective our actions are in creating what we need. Whether we look to the interior world of our feelings to know what we need or to the exterior world of our relationships with others to know what we need, we are looking for places where we are irritated. When we look inward, what we are looking for is our "bad" feelings as a clue to what we are not getting that we need. When we look outward, what we are looking for is the conflicts which arise in our relationships with others as a clue to what we are not getting that we need.

In either case the quality of esuba is evidence that we are not getting our needs met. As we shift to meet them, shalom is restored.

## Preventing Abuse by Knowing What We Need

Remember that abuse is a quality of choices we make when we have the opportunity, the permission, and the motivation to use the power we have over others to meet our needs at their expense . The motivation for any behavior is to get ourselves what we need. However, abuse is a strategy which doesn't work. Abuse doesn't create what we need.

Some people disagree with this. Some say that abuse does work. I don't see it. I can see that sometimes abuse can get others to do what we want in the short run. But even when that happens, it doesn't actually construct what we need. We are more likely to be content with abusing others if we don't actually know what we need.

When Joe told three year old Jack to leave him alone as he sat trying to read the paper in the living room, Joe only knew that he wanted Jack to be different and not demand his attention. He did not know what he actually needed in the moment. The best he could do was to bully Jack.

# Who Meets My Needs?

The chances of my being able to meet my needs are greatly increased when I know what it is that I need. Nevertheless, we find it hard to pay attention to our needs. We don't want to be needy. We don't want to be selfish. So we tune out our awareness of what we need.

This in no way diminishes what we need—it only tunes out awareness of what we need. If we don't know what we need we are much less likely to act in ways which construct what we need. If we aren't getting what we need, we are not able to function optimally.

Still, we can't always create what we need all by ourselves. We can't, for example, create intimacy all by ourselves. Some qualities are only available in the context of a relationship with another.

For this reason we think we get what we need from the other. In some instances this is true. At the lower end of Maslow's hierarchy the needs are mediated through actual material objects. If I am hungry and you have food and you give me some, you have met my need. Higher order needs are not things others give us, they are things we create together. We tend, however, to treat them as though they were objects which people give or withhold.

When Joe went to the wedding with Jamie and was left to fend for himself while she conversed with some old friends, he began to feel uncomfortable. Despite the festive setting, he found esuba arising for him. He knew that he was not getting attention from Jamie and he knew that when he gets her full attention he is not subject to these bad feelings. He concludes that what he needs is her attention. She has given it to him before but now she is withholding it.

As long as Joe is using a conceptual map that what he needs is something Jamie has but is now choosing to withhold from him, he is framing the problem in a manner that stops him from solving it. Worse, it is a map which creates the very problem he is trying to solve. If the conceptual map states that the problem is that Jamie is not as he wants her to be, not as she has been in the past, and not as he has a right to expect her to be; then he has a right to demand that she be who he wants her to be. But the more demanding he becomes, the less she is going to want to have a relationship in which she attends to him. Why would she want to give attention to someone who is telling her she is wrong and bad?

If Joe recognizes that he is not getting what he needs "from" Jamie so decides to create something "with" Jamie, a world of other options opens for him. He can go and stand beside her and enjoy the conversation she is having with old friends and even join in the conversation himself.

# Needs as Qualities

We want to get what we need and there are different kinds or levels of needs but it is even a bit more complicated than that. There are at least three distinctly different phenomena which we refer to as needs. There are 1) strategies or choices, there are 2) events or occurrences, and there are 3) qualities or ways of being. We mentioned this back in Chapter One. We have to understand these differences if we are to deeply know what we need such that we can make the choices which construct those needs.

## Strategy

"But what should I do?" is a question I often hear very early in conversations with a new client. Often I am told, "There is nothing I can do, I have tried everything." Or if I have been reflecting hope to someone who has decided there is no hope I may hear, "Okay, so what do you think I should do?" offered with the implied tone which adds, "so I can prove to you that it won't work." We want to know what to do but sometimes we also believe we have already tried everything.

Ultimately we must do something different if we are going to construct a change in our circumstances. But this is the place to end up, not the place to start. If we start by focusing on what to do, we will do what we have always done and thus get what we have always gotten. What I ultimately do arises as a 2° [Personal-material: choice] strategy. But if what I am doing isn't working–if I am going to construct a new way of being–I need to have access to some higher order perspectives.

## Events

Because we discover we are not getting what we need out of the awareness that the current events of our lives are as we want them to be, the natural assumption is that what we need is for the current circumstances to be different. When I tell my son to clean his room and his room isn't clean, what I need is for him to clean his room. I conclude that what I need is an *event* in which I become satisfied.

This shift from attention to *strategy* (I just need to…) to attention to *event* (I just need for others to…) hinders our ability to respond creatively as it focuses on what we cannot change (the behavior of others) and takes our attention off our own ability to act differently. Nevertheless, there are some ways this formulation of what we need as an *event* is an improvement over the idea of a need as a *strategy* because it moves our awareness off of an impulse to react and brings to our attention the cause of our distress. It brings our attention both to the event which caused the distress and to the awareness we have of what it is about this event which we find bothersome.

Let's look at an example in the lives of the Johnsons to help us see how this works. You remember that Joe told three year old Jack not to ride his tricycle in the street and then, upon returning from the store, saw Jack ride into the street and Jack saw his dad see him. This is the event which alerted Joe to the fact that he was not getting what he needed. So what does he need?

At the level of a strategy, Joe needs to send Jack to his room in fulfillment of the consequence which Joe constructed for Jack when he initially confronted him about riding in the street. But Joe also needs to put away the stuff he has just bought and he needs a happy relationship with Jack. He doesn't want to be always yelling at Jack and he wants to show Jane that he can contain his anger. There are many things here which Joe needs.

At the level of event then Joe needs for Jack to put his tricycle away and go to his room. He needs the supplies put away. He needs smiles from Jack and praise from Jane.

## Qualities in the Relationship

These events, if they should happen, will be evidence to Joe that there are certain qualities present not only in his relationships with Jack and Jane, but also with himself. It is these qualities which are the most durable goal for his striving as they are aspects of his relationships which are completely within his control to create and which are evidence that he is getting what he needs.

If Jack puts his tricycle away, Joe knows that he is consistent in his relationship with Jack and that they have a relationship in which his authority is secure. If the supplies get put away, Joe knows he is responsible for completing his tasks and is conscientious. If Jack smiles at him, he knows there is admiration and affection. And if Jane praises him, he knows he has approval. These are all valid and appropriate needs.

If Joe is able to discover out front the qualities he needs in his relationship with himself and his family, he is able to act easily to create those qualities. If he knows he needs to be someone who is conscientious and consistent, he will both put the supplies away and address Jack's transgression to ensure Jack knows what is and is not allowed. He needs admiration and affection so he will do it in a way which doesn't shame or belittle Jack and assures Jack that he is loved. And when he is able to do that he creates approval of his own behavior whether Jane sees it or knows of it. He is not waiting to get it from Jane but is creating it for himself.

The way I have laid out here the three perspectives on needs—strategies, events and qualities—make it seem as though they are three discrete things. As we explore them more deeply we discover they are more likes stages in a continuum of understanding. As we look at what strategies we might invoke, we look to what events we hope to create. As we look to what events we would like to see we discover the qualities we hope such events would generate.

You may recall at the end of Chapter Seven when Larry was steamed because his mother forgot his birthday. Larry didn't know that he needed certain qualities in his relationship with his mother but could only see how he wanted her to be different. Since he couldn't change her but didn't want to feel powerless, he chose to act in a way that created the opposite of what he needs. He chose to have nothing to do with her. "See how powerful I am," he seemed to say, "I can create distance in my relationship with my mom."

Larry's story is a vivid example of something nearly everyone does from time to time. We all make choices which get us the opposite of what we need. So let's use this progression from strategy to event to quality to event to strategy to look at how we can act more powerfully to construct what we need.

**Original Event:** I had a birthday and got no acknowledgement from my mom.

**Impulsive Strategy:** I will write her off and have nothing to do with her.

**Desired Event:** I want to have my mom honor me on my special day.

**Missing Quality:** I need a relationship in which we feel appreciated by each other and know that we honor each other.

**Expanded Event:** I want us to give honor to each other and to show our appreciation.

**Responsive Strategy:** I will honor my mother with a phone call of appreciation.

What we don't have in this sequence is anything about what is going on with Larry's mother. All we know is that she didn't call. She might be ill. Or maybe she is just angry. She may have noticed a pattern in her relationship with Larry that the only time he calls her is when he needs something. She may be so fed up with his taking her for granted that she has decided not to call on his birthday. He doesn't like what she is doing. She may not like what he is doing.

But while neither one may like the strategy the other is choosing, they are both looking for the same quality in their relationship with the other. They both want a relationship in which they feel honored and appreciated.

*Conflicts arise over strategies, not over qualities.* This is a very important point which helps us as we look for ways to resolve conflict creatively. We have conflicts about the strategies we propose, not about the qualities we need. As long as the focus of our attention is on the strategies, we are looking at the source of the conflict. We have to move our attention to the qualities we seek to create if we are going to construct the solutions.

This problem arises all the time in legislative bodies. Legislation is about passing bills. The bill says, "This is what we will do." They are strategies. Some legislators think we should pay more taxes and some think we should pay less. There is a conflict between strategies. All agree that we want a lean government which does for the community those things which are best done collectively

*Knowing What We Need*

and that such action should be as efficient and effective as possible. There is no conflict about the qualities we are trying to create. The only question is how we will get there…how do we act to create those qualities?

So we ultimately want to come together on a strategy. After all, if we only do what we have always done we will only get what we have always gotten. But before we figure out what we are going to do, let's be sure we know what we need.

## Three Perspectives on What We All Need: Health, Trust, and Justice

To help us more easily and readily identify what we need, we will look at three different templates for seeing what qualities are optimal for our wellbeing. What conditions best support health and wholeness?

You may recall in your junior year of high school in biology class looking through a microscope at a slide of some object in the natural world. There were several things you could adjust to see the slide better. You may have had a light. You certainly had a focus knob to adjust the length of the focusing tube. And there may have been a lens head just above the slide which you could turn to select the final lens to adjust the magnification power of the microscope.

As you selected the power of the lens by turning the head you could see the object on the slide at differing resolutions. If you haven't used a microscope you can get a similar effect by going to an online mapping program and looking at the same place up close or at a distance. It is the same place, or the same slide, but the way it looks may be very different depending on the lens through which you are looking. How we see it depends on the perspective even when the thing itself doesn't change.

We will look at the conflicts which arise for us from three different perspectives to see what each can teach us about what we need. These are not the only three perspectives. There are a theoretically infinite number of lenses through which we can look. I offer these three only as a guide to what we can become able to see when we look.

These three are ways of looking at what creates the quality of *health* in our relationship between self and other, what creates the quality of *trust* in a relationship with another, and what creates the quality of *justice* in a community.

## Personal

With the microscope set on the highest power we look at the relationship between what we perceive to be "self" and what we see as "not-self." We each have developed a "separate self sense" by which we perceive ourselves to be separate from the world around us. Where are the boundaries to self?

I have a cup of coffee on my desk. The coffee is not me. I take a sip. Now it is. In a bit I will walk down the hall to the little room and then the coffee will not be me anymore.

I breathe in air and with it oxygen. The oxygen passes through the semi-permeable membrane in my lungs and bonds with the hemoglobin which then carries it to my cells where it is traded for carbon dioxide. The hemoglobin returns to my lungs where it trades the carbon dioxide for another oxygen molecule. I breathe in and I breathe out.

We imagine ourselves to be far more separate from the world around us than we actually are. We have a boundary between self and not-self which is a sort of semi-permeable membrane.

In order to maintain health I need to be careful about what I let in through this membrane and what I let out. I must be careful that I don't expose myself to carbon monoxide as it bonds with the hemoglobin but the cells can't use it. I must be careful that I don't get diarrhea because I might get dehydrated. There are things I want to let in and things I want to keep out. There are things I want to let out and things I want to keep in. This is true physically and it is true emotionally.

Sometimes get what we need and sometimes we don't. There are four options here.

• **Let in what nurtures:** We can get what is nurturing and supportive for us and feel satisfied, or we can fail to get what is nurturing and supportive for us and feel hurt.

• **Keep out what is toxic:** We can protect ourselves from that which is toxic to us and feel safe, or we can be exposed to that which is toxic to us and feel hurt.

*Knowing What We Need*

- **Let out self expression:** We can express what is true and vital for us and feel satisfied, or we can be stifled from expressing what is true and vital for us and feel hurt.

- **Keep in what is precious:** We can protect that which is precious to us from being taken or defiled and feel safe, or we can fail to protect that which is precious to us from being taken or defiled and feel hurt.

So we are either *safe and satisfied* or we are *hurt* as a consequence of how well we construct our relationships with others. When we do well at establishing and maintaining boundaries, we get safety and satisfaction. When we don't do well, we get hurt.

I am not saying that if you get hurt it is your fault. I am saying that if you want to be responsible for your own welfare, you notice when you are hurt and seek to adjust your boundaries.

Now, this business of setting boundaries can be a source of great confusion. I have often heard clients of mine declare that they are going to "set a boundary" with some important person in their life. By this they mean that they are going to make clear to the other what the other may or may not do. This is not what I am talking about. Setting my boundaries differently is about defining what I will or will not do, not what I will allow or disallow from others.

> Joe is awakened from a deep sleep by the ringing of the telephone. He struggles to focus on the digital clock on his bed stand as he gropes for the phone. It is just after 2:00 AM.
>
> "Huh?" he grunts into the phone.
>
> "Joe, buddy, is that you? Hey, this is Jake. I know it is the middle of the night but I didn't know who to call. I am just getting back into town from a business trip and my car just broke down. I am about fifteen minutes from you and need a lift. Could you come and get me?"
>
> Jake was Joe's closest friend in college. They haven't seen much of each other since Joe and Jane married and Joe feels a little guilty about that. He resents being awakened but there have been lots of times when he and Jake were out

*partying well past 2:00 and Jake is single. He doesn't really know how much his call is disrupting things for Joe.*

*"Ungh, sure Jake I can help you out. Where are you?"*

Joe doesn't like being awakened but he sees this as chance to reconnect to Jake and he likes being someone that others can count on. This is his chance to be a best friend to Jake.

*A couple of weeks later Joe again gets a late night call from Jake. "Hey buddy; you won't believe what just happened. My car quit on me again. Can you help me out?" Joe again gets up and goes to help his friend but he notices that he is less sure he is doing the right thing. He is not sure he is being who he wants to be.*

*A week later Joe gets another late night call. This time he cuts Jake off in the middle of his explanation about what is wrong saying, "Fix your damn car," and rolls over and goes back to sleep.*

Joe has adjusted his own boundaries in relation to Jake. He is not expecting Jake to change. He is just changing who he is willing to be with Jake.

We gather data from our emotional and physical systems and notice whether we are getting what we need. When we are, we relax into whatever is transpiring. When we are not, we flinch and seek to pull away from whatever is hurting us.

We have already noted that it is important that we create what we need and we often resist because we don't want to be selfish. But there is another aspect of how we construct our awareness of ourselves which effects how we construct our relationships with others and the boundaries we create with them.

Who "I" am is whatever I identify with. What I identify with can change depending on the context. So, in the interplay between self and other, who is *self* and who is *other* can shift.

When I was a child I fought with my brother. I wanted to kill him. Our mother, being the compassionate woman she is, would say to us, "If you are going to fight, don't do it in the house. Go out in the back yard." So we would fight in the back yard. In this relationship with my brother I was my physical self and he was the hated other.

Except that sometimes, Blair, the kid who lived two doors down, would come up to play and would get into a fight with my brother. Well, nobody messes with my brother. So in this instance my brother and I were *self* and Blair was the alien *other*.

Except that Blair and I were on the same baseball team and so he and I and the rest of the team were *self* against the other teams in the league who were all *other*.

Except that we weren't the best team in the league so when the winner of our division went to State, who do you suppose we rooted for?

Who I constructed as the "self" whose needs I was dedicated to meeting and who I constructed as "other" with whom I was trying to construct a safe and satisfying relationship changed as the context changed. Sometimes this shift can come very quickly.

> *When Jesse started playing soccer, Joe got really excited about what a natural he seemed to be. Joe played in high school and college and Jesse's participation on a "select" team brought out Joe's pride and he greatly enjoyed the vicarious pleasure of watching his son on the field. Jesse played right wing, the same position as Joe played in college and Joe could really see himself in his son.*

> *Mid-way in the second half of a game against the best team in the league with the score at 1-1, Jesse got a long pass and was just barely on-side. He took it at full stride and raced down the field.*

> *Joe was on his feet yelling, "Yes, go, go!"*

> *Jesse sped down the field, far ahead of the defender who had been covering him, with no one between him and the goal but the goalie. With each step the shoelace on his left boot got longer and longer. As he did a little stutter-step to fake out the goalie, he stepped on his own shoelace and landed face first as the ball dribbled into the goalie's hands.*

> *Joe's glee turned to fury. "Stupid kid, can't tie your own shoes!"*

Joe was Jesse on the field heading to a big moment of triumph and glory. They were one. But when Jesse stepped on his shoelace, it was for Joe as though he had just been tripped. Joe was furious that his son had just stolen the goal from him. Joe went from being Jesse to being the one Jesse tripped. Who "I" am in my relationships with others can change and can do so in an instant.

## Relational

Now, let's adjust the head on the microscope to see a broader field. Instead of just looking at "I" let's look at "we." We construct relationships with others all the time. We can sit down on a bus and have a relationship with those around us. What is involved in constructing a relationship, especially a relationship in which we are able to construct what we need?

Through this lens of the microscope we focus on three concerns. What do we know about each other? How much respect do we have for each other? How willing are we to act on each other's behalf?

### Known

Having a relationship with another involves both knowing and being known by them. Even if we are only talking about the relationship we construct with another on the bus, we know what they are reading, where they got on or off, and, if we are sitting close, even how they smell.

It is fairly easy, in a new relationship, to find things to talk about because there is so little we know about each other. Over time we may find ourselves having less to talk about because we have already said what we want to say, or we may have things we don't want the other to know about us. We may discover that we are afraid of being better known for fear of being rejected or betrayed.

Ideally, we find that we can be both deeply known and fully accepted for who we are. But these are hard to balance. It turns out that deeply intimate relationships are hard to create and maintain.

As we let others know us, there are a series of problems which can develop.

One is that we find that we don't know ourselves well enough to tell the other who we are. As the relationship grows deeper we are invited to share more deeply. We may come to the limits of what we know about ourselves.

We may also find that the other has a sense of who we are that doesn't match who we believe ourselves to be. There are at least a couple of reasons this can happen. One is that we don't know aspects of ourselves which the other becomes able to see and name. Another is that the other may project on to us who they want us to be or who they are afraid we are. What they see in us is not some aspect of ourselves, but something they are working out by projecting that attribute onto us. In the first instance, when they know something true which we don't see, it is in our interest to open ourselves to their insight. In the second instance, when they project something which is not really about us but actually about something which is going on with them, we want to protect our own self image.

But when we have a relationship with someone who deeply knows us and with whom we feel free to let ourselves be known, we find that letting them know us actually helps us know ourselves. The relationship becomes a mirror by which we may see ourselves more clearly.

## Respected

A second aspect of a healthy relationship is that it is one in which we respect each other. Now *respect* is one of those words we use in different ways so I want to be clear about how I mean it. *Respect* can mean *obey* as in when a father says sternly to his son, "You better respect me." *Respect* can also be a synonym for *admiration*. But *admiration* has to do with how we feel about what another is able to do. If we really like what someone does or is able to do we may say we admire or respect that person.

Here I am talking about something different from *obey* or *admire*. What I mean by *respect* is the quality in a relationship when we acknowledge each other's worth. I respect someone whom I see as having value. The test is whether we can respect someone even if we don't admire what they are doing. Can I respect my son even when he is not obeying me?

In a healthy relationship we know that we each value the other no matter what they do. We still know the other to be precious and we know they honor our value as well.

## Cared for

A third quality of a healthy relationship is that it is one in which we care for each other. Now, *caring for* someone is not the same as *taking care of* them. They can easily go together, but it is possible for someone to have the job of taking care of another when they don't actually care for them.

Caring for someone is a quality which arises when we decide to pay attention to how our choices affect the other and we want what is best for them. This is not the same as doing whatever they want. We can easily care for someone and still not do what they want us to do. Even when we are not as they want us to be, we still notice how what we are doing affects them.

Knowing is a *cognitive* function. It has to do with how we think. Respect is an *affective* function. It is of the realm of our emotions. Caring for is a *conative* function. It has to do with our will and, thus, the way we make choices.

When Jack was three and made an object out of Legos and went to show his dad, and, when Joe was sitting in the living room reading the newspaper and Jack wanted his attention, and, when Joe told him to leave him alone and to go to his room for fifteen minutes; Jack saw that his dad didn't want to know what he was building, didn't value him, and wasn't going to act to care for him. If this were the usual way that Joe treated his son, Jack would not come to trust his dad.

## Systemic

And, finally, let's adjust the head on the microscope for the broadest possible view taking in the whole system of which we are a part. This may be the family, the neighborhood, a church or other organization, the city, region or nation, the globe or the cosmos. Any system is made up of many parts and there are certain qualities the system must have if each of the parts and the collective whole is to function optimally.

### Communication (Awareness)

First of all, the parts of the system have to know what is going on with the other parts. There has to be some mechanism by which the system creates shared awareness or consciousness.

As a body is a system made up of many organs, the nervous system links them all into an organism in which self-consciousness arises. Families have calendars on bulletin boards or online to help them keep track of when the games and the doctor's appointments are. Cities have newspapers and radio stations to keep citizens informed, and communities have elections to discover the will of the people. The State of the Union is presented by the President and the welfare of the globe is monitored by seismologists and climatologists. Every healthy system has a way of monitoring its own level of functioning.

## Competence

As we come to know what is going on in the system, we must be competent to respond to the needs of the system. We have to gather or create the necessary resources and then distribute them in the best possible way.

If I am hungry I need to identify edible roots and berries or else find a grocery store and have some money to buy food. If we have too much traffic trying to get across the river we need to build a new bridge. We have to identify the funds, the steel, the concrete, the laborers and engineers to build the bridge, and make and follow the plans.

## Conflict Resolution

In every system there are times when there are not enough resources. We will need a mechanism by which we can discover and distribute the resources, clarify the identity of the parts of the system, and solidify the agreements which build a constructive process for working together–for power with.

We may have the workers to build the bridge, but not enough money. Or we may know where the money will come from but we can't agree on where to build the bridge. There will never be enough so we will have to resolve the conflicts over scarce resources. We will have to be clear about the authority of various municipalities to approve right of way, and we will have to know how the bonds for building the bridge will be paid off.

> After the game in which Jesse missed the goal, Joe sat with him as he changed
> out of his soccer shoes. As Jesse pulled on his everyday sneakers Joe noticed

*that they were falling apart. Joe was aware that Jesse needed new shoes.*

*Joe checked and determined there would be enough time before they had to be home to start dinner to swing by the shoe store to see if there was a pair on sale that Jesse would like. Joe knew where the store was, had his wallet with the credit card and was able to drive the car. He marshaled all of these competencies to the service of new shoes for Jesse.*

*When they got to the store they found a wall of shoes arrayed before them. Joe started looking for the ones with the red tags that indicated they were on sale. But Jesse saw the pair that was the signature brand of his favorite basketball player. Joe looked at the price tag and almost choked. If they bought those shoes, Joe wasn't sure how they were going to make the mortgage. But Jesse really wanted those shoes and Joe felt badly for him for the missed soccer goal and the way he had yelled at him. He was conflicted about how to use the resources.*

When Joe heard the message communicated from Jesse's shoes about what Jesse needed, and responded to that awareness by managing time, money and space to get to the store, and, when confronted with the difference between the shoes Jesse wanted and the ones Joe could afford such that the needs of the whole system were best attended to, Joe was creating justice.

This is not the justice we create with the criminal justice system. That justice is about creating consequences for people who choose to do things which harm the welfare of others or of themselves; it is about identifying and punishing the bad guys. The justice we are talking about here is not a reaction to what is harmful, but a creative action to construct the qualities which allow for healing and wholeness.

## Good Emotional Hygiene

Let us return for just a moment to our process for becoming as emotionally healthy as possible. There are three skills we want to master. We want to know what we are feeling, even when we are feeling "bad." We want to identify the cause of the feelings–this is especially an issue when the intensity of our feelings is out of proportion to the event which evoked those feelings. Then, we want to harness the energy of the emotion, put it with the information about what we need, and use the two to launch an action which moves us toward what we need.

When Joe yelled at Jesse that he was stupid for not tying his shoes, Joe recognized that he was out of line. He saw the looks of those around him and he mentally replayed what he had just done and he knew that this was not just about Jesse's missed goal. This was mostly about something internal to Joe. So what was going on with Joe?

He knew that the feelings arose for him as Jesse was about to score and become the hero of the game. He knew that his feelings changed from excitement and anticipation to anger and disappointment but he also knew that the emotions were not in proportion to the event. This was just a bunch of kids playing together. This mistake on Jesse's part did not warrant such a display of contempt on Joe's part.

If Joe can figure out what is going on in him when he gets so worked up and identify what he actually needs, he may repair his relationship with Jesse. He may also be able to repair his internal conflict such that he doesn't keep doing this to Jesse. If Joe is able to remember how he has been striving to score at work, to acknowledge how angry he is at himself for not being able to follow through on his own, not taking care of the little details that support his own success, then he may see that this is really about him at work, not Jesse on the field. He will not only apologize to Jesse but address whatever is blocking his success in business.

It is just these skills that we turn to in the next chapter.

## Summary

Everything that grows does so through stages of development. One of the things which grows is our capacity to meet our own needs. We also grow in our capacity to know what we need. Our ability to create what we need is much stronger when we know what we need. When we don't know what we need we are much more likely to act in ways which are abusive to others. We sometimes assume others can meet our needs and we become demanding and controlling when they don't.

We use the word *need* to refer to the strategies we might choose (I just need to…), the events we hope to construct (I need for you to…), or the qualities we hope to evoke (I need…). While we benefit from paying attention to all three kinds of needs, we should be very wary of choosing a strategy before we are clear about the qualities we are seeking to create. Indeed, the conflicts we encounter around what seem to be competing needs are conflicts about strategies or events, not about the optimal qualities. We all need the same qualities.

To help us determine what qualities are missing when conflicts arise, we can use a variety of maps. We here reviewed three such maps, though there are many more.

From the perspective of a single individual in relation to a complex world: there are things we need to take in and things we need to keep out. There are things we need to let out, and things we need to keep in. When we do this well we have good boundaries. When we are hurt we know that there is a problem with our boundaries and we may decide to adjust them. If we do a good job of maintaining our boundaries we have health.

From the perspective of a person in a relationship with one other person: there are qualities the relationship needs if we are to function optimally. We need to know the other and know that the other knows us. We need to feel the respect of the other and to appreciate their value to us. And we need to pay attention to what is going on with them and act in a manner which is consistent with their interests and to know they do the same for us. When we can know, respect, and care for each other we create trust.

From the perspective of our role as part of a complex system like a family, organization or community: there are qualities the system must create to preserve the wellbeing of the whole and all of its parts. Each part must have a sense of what is going on with the other parts, the system must create or gather and distribute the resources that all of the parts of the system need, and the parts of the system must have a mechanism for addressing conflicts when there are not enough resources to meet the needs of each part. When we are conscious, competent, and can resolve conflict we create justice.

Knowing what we need allows us to repair any damage we may have done to others when we blame them for what we don't have, and frees us to act in ways which genuinely meet our needs. It supports our ability to create health, trust, and justice.

# Part Three:
# Tools for Transformation

If I am going to use the perspectives given by these conceptual maps in a manner that heals my Self, my relationships, and the world, I have to change what I do.

# 11

# Strategies: The Practical Disciplines

We have been considering how in theory it is possible to resolve a conflict. Nevertheless we don't get any positive benefit until we actually do something different. In this chapter we consider some practical things we can do to move us toward resolution.

I am often asked by impatient clients in a crisis, "But what should I do?" In general this is an easy question to answer. "Do what moves you toward what you need, being careful not to do it at another's expense." The problem is that the right thing to do in any given situation can be rather difficult to determine. We have a series of disciplines which help us figure it out; that is, they help us figure out what we want to do and then help us do what we decided. The more we practice, the more mastery we develop.

## Appreciating Discipline

You may recall that we introduced the idea of disciplines at the beginning of this book as we considered how difficult it is to change ourselves. Especially when the change we seek is a transformation to a more complex way of being, we are not able to create a durable shift in our behavior without a robust practice. This practice may include many disciplines but all of them have certain common features.

- They have a clear *intention* about how we are seeking to change.
- They require us to pay keen *attention*.

- We have to engage the practices through many acts of *repetition*.
- And while we initially structure our practice through the *guidance* of an *external* coach or teacher, we come to feel an *internal* sense of rightness and clarity through and towards the practice.

We tend to admire those who are disciplined but we have trouble appreciating the ways in which we ourselves are disciplined and, thus, have trouble seeing that we can take on a new discipline as a means to our own transformation. We just can't see ourselves actually doing these things. We say, "Yeah, I can see that this would be a great thing for me if I could do it, but I just don't have time."

Each of these disciplines takes very little time. They do require, however, full attention and consistent practice. It has universally been my experience, both professionally and personally, that the time these disciplines take is significantly less than the time which is created by the greater level of performance we achieve when we practice them. They are a great investment.

## Review of the Mindfulness Disciplines

We have already introduced the first five disciplines. These are the ones I call the Mindfulness Disciplines. They are simple little exercises which, when we do them everyday, dramatically raise the level of our awareness of what is going on with us, especially in the context of our relationships with others, but also in relationship to ourselves. Briefly they are:

1. **The Bothers Me Log:** spend five minutes a day writing down or otherwise recording whatever you have noticed bothering you since the last time you made an entry in the Log. This is not a diary. Just make quick notes about the events so that you can recall them. If you want to keep a diary, great. But this is not that. This is an attempt to make an exhaustive list of every little thing you notice. Try to capture as many items as possible and keep at it for at least five minutes.

2. **The Anger Workout:** spend at least 5 minutes but not more than 20 minutes in an activity which
   a. allows you to focus your attention on your physical sensations

as you become fully aware of your anger (or any other feeling you don't want to feel),

b.  is safe for you and others, and

c.  is a routine that you can do nearly everyday in much the same way.

3.  **Cultivating Critical Feedback:**  set aside some time everyday to list the critical feedback you hear from others.  If you can't hear any, ask for it.  Others don't like everything you do.  Notice and address your own resistance to hearing this.  Don't take it personally.  You don't even have to believe it.  But notice it.

4.  **Suspend Self-Soothing:** notice that you get anxious and that you sometimes do things to soothe the anxiety.  Anticipate the self-soothing but before you do it, stop yourself and notice the anxiety and see if you can identify what you are anxious about.  Don't self-soothe until you can identify your anxiety.

5.  **Self-Care Routine:**  make a list of all of the things you do everyday to care for yourself.  While you are at it, 2) make a list of the things you have sometimes done to care for yourself but don't seem to get to often enough.  And you might as well 3) make a list of all of the things you think you ought to do but have never been able to get yourself to do.  Now, put the second and third list away and just focus on the first one.  Turn it into a daily routine so you can more easily notice when you don't do what is good for you and see if you can identify that part of you which talks you out of doing what you have already decided was good for you.

[For a fuller summary, the class handouts are in the Appendix and more information is on the web site at JustConflict.com]

# Focusing On Conflict, From a Locus of Curiosity, Through the Lens of the Discipline

There is one other thing we want to keep in mind as we introduce the Practical Disciplines.  You recall that we talked about the different aspects of our awareness and that we can make choices about how we construct our awareness. We identified that we can choose what we look at—the *focus of our attention*. We can choose the stance or role from which we look—the *locus of our identity*. And we can choose the perspective—or *lens*—by which we make meaning about what we see.

The *focus of our attention* is the conflict. We notice that this circumstance is bothering us as we complete our Bothers Me Log, and we feel the emotions as we do our Anger Workout. We may have even received some Critical Feedback from others about the circumstance. We are paying attention.

We use the tools of the Mindfulness Disciplines as ways of focusing our attention on the conflict and now we are ready to use the tools of the Practical Disciplines to figure out what to do. We are ready to use the *lens* of the discipline as a framework with which to address the conflict.

What is the *locus of our identity*? Ideally we come from the highest Order of Self available to us. If this is a persistent conflict in a significant relationship we must bring our best to this problem. We want to have available to us the highest qualities of the Self.

Internal Family Systems therapy identifies several qualities of the Self. The Self in IFS terminology is roughly analogous to the 6° of Self as we named them in Chapter Four, but also incorporates qualities from Seventh and Eighth Order as well. IFS has identified eight of these qualities. They include calm, curiosity, compassion, confidence, courage, clarity, connectedness, and creativity.[26]

While these are all very helpful and necessary qualities, we want especially to focus on the quality of curiosity. As we try to construct resolution of conflicts we have to be curious about what we need, about how our behavior is affecting others, and about what maps they are using to make meaning of the events in our shared experience. As important as our curiosity is, however, it can lead to behavior which is very damaging to our efforts to construct resolution.

## Being Curious Without Asking Questions

Back in Chapter Seven we introduced the paradoxical notion of "Fighting without Fighting." Similarly we now suggest that we "Be curious without asking questions." To do this we have to examine what a *question* is.

---

26   Center for Self Leadership, 2006

A question is a kind of statement which calls for the punctuation of a question mark at the end of a sentence. It is a brief statement of what we want to know. It leaves out some information for the purposes of brevity so that we can simplify our conversation. So we say, "Will you pass the salt, please?" rather than saying, "I would like to have the salt but can't reach it and I am wondering if you would be so kind as to pass it to me."

It most circumstances we don't need the detail of the longer statement to know what someone means and we appreciate the brevity. But when we are addressing a conflict the brevity may leave out some very helpful information and may add layers of conflict to an already complex situation.

> Joe and Jane decided to let Jack stay at a friend's house to watch the end of a championship game even though it was a school night. Jack is normally expected to be in bed by 10:00 but the game wasn't going to end until 10:00 if it didn't go into overtime. They set the curfew at 11:00.

> Jane went to bed but Joe stayed up waiting for Jack's safe return. 11:00 came and went and Joe started to pace. When Jack came it the door at 11:15, the first thing out of his mouth was, "What time is it?"

Joe really didn't need to know what time it was. He was very aware of the time. He may have wondered whether Jack knew what time it was. Or he may have wondered if Jack cared enough to keep the curfew. He may have only been expressing his relief that Jack was okay.

For Jack's part, if he just answers the question, he is only going to make the problem worse. He is invited to give a reason for being late, but this won't be an answer to the question so he will be seen as disrespectful. This isn't going to move them toward resolution.

While there are no specific behaviors that are always helpful, there are some that are always a problem and will tend to hinder resolution of the conflict. In particular:

- Don't ask questions to which you already know the answer. These are clearly a way to make the other lose. Either the other knows the answer you are looking for and gives it, proving you right. Or the other doesn't know the answer you are looking for and is proven wrong.

- Don't ask questions you know the other person can't answer. These are also a way to make the other lose but they are often not actually questions at all but statements of what we believe to be true. If we ask someone, "What makes you so stupid?" we aren't actually looking for an answer. We are making a statement of contempt toward the other.

- But most especially, don't ask why. Anyone who has ever had a three year old in the house who has discovered the power of why knows how irritating this can be. The answer to *why* is always *because…* and that is not an answer. *Why* makes us defensive. The question assumes there is something amiss. If someone were to walk into the room where you are reading at the moment and ask, "Why are you sitting in that chair?" how would you feel? When we ask why, we don't come across as curious, but as critical. If instead someone walked in and said, "I am worried that you are not getting good light where you are sitting and suggest you might see better if you moved to a chair closer to the window," you would have a very different response.

For these reasons I strongly encourage you to notice when you begin to ask questions and to avoid them whenever there is some tension in the relationship. Instead, focus on what is going on with you and seek to illuminate for the other how you are feeling and what you need.

> *When Jack finally walked in at 11:15 Joe said to him, "Jack, I have been really worried about you. I don't know for sure when the game ended but I believe you had plenty of time to get home and so when you are late it doesn't encourage me to trust you with an extended curfew in the future. I would like to know what happened that kept you from being home on time."*

To this Jack can respond easily. He either knows what happened or he is invited to figure it out. It creates a quality of curiosity in the relationship rather than one of suspicion and attack. Being able to do this takes practice.

The other side of this observation is that most of the people you have conflicts with will not have read this book. They will continue to ask you questions when they are stressed and you will continue to get defensive. So let me offer some suggestions about how to respond when you are being questioned in ways that raise your hackles.

You do not have to answer the questions that others ask you. When we are afraid that a situation is going to escalate, we often try to please others. If they ask us questions, we try to answer them. But when the questions are ones we can't answer, or ones they already know the answer to, then our attempts to answer them will only fuel the fire. If we can notice either our own defensiveness or the format of the question being asked and realize that we don't yet know enough about the other's curiosity, we can get curious about their curiosity.

Jesus is depicted in the Gospels as doing this often and with great skill. When asked a trick question, he would respond with curiosity about the question. One of the best examples of this was when he was asked about paying the tax to Caesar. Since Caesar claimed to be a god, paying tax to him was worshipping a false god, it was idolatry. But not paying the tax was a crime and telling others not to pay the tax was treason. So Jesus asked to see the coin by which the tax was paid. On it was the image of Caesar. He simply stated, "Give to Caesar what is Caesar's and to God what is God's." At one level this seems like a clever way to dodge the question, but it actually goes to the heart of the issue. While his questioners may have been trying to trap him, his response illuminated the real issue at stake.

Similarly when we are being questioned by others and we sense a trap or that the questions aren't really the issue at hand, we can respond with curiosity about the question.

> Jack knew he was late but he didn't expect his folks to wait up for him. He figured if his dad was up it was to watch the game so he would know that it went into double overtime. He was caught off guard when he walked in and was immediately confronted with, "What time is it?"

> Jack started to answer and then paused. He could tell his dad was angry and he was aware that this seemed like a big deal about 15 minutes. So he knew he the emotion was about more than being late. Instead of telling his dad about the time or trying to explain why he was late, he said, "Dad, I can see that you are pretty upset and I am wondering what you need to know from me to help you get what you need."

Okay, okay, no teenager is actually going to say something like that. Heck, most adults don't have the maturity and presence of mind to respond that way. But what would it be like if we did?

## The Five Practical Disciplines

So, remembering that we want to keep our attention focused on the event or circumstance that is causing esuba to arise in our awareness, and we want to come from a space within ourselves which approaches the world around and within with an attitude of curiosity, let's try looking at these events with a variety of lenses which can help us identify what we might do to create resolution.

Let's also remember that these disciplines are designed to make conflict resolution as simple as possible. But simple is not the same as easy. This will be the hardest work you ever do. And let us also remember that none of these disciplines will get the people around you to change. Your only reason to use these is to get yourself to change. If you start to say to yourself, "Oh, this won't work," check to see if you believe it won't work because it won't get others to change. If so, you are right. It won't.

## Discipline #6: ACE - When We Notice It Is the Same Thing Again and Again

Since you have been paying keen attention to the conflicts which arise in your awareness, you have noticed that these are mostly the same things over and over. Use of the Bothers Me Log has clarified for you the events which keep happening which bother you. Pick one that is big enough that you have some energy to address it but not so big that it scares you.

Now notice that this is something that happens often and you know something about when it is going to happen next. It may be an event that happens every Friday, or right after your mother-in-law leaves, or when the moon is full; there is something predictable about when it will come up. You can anticipate when this will happen again or, at the very least, that it will happen again.

Since it will happen again, it is in your interest to be ready for it. You remember what happened last time and you don't want that to happen again.

If you are going to handle it differently next time you will have to be ready... you will have to have a plan. We will come back in a moment to the matter of developing a plan.

Once you have a plan, you will have to implement it. Just because we know what we would like to do, doesn't mean we are going to do it. Part of your plan involves identifying how you will do what you planned.

Then after the event happens, given that things never go the way we want them to, evaluate how well your plan worked at creating what you need including evaluating how well you were able to show up the way you intended to show up.

In short, the discipline requires that you;

*Anticipate* the next iteration of the circumstances which evoke the conflict;

*Create* and implement a plan; and then

*Evaluate* how well the plan works and how well you are able to work the plan.

Then roll this entire awareness up and start again. When will it come up again? What will you do then?

> Jane walks out of the living room on an autumn afternoon after reminding Joe once again about his dirty clothes on the bedroom floor. She notices her resentment and her expectation that nothing she has just said to Joe is going to change anything...he will continue to be the same slob he has always been.

Jane notices that this is a pattern of conflict in a significant relationship and that she will have more opportunities to address it. She can keep trying to get Joe to change, or she can decide to let the conflict solve her. As this is a persistent problem which Jane sees as one in which she is over-reacting, this may be a fertile opportunity for growth.

For Jane to move forward she needs a plan.

# Three Parts to the Plan

As we seek to construct a plan for what we are going to do differently next time, it helps to separate out the plan into three parts. What do I wish I had done last time? How will I know next time when it happens? What do I need to do before next time to be ready for it?

- *Last time:* If I had it to do over again, what would I want to have done differently? Of course, we can't go back in time. Time only moves in one direction. But *last time* has some important information for us and we don't want to lose the lessons we learned. I was there. I was paying attention. I know what I did and said. I know what others did and said. I have a lot of information about this dance we do together from time to time. So the first thing I want to construct is a sense of what I could have done which would have gotten me more of what I need. It doesn't have to be a plan which would make everything perfect. But it does need to be something which I believe I could have done which would have gotten me more of the qualities I need.
- *Next time:* Once I am clear about what I wish I had done, then I can prepare for next time. *Next time* I want to do what I wish I had done *last time*. Except that *next time* might look somewhat different from *last time*. How will I know *next time* when it comes? What are the markers which will alert me that this is the time to invoke my plan for a new way of being? I want to be very clear about this so I won't miss it.
- *Before next time:* One of the things I know about *next time* even before it comes is that when it shows up I am going to be tense. I will feel anxiety about the event itself and about my ability to do what I have decided to do. What can I do before then to be as ready as possible when these circumstances arise in the future?

Let's see how Jane can prepare a plan for addressing her issue with Joe when he says he will clean up after himself and then watches TV instead of following through on his commitment to her.

*Jane feels like she is becoming a nag. She remembers feeling nagged by her mom and she knows Joe doesn't like it. When she gets that way she just feels*

*Strategies: The Practical Disciplines*

*the resentment building in both of them. She decides that next time she will have a pleasant tone of voice and only try to get Joe to make a commitment to when he will pick up his clothes and not insist that he do it immediately.*

*Jane knows that this will be an issue next Sunday afternoon but is aware that it could come up sooner if he doesn't pick up his stuff. She decides that if his clothes aren't picked up by the time they go to bed Monday night she will try out her new plan.*

So Jane has in her mind an idea of what she is going to do. As we proceed we will check in with her and see how she is doing on implementing her plan.

## Discipline #7: Statement of Accountability- When We Notice Our Own Regret and Want to Be Certain About the Future

It is far easier to address conflicts when they are small; that is, when the energy we carry from the emotions we have toward the event and towards others who have a different perspective on the event are small. We are far more likely to do what we have chosen to do when we are calm and centered.

But around the little things it may be hard for us to figure out what the issues are for us. There just isn't enough energy there to get past our barriers to self-awareness. It is too easy to remain in denial. For this reason it can be very helpful to work on some bigger issues. The big issues have enough energy around them to help us go deeply into Self-awareness.

Consider the times in your life when you did something you regret. Think of a time when you harmed someone you care about. Think about the time when you did the most harm to someone else which you now most regret.

We have all done things which are harmful to others. We all have regrets. What we are looking for here is an event that has both. If you have done things which harmed others which you don't regret, that doesn't count. If you have done things which you regret but which didn't harm anyone else, that doesn't count either. It has to be an event for which both are true.

I hope before you read on you will bring to mind a specific event in when you acted in ways that were harmful to another which you now regret. This is hard to do. We don't want to think about those times. But if you want to be as certain as you can be that you won't again do something like that, this is worth the effort, and the explanation of the discipline will make more sense if you have before you an example from your own life.

> After Joe's accident the night Jesse went off to his girlfriend's house without permission, their relationship became very strained. Joe felt bad about himself for not being able to work and got really tired of being cooped up at home. Jesse's guilt about not being present when the news came about his dad turned into anger at his girlfriend and they broke up.
>
> After one particularly contentious day, Joe lay in bed not being able to sleep. Though he normally didn't drink on a weeknight, he had had a few beers to settle himself down. He didn't like the feelings he was having toward his son and he knew they were at least partially to do with things which were not Jesse's fault. He decided to talk to Jesse if he was not already asleep.
>
> Jesse was relieved when his folks went to bed. His bedroom was upstairs next to Jack's and they could each shut their doors and have some privacy. Jesse was feeling really lonely and was missing his girlfriend. He wrote her a letter and read it and decided it was stupid and decided to burn it. He found some matches and a dirty plate he had brought to his room with some nachos and lit the letter. Just as it started to burn he heard his father coming up the stairs. He quickly locked the door.
>
> Joe noticed the smell of smoke coming down the hall and could tell it was coming from Jesse's room. He knocked on the door and called Jesse's name. Jesse didn't respond.
>
> Inside the room Jesse had the window open and was trying to air out the room. He hoped his dad would just think he was asleep and would go back to bed so he tried to be as quiet as possible.
>
> Joe pounded on the door now worried that Jesse might be hurt. Getting no response, he broke down the door.

　　　　　　　　　　*Strategies: The Practical Disciplines*

*Stepping into the room Joe found Jesse standing by the open window looking a bit surprised but with a feigned look of nonchalance. Joe turned back to the door and ripped the remains of the door out of the door jam.*

Joe was not in the habit of ripping his house apart. This wasn't something he planned to do and is certainly not something he wants to ever do again. But he knows he is capable of it. He did it.

So holding in mind the choice you made which was harmful to someone else, let's walk through the steps of the Statement of Accountability using Joe's choice as an example. There are four parts to the Statement of Accountability: What was the choice you regret? What was the harm you did? What was going on with you that supported your making that choice? What do you have in place in your life now to protect from making that choice again?

## What Was The Choice You Regret?

Our first step is to separate out from all of the choices we and others made the one we most regret. Which part of this do I most wish I had never done? Every event is constructed out of many choices, both ours and others. But what is the one I made that I now most regret?

> *Joe did not regret getting out of bed and going to Jesse's room to try to smooth things between them. He did not regret pounding on the door and calling to Jesse when he smelled smoke. He did not regret breaking through the door when he found it locked and got no answer from Jesse. What he regretted was then turning around and destroying the rest of the door once he knew Jesse was safe.*

To be sure, Jesse also made some poor choices which also constructed this event, but those are things he can work on in his Statement of Accountability. We may have a tendency to excuse our own behavior when others are also acting badly, but that won't help us with our own transformation.

## What Was The Effect Of Your Choice On Others And On Your Relationships With Others?

We have already determined that this choice was harmful to others, but can we be more specific about that. What was the harm? And what was the harm, not just to the person we acted toward but also to others who may have come to know about it? And what was the harm, not just to the people, but also to our relationships with them?

> Joe saw the expression on Jesse's face when he broke down the door. When he then turned and pulled the remains of the locked door from the door jam, splintering the wood as he did so, he saw Jack burst out of his room having been awakened from sleep. He knew that neither of his boys had ever seen him this way. He always tried to be calm whenever he got angry. He didn't want to show them that it was okay to be violent when angry. He knew this scared them both, but especially Jesse. It was not hard to imagine that Jesse saw his dad's ripping the door apart as a redirection of his wish to tear him apart. It was terrifying.
>
> Downstairs Jane heard the noise and came up to try to intercede. She was relieved to find that no one was physically hurt, but she had never seen Joe like this and had a flash of wondering if she really knew him at all.

So the effect of Joe's choice to destroy the already damaged door was that it terrified his sons and it modeled for them a way of being when angry which was something he had tried to avoid. It scared his wife and left her wondering who he was.

It also meant that he had to fix the door, but that is not where we want to focus. This is not so much about how Joe was harmed but how those around him were harmed.

## What Was Going On With You When You Made That Choice That You Said You Wouldn't Make?

Typically these choices are a kind of perfect storm. There are almost always multiple issues which come together to induce us to make choices we would

312                                                *Strategies: The Practical Disciplines*

not normally make. The trick here is to try to identify as many of them as possible. This is where we find the greatest benefit from this discipline. The more patterns we can find which contribute to the choices we want to avoid in the future, the more benefit we get from this exercise.

> *Joe became clear upon reflection that his inability to work weighed heavily on him. Even though they were alright financially, he just didn't feel like he was supporting his own family. The worker's compensation checks felt like welfare to him. When he looked more closely at that he discovered that he was angry at himself for the accident. He should have known better. Heck, he did know better, he just did a dumb thing. The fact that his family was getting insurance payments to make up for his stupidity seemed almost like theft. He was disgusted with himself.*

> *He was also aware that he and Jesse had grown apart and that this had really started even before the accident. He and Jack had always been close in a way he had never been with Jesse and this fact seemed like an accusation that he wasn't really a good enough father. He and Jesse just couldn't talk the way he could with Jack.*

> *And he was aware that the beer he drank to help him relax that evening hadn't actually helped. He knew there was a difference between drinking for the taste and drinking for the mood altering effects and he knew this was the latter.*

So Joe could identify three sets of issues in three different relationships which were impacting his ability to clearly and calmly choose how he wanted to show up in his life when he smelled smoke and Jesse's door was locked. How many issues can you identify as having affected you when you made the choice you regret?

## What Strategies Do You Have In Place Now To Address Each Of The Patterns Which Contributed To You Having Made The Choice You Most Regret?

If we are to be as certain as we can be that we are not going to make that choice again, we want to have in place a specific strategy for addressing each of the issues which contributed to our having made the choice. We want to have something we can do every day which addresses the causes of the choice. What did we use to give ourselves permission to behave in a way we don't want to behave?

*Joe discovered two important patterns in his response to being laid up by the accident. One was that his image of himself as a provider for his family was a very central aspect of who he sees himself as being. And the second was that he has a part of himself which is very self-critical even to the point of being unforgiving if he makes a mistake.*

*This aspect of himself as provider is a 3° construction of himself. His role is to provide for his family. He is responsible for their welfare. If he is not doing this he is failing to fulfill his obligations. The self-critical part is more reactive, less well developed. It is a 2° part which is trying to bully him into being better.*

*For Joe to become aware of these aspects and how they are shaping his behavior, he has to have a 5° self awareness. He has to be aware of these apparently conflicting parts. He will continue to notice these parts and appreciate what they are trying to do for him but not let them get pushed to such an extreme position that they act out in anger. Were Joe to read this book he would discover the Anger Workout as a tool for helping him befriend his anger without letting it act out.*

*Joe is not as intimate with Jesse as he would like to be. He is confused because it has always been easier to be close to Jack. One strategy Joe could invoke is to consciously set aside time every week to do something with Jesse that Jesse enjoys.*

*And Joe will want to take a close look at his use of alcohol. Even if he decides that he is not an alcoholic, it is true in this instance that he has a problem with drinking. First of all he was choosing to use alcohol as a medication. And then he used it as a disinhibitor to give himself permission to do something he might not have done if he weren't a bit drunk.*

So Joe can identify a strategy for each pattern that supported his having made the choice he regrets. As long as he is using these strategies everyday he can minimize the likelihood that he will make this bad choice in the future.

෫

Let's check in with Jane and see how she is doing with her plan to address the conflict she has with Joe over his clothes on the bedroom floor.

> Jane watches to see if Joe picks up his clothes and to her surprise he gets up from the couch during half time and puts them away or in the clothes hamper. While one part of her is pleased and surprised, she is also aware that she is disappointed that she doesn't have a chance to try out her plan. She forgets about it.

> Friday evening Joe takes the boys to a sports banquet for fathers and sons. Jane is pleased that Joe is spending the evening with the boys and she gets some time to do a few things around the house she has been putting off. After finishing the dinner dishes she goes into the bedroom to change and finds Joe's clothes all over the bed and the floor. She fumes. She decides to leave them right where they are.

> When Joe and the boys get home Jane is sullen. They act like they don't notice but the boys don't put up any resistance when they are told it is bedtime. As soon as Jane and Joe are alone in the bedroom she unloads on him. "I can't stand it that you are so selfish and inconsiderate," she hisses at him. He is bewildered. He has no idea what she is talking about. She throws on her robe and goes into the living room with the thought that she will just spend the night on the couch.

> Even as Jane is fuming there is a part of her that is surprised at how angry she is. She curls up on the couch and tries to figure out what is upsetting her so much. As she just sits with her feelings she remembers a similar outburst with her college roommate.

*Sandra was from a wealthy family and only ended up at State because she was so casual about applying for college that by the time she got around to it she had missed all the deadlines to the schools she wanted. Jane's best friend from high school was going to be her roommate and then changed her mind at the last minute so Sandra was the luck of the draw.*

*Sandra had never really had to take care of herself and she allowed her side of the room to become a total mess in Jane's eyes. One night Jane was up late working on a paper which was due the next day. She carefully trained her work light onto her books so it wouldn't bother Sandra as she tried to sleep. Jane knew Sandra had a paper due as well but Sandra had decided she was going to ask for an extension and assumed she could get it. Out of the corner of her eye Jane saw something flit across the floor. It took a moment for her eyes to adjust to the dark but then she clearly saw a mouse staring back at her. She shrieked.*

*When Sandra sat up in bed startled, Jane turned the full force of her fury onto her. She told her that the reason there were vermin in the room was because Sandra was such a pig. She told her she was lazy, inconsiderate, and selfish.*

*The next day others on the floor asked about what had happened. Jane was so loud that many awakened to her tirade. Jane was mortified.*

As Jane sat in the dark in the living room nestled in her robe on the couch, she remembered the rage against Sandra and realized how much it felt like the rage she had just leveled at Joe. She decided to do a Statement of Accountability to see what she could learn.

She identified a couple of ways that her relationship with Joe reminded her of her relationship with Sandra. She recognized some of the same patterns. She saw each as entitled and lazy and a slob. But when she really looked at it, she realized that this didn't really apply to Joe most of the time. There were just these moments when she was feeling left out or ill considered when she would project onto him that he was just like Sandra.

One pattern then was that she would take on responsibility for another's mess and then resent it. So one strategy could be that she could work to notice when she was over-functioning. Another pattern was when others got to enjoy a privilege which she wanted but denied herself—as with Sandra sleeping or Joe getting to go to the banquet—she would feel resentful. Never mind that this was a father and son event. She wasn't being rational. And a third was that someone else's inattention to care for their own possessions became a sign that they did not consider Jane. She took it personally. She could work at realizing that Joe was normally very considerate of her and that this was one area where he just didn't see how he was affecting her.

## Discipline #8: Apology and Forgiveness - When We Want To Heal a Damaged Relationship

Jane's relationship with Sandra never recovered. Jane put in a request for a new roommate but Sandra transferred schools at the semester. While they each tried to be cordial, they never spoke about anything of substance again. Some relationships just aren't worth fixing. But some relationships are very precious to us and we want to do everything we can to repair them when they are damaged. Our next discipline is designed to give guidance to what we need to do to repair the relationships we want to restore when they are damaged.

*Event:* Relationships are damaged by events which cause harm to the parties. These can be discrete events or they can be a series of events. In either case, healing begins with the identification of the events which did the harm. What actually happened?

This is the essential first step in any attempt to resolve a conflict. What is the actual shared reality? What can we all agree happened or is happening? This is the point of our departure. We can pick any point we want, but we have to pick a point. If I am going to address this conflict in such a way as to heal a relationship with another, we have to start at the same point.

*Choices:* Events arise as a result of the many choices which construct them. Therefore, our next step is to identify those choices. One of the things which harm relationships is the denial of the significant role that some choices have had in constructing a given event. The most obvious way we do this is with blame. As we noted in Chapter Nine, blame is a way of denying accountability and is a statement which says that only one person or party's choices matter in the construction of a given event.

Therefore we have to name both the choices we made which contributed to the event and the choices others made which contributed to the event. We have to have both fully in mind.

When Joe broke down Jesse's door and then pulled it out of the door jam it was entirely Joe's choice to so act. He is fully responsible for his own actions. And it was not incidental that Jesse was burning something in his room, locked the door, and didn't answer when his father called to him.

*Consequences:* These choices were *causes* which have *effects*. What can we know about the effects of these choices on the other, on ourselves, and on the relationship? These are all relevant concerns.

We already know they did harm. But what was the harm? How specific can we be? The greater the clarity we have, the more effectively we can act to repair the damage.

Jesse's choice to burn something in his room scared Joe because it put the safety of the house and its occupants at risk. Jesse's choice not to answer the door when his dad knocked on it left Joe uncertain about whether his son was conscious. It scared him. Joe's choice to break through the door, even though it was not the choice he regretted, did scare Jesse, but what really terrified Jesse was when his dad proceeded to tear the rest of the door apart. Jesse believed his dad wanted to tear him apart.

*Clean-up:* If we are to repair the damage that has occurred in the relationship we must clean up the mess. If I spilled the milk, I have to wipe it up. So, for each of the consequences we are able to identify, there should be an action we take to ameliorate those effects. There are essentially two sets of actions which we are looking at here. One is the action we take to address the effects of the choices we made. The other is the action we take to address the effects of the choices the other made. We explore those a bit in a moment, but first, there is one other step in the process we want to include if we are to really do everything we can to repair the relationship.

*Pattern:* Especially when this event is a part of a pattern of events (and any event can be seen as part of a larger pattern) we want to figure out what the pattern is for the choices which are doing the harm and try to alter that pattern so we no longer make those choices. If we keep doing the same harmful things, or keep ignoring the harm which is being done to us, we won't actually heal the relationship.

So we end up with a series of steps in addressing a damaged relationship:

- Identify the Event
- Acknowledge the choices
- Appreciate the consequences
- Clean-up the mess
- Alter the patterns

While these steps are the same for all relationship repairs, we have different names for what we are doing depending on whether the focus of our attention is on the choices *we have made* or if we are focusing on the choices *the other has made*. If I am naming my own choices which damaged the relationship, we call this an *apology*. If I am naming the choices the other made, we call this *forgiveness*.

To be sure, this is not what most people normally mean by *apology* and *forgiveness*. Indeed, I often hear back from people when I suggest that the tools of apology and forgiveness are immensely powerful agents of healing, "I've tried that and it doesn't work." So I want to be clear about what I don't mean as much as what I do mean.

Many people confuse an apology with the statement that they are sorry. Certainly regret or remorse are important components of an apology, but they are not sufficient. For me to say I am sorry is an expression of sorrow and may be something that another finds reassuring but, if that is all I am saying I am stopping far short of what I am able to do. In some circumstances, I may even make things worse.

If you have a loved one die and I say to you, "I'm sorry," it may be comforting to know that I am concerned for you and your loss, but I am certainly not taking responsibility for any part of the event. If you have expressed distress at a choice I have made and I tell you, "I'm sorry you're upset," you may be appreciative that I have heard you and acknowledged what you have told me but you also might rightly be angry at me. I have in essence said, "I'm sorry you have the bad judgment to tell me how my behavior is affecting you." That is certainly not what I am suggesting we mean by an apology.

Similarly, we may confuse forgiveness with an offer to forget all about it. We may believe we are to "forgive and forget." As nearly as I can tell this notion comes from a passage in Hebrew scripture in which we are admonished to "forgive and remember not." Let me suggest that for us to not re-member an event is not the same as not holding it in our memory. I am not a Hebrew scholar, but I believe what is meant by this passage is that we are not to re-member, that is, not to re-create the event. When we are harmed and we feel an urge to get revenge and thus extract an eye for an eye, we are re-constructing or re-membering the event. So, no, we are not getting revenge, but neither are we forgetting. Better to forgive and remember in the sense of holding the event in our memory rather than reconstructing it in our relationship with the other.

In any case the reason to forgive is not to let the perpetrator off the hook. We do not forgive to change the other; we forgive to change ourselves. In just the same way we do not apologize to get the other to forgive us; we apologize to change ourselves in the wake of an event we regret so that we are less likely to construct a similar event in the future. The reason for me to apologize is to change myself. The reason for me to forgive is to change myself.

## Apology

> Joe started working on repairing the door frame and door the day after he tore them apart. The job took a couple of days. It gave Joe time to think about the events of that evening and what he wanted to do to repair his relationship with Jesse.
>
> Jesse knew that his dad wasn't just ignoring what had happened. He was, after all, fixing the damage. And it was reassuring that the matter of his door was being addressed as his privacy was important to him. But the work on the door and frame also kept Jesse's attention on the events of that evening and on the choices he had made.
>
> A couple of days later, as Joe was putting the hardware back on the door since the paint had dried; Jesse came into his room with his school books. Joe had been waiting for a good chance to talk and this was it.
>
> "Jesse, I am really sorry about the way I acted in here a couple of nights ago. I was really angry and I took that anger out on your door and I expect that was

*pretty scary for you to see your dad lose it like that. It cost you your privacy this past couple of days but, more than that, I expect it may have made it hard for you to trust me. I want you to know that this is not the way I want to act when I am angry and I am working on paying more attention to my feelings so they don't surprise me like they did that night."*

*As Joe said this he was calm and looked right at Jesse. Then he paused. Jesse waited for the rest of it. He was expecting that his dad was going to launch into telling him all of the things he was mad about. But Joe just stood there and waited.*

*Jesse decided he would have to speak. "Well, Dad, thanks for fixing my door. And I know you were really angry... and I understand why... and I shouldn't have burned that paper in here... and I know it scared you when I didn't open the door but I was afraid and just wanted to be left alone... cause I was upset about breaking up with Lisa..." and as Jesse said this he felt his tears well up and his voice choked. Joe came towards Jesse and gave him a hug. He didn't say anything, just held him.*

The best first thing to do to repair a damaged relationship is always to apologize. It must be a genuine apology for a choice you actually made which you fully regret. Joe really did regret tearing the door apart. So he started by cleaning up the mess. He fixed the door. Then he addressed the mess he had made with his son in his expression of rage by a full and clear apology.

Jesse knew what event his dad was talking about. He heard his dad be clear about which choice he was apologizing for. He knew his dad was aware of some of the consequences to him around fear, trust, and privacy. He had seen his dad fix the door and was now apologizing to him. And he heard his dad's commitment to continuing to pay attention to how he felt and expressed his anger.

Once Joe had done his work in making his apology he just waited in the space he had created. He didn't rush in to talk about all of the things Jesse had done. He simply enjoyed the fruits of his labor, the repaired door and the full apology. Jesse had not been consciously working on what he planned to say to his dad. In fact, he hoped they would never speak of it. But the quality of the emotional space which his dad had created drew Jesse in. He found himself stepping in and stepping up and opening up. And Joe was waiting to welcome him.

For Joe to do this he had to be clear about several things. First, he had to know that he was the only person he could change and to trust that that was enough. Second, he had to get clear that he was more committed to healing the relationship with his son than he was to being right or showing Jesse how he was wrong. If Joe had been hanging on to any shred of self-righteousness, his conversation with Jesse would not have ended in a hug.

## Forgiveness

You remember that in Chapter Nine as we discussed accountability we observed an incident between Joe and Jane shortly after they married. Joe surprised Jane as she was cutting onions and she had a flash back to the time she was raped at knife point when coming home through the park. After that incident Jane decided she wanted help with her healing and joined a rape survivors group.

> *Just being in the presence of other women with similar experiences was comforting and upsetting. The leader of the group gave Jane time to get accustomed to the group and the women in it and didn't press her to talk about her experience for the first couple of meetings, but Jane knew her turn would come to her as she heard the stories of the other women. At some point she would have to describe the event.*

We tend to resist reliving trauma. It was horrible the first time, why should we have to do it again? We can't change the past, so why not leave it alone? But there is an important shift which is necessary for healing. We need to go from *being in the event* to *witnessing the event*. We want to move the locus of our awareness from the center of the experience to a place outside of but focused on the events. Talking to others can help us do this. They are witnesses to the event. No, they cannot know what it was like. It is not their job as witnesses to *have* our experience. It is their job to help us *become a witness* to our own experience.

*When it became Jane's turn to talk about what it was like for her that evening as she walked home through the park, she found that it was easier than she feared. She knew they would not blame or judge her. She had come to trust their strength and so was not worried that her story would be harmful to them. But she also found their curiosity to be soothing and enlightening. They wondered about things she hadn't really thought about.*

*One of the women asked her about her anger at herself for walking alone through the park. She found herself getting angry at the question. It seemed as though the question suggested that she shouldn't have been so bold as to walk by herself in a secluded area. She felt judged. But as the woman just stayed curious, Jane discovered that she was not being judged; the woman really wanted to know if she were angry with herself and she discovered to her surprise that she was. There was a part of her which was very critical of herself for her choices which put her at risk.*

One very important aspect of healing for trauma survivors, especially for those who have been assaulted, is being able to look at the choices they made and come to clarity about whether those choices make them to blame for the harm which came to them. Yes, Jane chose to walk through the park. But, no, that doesn't mean she "asked for it."

*Jane told the group about her meltdown in the kitchen when Joe came up behind her and found that she came to see her behavior as perfectly understandable and acceptable and, at the same time, confusing and blaming toward Joe. She was able to see that one of the consequences of the rape was defensiveness and anger in her relationship with Joe. She was clear that she wanted to dissolve those qualities as they arose with her beloved.*

As we become aware of the consequences of the harm which has been done to us, we become clear about what we want to become able to clean up. We have to identify the mess before we can clean up the mess.

*As Jane looked at the larger view of how her life had changed since the rape she could see that she was careful not to be alone in public places — she never went to the park when it wasn't crowded unless she had a companion—and she became a financial supporter of the rape crisis center. But she also watched to see that she not put onto Joe her feelings about the rapist. It still bothered her that he had never been caught and she found herself being angry that she hadn't been able to give a better description of him.*

So Jane engages in healing of herself in the context of the event of the rape by working through a process of forgiveness. She becomes a witness to the event rather than only the one who experienced it. She clarifies which choices she made and whether those choices caused the event. She discovers all of the consequences of the event and does what she can to clean up from it. And she discovers the patterns in her life which the event had created and determines which she will continue and which she will work at changing. And she does all of this work of forgiveness without ever even knowing who her assailant was.

## Directly Addressing Others: Two Techniques

In some cases we can fully address and heal from a traumatic event without ever having contact with the person who has harmed us. In Jane's circumstances the event was very important but the relationship was not. But when the event which did harm is in a relationship we want to preserve, it becomes necessary to address the event in the relationship. We have to talk about what happened.

It would not have worked for Joe to simply fix the door and never say anything to Jesse. Joe had to voice his apology to his son. Once he had done so it didn't matter what Jesse did. Joe wasn't offering the apology to get Jesse to do anything. Joe offered the apology to create something: a quality in his relationship with Jesse.

Still, sometimes it can feel very threatening to speak with others about an event which has damaged our relationship with them. We can be putting ourselves at risk. They may deny the event occurred. They may justify the choices they made which were harmful. They may ridicule us when we identify the ways we were harmed. They may not only refuse to clean up the mess, they may make it larger. They may just continue the patterns which created the problem in the first part. And we are appropriately worried that these things may happen and we resist putting ourselves at risk.

One reason for this resistance is that nearly all of us have been bullied at some point in our lives and we are still struggling to recover from the trauma. To do this work, we have to believe that there is something we need which we can create for ourselves by addressing an issue with someone who is consistently making choices which hurt us. We have to become able to stand up to the bully in a manner which feels safe.

When we were second graders on the playground at school and the bully was picking on us, we knew better than to let the bully know we were scared. We knew instinctively that to let the bully know that the bully's choices were hurtful to us would only make the hurtful behavior continue. This is one of the techniques we learned as a child which was adaptive at the time but which no longer works now that we are adults. We think we have to learn not to let them see us sweat.

There are things we learned to do as kids that no longer work for us as adults; however, we keep doing them hoping they will work. We are using a tool which was designed for a different problem and, thus, is a strategy that is a cognitive distortion.

> *Jane gets really irritated by Joe's dirty clothes on the bedroom floor. Joe knows it and yet he still leaves his clothes on the floor from time to time. Jane wonders if maybe Joe does it because he knows it bothers her. Maybe he wants her to be angry and to know that she is powerless to stop him from leaving his clothes there. If she pretends it doesn't bother her, maybe he will loose interest and start cleaning up after himself.*

This way of thinking keeps Jane stuck on two fronts. One, it tries to get Joe to change. And two, it assumes he is doing this *to* her and that, if she ignores him, the behavior will go away. This starts to look like a bad idea but it is very common for people to decide not to tell others when the other's behavior is upsetting in some way. So let's look at this logically.

Either Jane tells Joe how his behavior affects her or she doesn't.

Either Joe means to upset her or he doesn't.

So we have four sets of options for how this might play out. Let's look at each of them.

Assuming Joe doesn't mean to upset her and Jane doesn't tell him she is upset, it is most likely Joe will keep doing what he is doing. From Jane's perspective, that is a negative outcome.

Assuming Joe doesn't mean to upset her and Jane tells him she is upset, Joe will likely make more of an effort to change his behavior because it is not creating the outcome he desires. From Jane's perspective, that is a positive outcome.

Or suppose Joe does mean to upset her and she doesn't say anything to him. In this case he is likely to keep doing this or he may do even more to upset her. This is certainly a negative outcome.

Then suppose Joe does mean to upset her and she lets him know that the behavior is bothersome. What are the options here? Joe could decide that he has gotten what he wanted—Jane is bothered—and he can now quit. That would be positive. But he also might be pleased that he is successfully bothering her and decide to keep it up. Is this a positive or a negative outcome? If Jane is hoping to get Joe to change, she will likely see this as negative. Joe didn't become more the way she wants him to be. But if she is only looking to change herself, this is a positive outcome. She discovers that Joe is not a safe person— he is actively seeking to upset her—and that is very important information.

Thus, in every case it is in Jane's best interest to let Joe know how his behavior is affecting her. Even if she is confirming that he is getting to her, she can then see what he chooses to do with that information. While we have good reason to fear based on our childhood experience, as we are now adults who can care for ourselves, we are better served by letting others know how we are being affected by them.

Here, then, are two techniques or strategies for addressing conflicts in significant relationships when we are afraid that to do so will only recreate the trauma. We call them *addressing onions*, and *predicting the unwanted outcome*.

## Addressing Onions

Some conflicts are like onions. If you slice them open they are wet and sticky and they make you cry. So we naturally want to avoid the onions. But if we are committed to healing ourselves in the context of our most significant relationships, we have to find a way to address them.

*Jane found she was so surprised by her reaction to Joe coming up behind her in the kitchen that she became strongly committed to doing everything she could to heal all aspects of her life in the wake of the rape. But one of the choices she made which her work in the group helped her to discover was that she did not immediately report the crime. She went home and took a shower and went to bed and it wasn't until the next day that she went to the doctor fearing that she might have contracted a disease. It was her doctor who persuaded her to tell the police and by then much of the evidence had been destroyed.*

*When Jane looked at what was going on with her that she didn't immediately report the crime she remembered when she went to her mom to complain when her brother was spying on her in the shower. Her mother's response was, "Jerry is a good boy and would never do anything like that."*

*As Jane considered her relationship with her mother she realized that her mother typically shut out any description of the world which didn't already fit what her mom expected. If Jane saw things differently, she was being silly or stubborn or rude. Jane came to see that this was still true and was a big barrier in her relationship with her mom. She wanted to address it but couldn't see any way to bring it up that wouldn't just make things worse.*

Jane's problem is that she can't conceive of a *strategy* which will construct an *event* which will create the *qualities* she is looking for in her relationship with her mother. But what are those qualities? She would like her mother to be more open to her reality but that would require her mother changing and she is very clear that she can't change her mother. She *wants* her mother to acknowledge her reality, but she *needs* a relationship in which her reality is acknowledged. She can be the one to acknowledge her reality but she has to become able to do this in her relationship with her mother.

The quality she is looking to create in her relationship with her mother is one which affirms as valid her own perceptions even when they are not the same as her mother's. The task then is to design a *strategy* which constructs an *event* in which these *qualities* are created.

One important aspect of an onion is that it is layered. The inner part of the onion is wet and sticky and makes us cry, but there is an outer layer which is dry and brittle and allows us to address the onion without getting our hands sticky. Relationships are layered. The outer layers are the parts we can easily talk about. As we go deeper, the risk becomes greater. Jane wants to find that outer layer with her mom.

The process for identifying the outer layer of an onion seems complicated but it is actually just a series of simple steps repeated over and over. It is a recursive loop, like in a computer program, where we do an operation over and over until a certain condition is met. In this case the condition we are looking for is one in which Jane has a statement she can make to her mom which is an expression of her truth which she can feel safe expressing to her.

We start with any expression of Jane's truth. This is especially important in this case as Jane is concerned about her truth not being acknowledged, but no matter what the issue is, it is essential that we speak the truth about it. We do not heal through falsehood. You recall the poem about the blind men and the elephant. There are many correct perspectives. There are many truths. We will not know, much less name, every correct perspective. But it only takes us away from healing when we say something is true when we know it is not.

So we may wonder with Jane what is true for her when she considers this pattern of conflict in her relationship with her mom.

> *"I feel like telling her that she is selfish and petty and that she pushes me out of her life."*

Okay, that is a true statement. Jane does actually feel that way. But is there any part of Jane which doesn't feel comfortable with that plan? Sure, there is a part that labels talking that way to her mom as disrespectful and rude. So, finding the part that doesn't want to be disrespectful and rude, what is that part's truth?

> *"I want a relationship in which my mom and I are respectful and courteous to each other."*

Yes. And so, as you imagine saying this to your mom, are there any parts which are not comfortable with this plan? Can you find any parts which do not approve of you saying this?

*"Yes, it feels like this is dodging the issue. She will say, 'Sure, and I want you to be courteous too, dear.' She won't know what this is about."*

So there is a part which wants her to know what this is about. Can you find that part and speak its truth? What would that part like to say to your mom?

*"Mom, sometimes when we are talking it feels to me like the only perspective there is space for in the conversation is yours. Sometimes I have a point of view which is different from yours and I wish we could acknowledge that we sometimes see things differently."*

Yes, and so, as you imagine saying this to your mom, are there any parts which are not comfortable with this plan?

We continue this process over and over until we have a plan for what Jane wants to say, which is true, and which is comfortable for all of the parts. When we have that we then check to see if this is really a plan we want to try by asking one more question.

"Imagine yourself saying this to your mom and imagine what her response is likely to be. There may be several options for how she might respond. Just see what all the options are and see if you are comfortable with how she might respond."

In Summary: Addressing an Onion

1. Find the outer layer
   a. Bring to mind a true statement in the language of complaint
   b. Imagine what it would feel like to voice that true statement
   c. Find any parts which are not comfortable with voicing that true statement
   d. Identify that part's truth and go to 1)b)
2. When you come to a true statement which all of the parts are comfortable with voicing, imagine how the other is likely to respond and see if there are any parts which not be comfortable with that response. If so, go to 1)d)
3. When all of the parts are comfortable, speak that truth
4. Suspend the conversation if it starts to go too deep

When you get to this point you may find that no matter how clearly or well you state your own truth, there are still parts of you that are so afraid of the outcome that you don't think you can address this issue. In these cases we want to try to predict the unwanted outcome.

## Predicting the Unwanted Outcome

This technique is designed to help us actually address what we need in our relationships with others when there is a part of us which is very afraid of what will happen. We do this by creating a binary choice—either this or that—in which one of the options is the outcome of which we are afraid, and then predict that this is what will happen.

Let us suppose here that there is a part of Jane who is terrified that Mom will respond to her true statement by insisting that Jane always wants it her way. She doesn't really know whether Mom feels that way but she is so afraid she does that she can't raise the issue with her. So what might Jane say that was a prediction of what she is most afraid might happen?

> *"Mom, I would like to talk to you about some feelings I have about whether my point of view can be respected in our relationship, but I am afraid that if I do you will insist that I often demand that you see things my way."*

If Jane were to say this to her mom, her mom might respond, "Yes, you always have to have it your way," or she might say, "No, I don't think you are demanding." If Mom responds the first way, she will be proving Jane right. If she responds the second way, she will be proving Jane wrong. Either way, Jane wins.

If the worst happens Jane can say to herself, "Yes, I was right, Mom can't allow in any perspective but her own." This confirms for Jane that her cognitive map for making sense of her relationship with her mom is correct.

If the best happens Jane will learn that she misunderstood her mom and that there is room for Jane's perspective. This opens up for Jane a new way of looking at her relationship with her mom that can be much more satisfying. Either way moves Jane toward what she needs.

These two techniques are tools we can use to help us address what we need in relationships we want to heal when we are having trouble getting ourselves to speak our truth in the context of the relationship. In both cases, though, we may find these tools work too well. We may find that once we present the onion, even though we are only holding the dry outer cover, the other will want to go deeper. We need to decide before we initiate the conversation just how deep we are willing to go.

If Jane tells her mom that she wants a relationship in which her perspective is accepted, her mom might say, "Of course you do, dear. Have there been times when it felt like I didn't want to hear what was going on with you?" If this happens, Jane has to be ready if she wants to say, "When Jerry spied on me in the shower when I was twelve and I told you about it, you insisted that I was wrong." Maybe that will be too threatening. Maybe there are other layers she can address first. But in any case, she will want to be prepared to say, "I really do want to talk with you about this mom, but I am just not quite ready yet." It is important that we know how deeply we are ready to go into the onion and be prepared with how we will suspend the conversation if it starts to go past where we are comfortable.

The very best way to initiate a conversation with someone about the events in the relationship which have harmed the relationship is to apologize.

- If you can find something you have done which you genuinely regret,
- If you can fully own and accept the harm you have done,
- If you can name it to the other and do all you can to acknowledge the effects and to clean up the mess while committing to address the patterns which allowed it to happen in the first place,
- If you can do all of this without any expectation about how the other will respond but do it only to construct your own integrity in the relationship,
- Then you will have powerfully constructed a space for healing.

This is all you can do. It is a lot. It is enough.

## Discipline #9: The Framework for Creative Conflict Resolution. When We Are Willing To Address a Specific Conflict Before We Have an Agreement with the Other

We introduced the Framework in Chapter Seven when we explored what it might mean for us to be assertive. We will not go into detail again here but there are a couple of things we want to point out.

All of the disciplines come together in Discipline #9. We must have sufficient awareness to know what is bothering us in the context of our most significant relationships and to know whether this is an example of a troublesome pattern. We have to know how it is that we are being affected and how this impact is related to difficulties we have had in past relationships so we can know what we need. Then we have to design a way of being which responds to the event such that we are creating what we need without in anyway expecting or depending on others changing. Once we have the plan we have to implement it in a manner that is fully sensitive to the impact we are having on others, taking care that we are not in any way trying to get what we need at the expense of another. This is very simple, and very difficult to do.

> ### Framework
> - Significant Relationships
> - Pattern of Conflicts
> - Event
> - Effect
>   - *Sensation*
>   - *Thought*
>   - *Emotion*
>   - *Wish*
> - Need
> - Action

The Bothers Me Log (Discipline #1) helps us to identify the patterns of conflict in our most significant relationships. The Anger Workout (Discipline #2) helps us implement our plan even when we are most aroused by our passions. Cultivating Critical Feedback (Discipline #3) helps us know how what we are doing affects others. Suspending Self-Soothing (Discipline #4) helps us recognize our deeper feelings and anxieties. Developing a Self Care Plan (Discipline #5:)helps us know when we are stopping ourselves from doing what we have already decided is in our own best interest. When in the process of using ACE (Discipline #6) we get to the point of devising a plan, implementing the Framework is the way we come to the plan.

> *Jane sat on the couch in the living room in the dark and considered her blow up at Joe. She could see that it was about more than just what Joe was doing and especially how it was related to her college roommate Sandra. She didn't want to spend the night on the couch in her robe, so she pulled herself together and went back to the bedroom.*

　　　　　　　　　　　*Strategies: The Practical Disciplines*

*"Joe, you still awake?"*

*"Yeah, I can't sleep."*

*"Well, I don't want to keep you up but there are a couple of things I would like to tell you if that's okay."*

*"Okay."*

*Jane came and sat on the side of the bed so that she could look at Joe while she spoke. "I am really sorry for blowing up at you like that. You are not selfish and inconsiderate. It really bothers me when you don't pick up your clothes in here, but my feelings are way out of proportion to what is going on. I know a part of it is some stuff with a college roommate and I will have to work that through."*

*Jane paused a moment to see if Joe wanted to respond. Joe was just relieved that she wasn't still mad at him. He thought about committing to doing better in the future but he knew he had already made those promises and hadn't kept them.*

*Jane went on, "I was really glad you got a chance to be with the boys at the banquet tonight. I kind of needed an evening by myself but I was also lonely and when I saw your clothes all over the room I got to feeling sorry for myself and taken for granted. I know that isn't what you meant, but that is what it meant to me... that I was just here to clean up after you. Anyway, I'm just really sorry about blowing up at you."*

*Jane got up from the bed and walked around to her side, slipped off her robe, and climbed under the covers. Joe rolled towards her, pulled her close, and they fell asleep.*

Jane knows that her relationship with Joe is the most important one she has currently. This business of his leaving his clothes on the floor is a pattern, but so is her ire at him when he does. When the event happened this evening she felt the old familiar feelings arising. She felt hollow inside, and abandoned. This meant Joe didn't care about her and that she was just a maid to him. She wanted him to be someone who cleaned up after himself, but what she needed was a relationship in which they each felt appreciated.

Since Jane needed appreciation and acknowledgement in the relationship and she wasn't getting it from Joe, she decided to create it for herself. She used the insights about herself which she had gleaned by doing the Statement of Accountability and then created a tone of openness and acceptance by starting and ending her statement to Joe with an apology. She didn't demand or even expect that he was going to change. She created what she needed by respecting the validity of her feelings even as she apologized for her behavior.

## Discipline #10: A Conflict Resolution Meeting - When We Have an Agreement to Address a Specific Conflict

So we come to the last and the most complex of our ten disciplines. This one is different from the others in a couple of respects. It is one we do with the other party to the conflict and it is one we already know how to do; indeed, we do it all the time.

Each of the prior disciplines are things we do on our own either to become more mindful about our conflicts or how we might begin to address them, or they are things we do on our own to prepare for addressing a conflict with another. We don't need the participation of someone else in order to apologize to them. In fact, when we are in a relationship with someone who is being short with us or is avoiding addressing an issue with us one of the best ways to open up the relationship to healing is to offer a genuine apology.

But the Conflict Resolution Meeting is something we do with the other with whom we are in conflict. Thus, this discipline may not be available to us. We can't do it on our own.

On the other hand, it is simply a series of steps we already do all the time. It only becomes difficult as the intensity of the conflict increases. Remember that the intensity of a conflict is a function of the level of commitment or attachment the parties have to the issue or event (ownership), and the degree of separation they perceive between their perspective toward the issue and that of the other party (discord). When the level of conflict is high we get flustered. When the intensity of the conflict is low it is really quite easy to resolve conflict. One of the strengths of this discipline is that it reminds us that we really can do this… we do it all the time.

Conflicts are resolved to the degree to which the parties involved can move from a stance of opposing each other's ways of approaching a given issue to one in which they are acting together to meet their mutual needs. We do this by becoming clear about the nature of our relationship to each other, naming the issue or the event which is the occasion for the conflict, hearing how each other makes meaning about the event, discovering common needs, and agreeing to act to support those shared needs. Let's take each of those steps in turn.

## Clarifying the Nature of the Relationship

For our purposes here we are going to assume a conflict between two persons. The same principles apply for more complex situations, but they become harder to talk about.

The relationship is the matrix in which the conflict arises. If we don't have an agreement about the nature of the relationship itself, we can never come to an agreement about the conflicts which arise as events within the relationship. And even if we do, it won't resolve the underlying conflict. If I insist that I have a right to assault you if you don't do what I tell you to do then we can't begin to talk about what we are going to have for dinner and assume that a genuine agreement is possible.

In many if not most relationships there is already a high level of agreement about who we are to each other. We are clear about how we share rights and responsibilities. We know the ways in which the relationship is mutual and whether there are aspects in which we have a fiduciary responsibility to each other.

But when we construct the relationship out of a different set of assumptions, or when we construct it in a way that does not balance rights and responsibilities, then we cannot have a stable and just relationship and none of the following steps are going to work. This is the reason why we don't do couples counseling in battering relationships. It is not just because there is a high level of violence or because the conflicts have a high level of intensity. High conflict relationships can benefit from intervention which addresses both parties together. It is because the fundamental problem is the structure of the relationship itself and nothing we do will repair the events in the relationship when the framework is itself oppressive.

## Naming the Event or Issue Which Is the Occasion for the Conflict

Assuming we are in basic agreement about the nature of the relationship and it is constructed in a manner that is just and stable, then the question is, "What is going on that we find ourselves in conflict?" Can we be clear about what the problem is and agree about where we disagree?

We must keep in mind that each party is likely to react most strongly to different aspects of a shared event or issue. Any circumstance is a complex web of events and concerns. There are many conflicts in the context we are considering. Can we acknowledge that each party may respond with different intensity to different aspects of a given event or issue?

Sometimes we find that we cannot agree on what happened or what is happening. It may be that we are just on such different pages that the event itself gets lost. Then the issue is not the event itself but the way we are addressing it. It may be that the place to start is with the event which is *when we can't agree on what happened.*

## Honoring How Each Is Affected By the Event or Issue

We already know that we see the event differently. We know we take different sides of the issue. If we weren't, we would not be experiencing this as a conflict. If we are going to come to resolution, we have to see the other's perspective and to recognize how the perspective of the other is valid for the other. It is not necessary that we adopt the perspective ourselves, though we should feel free to do so if it makes sense to us, but we need to know how this makes sense to the other. If a blind man wants to get the fullest picture of what an elephant is like, he does well to listen to his fellows' perspectives and imagine how they might be accurate.

To do this each party must do five things marginally well. This is the hardest part of this otherwise simple process.

*Each know how he or she is affected by the event or issue:* The event which is the core of the conflict has caused a set of feelings in each party and each has made the event mean something. When something troubles me I may have to do some work to figure out what it is that is bothering me. It may not be the event itself.

It may be that it reminds me of something else about which I have strong feelings. So I have to figure out what the sensations, emotions, thoughts and wishes are which arise for me in the wake of this event or in the midst of this issue.

*Each be able to express clearly the effect:* When each has clarified what each is feeling and thinking, then each has to find a way of talking about, or otherwise expressing, the internal content such that the other can come to understand it. I have to have the words to say what is going on with me such that I can convey it to the other. I have to have sufficient self-awareness and self-expressiveness that I have some hope of being understood.

*Each find it safe to be known to the other when each is not who the other wants him or her to be:* The fact that there is a conflict arising in the relationship may be so threatening to either party that to express a difference may feel unsafe, either to the person or to the relationship. I have to know that I can be known and not have it put me personally or the relationship itself at risk. There may be an "onion" which will have to be addressed before it becomes safe to be known.

*Each be able to tolerate her or his own anxiety when confronted by another who is different:* Being with others who are different from us is inherently anxiety provoking. If each is going to hear fully the perspective of the other, each will have to self-soothe in the midst of that anxiety well enough to genuinely hear the other. If I am so anxious about the fact that we see this event differently that I can't actually let myself hear your perspective, I am not going to see it as valid for you. I have to take good enough care of myself emotionally that I can be present to your reality.

*Each be able to mirror back to the other the other's perspective well enough that each knows that each is heard by the other:* When we hear the other tell back to us what the other has heard, we get a chance to test whether what we said was what we meant, and it gives us a chance to hear whether we were heard accurately. We can then correct what we meant, perhaps even discover a nuance of meaning we had missed before. This is what intimacy is about.

Once we have each had a chance to do these five tasks in the wake of the event or issue, we then each have a clear picture of both what we bring to the event—what is our own perspective—and also what the other brings—how the other sees this shared event. We are then free to appropriate aspects of the others meaning into our own cognitive map if we so choose. It's our choice.

## Finding Common Needs

Given the differing cognitive maps about the meaning and effect of the event held by each party to the conflict, we can now identify where it is that we have common needs. This is always possible. The conflict is not about what we need, but about the strategies we have in mind to move toward what we need. The process of coming to see our own and each other's perspective has taken us deeper into our awareness and we are now closer to identifying the qualities we are missing when the conflict arises. All we have to do now is to name what those missing qualities are for each of us such that we can both hold them in our awareness.

## Agreement about What We Will Each Do

Finally, it falls to us to each make a commitment to construct what we need. This usually requires each of us follow a different course of action, but this is a matter of constructing a reciprocal agreement about how we each accept responsibility and express our rights. It may be that we will have to return to the agreement to reconstruct it from time to time. Few agreements are so durable that, once constructed, they stand forever.

# Some Examples

You may well be thinking that this doesn't seem so simple and that it isn't the way you normally resolve the conflicts which arise in your experience. Some examples may help to clarify what this looks like in practice.

You may remember when Joe and Jane had a conversation about dinner and identified that they needed milk and lettuce but not who would be responsible for getting them. They each thought the other would. Upon them both being home and neither having stopped to get groceries, Joe grabbed his keys and went to the store. They have an agreement that they share responsibility for feeding the family and buying groceries. This was not something only one of them could or would do. They agreed that the issue was food for dinner and the event was that neither bought milk and lettuce. They each had a responsibility to the family at the moment and Joe offered that he be the one to go to the store. Jane agreed that she would stay home and tend to the boys and get the rest of dinner started. They each felt comfortable with their role. They both needed dinner but they also both needed to act responsibly on behalf of the family.

Notice that most of these steps were assumed or expressed and negotiated with few, if any, words. There was a very low level of intensity of the conflict. They have a high level of attachment to the issue, but a low variance in perspectives. If Jane had a sense that Joe routinely shirked his responsibilities, this might have gone very differently. As it was, it reaffirmed their capacity to work well together. They would likely not even see this as having been a conflict.

So let's see what this looks like with a slightly higher intensity of conflict.

> When Jack was first learning to drive he rode with his mom to an appointment after school which took them down a busy stretch of road which was once a country highway but which had become burdened by recent construction in the area. Jane was stressed by the traffic and by a fear of being late to the appointment. Aware of her wish to drive faster but her concern for safety and her awareness that in a few months Jack might be making this drive on his own she commented, "This is a really dangerous stretch along here. You should never go faster that 50 here."
>
> Jack responded, "Dad says it is okay to do 55 here."
>
> "What, no way, you listen to me. If you ever want to drive this car you are going to have to be cautious and responsible."
>
> "Mom, why do you have to be so critical of me all the time? I am not even driving and you are accusing me of being irresponsible."
>
> They rode in silence for a few minutes as each fumed. Finally Jane broke the silence with a change of tone in her voice. "When I think of you driving along this stretch of highway I get scared. I know that learning to drive is important to you and I want you to be a good driver. You are mostly pretty careful, but I am still afraid."

*Jack answered back, "I just wanted you to know that what I hear from you sometimes is not the same as what I hear from Dad. He sees things differently from the way you do. I want to try to please you both but I can't if you don't expect the same things."*

*"Well," Jane responded after considering what Jack had told her, "I can see that we may not be giving you consistent expectations. I will talk to your dad about this, but I want you to promise that you will be a safe driver."*

*"Of course, Mom, I know that driving is dangerous and I don't want to get hurt either."*

Jack and Jane are clear that they are mother and son. There is no question that Jack will not drive without his mom's permission. The event is Jack's reply to his mother's caution about speed by telling her what Dad has said. Jane is afraid for Jack's welfare. Jack is confused about parental expectations. They both want a relationship in which there are the qualities of safety and clarity of expectations. Jack will drive carefully. Jane will have a talk with Joe.

The more intensity in the conflict, the harder it is for the parties to work through each of these steps. By the time we get to the intensity of two nations who share a commitment to living on the same land but deny the right of the other nation to exist we can find such intensity that the conflict may seem impossible to resolve. Nevertheless, if resolution is to be found it will be through following these simple but very difficult steps.

## Time Outs

There is one other technique Jack and Jane used in the vignette above which is worthy of mention. They took a time out. They were in the car having a fight and they stopped and let the silence wash over them as they each focused on what they were feeling and needing. Then they were ready to come back to the conversation from a more centered place in their awareness.

Many couples find that they have the same fight over and over. It is not just that the same conflict keeps arising. That is true for all significant relationships. But they respond each time in much the same way… and one aspect of the same reaction is that they are each trying to make the other lose. As we have seen, this typically works in the short run. We are able to make the other lose. But this doesn't actually get us what we need in the long run. So this is a pattern in the relationship we would do well to abandon. We have to stop doing what doesn't durably work to make room for things which actually move us toward what we need.

It is possible, and sometimes necessary, to take a unilateral time out. We may not be able to negotiate this with our partner. It would be better if we could, but when we don't have the same understanding of the nature of our relationship or when the other is so impulsive that an agreement won't hold, we just may have to take a time out all on our own.

In essence this is what battered women do when they pack up and move to a shelter. Having found that they can't construct an agreement with their partner to address and resolve the conflicts mutually, they take a time out. It is a sad reality that this is so often necessary and I want to be clear here that it is not my intention to minimize the validity of that choice in some circumstances.

Still, there are relationships in which there is a high level of conflict but a mutual commitment to healing in which it is possible to come to an agreement about using Time Outs to stop the fighting and still address the conflicts. It is to those couples that I address this next section.

## Identifying the Fights

The first step is to recognize the pattern of fighting. Do either of you see a pattern to arguments you get into in which you have a sense of déjà vu. Is this the same thing you have been through before? Do you already know what you are going to say, and what your partner will say, and how it will all end? Do you already know you are not going to feel good about it?

You may find that you both have this sense but it is about different patterns; you each have different aspects of the relationship which you are tired of replaying. The important thing is to see if you both see it, or, even only one of you sees it, you are both willing to address it.

## Agreeing To Stop Them

Just because you see the patterns doesn't mean you agree to stop them. Either of you may have a concern that there is nothing else you can do to address these conflicts so to agree to stop them may feel like an agreement to give up. There has to be enough trust that the plan you develop will be more helpful and satisfying for you each to sign onto a plan to respond differently.

## Making a Plan

Each couple has to devise their own plan. There is no "plan in a can" that we can open up as a sort of "one size fits all" recipe for a Time Out. But there are some components I have found that are necessary in nearly every case I have worked with.

1.  The Time Out has to have an end point. You are suspending the conversation temporarily until you can each get centered and clear. You are not agreeing to never talk about it again. You will not find that to be a satisfying agreement even if you are able to keep it. Part of what you have to do is to agree on when you will return to the conversation.

Typically one person wants to stop the fight and the other wants to get things settled. One is fleeing and the other is pursuing. The pursuer won't give up the hunt without a commitment to return to the issue at a time certain. This may be in five minutes, this may be after the kids are in bed tonight, or this may be "when we meet with our counselor next week."

2.  It must be clear how the Time Out will be called and that each has a right to call the Time Out. Usually one person has more of an inclination to call the Time Out than the other, but each must be free to use it. It cannot be a tool that one uses to control the other. If it begins to feel to one that the other is just trying to avoid a necessary but difficult conversation, that should become the focus of the conversation.

Some couples simply say, "Time Out." Others use a hand gesture or a secret phrase. I suggest you not plan to say something like, "I need a break." That may be true but it may not be something the other hears as a clear indication that "this is that thing we agreed to do."

3. The plan should make it clear what each of you will do during the Time Out. Where will you each go? What will you do about other responsibilities during the Time Out? Is communication about other things allowed during the Time Out or will you not speak to each other?

4. The plan should include what you will do when the Time Out is over. My suggestion here is that you use the discipline of the Conflict Resolution Meeting to address the event that raised the need for the Time Out. What happened? What set each of you off? How were you each affected? Can you each reflect back what was going on with the other? What do you both need? What will you each do?

When it comes to taking turns sharing perspectives, I suggest the person who is the most upset be the one to go first. It is hard to hear the other when we are feeling intense feelings, so the one most affected should start. If there is a disagreement about who is most upset, I suggest the one who called the Time Out should decide.

## Implementing the Plan

As we have seen, having a plan is not the same as implementing the plan. This is no different from plans we make as an individual. Indeed, you may have noticed that this is essentially a way for a couple to use Discipline #6: (ACE ) collaboratively. We can't implement a plan we haven't made, but we can easily make a plan and not implement it.

Therefore, I strongly suggest you have a "fire drill." Once you have developed the agreement about how you will call it and where you will go and what you will do when you come back together, have a few practice runs. Each of you should call a Time Out whenever it occurs to you. When you get back together, share what it felt like to call the Time Out, to take it, and how it feels to contemplate doing it in the midst of intense conflict. It is very hard to do a new thing even under the best of circumstances. If you can't call a Time Out when there is a low level of stress, you will certainly not do it when the stress is high.

# Summary

We know that gaining the skills to be masterful at conflict resolution helps us create whatever we and those around us need and, thus, is worth the effort. We have discovered practices which enhance our ability to be mindful of the need for resolution and now have turned to some practical disciplines which we can use as maps for getting to the resolution we desire.

We have noticed that there are patterns of conflicts which arise for us and we know they continue to arise so we prepare for the next time by anticipating when a pattern will appear, creating a clear image of how we want to deal with the pattern and then doing our best to implement our plan. We evaluate both the plan and the implementation and prepare for the next time. We have resolved to do this over and over, each time learning and growing and improving how we show up for the conflict.

We have noticed that, at times, we make choices we regret which are harmful to others. While we hope we never make those choices again, we also know we never meant to make those choices in the past. We have to explore deeply what was going on with us when we made the choice so we can be as sure as possible that we won't make that choice, or one like it, again. We identify what the choice was, how the choice impacted others and our relationships with others, what was going on with us at the time which gave us permission or otherwise prompted us to act badly, and then find or develop a specific strategy for addressing each of the patterns which contributed to the bad choice.

We know we can just leave some damaged relationships but others are worth restoring. To do so we have to both apologize and forgive. We have to be clear about the choice which did the damage and who it was that made the choice. We have to be clear about the consequences to the other when the choice was ours or the consequences to ourselves when the choice was someone else's. We have to be committed to cleaning up the mess made by the choice and then be sure we are doing everything we can to address the patterns which supported the choice or which may have arisen from it.

We see conflicts arising continually in all of our relationships but especially notice them in the relationships which are most significant to us. We notice the patterns which are most troubling to us and we identify the events which are elements of the pattern. We become able to clearly name the event such that others know to what we are referring and agree that this is something which happens. We clarify for ourselves how these events affect us and what it is we need and then develop a strategy which moves us toward what we need and which in no way depends on others changing.

We become able to engage others in dialogue about our patterns of conflict and clarify with them the nature of our relationship when these events arise. We affirm how we each see the events and hear how we are each impacted by the events. We then agree on what we both need and to form agreements about what we will each do to construct what we both need. When the agreements are not kept, we return to them and repair them as we are committed to our common wellbeing.

ॐ

The key to using any move in a martial art is to learn it so well that your body knows it, not just your mind. In a given situation, you simply respond. You have repeated the move so many times that your action is an impulse, not a conscious choice.

If you practice these disciplines over and over, you will find that you begin to see the world through a different perspective and that you naturally act differently as conflicts arise. You will no longer be afraid of them. Or perhaps you will still be afraid but you will also have the confidence to know that you can address them productively. You can use these disciplines to create what you need, confident that you are creating what those around you need as well.

# 12

# Technologies for Transformation

Have you ever played the game "peek-a-boo?"
In the unlikely event that you don't know, this game is one in which one person places his hands over his own eyes so that he cannot see the other and then removes his hands and says, "peek-a-boo!" The person he is playing with then mimics that action and, at the point of removing her hands, bursts into laughter.

So, when you have played this game, who do you normally play it with?

We only do this with very young children. Older children and adults just don't seem to enjoy it anymore. This game is only fun for us when we play it with people who are just learning to negotiate the shift from First to Second Order. At 1° [Personal-material: perception] I am whatever I am experiencing. If I put my hands over my eyes so that I can't see you, you are no longer there. When I pull my hands away, I can again experience you and you come back. By the simple act of covering my eyes with my hands I can make you go away and come back[27].

Mastering this ability to make you go away and come back is a 2° [Personal-material: choice] task. So what we are doing when we play peek-a-boo with children is to engage them in a game which teaches them a perspective which supports their transformation from 1° to 2°. It is a technology for transformation.

There are many technologies for transformation. The job of a teacher is to create opportunities for transformation in the lives of her students. Coaches

---

27 Knowing that something is there even when we don't experience it directly is called object constancy.

and therapists and pastors are all expected to construct relationships with others which support their growth and change in some dimension of their lives. We all do it from time to time.

But didn't we say that we can't make others change? Hasn't one of the fundamental principles we have been asserting that, when we try to make others be different, we are investing in something we cannot do and, thus, are setting ourselves up for feelings of helplessness and hopelessness?

Yes, that is true. But when we play peek-a-boo with a child we are not making the child be different. We are engaging the child in an examination of what is already true for the child. We are joining with the child in observing how her reality is arising in her experience. We are not making her change; we are joining with her in a way that supports her own transformation.

So while we cannot make others change, we can work to create the circumstances which support the other's transformation, recognizing that transformation occurs naturally and easily when all of the necessary conditions are met.

What then are those necessary conditions? We have been supporting our own transformation by practicing disciplines which have a clear intention, which focus our attention, which we reinforce by repetition, and which are structured by the guidance we get from others and from within. It is that guidance from others we are considering here. What do we look for in a relationship in which we get guidance for our own transformation? How do we construct relationships which support the transformation of others?

## Three Steps in the Transformational Relationship

There are many kinds of relationships in which it is appropriate for one person or party to work toward the transformation of another. And there are many in which it is not. In general I am only able to support the transformation of another if I am in a fiduciary relationship in which their growth is my responsibility. We have already named teachers, coaches, therapists and pastors as roles in which this kind of relationship can be appropriate. Perhaps the largest group of transformation agents is parents. We may even see that the broader society is responsible for the development of all of its citizens thereby having a responsibility to create mechanisms for transformation such as quality public education.

In most marriages, however, such a role is outside the bounds of the relationship. I am not responsible for the development of my spouse. That is, unless we have specifically agreed that we are going to support each other's transformation.

Because there are so many different roles and relationships in which this process can happen, I am going to speak of the two parties as the *seeker* and the *guide*. The *seeker* is the one who desires support for growth and the *guide* is the one who supports that growth in the seeker. If I decide I want to learn to paddle a kayak safely and so sign up for a class from a local sporting goods store, I am the seeker and the teacher is the guide. If I decide to help my nephew learn to hit a baseball, I am the guide and he is the seeker. That is, if he wants my help.

The first step in the technology of transformation is the creation of the supportive relationship. In some cases this may be done formally as when a therapy client interviews a potential therapist and then the therapist gathers information about the client's history, current circumstances, and goals. In other cases the relationship is constructed informally as when an adult engages a toddler in a game of peek-a-boo.

As we create an alliance with the person whose transformation we are seeking to support, we have to build a relationship with the seeker which assures the seeker that we know what it is like to be where the seeker is. We have to appear to our seeker as someone who "gets it."

If I want to help my nephew be a better hitter, I have to let him know that I see how it is going for him, that I care about how he is batting the ball, and it helps if he knows that I also had trouble learning to connect with the ball.

The second step is to support the seeker's capacity to look at the seeker's current best map and to see the ways in which it is not adequate to the tasks of living she or he is confronting. This may be pointing out to the seeker that what the seeker is doing isn't working, but it may also simply mean being present with the seeker and encouraging the seeker to explore his or her own experience.

I may just ask my nephew about his batting average or ask him if he is interested in becoming a better hitter. If he isn't interested in hitting the ball better, I will not be able to help him. But if he thinks he just can't hit—he doesn't see batting as something which he could improve on—then I can assure him there are some things we can do to support him becoming a more effective batter.

The third step is to provide a map which is both better than the one the seeker is currently using and one which the seeker can actually use. If I am simply giving the seeker my map, even if it is a great map for me, but the seeker doesn't know how to use or see how it addresses the seeker's problems, it will not support the seeker's transformation. Another way to say this is that the seeker has to know that what I am seeing and saying actually fits the seeker's needs.

I can give my nephew all kinds of advice, even good advice, but if he doesn't know what it means to "choke up" on a bat, he won't follow my instructions. And if he knows I can't hit the ball myself he probably won't listen to me.

Let's look at this process in a somewhat more complex but well known and tested program: that of addressing addictive behavior.

AA is the best known of the many 12 step-recovery programs. Each is tailored to a specific addiction but all have common elements. Whether the drug of choice is alcohol, food, or sex, there are certain elements of the technology which can dependably move us toward health and wholeness. But, as with all programs, it only works when you work it.

1. Entry into the program is generally through attending a group in which the only requirement for belonging is being able to say that you belong. New members are greeted and supported and given a list of people they can call if they have questions or need help. Every effort is made to let newcomers know they are understood and welcomed.

2. While members can and do continue to use while they work the program, the purpose of the program is to gain sobriety. They are supported in knowing what sobriety means to them and to identify when they lose it and be helped to regain it. Hearing how others maintain their own sobriety challenges them to do the same.

3. They look for those who have been able to construct and maintain their own sobriety and they look to see what those others are doing and even ask them to give them direct support by being a sponsor. They know that the experience, strength, and hope of others can help them become more of who they choose to be.

12 step recovery is a tried and true technology for helping people move from 2° [Personal-material: choice] to 3° [Interpersonal-relational: perception]. When the demands of my life get to be too great and I am not having the experience I want I may find that moving up to 3° is just more of a step than I can take. "I can't even seem to know what it is that others expect of me, so to heck with it, I'll just get drunk." That is, I will make a choice that changes my experience rather than transforming my relationships.

By entering the program I receive support to practice showing up at 3°. The rules are clear and no matter how many times I break them, I can always come back and try again. There is no limit on forgiveness in a 12 step program. I will get confronted when I abandon the program, especially if I am seeking the guidance of a sponsor, but it is just that sort of external guidance which supports transformation.

## Skills of a Transformational Guide

These three steps unfold as stages through which the seeker-guide relationship moves on the way to transformation for the seeker. Each of these calls for a distinct set of skills on the part of the guide. Again, we all have these skills to some degree. The degree to which we want to become better able to support the transformation of others—and by that to help them become better able to resolve the conflicts in their lives—is the degree to which we have to become masterful in these three sets of skills.[28]

## Bridging

The first step is the creation of an alliance or resonance between the seeker and the guide. This requires that the guide have some facility with a skill we call *empathy* or *compassion*. This is the ability to be emotionally present with another in such a way that the other feels known and cared for.

Let us remember that being able to master this skill depends upon the

---

28   These three stages can be named in many different ways. I have generally referred to them as bridging, challenging and modeling. Those who like alliteration may prefer melding, meddling and modeling; or resonance, rupture and repair; or alliance, alarm and alleviation.

guide's ability to know and care for the guide. We cannot relate to other's feelings better than we relate to our own. For this reason, if we aspire to be skillful at helping the development of others, we must first be well centered in our own experience.

Developing a capacity for compassion requires being with others even when, or especially when, they are having experiences with which we are uncomfortable. They could be having pain from an accident or a disease. They could be in a circumstance that is confusing or frightening to them. Or they could be adopting a position that is alien or dangerous to what we see as our own interests.

Compassion is easier in some circumstances than in others. We can more easily find compassion for a sick child than for a thug who is robbing us. It is easier to find compassion for the innocent than the guilty. It is easier to find compassion when we are safe and satisfied than when we are scared or angry.

Assuming that we each want to develop a greater and greater capacity for compassion, here is a map for the stages we move through as we grow our capacity for caring for and with others. As with any developmental map, it is important to remember that these are not discrete stages but snapshots along the way in a seamless flow. It is also important to remember that we tend to be at higher levels or stages on our best days, but when we are stressed physically or emotionally, we tend to regress to an earlier stage. Thus I am sometimes able to have empathy for what my spouse is experiencing at work, but other days I am going to insist on trying to fix it, or even, if I am really stressed, I may just say that don't want to hear about it.

**Repulsion** – $(2>1)$[29]: The other is different from me in a way that would be dangerous for me to understand or connect to. The other is a threat to me and I reject or avoid the other in order to protect myself and my point of view.

---

29   The numbers in parentheses refer to the stages in the Orders of Self. At the odd numbered orders we are constructed by our perceptions; at the even numbered orders we are constructed by the choices we make. Thus, our approach to others is an even numbered response to an odd numbered circumstance. From the state of mind that is 4° [Interpersonal-relational: choice], for example, looking toward 3° [Interpersonal-relational: perception] results in a slightly different perspective and behavior than when looking toward 5° [Intrapersonal-internal: perception]. The numbers in parentheses identify this perspective as a result of the locus of identity > and the focus of attention.

**Pity** – (2>3): The other is suffering in a way that I understand. I may have had similar experiences and I know what it is like to have that experience and I am glad it isn't happening to me now. I keep my distance in order to protect myself from having those feelings return.

**Sympathy** – (4>3): The other is suffering and I think I can be present to the other in a way that is designed to help the other through the suffering. I should help the other by showing the other what to do.

**Empathy** – (4>5): I cannot fully know the experience of the other but, to the degree to which I know my own experience, I can relate to the other's experience. I am not interested in telling the other how to be but only to be present to support the other.

**Compassion** – (6>5): From what I know of my own resourcefulness, I have a high confidence that the other has within the resources for the other's growth and healing. I want to be with the other in the other's process of healing knowing that to do so supports my own self-discovery and growth.

**Deep Compassion** – (6>7): I am more and more aware that the ways we are different are simply aspects of the accidents of our coming into the world—our race, our sex, our abilities and disabilities—and the ways in which we are the same are far more significant than the ways we are different. When others do not share this awareness I feel a deep sadness and wish to support the other's coming into an awareness that frees the other from the other's suffering.

**Identity** – (8>7): What appears as suffering is the longing of creation for wholeness. I am not other than a manifestation of the divine energy and intelligence that arises in all. Every face is my one true face.

It is instructive to note that there is a series of transformations which arise for us as we develop the skills of compassion.

- *Not safe* to *safe*: at first the other's distress is felt to be a threat to our own wellbeing but as we grow in this skill we find it safer and safer to be around those who are suffering. It is not that we are less affected by their suffering, but that we are more and more confident in our own ability to relate constructively and to remain centered.

- *Don't understand* to *understand* to *affiliation* to *unity:* a second more complex transformation is that we move from not understanding the other to a sense of understanding to actually feeling a sense of kinship with the other and finally to a place of understanding ourselves to be in solidarity with or unity with the other.

- *Confidence that I know them* to *awareness that I do not:* Still, though we have a greater sense of understanding the other we also go from *certainty that we know what they are going through* to *recognizing the uniqueness of their experience* and a *curiosity about their experience* and a *respect for them as the sole interpreter of that experience.*

- *Doing for* to *being with:* While we have a concern for the other's welfare, we come to see that we are not taking care of them (which can feel oppressive to them), but simply being present with them.

- Differences transform from being *something we believe can harm us,* to *something which doesn't affect us,* to *something we might learn from,* to *something of great value to us.* The fact that the other or the other's experience is different from who we are or what we are experiencing or what we are making events mean shifts from being a threat, to being neutral, to being informative, to being vital (life giving).

- The other is dangerous, stupid, hurt, creative, beloved: Who the other is seen by us as being transforms from *someone who presents a risk to us,* to *someone who is beneath us,* to *someone who has been harmed,* to *someone who has potential,* to *someone we deeply care about.*

## Challenging

The second stage is the discovery of the place or places where the seeker's perspectives and strategies are not creating what the seeker needs. This requires *insight* and *wisdom* on the part of the guide, insight to see what is going on for the seeker and wisdom to know which part of the problem should be addressed first.

It is the nature of this stage in the process of supporting another's transformation that errors or shortcomings are identified. But there is not just one shortcoming which we can identify. And we can't deal with everything at once. Where do we start?

In some cases, addressing a problem may require a series of actions. The place to start is the first or next step in that series.

> *Many years ago I was the Director of a summer camp which had fallen into disuse and disrepair. I had a team of workers busy repairing the camp when I was notified that a group would be coming for the weekend and would be using the upper cabin. They wanted to be sure that there were screens on the windows.*

> *For several years teams had repaired the cabin with sheets of screening and a staple gun. These repairs lasted a few weeks or months at most. Each year the screens had to be replaced. The siding was loose. The roof needed a new layer of tar paper. All of these projects required power tools and the power line was down because the dead oak kept dropping limbs on the line.*

> *When the President of the Camp Board of Directors arrived he was very upset to see that we were working on cutting down the oak tree rather than putting screens on the windows.*

One of the distinctions we can make to help us see where to start on any project is between importance and urgency. In the series of tasks related to having screens on the cabin windows taking down the oak tree was more important because failing to do so would just result in the same problem coming up again and again. But the arrival of the kids for the weekend made the screens more urgent.

> *The President picked up a roll of screen and a staple gun and got to work.*

When a guide is trying to help a seeker find the place to start on addressing a problem there will be competing demands for addressing what is most important (what is first in the series) and what is most urgent (what will create the greatest problems if it isn't addressed soon).

When I am trying help my nephew hit the baseball and his stance isn't right and he isn't following the ball all the way in with his eyes, I may have to set both concerns aside until we deal with the fact that the bat he is holding is too heavy for him but he insists that he wants to use that one because it was signed by his favorite player.

A part of the guide's job is to help the seeker discover the first thing to work on. This is complicated by the common experience that what the guide sees as the biggest problem is the one the guide is most comfortable addressing. When the only tool you have is a hammer, the whole world looks like a nail. This may be a problem that the guide is good at addressing and wants to display expertise, or it may be a problem the guide has been addressing in her or his own life; however, if it is not the problem which is first for the seeker, it should be put aside.

It takes insight to see what the problems are and it takes wisdom to know which of the problems should be addressed first. Sometimes the first thing is the first step in a developmental series or a hierarchy of needs, and sometimes the first thing is a response to an impending crisis. The task of the guide is to offer guidance about priorities.

## Modeling

The third stage is holding out for the seeker the perspectives and strategies which construct what the seeker needs. This requires that the guide have some skill at showing the seeker a way of being which is not yet available to the seeker but which the seeker is able to see as being within reach. This means that the guide has to model this way of being.

If I tell my son he should clean his room because then life will be easier for him and he will find things and they won't get broken, but my room is always trashed, he is not likely to be persuaded. It is well known that, especially in relationship to our children, we teach by example. And it is also well known that we often fail to set the example we want others to follow. Some popular phrases which speak to this include, "Do as I say, don't do as I do," and "It is easier to coach than it is to play." But if we are to be good coaches we have to be good players. If we are to be good guides, we have to be good seekers.

When I first began my clinical training to become a pastoral counselor I was surprised to learn that a requirement of the program was that I be in therapy myself. I was troubled both because I had not budgeted the expense and because

I didn't know what I was going to work on in therapy. As far as I was concerned I didn't have any problems. I just wanted to help others with theirs.

As I now look back on the various events and circumstances in my life which have led me to be a skilled psychotherapist, I can affirm without hesitation that the most important has been my work as a client in therapy. That is where I learned the skills to deal well with my own life and to support others in their efforts. You cannot be a good teacher if you haven't had good teachers. You can't be a good coach if you haven't had good coaching. You can't be a good guide if you aren't a good seeker.

So, at the core, what the guide is modeling for the seeker is how to be a good seeker. When the guide is trying to support the seeker through a difficult transition, and the seeker isn't getting it, the guide may become frustrated at trying to create change in the seeker. This is the point at which the guide must seek the guidance of the seeker. The guide has to figure out how the guide can be different in the relationship, not how to get the seeker to be different.

When Jane wants five year old Jack to clean his room and he doesn't do it to her standards, she is likely to become frustrated and try to push him harder. When instead she wonders what it is that *she* needs and what she can do to transform the relationship rather than to bully Jack, she can discover a different way of being for herself.

She may learn that she is anxious about being a good mom and worried that she can't teach her sons to be responsible. She may discover that she is feeling overwhelmed by the tasks of housekeeping and that she resents Joe for not doing more and is taking it out on Jack by expecting things of him he is unable to do. She may discover that Jack is angry with her about something but is not able to address it directly and so is expressing his anger by defying her. Each of these would call forth a different way of being which would result in a strategy to move her toward what she needs which is also in Jack's best interest.

In each of these instances the focus must be on clarifying the issues and refining the process for addressing them while detaching from the outcome. We can't determine what will happen, but only how we will enter into the circumstance which will inform the outcome. We must keenly focus on what arises for us and how we respond to it and then we must surrender to the outcome. It is just this stance of focused surrender which allows us to create the greatest good.

# Being a Helpful Bystander

Very often we find ourselves in relationships in which we observe others, others we care about, making choices which are not in their best interests. We care about them so we want to help.

At times we may even witness one person being abused by another and, because of our concern for the victim or the perpetrator or for the wellbeing of the relationship or the society, we decide we want to intervene. We are a bystander who has a stake in the transformation of others. How can we intervene in a way that is genuinely helpful?

Throughout this book I have been pointing out that this process is simple but not easy. Nowhere is this more true than here.

Remembering that we can't change others and that the only problem we can solve is our own, we can become good seekers rather than trying to be a guide to someone who hasn't asked us for help. We can notice that we are troubled, identify what is bothering us, figure out what we need, and then act to create what we need.

*Several years ago I was in Anchorage visiting my sister. I got tired of the curio shops she and my wife were browsing so I took a walk around the block. I came across a woman and a girl. The woman was cursing and belittling the girl. The woman appeared to have been drinking.*

*The girl looked to be in her early teens and I presumed she was the woman's daughter. I found the language and the demeanor to be very abusive and a part of me wanted to pretend it wasn't happening. As I noticed that wish to look away I also became aware of a part of me that wants all abuse to be witnessed and addressed and to live in a society that doesn't divert its eyes from abuse. So I stood and watched. As I did so it occurred to me that the girl was taking it as though she thought she deserved to be treated this way and I became concerned that she was learning to blame herself for the abuse of others.*

*At this point the girl looked over at me and her mother whirled at me and spat, "What are you looking at?"*

*"I am watching you," I answered.*

*"This is none of your business."*

*I thought about that for a moment and answered, "When one person abuses another, especially in a public place, I think that is everyone's business."*

*The woman turned toward the girl and breathed heavily. The girl shook her head at me as if to say that I was making things worse and that I should leave them alone.*

*"Okay," I said looking straight at the girl, "but I want you to know that no matter what you have done, you do not deserve to be treated like this," and I turned and walked away.*

*I found my sister who worked as a supervisor in juvenile probation and inquired about how social services might respond and then contacted the police. When I returned to the site they were gone.*

What I was doing throughout this interaction was to address my problem, not theirs. I don't really know what their problem was. But my problem was that abuse was occurring without a witness and without a public voice saying that it was wrong and unjustified. That was my problem and that was a problem I could address.

It is hard to let go of trying to change others. We all know we can't change others but it doesn't stop us from trying. It is hard to trust that we can create what we need by changing ourselves and that, by so doing, we also create what others need.

## Summary

Among the many abilities which grow as we mature is the ability to guide others in their ability to do the things we know how to do. We can be a guide to them to the extent that they want our guidance and to the extent that we can model for them what it is like to be a seeker.

There are stages or waves in the development of the relationship between guide and seeker. First, the two must have enough of a resonance that the seeker can feel that the guide is able to identify with the seeker's experience. This requires compassion on the part of the guide and is itself a skill which can be learned and which grows through practice.

Second, the guide must determine the best place to give attention to help the seeker get unstuck. There are likely many growing edges for the seeker. The guide's job is to help find the one the seeker will benefit most from addressing first. This may be hard for the guide to see because the guide may so closely identify with the seeker that it is the guide's growing edge which gets identified.

And third, the guide must model for the seeker the solution to the problem. The guide has to be able to show the seeker a way of being which, when emulated by the seeker, results in a resolution of the seeker's problem. At this point guides can get very frustrated and try to push the seeker into resolution instead of trusting the process. Transformation is natural and normal and will happen as conditions are right. You can't push the river.

As much as we may desire transformation for those we love, we cannot make them change. The more we try, the more resistant they are likely to become. If, instead, we see the problem as our own and seek to address the problem we each have when those we care for are not able to "get it," we model for them what it means to be a seeker. We become more and more able to create what we need and, in the process, to create what they need.

# Epilogue

Eddie was able to return to the home with his wife a daughter after two years of separation. He left his dad's home feeling much better about himself and with what turned out to be a better relationship with both his parents.

Larry never did call his mom. He left the group not long after his birthday and before Christmas so we never knew if he and his mom celebrated together. He was never able to do the Anger Workout and remained terrified of what he might do if he spoke directly with anyone he was angry with.

Saturday afternoon after the Friday night sports banquet Joe caught Jane in the living room folding and sorting clothes onto the sofa and chairs while the boys were off with friends.

*"Jane, can we talk for a minute?"*

*"Sure," Jane replied while pulling T-shirts out of the laundry basket.*

*"Can you stop for just a minute?" Joe motioned to one of the chairs that was still open while he sat opposite it. When he had Jane's eyes he went on. "I'm not sure I understand all of what was upsetting you last night, but I know a part of it was from my leaving my clothes lying around our bedroom. I know that makes you feel like I am expecting you to clean up after me but that really isn't the case. I was in a hurry and didn't want to be late to the banquet and I also needed to get the boys moving and I just didn't think about the fact that you*

would have to look at my mess all evening. I really expected that you would do something to relax instead of doing housework."

Joe paused to see if Jane wanted to respond before going on. "I am worried that you are so driven to get things done around here. You are a great mom and you keep a great house but you aren't doing so well in caring for Jane. I really love Jane and I think she needs some time off and I hope you will agree to let her do something fun today. It's a Saturday and here you are still working."

Jane felt a weight lift from her as Joe said these things. She was still holding some of her anger at him and expected that he was going to be mad at her. When he chose instead to express concern for her she was surprised and relieved. She smiled.

Joe stood and took Jane's hands and pulled her up to him. He gave her a hug and then added, "So can you think of what you would like to do after I finish folding these clothes?"

Noticing that she enjoyed his embrace and aware that the boys were gone for the next few hours she said, "Well, I didn't get enough sleep last night. Maybe we could both get a nap," and she kissed him.

# Annotated Bibliography

*CCCR Home Page*. Center for Creative Conflict Resolution. Web. 16 May 2009. <http://www.creativeconflictresolution.org>.

> The main site for the Center for Creative Conflict Resolution was updated in May 2009 and includes a link to the site for this book (Also at http:// JustConflict.com) with other resources for information about Creative Conflict Resolution.

Fowler, James W. *Stages of Faith The Psychology of Human Development*. New York: HarperOne, 1995. Print.

> James Fowler was among my first sources for an understanding of developmental lines and how they construct transformation in our perceptions and conflicts in our personal relationships. I discovered his early work just as I was personally struggling with being faithful to the community which nurtured me even as I was having trouble with the beliefs I thought I was supposed to hold.

Goleman, Daniel. *Emotional intelligence*. New York: Bantam Books, 1995. Print.

> Goleman was able with this book to raise to public awareness that rational thought is not superior to emotional competence. He vividly makes the point that emotions matter, that we suffer when we are not aware of them, and we can learn greater facility with them by concerted effort.

Gottman, John Mordechai. *Seven principles for making marriage work*. New York: Three Rivers, 1999. Print.

> This is a nice summary of the findings of Gottman's research. I agree with almost everything he says about conflicts in intimate relationships except that some cannot be resolved. Our difference here is actually somewhat semantic. I think we disagree about what resolution means. He notes that we can't always get our partners to want what we want. Yes. But we can construct harmony even when the other is not who I want him or her to be. On that, we heartily agree.

*Groundhog Day*. Dir. Harold Ramis. Perf. Bill Murray, Andie MacDowell. Columbia Pictures, 1993. DVD.

> This perfect movie introduces us to a day in the life of Phil Collins, played by Bill Murray. He gets stuck in the same day being consigned to repeat it over and over. As he is presented with the same conflicts in the same relationships he slowly learns that he is the only person he can change. And when he does, he not only transforms himself but all of the relationships in which he finds himself.

Hall, Sue Parker. *Anger, Rage and Relationship: An Empathic Approach to Anger Management*. New York: Routledge, 2009. Print.

> Anger management is big business because so many people are angry and they do so much damage with it. There are many books about anger but this is the first I have seen that fully appreciates the difference between the feeling of anger and the behavior of anger. Sue Parker Hall calls the feeling of anger, anger, and the behavior of anger, rage. It is just this distinction I am trying to make here.

Hendrix, Harville. *Getting the Love You Want: A Guide for Couples*. New York: Perennial Library, 1990. Print.

> This straight-forward guide for couples has been one of the first books I recommend for nearly twenty years now. Of great value are the exercises found in the back. One of central insights Hendrix holds up for us is that a marriage is something we construct and that we get to decide what it will look like.

Kegan, Robert. *In Over Our Heads The Mental Demands of Modern Life.* New York: Harvard UP, 1998. Print.

> I took this book with me on vacation several years ago. Kegan taught be first of all about the evidence based research about how we all transform in our perceptions of who we are but also about the necessity that we have help in our transformation. If we want a better world, Kegan argues, we have to be intentional about creating the structures which support the transformation of everyone into a higher way of being.

Maslow, Abraham H. *"A Theory of Human Motivation."* Psychological Review 50 (1943): 370-96. Print.

> This article is one that surprised me when I read it because it asserts so many ideas that we now take for granted. It summarizes work in developing a theory of human motivation and separates motivation from behavior. It explains how what may appear to be deviations from the hierarchy are in fact examples of where a behavior may be motivated by multiple needs, and it suggests the importance of understanding the true motivation of our behavior.

Rosenberg, Marshall B. *Nonviolent communication a language of life.* Encinitas, CA: PuddleDancer, 2003. Print.

> I actually met Marshall many years ago when he conducted a workshop at Eden Seminary when I was a student there is the 70's. I remember he taught us to caution statements which were only true when "should" was included. A couple of years ago I found his more recent work and am delighted that we are mostly saying the same things. It confirms the validity of my perspective when I find other who see from the same vantage point.

Rothman, Jay. *Resolving identity-based conflict in nations, organizations, and communities.* San Francisco, Calif: Jossey-Bass, 1997. Print.

> Rothman was the one who turned me on to the idea that conflicts have a complex agenda. In addition to the obvious resource-based origin of conflicts, Rothman pointed out how we fight about identity-based issues as well. I later discovered that there are also process-based issues.

Schlitz, Marilyn M., Cassandra Vieten, and Tina Amorok. *Living Deeply: The Art and Science of Transformation in Everyday Life*. Oakland, CA: New Harbinger, 2007. Print.

> Working on behalf of the Institute of Noetic Sciences, these authors did a review of what we know about how we can construct our own transformation. This book not only catalogues some excellent practices, it also constructs a meta-analysis of how transformation happens and what we can do to support it for ourselves and others.

Schwartz, Richard C. *You Are the One You've Been Waiting For*. Chicago: Trailheads Publications, 2008. Print.

> This is only the most recent of Dr. Schwartz's books about Internal Family Systems therapy. It is accessible and a good summary of the theory in the context that most of us need to hear it. How do I fix my intimate relationship when my beloved is such a dunderhead? By seeing the conflicts as opportunities for Self transformation.

Walsh, Roger. *Essential Spirituality The 7 Central Practices to Awaken Heart and Mind*. New York: Wiley, 2000. Print.

> What Dr. Walsh refers to as practices are the qualities that each is intended to create in the life of the practitioner. What he refers to as disciplines are the actual behaviors intended to create the transformative outcome. As a result these are far more than seven activities, but many disciplines culled from the religions of the world to create qualities that we all need for our spiritual wellbeing.

Wilber, Ken. *Integral Spirituality A Startling New Role for Religion in the Modern and Postmodern World*. Boston: Shambhala, 2007. Print.

> If you are not versed in the work of Ken Wilber, this is probably not the place to start. But if you do know about AQAL and Integral Philosophy and you have concerns about how we develop spiritually, I suggest you not miss this one. More than any other single source, Wilber's work has been a guide and an inspiration to me. The left column of the Chart of the Orders of Self is his. [http://www.creativeconflictresolution.org/jc/images/Orders%20of%20Self%20chart.pdf]

# Appendix

## Handouts on the 10 Disciplines

Discipline #1 – Bothers Me Log

**Injunction [What to do]:**
Spend five minutes every day making a record of what you can identify as having bothered you since the last time you did this discipline.

**Why do it [Rationale]:**
Paying attention to our feelings connects us to ourselves…to what is going on with us. We don't like the feelings of being bothered and there are powerful influences in our lives that tell us not to pay attention. We learn to try very hard to keep things from bothering us. As a consequence we become increasingly disconnected from ourselves. Noticing what is bothering us is a simple but powerful way to reconnect.

**What it will get you [Promises]:**
While in the short run you will be more aware of being bothered by the events around you, and thus will feel more bothered, in a short time [usually a couple of weeks] you will notice the "bother" subsiding. This is because most of what bothers us are things we already know how to address but haven't simply because we haven't given those things sufficient attention. Over time you will feel more confident and will be better able to anticipate problems rather than having them sneak up on you.

**Suggestions:**

Try to do the journal at the same time everyday. Build it into your routine. Most people find that doing it in the evening while looking back over the day works best, but find your own rhythm.

Don't do an extended narrative about each item. Keeping a diary is fine if you want, but this is something else. Just note each item with enough detail that you can identify it and then ask yourself, "And what else?" Try to find as many items that are bothering you as possible.

You likely find the same emotional issues coming up day after day. If you make a chart of these you can just check off the events that happen over and over again. Try to group them into categories.

Some bothers are easier to identify than others. We can usually identify "when others do things I don't like" as things that bother us. A bit harder to find are the "things they don't do that I wish they would." Harder still to recognize are the "things I do that I wish I hadn't." And hardest to indentify are the "things I leave undone that I wish I had done."

If you find yourself feeling overwhelmed by all of the events that are bothersome, make a second log of all of the things that satisfy you. Do it in a similar manner where the goal is to notice as many items as possible.

## Discipline #2 – Anger Workout

**What to Do [Injunction]:**
Spend five minutes a day [not more than twenty minutes at a time]

- focusing your awareness on your most intense feelings of anger
- while you are doing something physically active [and thus are aware of your physicality]
- which is safe [both for you and for others].

**Why do it [Rationale]:**
Paying attention to our feelings connects us to ourselves…to what is going on with us. But we don't like the feelings of being angry so we stuff those feelings until they spew out in an over-reaction to a situation or they fester and poison us and our relationships with others. Anger is simply the feeling we have when we are hurt by what we experience to be the choices of others. Anger is a natural and normal response to some events in our life. But we don't like what we do when we are angry. We don't like what others do when they are angry. We don't like how others treat us when we are angry. So we stuff it…and stuff it…and stuff it. And then, when we give ourselves permission to be angry and so reach for a pinch of anger, we instead pull up a fist-full.

The anger workout is a way to empty the anger bag so that we are not burdened by carrying all that around with us everywhere we go. It frees us to feel our anger and to express it appropriately.

**What it will get you [Promises]:**
We have spent many years learning to deny our anger and to stuff it. We have very few models for how to be angry in creative ways. Don't expect there to be a rapid shift in how you feel or express your anger. At the very least, you should expect to do the anger workout every day for a couple of weeks before you begin to see a change. But look for these three shifts in your feeling and behavior:

- You become less likely to over-react. When you are angry, you will only be angry about the event that just happened and not all of the other events that it reminds you of that you haven't addressed.

- You become more aware of being angry. While this may not seem like a good thing at first, you will be able to address issues before they become so overwhelming.
- You become more creative with how you express your anger. You become more comfortable with the feelings of anger. This assists you in trying new ways of being versus going back to doing the same old strategies.

**Suggestions:**

Try to do the anger workout at the same time everyday. Build it into your routine. Many people find that doing it in the morning as a way to start the day works best, but find your own rhythm. Try to do the same activity at the same time. Walking is probably the best thing to do, but it is possible to do an anger workout doing anything that is physically active, even breathing. Just remember, it has to be something that is safe. Don't rehearse violence. Don't put yourself at risk.

Don't get lost in thinking about the events that make you angry or in trying to figure out what to do. Stay in the emotions and sensations as much as possible. Problem solving comes later. This is not about developing a strategy, but about becoming more connected to yourself.

This is not something to do only when you notice being angry. It is fine to take a walk to cool off when you are angry, but this is different. This is spending time every day to go and look for the anger, feel it as intensely as you can, and then put it down and go on with your day.

It may help to think of your anger as being like a big dog, a working dog. It has a job to do and it is happier when it knows what its job is and how to do it. The anger workout is the time each day when you work on training your anger dog. Take it out for a walk and be fully present to it, but in a way that you both know you are in charge. The problem is that sometimes your anger dog leads you around instead of you leading it around. It takes some time to train it but if you don't spend time with it everyday it will get restless and start chewing things up.

Some people have too much anger and some have too little. The anger workout serves to moderate anger one way or the other. People with too much anger harm their relationships with others, but people with too little anger get harmed by others. They can't take care of themselves. The anger workout helps them to know their own anger.

Anger is the feeling most of us are having when we are doing the strategies that we will later regret. But there are other feelings that can be a problem for us. You may want to do a workout around other feelings as well. In general it is best to try to feel the feelings you most don't want to feel. Those are the feelings that are the most repressed and are likely to do the most harm.

## Discipline #3 – Cultivating Critical Feedback

**What to Do [Injunction]:**

1. Notice when those around you see things differently than you do. Especially notice when you are doing or seeing things differently than they expect or want you to.

2. Make sure you clearly understand how they see things differently, how they want you to see things, and how they want you to act. Summarize what you hear them saying and ask them to confirm that your understanding is accurate.

3. Thank them for giving you this valuable information.

4. Think about how you want this information to affect you.

**Why do it [Rationale]:**

We all have cognitive distortions. We cannot see our own cognitive distortions. We need critical feedback from others to be able to identify them. If we fail to identify them we will continue to act as though the world around us is different from the way it actually is and we will continue to fail to create what we need.

A cognitive distortion is a way of thinking about the world that doesn't match the way the world really is but which we cling to for reasons that may well not be consciously available to us. We are always working to make the way we think about the world match the way the world really is. And we adjust the "map" we have of the world around us as we get new information. Except that sometimes, in spite of the data we are getting, we cling to an old way of seeing things instead of updating the map.

We don't know that we are doing this. We are unconsciously disregarding some of the information that we are getting in order to cling to a particular way of seeing things. Since we don't know we are doing this, we can't fix it without some input from outside of the system we have created. For this reason, we need critical feedback from others.

**What it will get you [Promises]:**

- There is a part of all of us that resists getting critical feedback from others. This discipline helps you become more aware of that impulse. That part thinks you already know what you need to know so critical feedback will only be confusing or harmful to your self-esteem.

- You will discover that there are other perfectly reasonable ways of looking at the world, and at what events mean, that had not occurred to you. You will be surprised that you hadn't thought of these new ways of seeing things.

- You will find that openness to other ways of looking at things doesn't actually diminish you, but, on the contrary, allows for appreciating a greater richness and depth in how you approach the world.

- You may be being perceived differently than you are trying to project. They may also see things more objectively than you and offer it up as critical feedback. Both are potentially valuable to you.

**Suggestions:**

The key to this discipline is to know that just because you hear critical feedback from others doesn't mean that you have to accept or "own" that feedback. Some people will only be giving you their own cognitive distortions. You don't have to believe what they say to have their feedback be of benefit to you. They may be completely wrong, have terrible advice or give critical feedback in an effort to get you to change or forfeit your needs or boundaries. There is a difference between soliciting and accurately understanding their feedback and automatically taking it all to heart.

Listen to the way that you talk about the way the world is. Especially listen for the words *should*, *ought* and *supposed to*. These are indicators that the idea is a distortion because we already know that this is not the ways things actually are.

Be sure to thank others when they give you critical feedback. This will both increase your ability to take in and learn from the feedback and will increase the chances that they will continue to offer it.

# Discipline #4 – Suspending Self-soothing

**Injunction [What to do]:**

1. Identify the activities that you do that soothe you when you are anxious. These may be actions that are ways of being that are intrinsically relaxing or they may be actions that are a form of acting out or an addiction.

2. Before you do the activity that soothes you, feel the anxiety until you can clearly name what you are anxious about. If you can't identify it, try to stay with the feeling for a while and just let yourself feel the anxiety.

3. If the feeling gets too strong, simply do what soothes you.

**Why do it [Rationale]:**

We all feel anxious. From time to time, the anxiety gets so strong that we act in ways to soothe the anxiety…to make it go away.

Anxiety is a natural and normal response to our inability to resolve problems in our life. The purpose of anxiety is to draw our attention to the problem so that we can give it attention and solve it. But sometimes the anxiety gets so intense that it gets in the way of our ability to act creatively. At these times, we need a break from the anxiety.

We all have ways to soothe ourselves. Some of these strategies are ways of being that offer a genuine alternative to the way of being that generated the anxiety. But some of these strategies are things we do to mask or mute the anxiety itself. In any case, we are not going to address and resolve the problem until we know that we have a problem and we know what the problem is. The point of this discipline is to stop the self-soothing until we are sufficiently aware of the problem such that we can do something to address it, rather than simply masking the symptoms of the problem.

**What it will get you [Promises]:**

You will *feel more* anxious. We are mostly unaware of our anxiety. As we pay attention to it we discover that we always have at least a low level of anxiety. This is perfectly appropriate. If you have no anxiety at all, you are dead. But when you pay attention to it, you will notice it more and more. So the first promise is that you will become more aware of your anxiety. That doesn't really sound like a good thing.

**You will *be less* anxious.** But the second promise comes from the awareness. That is, the more aware you are of your anxiety, the less of it you will have. You will naturally mobilize your resources to address the problems that are the sources of the anxiety in the first place. Alternately, the less attention you give to your anxiety, the more of it you will have.

**You will have more energy.** The third promise is that, as you become more aware of the anxiety, you will put more of your time and attention to addressing the problems, and you will spend fewer of your resources on avoiding the anxiety in the first place.

**Suggestions:**
Notice what you find boring. Boredom is the feeling we have when what we have been doing to avoid the anxiety isn't working any more. Just notice: are you ever bored watching TV? How can that be? They spend millions on making every instant powerfully engaging. But when we are choosing to watch TV as a way to not feel the anxiety, after a while the anxiety builds up and the TV watching doesn't work anymore to mask the anxiety. We feel bored with it. Whatever you are bored with is something that you are doing to mask anxiety or it is something that generates anxiety. Try to notice when you are bored and to find the source of the anxiety.

Keep a list of what you do to self-soothe. You probably have many things that you do. Some of them are just *ways of being* [taking a walk, listening to music] but some of them are *ways of doing* that are designed to hide the anxiety [eating compulsively, smoking cigarettes]. Try to identify as many of the strategies that you use to self-soothe as you can.

When you notice yourself using one of the strategies, stop yourself and see if you can identify what you are anxious about. Practice feeling the anxiety and work on being able to tolerate more and more of it until you can feel it very clearly. Remember, you can always return to what you do to self-soothe if the anxiety becomes too much for you.

When you do use one of your strategies to self-soothe, don't be critical of yourself. You are just doing what you do to care for yourself. It isn't bad to care for yourself. Simply notice what you are doing. Don't beat up on yourself.

# Discipline #5 - Barriers to Self Care

**Injunction [What to do]:**
- Make a list of all of the activities that you do everyday to take care of yourself that benefit you directly and others only indirectly.
- Make a second list of strategies that you have done routinely to take care of yourself but which you aren't able to get yourself to do consistently even though you believe that you are benefited when you do.
- Make a third list of actions that you believe would be good for you to do but which you have not been able to get yourself to do at all.
- Now take list #1 and turn it into a schedule that is specific enough that you will notice when you depart from it. For example, one of the strategies that you do everyday to take care of yourself is to sleep. Decide when you are going to go to bed and when you are going to get up.
- You are not going to always do as you have planned. Simply notice when you depart from your plan. If you stay up later than you planned, notice how you talked yourself into straying from your routine. See if you can find the part of you that persuaded you to depart from what you already decided was in your own best interest.
- As you find yourself doing what you decided to do, you can add items from list #2 and then #3, but only when you are mostly doing what is already on the schedule. Don=t overwhelm yourself.

**Why do it [Rationale]:**
The barrier that tends to keep us stuck around not taking care of ourselves is that we A*should* on ourselves.@ We have one part that tells us what we should be doing and another that resists. This becomes a struggle for control and we repeatedly thwart ourselves. Each takes a turn at dominance and submission. Instead, if we build a relationship between those two parts, they are able to bring both of their sets of skills and perspectives to the task of self-care.

For example, most of us have a part that tells us that we should do certain actions to care for ourselves. This part may not do anything more than gripe at us for not caring for ourselves or it may actually have been able to get us to do strategies that are good for us for fairly long periods around specific activities.

We also have a part that is more spontaneous and impulsive that says that we don't need to do the self-care now (or perhaps at all). It just wants to play, or it may be a part that is busy taking care of others, so we don=t have time for ourselves.

Rather than allowing these parts to fight it out, we can be more satisfied if we can establish a relationship with each of them and then allow them to relate to each other in such a way as to meet both of their needs. For some folks there are more than two parts here. There can be a whole complex of parts and issues that compete for our attention.

**What it will get you [Promises]:**
There are actually several results that will happen for you as you consistently apply yourself to this discipline.

- The simple act of writing down what it is that you do for yourself will remind you that you do act on your own behalf and that you are someone who is worth taking care of. Your self-esteem will rise.
- You will become more conscious of what it is that you want to do to care for yourself. Most of our failures to adequately care for ourselves come from our failure to plan to care for ourselves. Simply having the plan increases greatly the chances that you will act on your own behalf.
- Having the plan and then noticing when you don't follow it highlights the tension between the parts of you that are trying to care for you responsibly and the parts that are caring for yourself impulsively. This tension, this conflict between the parts, is a crucial starting place for our inquiry into our own interior life.
- By attending to the issues of the more impulsive parts of ourselves we become less impulsive and also to discover important ways that we are not doing the best job of caring for ourselves.

**Suggestions:**
The key to this discipline is that the goal is not to make yourself take care of yourself but to notice how you stop yourself from taking care of yourself. This is about getting to know the part that sabotages the plan and to appreciate what it is that that part is trying to do for you. This is a difficult point to get so I am going to say it again. The point of this discipline is not to shame

ourselves into doing a better job of caring for ourselves. We have plenty of shame already. The point of this discipline is to discover what may be in the way of acting on our own behalf and to remove those barriers. At the same time, we are likely to discover that there are needs that we have of which we are unaware. By becoming aware of those needs we can begin to act in ways that address them.

## Discipline #6 – Anticipate, Create, Evaluate [ACE]

**Injunction [What to do]:**
Recognizing that in our relationships with others there are patterns of conflicts that arise with them; and recognizing that the most distressing conflicts are those that arise over and over again in the context of our relationships with those with whom we have the most significant relationships; select a single pattern of conflict in a particular significant relationship.

- Anticipate when the next time will be that this conflict will arise. Identify how you will recognize it. This may be because of some response in you or it may be because of some specific behavior on the part of the other or it may simply be because a certain time has come.
- Create a new way of addressing the conflict. You can remember what you did last time and what effect the choices you made then had on you and on the relationship. How do you want things to be different next time? This step has two parts to it:
- Plan for what you intend to do.
- Implement the plan.
- Evaluate how well the plan worked. In what ways did it move you toward what you need and in what ways did it fall short? How well were you able to do what you planned to do and how were you acting differently than you expected to act?

Then, trusting that the pattern will reappear, begin the process again by anticipating the next occurrence.

**Why do it [Rationale]:**
The experience of having the same conflict come up over and over again can be a great source of frustration, helplessness, and anxiety. This is mostly because the focus of our attention is on what the other is doing and thus is on something that we can't change. When we shift the focus onto what we are doing and onto the qualities that we are trying to create in the relationship, we discover that we are actually very powerful.

We often have the goal of making the conflict go away. This is an unreasonable expectation. We can't really change the pattern. But we can change the present event. We do that by changing how we act...what we choose.

Doing things differently turns out to be much harder than it seems at first. We may have a clear idea of what we want to do but then find that we can't get ourselves to do it. While this can be its own source of frustration, it can also be a way to find how we are blocked from acting more assertively on our own behalf.

**What it will get you [Promises]:**

As you practice this discipline, you will find that you have been doing it all along in some form or another, just not with as clear an intention. When you smash your thigh into the desk drawer when you get up, you vow to make sure that you close it all of the way next time. You anticipate that there will be another time that you open that drawer and that sometime after that you will get up from your chair and that you will whack yourself if you haven't closed the drawer. If you make the plan but don't implement it, you will get another bruise on your thigh and will have a chance to figure out why you can't remember to close the drawer.

But as you do the discipline with greater intention and with more and more complex conflicts you will find that;

• The hesitation that you have about addressing conflicts will diminish as you recognize that the conflicts are going to arise whether you anticipate them or not and that, when you do, you are better prepared to deal with them.

• You will begin to feel more and more powerful and less frustrated and helpless. You will notice that each time the pattern emerges you respond with greater and greater clarity and calm and the outcome will be more and more satisfying for you.

**Suggestions :**

It is important to avoid some common pitfalls.

• Some people try this discipline and then report "that it didn't work." If you think that the outcome is going to be that you will change the other or to make it so that the conflict doesn't ever happen again, then, true, this won't work. The gauge of whether it works is whether you were able to be different in the way that you decided to be different. Even then, if you are not able to change what you do, simply noticing how hard this is can be a first step toward profound transformation.

- Some people come up with a plan and then find that they can't get themselves to implement it and give up. They think that because they couldn't do what they decided to do, this won't work. In fact, these are the very things we most want to identify. When we find the places where we want to respond differently and are stuck, we have found a core block in our own behavior. [See discipline #5 for more on this.]

## Discipline #7 – Statement of Accountability

**Injunction [What to do]:**

Think over the choices that you have made in your life and select one that was harmful to others that you regret. While there may have been several things that you have done, start with the one that you most regret that was the most harmful to another. [If you cannot think of any choice you have made that was harmful to others, or can only think of things that while harmful, you don't regret the choice, then you will not be able to do this discipline. See rationale below.]

1. Clarify the <u>choice</u>. Get very clear about exactly what it was that you chose that you regret.

2. Identify the <u>consequences</u> to others. How did this choice that you made affect others and your relationships to others?

3. Name the <u>patterns</u> that permitted this choice. Since this is something that you regret, there were things going on with you at the time that allowed you to do something that you would ordinarily not do. What were all of things that were true for you at the time of the choice that gave you permission to act in this way?

4. Identify the <u>strategies</u> that you have now for addressing these patterns. In order to ensure that we won't again do the thing that we regret that was harmful to others, we have to have strategies for addressing the ways that we permitted ourselves to make the poor choice in the first place.

**Why do it [Rationale]:**

We all make choices that are harmful to others. Unfortunately, not everyone is able to identify these choices or to feel regret for having done them. If you are able to identify the choice and to know that you have done harm and to feel guilt for the choice, then you are able to address the choice in a way that will help you avoid such behavior in the future.

Oftentimes we will simply assure ourselves that we know better now and will never do that again. This is not a safe strategy. For one thing, if someone had asked you before you had made that choice if that were something you were likely to do, you would no doubt have said you would not. "Knowing better" was something you had in place before you did it. Still, you did it.

Further, there are those things that come up for you from time to time that give you permission to do the things that you don't want to do. Ignoring them won't make them go away. Addressing them holds out the promise for improving other areas of your life as well.

**What it will get you [Promises]:**
- While this is a fairly straightforward discipline, it is very hard to do for emotional reasons. It is hard to admit, even to ourselves, much less to others, that we have made choices that seriously harmed others and our relationships with others. Nevertheless, this discipline is well worth the effort. There is a lot that we can learn about ourselves by looking at what we have done when we were at our worst.
- These most regretted choices tend to be a sort of "perfect storm" in which several sets of influences come together around a single event. For example if I have too much to drink and have a fight with my wife when I am scared about losing my job shortly after my mother dies, the fear and anger and grief may be released by the inebriation in ways that permit me to make some very bad choices. Each of these issues demands my attention, but I may not see the need to attend to them without the consequences of my regrettable choices to focus my mind. I have not fully grieved the loss of my mother. I have not attended to problems at work. I don't have good ways of addressing conflicts in my marriage. And I have a tendency to drink too much when I am anxious. All of these are problems worthy of my attention. Thus the central promise of the Statement of Accountability is that by using the energy in the guilt that I feel I can transform my behavior into constructive action.

**Suggestions:**
The key to this discipline is to pick the thing that we really regret, rather than what we think we ought to regret or what others believe we did wrong. The energy for transformation comes from the shame that we feel about who we are

when we behave badly. The process is to take the energy from the shame, turn it into guilt about what we did [thus getting very clear about the choice that we made] and then fully addressing the aspects of our behavior that allow for us to behave that way so that we can really be confident that we have fully addressed the issues that allowed for the harmful action.

For this to work we have to be careful to:

- Be very specific about the choice. A general description of what happened won't do.
- Be clear about all of the consequences to the other and to the relationships with others. While it is helpful for other reasons to note the consequences to you, for the purposes of the Statement of Accountability, those aren't really relevant.
- Identify all of the patterns, even the most subtle. Squeeze all of the benefit out of this process that you can. See if you can name at least half a dozen patterns that you can see coming up in other areas of your life as well.
- Be very clear about the strategies. These should be observable behaviors. "Being careful that I don't drink too much" is not as good as "attend my AA meeting every week and talk to my sponsor every other day."

# Discipline #8 – Apology and Forgiveness

**What to Do [Injunction]:**

**Event:** Identify an event or a series of events which have done harm to you or to another in a relationship you want to repair. (If you have been harmed by the choice of another then the relationship you are repairing is primarily the one you have with yourself.)

**Choices:** Clarify as precisely as you can the choice or choices you or another made which was the cause of the harm. There may be several choices and those may have been made by you or the other or both.

**Consequences:** Taking each choice in turn discover all you can about how that choice affected you and the other and your relationship to the other. Take this as deep as you can.

**Clean up:** Identify what you can do to repair the damage that has been done by the choices even if you were not the one who made the choice.

**Patterns:** Identify what patterns of choosing supported making the damaging choice in the first place and what patterns have been created by the effects of the choices and identify what you can do to dismantle those patterns.

**Why do it [Rationale]:**

Sometimes we find ourselves being harmed in our relationships with others or we discover that we have done things which are harmful to them. While we sometimes will just choose to have nothing to do with those who harm us, or they may decide not to have anything to do with us, there are many relationships which are too valuable to lose. So we want to repair relationships in which the damage has occurred. What we normally do is to act as though the damage hasn't happened. If we acknowledge the damage at all, it is to say, in effect, let's act as though this didn't happen. This is what often passes for an apology or forgiveness. But in order to actually repair the relationship, we will have to address the harm which was done. We will have to clean up the mess and that includes doing everything we can to be sure we don't make a similar mess in the future.

The reason to apologize and forgive is thus twofold. First, it is to seek to repair a damaged relationship or to repair our relationship to ourselves when we have been damaged by someone close to us; and second, to discover what was going on that allowed for the harm in the first place and to make the changes that will protect against such harm in the future.

**What it will get you [Promises]:**
The first thing you will get is a repaired relationship. Sometimes people respond to this promise by asking, "But what if the other doesn't accept my apology?" I have never known anyone to reject a genuine apology. We all long to have our experience validated and no one can do that more effectively than someone who has harmed us. What people reject are efforts at reconciliation which don't acknowledge the damage and are not genuinely motivated by a wish for full accountability. If your apology is experienced by the other as an attempt by you to get them to absolve you of accountability for your actions, then, yes, it will be rejected.

Remember that the reason to apologize is not to get the other to forgive you. That is trying to change them and they will resist your manipulation. The reason to apologize is to change yourself in the wake of choices you regret. The reason to apologize is to minimize the chances that you will again make this regrettable choice.

The promise then is that you will not only heal the relationship, you will also heal yourself and you support your own transformation into someone who doesn't do the things that harm others or your relationships to them.

**Suggestions:**
Carefully plan your apology. If you make lots of apologies for the same transgression people come to think that you are not sincere. Also, apologizing is often hard and painful. It is not the sort of thing we want to have to do over and over. So plan it out and do it with care.

Make sure you are offering your apology at a time and in a place that the other is fully available to hear it. In the song by Paul Simon, *Slip Slidin' Away*, the father goes to his son to apologize but instead kisses him while he is sleeping and then leaves. This is important. Do it well.

You will have lots of chances to practice apologizing if you are careful to notice whenever you do things that harm others. Being able to apologize well is a very valuable skill, so don't pass up any chances to practice. Whenever you want to talk seriously to someone about a circumstance or quality in a relationship, an excellent way to set the tone is to apologize for something. This has to be genuine. You can't apologize for something you haven't done or don't regret. But if you can find something about which you can apologize with integrity then you will have much better luck connecting with the other.

Finally, remember that the reason to apologize, as in all things, is to change yourself. The success of the apology is gauged by how well you offered it and how fully it transforms you, not whether the other does what you want with it.

Similarly, the reason to forgive is not to let the offender off the hook or to in any way get the person who harmed you to change. The reason to forgive is to transform ourselves in the wake of choices which have harmed us.

## Discipline #9 – Framework for Creative Conflict Resolution

**Injunction [What to do]:**

Remembering that you cannot change anyone but yourself, identify something which is arising in your life that is so troublesome to you that you are willing to change what you do in order to create what you need.

1.  Identify the Significant Relationship. There may be several relationships which are implicated in this troublesome circumstance. Pick one. We can't address them all, all at once.

2.  Identify the Pattern of Conflict. There is something about this circumstance which keeps happening over and over. There may even be several patterns. Again, pick one. We are trying to take something very complex and tease out a part of it which will be simple enough to resolve.

3.  Clarify the Event. Describe the event is such a way that all parties to the event will agree that this is what happened. If you can't agree on the event that already happened, you will never come to an agreement with yourself about what you hope to have happen.

4.  Feel the effects of the event. Notice the impact the event has on you. What are your sensations, emotions, thoughts, and wishes? When have you had these feelings before?

5.  Identify the qualities that you need when this event occurs. Yes, you want others to be different; but if they were as you want them to be, what qualities would arise in the relationship?

6.  Choose an action. Nothing will change until we change our behavior. What can you do which will move you toward what you need without expecting or depending on the other to change?

**Rationale [Why do it]:**

The reason for steps #1-5 is to get to #6. We can't count on anything changing until we change. But we are often in a hurry to get to *what we are going to do* before we know *what we need*. We put step #6 ahead of the others. When we do so we risk making a choice that will get us the opposite of what we need. We can't know what we need until we know how we are being affected. And there are many events causing many effects, so which one are we addressing first? Each of these steps is essential to discovering what we need so we can act to create it.

Conflicts can be very complicated. Sometimes the complexity of the conflict leaves us certain that it can't be resolved. When we go to the trouble to tease the complexity apart and only address one part of it at a time, we discover that it is manageable in small pieces. The only way to eat an elephant is one bite at a time.

### Promises [What it will get you]:

We imagine that we can't resolve conflicts unless the other changes. By consistently using this discipline to change how we are choosing to show up in the conflicted relationship, we not only discover what we need and thus what we might do, we discover how powerful we really are and how effective we can be at constructing what we need.

The truth is we can only change ourselves. It turns out this is an immensely powerful thing to do when the transformation we create for ourselves is one which moves us closer to our own center. This discipline is designed to help us become more Self aware at those very times when we are going to be most inclined to focus on the other.

If you resist the temptation to try to manipulate the other into changing but instead pay keen attention to how the conflict is affecting you, what you are feeling, what you are making these events mean, what they remind you of from your past, then you will draw yourself closer to your Self. As a figure skater in a spin gains speed when she draws her arms in, so will you gain power when you move more of yourself towards your own center. When you focus only on others and how you want them to change or what your judgment of the them is, then you move away from your own center and you pull yourself out of balance.

### Suggestions [How to do it better]:

Go back and take another look at step #3. Are you sure that the way you are describing the event, even if it is just to yourself, is a way that others would agree is an accurate description? If it isn't then you aren't ready to move onto step #4. Be curious about how others describe what is happening. See if you can hear the other's account of what is happening.

Be patient with yourself as you work at mastering this discipline. The first few times you try it you will almost certainly feel as though it isn't working. Check to see how you know it isn't working. What is your evidence? Are you waiting to see if the other is going to change? If so, you are trying to change them. If instead you are looking to see if you have been able to change your own behavior and you find that you can't yet, then you are not yet able to see some of the motivators for your own behavior. You may have decided what you want to do but can't get yourself to act the way you decided. That is fine. Just focus your attention on the part of you that doesn't want to do what the rest of you decided was the best thing to do. As long as you are moving to greater self awareness you are making progress in addressing the conflict.

Only very rarely are we able to make a shift in our behavior and sustain the shift in a way that fully resolves a conflict. When we are able to do so, we have reason to celebrate. But more commonly we find we have only been able to address a part of the problem or we find that we were able to show up differently for a while and then slipped back into old habits. Be gentle with yourself. You have been doing what you have been doing for a very long time and it is hard to change our habits, especially when we are under pressure. For that reason it is especially important that you notice any small success you have at shifting what you are able to do and to enjoy how it opens things up for you. Give your self praise for your successes, no matter how small. This will help you gain momentum in your transformation.

## Discipline #10 –Creative Conflict Resolution Meeting

[This is the only one of the ten disciplines that is done with the other party. As such it requires both parties be committed to working together to resolve the conflict. If at any point it becomes clear this is not the case, go back to Discipline #9.]

**Injunction [What to do]:**
[Each of these steps must be taken but they are not always taken is this order. You may find yourself skipping over steps because they are already resolved but if you find the process getting bogged down, you will do well to address them in order.]

**Clarify the nature of the relationship:** The resolution happens in the context of the relationship as it is defined by the parties. If there is not a clear understanding of the nature of the relationship, or if there are differing perceptions of the nature of the relationship, then the conflicts that arise within it are not resolvable. Indeed, the differing perceptions of the nature of the relationship are a conflict in and of themselves.

**Clarify What Actually Happened:** The conflict to be resolved stems from the shared reality within the relationship. When there is no shared reality or the parties are not dealing with the reality they both experience, the conflict is not resolvable.

**Discover How the Shared Experience Affects Each Other:** Even when there is agreement on what happened or what happens, the way the event affects the parties is different. That is intrinsic to there being a conflict. There are five sub-skills to this task.

1. Each party must have the capacity to know how it is being affected and

2. be able clearly describe the effect in such a way that the other parties can know that experience.

3. It must be "safe" to let the others know what is going on with each party.

4. The parties must be able to tolerate hearing that the others are different and to see the difference as valid.

5. Each party must be able to reflect back what the other is saying so that the speaking party knows it is being heard.

**Identify Shared Goals:** Though there are real differences, there are also shared goals. Without shared goals, there is no basis for a relationship. Identifying those shared goals creates the glue that holds the relationship together.

**Commit to Individual Action:** Each party has a role in furthering the shared goals. Each will identify a specific course of action that will promote the shared goal. If each party commits to an action and follows through, the common goal is created as well as trust in the relationship.

**Why do it [Rationale]:**

The truth is we all do this discipline all the time. We just don't usually break it down into its constituent steps. The reason for listing it is that this one is very hard to do when we are under a lot of stress, and so it really helps if we can identify each of the steps and recognize that we already know how to do this.

We do this because we come across situations in our significant relationships in which we are looking at the same event from very different perspectives and we become afraid that we are going to get stuck. We are going to have bad feelings and we aren't going to become able to act together to create what we both need.

**What it will get you [Promises]:**

Done well this will get you a clear sense of what is happening, an understanding of how the other understands what is happening and what it means to them, the knowledge that they care to know what your experience is and are able to see how it is valid for you, a clear sense of what you both value and what qualities you are both committed to creating in your relationship, and an agreement about what you will both do.

**Suggestions:**

The agreement that this process can create for you is not one that will be easy to maintain. Don't assume that it will be durable. You will likely have to continue to reconstruct it. Notice if this is a problem for you. Sometimes we take such pride in having created the agreement that we feel resentment when it is damaged or broken.

Instead I encourage you to focus on the process of creating the agreement rather than on the agreement itself. See the process as the goal. When the agreement is damaged you then have another opportunity to engage in the process. The more you engage in the process the more clearly you are each able to see the qualities you are trying to create together and the more you have a sense of partnership in creating the relationship.

Remember that at the Interpersonal tier we are not trying to make the conflict go away. We are trying to construct relationships in which we can clearly see and honor the validity of each other's perspective.

If you and your partner create an agreement and it is not kept, then either or both of you are not of one mind about the agreement. This is an opportunity to discover how you are each at odds with yourself over how you each want to be. This is a creative opportunity.

# Intimate Justice Scale

Read each item below to see if it describes how your partner* usually treats you. Then circle the number that best describes how strongly you agree or disagree with whether it applies to you. Circling a one (1) indicates that you do not agree at all, while circling a five (5) indicates that you agree strongly. Your answers are confidential.

1. My partner never admits when he or she is wrong.
   1   2   3   4   5

2. My partner is unwilling to adapt to my needs and expectations.
   1   2   3   4   5

3. My partner is more insensitive than caring.
   1   2   3   4   5

4. I am often forced to sacrifice my own needs to meet my partner's needs.
   1   2   3   4   5

5. My partner refuses to talk about problems that make him or her look bad.
   1   2   3   4   5

6. My partner withholds affection unless it would benefit her or him.
   1   2   3   4   5

7. It is hard to disagree with my partner because she or he gets angry.
   1   2   3   4   5

8. My partner resents being questioned about the way he or she treats me.
   1   2   3   4   5

9. My partner builds himself or herself up by putting me down.
   1   2   3   4   5

10. My partner retaliates when I disagree with him or her.

    1   2   3   4   5

11. My partner is always trying to change me.

    1   2   3   4   5

12. My partner believes he or she has the right to force me to do things.

    1   2   3   4   5

13. My partner is too possessive or jealous.

    1   2   3   4   5

14. My partner tries to isolate me from family and friends.

    1   2   3   4   5

15. Sometimes my partner physically hurts me.

    1   2   3   4   5

Scale developed and validated by Brian Jory, PhD., PO Box 495019, Mount Berry, GA 30149-5019. BJory@berry.edu

*The term partner refers to your most significant mutual relationship. This may be a spouse or former spouse or even a best friend. If you are not in a marriage currently or recently, or have a girlfriend or boyfriend, use your most intimate friendship when answering these questions.

# Significant Relationships

Name your five most significant relationships.

"Significance" is determined by;

- degree to which the other=s decisions affect your life;
- amount of time you spend with the other; and
- intensity of feeling you have for the other, whether positive, negative or both.

These five people should include;

- at least one parent or parent figure;
- your primary significant other;
- the person you have the strongest feelings about;
- the person you spend the most time with; and
- the person whose decisions have most powerfully affected your life.

## Worksheet:

Who is the parent or other care giver in your childhood who had the biggest impact on you whether positive or negative?

Who is the person in your life now with whom you have the most intimate mutual relationship?

Who is the person who, when you think about him or her, evokes the strongest feelings in you?

Who do you spend most of your time with in the average week?

Who is the person from you past whose decisions have had the most impact on you... how you see yourself, what you have chosen to do, who you want to be or to not be?

# Patterns of Conflict

Fill out one of these worksheets for each of your significant relationships.

Name of the person with whom you have the relationship [Sometimes the person is not known to you or is not the same person each time. For example, one of your patterns may be with the person who cuts you off in traffic or calls you to sell you something at dinnertime.]

_____

## Power dynamics:

List the ways that you have power over the other.

List the ways the other has power over you.

List the common goals that you share with the other. You may identify these by considering the ways you share power with the other, or the agreements or understandings that you have.

## Conflict Log:

Keep a log of the times, places, feelings, and anything else that seems relevant about the times that you feel annoyed at the other person or when you become aware that the other is annoyed with you.

Log the responses that you each make to the annoyance. Be specific. What do you each do?

# Conflict Log

Use this log to reflect upon and to document the conflicts that arise in your significant relationships from time to time.

**What Happened?** Describe the event that you experienced as a conflict from the point of view of someone watching it. Include only the parts of the event that anyone could have seen.

**What were you thinking?** What thoughts came to mind for you as this happened? What did you say to yourself about it?

**What were you feeling?** What sensations did you have in your body? What emotions came up for you?

**What was the issue for you?** How was this affecting you?

**What did you do?** What action did you take that anyone could have observed?

**What might you have done?** If you had it to do over again, what other choices might you have made that would have created a different or better outcome?

# Index

## H

## I

## L

## M

## N

## O

8th Order  109

## P

## R

## S

## T

## W

LaVergne, TN USA
23 October 2009
161914LV00003B/2/P